This book provides novel insights for the understanding of crimes against the environment, and offers a methodological blueprint for future studies. It is essential reading for anyone interested in this area of research, students, academics, practitioners and campaigners alike.

Rebecca W.Y. Wong, City University of Hong Kong

Environmental crimes and harms are likely to become increasingly pressing issues in the future. Awareness of them and their long-term consequences, and how to tackle or reduce them effectively, will consequently be on the agenda of criminologists, law enforcers, and policy makers. This book is a valuable contribution to the fast growing field of green criminology.

Tim Boekhout van Solinge, Utrecht University, The Netherlands

Environmental Crime in Transnational Context

Environmental crime is one of the most profitable and fastest growing areas of international criminal activity. The increasing cross-border scope of environmental crimes and harms is one of the reasons why governments and the enforcement community have trouble in finding the proper responses. Law enforcement cooperation between western industrialized states is often time consuming and problematic, and the problems increase exponentially when environmental criminals take advantage of situations where government and law enforcement are weak.

This book provides an overview of the developments and problems in the field of transnational environmental crimes and harms, addressing these issues from perspectives such as enforcement, deterrence, compliance and emission trading schemes. Divided into four parts, the authors consider global issues in green criminology, responses to transnational environmental crimes and harms, alternative methods to combat environmental crime, and specific types of crimes and criminological research.

Discussing these topics from the view of green criminology, sociology and governance, this book will be of great interest to all those concerned about the transnational dimensions of crime and the environment.

Toine Spapens is Full Professor of Criminology at Tilburg University, the Netherlands. He received his PhD in criminology in 2006. Since the early 1990s, Spapens has done extensive empirical research on (organised) crime and its containment, and on international law enforcement cooperation. His studies include illegal firearms trafficking, ecstasy production, large-scale cannabis cultivation, illegal gambling and environmental crime. His theoretical work focuses on regulation of illegal markets and network theories of crime.

Rob White is Professor of Criminology at the University of Tasmania, Australia. He has written widely in the areas of criminology and youth studies, and has a particular interest in issues related to environmental harm, ecological justice and green criminology. His recent books are *Transnational Environmental Crime: Toward an Eco-global Criminology* (Routledge, 2011), *Climate Change from a Criminological Perspective* (Springer, 2012) and *Environmental Harm: An Eco-Justice Perspective* (Policy, 2013). He is the author of *Crimes Against Nature* (Willan, 2008).

Wim Huisman is Professor of Criminology and chair of the Department Criminology at VU University Amsterdam. His main research interests and expertise lie in the field of organized and corporate crime and regulatory enforcement. Huisman is also editor of the Dutch *Journal of Criminology* and a member of the board of the European Working Group on Organizational Crime.

Green Criminology

Series Editors:

Michael J. Lynch

University of South Florida, USA

Paul B. Stretesky

University of Northumbria, UK

Now two decades old, green criminology – the study of environmental harm, crime, law, regulation, victimization, and justice – has increasing relevance to contemporary problems at local, national, and international levels. This series comes at a time when societies and governments worldwide seek new ways to alleviate and deal with the consequences of various environmental harms as they relate to humans, non-human animals, plant species, and the ecosystem and its components. Green criminology offers a unique theoretical perspective on how human behavior causes and exacerbates environmental conditions that threaten the planet's viability. Volumes in the series consider such topics and controversies as corporate environmental crime, the complicity of international financial institutions, state-sponsored environmental destruction, and the role of non-governmental organizations in addressing environmental harms. Titles also examine the intersections between green criminology and other branches of criminology and other areas of law, such as human rights and national security. The series is international in scope, investigating environmental crime in specific countries as well as comparatively and globally. In sum, by bringing together a diverse body of research on all aspects of this subject, the series makes a significant contribution to our understanding of the dynamics between the natural world and the quite imperfect human world, and sets the stage for the future study in this growing area of concern.

Titles in the series include:

Exploring Green Criminology
Toward a Green Criminological Revolution
Michael J. Lynch and Paul B. Stretesky

Animal Harm
Perspectives on Why People Harm and Kill Animals
Angus Nurse

Eco-global Crimes
Contemporary Problems and Future Challenges
Edited by Rune Ellefsen, Ragnhild Sollund and Guri Larsen

Environmental Crime in Transnational Context

Global Issues in Green Enforcement and Criminology

Edited by Toine Spapens, Rob White and Wim Huisman

Routledge
Taylor & Francis Group
LONDON AND NEW YORK

First published 2016
by Routledge

2 Park Square, Milton Park, Abingdon, Oxfordshire OX14 4RN
711 Third Avenue, New York, NY 10017

Routledge is an imprint of the Taylor & Francis Group, an informa business

First issued in paperback 2018

British Library Cataloguing in Publication Data
A catalogue record for this book is available from the British Library

Library of Congress Cataloging-in-Publication Data
Environmental crime in transnational context : global issues in green enforcement and criminology / by Toine Spapens, Rob White, Wim Huisman.
pages cm. — (Green criminology)
Includes bibliographical references and index.
ISBN 978-1-4724-6962-5 (hardback : alk. paper) 1. Offenses against the environment. 2. Offenses against the environment—Law and legislation. I. Spapens, A. C., editor. II. White, R. D. (Robert Douglas), 1956– editor. III. Huisman, W. (Wim), editor.
HV6401.E587 2016
364.1'45—dc23

ISBN: 978-1-4724-6962-5 (hbk)
ISBN: 978-1-138-60656-2 (pbk)

Typeset in Times New Roman
by Apex CoVantage, LLC

Contents

Figures and Tables

Figures

Tables

Notes on Contributors

Lorraine Elliott is Professor of International Relations and Public Policy Fellow at the Australian National University. She is also a senior research fellow with the Earth System Governance programme, the largest social science research network in the area of governance and global environmental change, and adjunct faculty for the PhD programme in Human Security and Global Governance at the University of Massachusetts Boston. From June 2015 to June 2018, she holds the role of Chair of the Board of the Academic Council on the United Nations System.

Floor Fleurke is Assistant Professor of Environmental Law at Tilburg Law School, Tilburg University (the Netherlands). Floor is a member of three research schools within Tilburg University, namely the Center for Transboundary Legal Development (CTLD), the multidisciplinary Tilburg Sustainability Center (TSC) and the Tilburg Institute for Law, Technology and Society (TILT). Her research focuses on European environmental law, with a specific interest in the relationship between science, technology and environmental law.

Carole Gibbs is an Associate Professor at Michigan State University with a joint appointment in the School of Criminal Justice and the Department of Fisheries and Wildlife. Her research interests include conservation criminology, environmental justice and white-collar crime. Recent publications appear in the *Journal of Criminal Law and Criminology* and *Law and Policy*.

Jan Glazewski is Professor in, and Director of, the Institute of Marine & Environmental Law at the University of Cape Town. His research interests include marine law, environmental law climate change and energy law. He is a founder member of PescaDolus – a transnational fisheries crime research group.

Cameron Holley is Associate Professor, Faculty of Law, member of Connected Waters Initiative Research Centre and National Centre for Groundwater Research and Training, UNSW Australia. His research is partially funded by an Australian Research Council Discovery Early Career Researcher Award (DE140101216), an ARC Linkage Grant (LP130100967).

Wim Huisman is full professor of criminology at VU University of Amsterdam and chair of VU School of Criminology. He conducts research in the programme 'Empirical and Normative Studies of Delinquent Behaviour and Criminal Law Enforcement'. Huisman studies the nature and causation of regulatory non-compliance in companies and other types of organizations ('white-collar crime'), as well as the consequences for corporate crime control. His research projects focus on, for example, criminal careers of white-collar offenders, corporate involvement in gross human rights violations and international crimes, environmental crime and food crime.

Janine Janssen is a cultural anthropologist and criminologist with a special interest in the intersection between the study of multicultural society and green criminology. She is Head of Research of the Dutch police force's National Centre of Expertise for Honour-related Violence and is Professor of Violence in Dependency Relationships at the Avans University of Applied Sciences in the Netherlands.

Lorenzo Natali holds a PhD in Criminal Law and Criminology and is currently a research fellow at the Department of Criminology of the University of Milano-Bicocca (Milan, Italy). His main fields of research so far have focused on violent crime, environmental crime, symbolic and radical interactionism, green criminology, cultural criminology, qualitative and interdisciplinary approaches on green crime, including visual green criminology.

Pasquale Peluso is Associate Professor at the Guglielmo Marconi University of Rome, where he teaches Criminology, Sociology of Deviance and Juridical Psychology. His research fields are urban safety, organized crime and green criminology. He is a member of the editorial board of several Italian and international journals about criminology and he is a referee for several international journals. He is author of several publications on criminology, organized crime and urban security.

Grant Pink is Director of Regulatory Capability and Performance, in the Department of the Environment, Australia. He is also an Adjunct Research Fellow, in the School of Law at the University of New England, Australia. As a practitioner and academic he has written extensively on environmental regulation and enforcement, environmental and transnational environmental crime, environmental enforcement networks, and capacity building within environmental regulatory agencies. He also recently served a term as vice chair of Interpol's Environmental Crime Committee.

Giuseppe Rotolo is Assistant Professor of Criminal Law at the Faculty of Law of the Università Cattolica del Sacro Cuore – Milan (Italy), from which he received his PhD. He is currently Lecturer in Criminal Law at Università Cattolica del Sacro Cuore – Piacenza (Italy). As a member of the *'Federico Stella' Centre for Research on Criminal Justice and Policy*, he takes part in many scientific national and international projects. He dedicates his research especially to the field of environmental crimes and the theory of justice, but medical malpractice, culpable offences and corporate crimes are also included among his interests.

James Sheptycki is Professor of Criminology at York University, Toronto. His special research expertise revolves around issues of transnational crime and policing. He has written on a variety of substantive criminological topics including domestic violence, serial killers, money laundering, drugs, public order policing, organized crime, police accountability, intelligence-led policing, witness protection, risk and insecurity. He is currently engaged in research concerning 'guns, crime and social order'.

Nigel South is a Professor in the Department of Sociology and Centre for Criminology, a member of the Human Rights Centre and, from 2005 to 2013, a Pro-Vice-Chancellor, at the University of Essex, Colchester, UK. He is also a visiting adjunct professor in the School of Justice at Queensland University of Technology, Brisbane. He has published widely on green criminology; drug use, health and crime; inequalities and citizenship; and theoretical and comparative criminology.

Toine Spapens is full Professor of Criminology at Tilburg University, the Netherlands. He specializes in research on organized crime and international police and judicial co-operation. His empirical studies include the trafficking in illicit firearms, ecstasy production and trafficking, large-scale cannabis cultivation, environmental crime, illegal gambling and match-fixing. His theoretical work focuses on organised crime networks, the regulation of (former) illegal markets and multi-agency approaches to serious and organized crime problems.

Daan van Uhm is a junior assistant professor in criminology at the Willem Pompe Institute for Criminal Law and Criminology of the Utrecht University. He has conducted research in the area of flora and fauna crimes and recently defended his PhD research on the illegal trade in wildlife with a focus on the EU.

Jonathan Verschuuren is full Professor of International and European Environmental Law at Tilburg University (the Netherlands) and faculty member of the Tilburg Sustainability Center. His research mainly focuses on the role of international and EU environmental law in legal practice, on issues such as biodiversity conservation and climate change. Some of his recent publications include *Research Handbook on Climate Change Adaptation Law* (2013) and 'Hydraulic Fracturing and Environmental Concerns: The Role of Local Government', *Journal of Environmental Law* (2015).

Rob White is Professor of Criminology at the University of Tasmania, Sandy Bay, Australia. He has written widely in the areas of criminology and youth studies, and has a particular interest in issues related to environmental harm, ecological justice and green criminology. His recent books include *Transnational Environmental Crime: Toward an Eco-Global Criminology* (2011), *Climate Change from a Criminological Perspective* (2012) and *Environmental*

Harm: An Eco-Justice Perspective (2013), and he is also the author of *Crimes Against Nature* (2008).

Karin van Wingerde is Assistant Professor of Criminology at Erasmus School of Law, Erasmus University, Rotterdam, the Netherlands. Karin's research interests include the regulation of corporate behaviour, and corporate, financial and environmental crimes. Particularly, she is interested in the relationship between various legal and extra-legal mechanisms of social control, and the behaviour of business firms.

Preface and Acknowledgements

This book focuses on the questions that follow from transnational environmental crimes and harms from the perspective of enforcement as well as green criminological research. The increasing cross-border scope of environmental crimes is one of the reasons why governments and the enforcement community have trouble in finding the proper responses. Law enforcement cooperation between western industrialized states is often time consuming and problematic and the problems increase exponentially when environmental criminals take advantage of situations where government and law enforcement are weak. In addition, developments such as climate change and loss of biodiversity affect the entire planet and may lead to all sorts of criminal behaviour and spark migration and conflicts, but are as of yet hardly studied from a criminological perspective.

As editors, we wish to thank Tilburg University and VU University for their financial support, which made the book possible. We would also like to thank Ashgate Publishing and the editors of the Green Criminology Series, Michael J. Lynch and Paul B. Stretesky, for enthusiastically agreeing to publish this volume in the series.

Tilburg, Hobart, Amsterdam.
Toine Spapens
Rob White
Wim Huisman

Introduction

Toine Spapens, Rob White and Wim Huisman

Environmental crime is in many ways a cross-border crime and the same applies to environmental harms that have not (yet) been criminalized. To begin with, such harms and crimes may be transnational in their effect, such as the pollution of air and water. Second, they may involve international commodity chains, for instance of waste that is being transported or trafficked illegally from one part of the world to another. Third, persons may travel from one country to another and commit environmental crimes or cause environmental harm in more than one jurisdiction or in international waters. Finally, cross-border environmental crime may even take place in cyberspace, for example by committing fraud in emission trading schemes (Spapens 2011). This transboundary and even global scope often also applies to environmental harms that have not (yet) been criminalized as such, with climate change as the most notable example.

Investigation and prosecution of transnational environmental crime requires cross-border cooperation between competent authorities. The central instrument in traditional law enforcement cooperation is rogatory letters, or requests for mutual legal assistance. How such requests are exchanged is laid down in an extensive patchwork of treaties and conventions drawn up for example in the context of the United Nations, the Commonwealth, the Council of Europe, and bilaterally between states. In addition, the police can exchange information through the Interpol channel. In this system, sovereignty is the basic principle and only the competent authorities of nation states may exchange rogatory letters (Michalowski and Bitten 2005). This system is in many respects insufficient to tackle transnational environmental crimes and harms effectively and we urgently need to think about feasible solutions for the problems experienced and the role criminologists may have in this process. Here we just mention a few aspects.

To begin with, many environmental crimes take place in territories that can be seen as 'ungoverned spaces', where the legitimate government is unable (or unwilling) to enforce laws or where state institutions have ceased to function altogether (Clunan and Trinkunas 2010). However, while the international community can decide to send peacekeeping forces, there is as of yet no possibility to mount missions to stop serious harms to the environment. There also exists no globally competent police force to enforce international environmental treaties, such as the Convention on International Trade in Endangered Species of Wild Fauna and Flora (CITES) and the International Convention for the Prevention of

Pollution from Ships (MARPOL). In some cases, non-governmental organizations have taken on the role of an alternative enforcement agency in situations where the legitimate government was no longer effective or as collectors of intelligence and evidence. Clearly, such operations are not only dangerous for those involved but they come with other potential problems as well, such as a lack of training and accountability (White 2012b).

Second, even in countries with a functioning *Rechtsstaat* the police and judicial authorities face many problems. In many countries, environmental crimes have low investigative priority and the agencies responsible therefore lack resources and personnel. Environmental crimes often do not produce immediate victims or visible pollution and thus require proactive and intelligence-led policing, whereas in many countries such concepts have yet to be developed or to be implemented successfully (Spapens 2014). Specialist knowledge on the part of the police and the public prosecution service is highly necessary, particularly because the perpetrators are sometimes corporations which do not hesitate to spend millions to hire the best lawyers, but expertise is often lacking. Furthermore, enforcement of environmental laws involves law enforcement agencies as well as administrative authorities but cooperation is sometimes problematic (Spapens 2014). This is also true for cases of cross-border crime when information must be exchanged between law enforcement and administrative authorities, for instance to enable the latter to revoke or refuse a license. Even within the EU there exists no clear legal framework for this (Peters and Spapens 2015).

Third, specific harms to the environment may not be defined as criminal offences at all. In other cases, the maximum penalty may be so low that proper investigation and transnational law enforcement cooperation may become impossible. For example, the application of special investigative methods such as wiretapping and surveillance in many countries requires that the offense is considered serious and penalized accordingly. In the Netherlands, for example, covert investigation methods can only be applied if the offence is punishable with a minimum of four years' imprisonment. A minimum of four years also applies to the United Nations Convention on Transnational Organized Crime, now the most comprehensive treaty for mutual legal assistance in terms of the number of states that are party to it. However, an offence does not qualify as 'organized crime' if the maximum prison penalty is lower than four years, which often applies to environmental crimes.

The examples clearly illustrate that enhancing the enforcement of cross-border environmental crime is already a Herculean task. However, we must also think about expanding criminalization to environmental harms, for instance by introducing the concept of 'ecocide' in international crimes as Polly Higgins (2010) and others have suggested.

If such crimes were introduced at the international level, criminologists also know that even in an ideal situation, only a small percentage of all crimes that are committed end with a conviction (Van Dijk et al. 2014). We must therefore also consider alternative approaches in the broadest possible sense at the level of international institutions, sovereign states and actors within states. This for instance may include taking action against corruption and promoting good governance in weak states; reducing demand for protected wildlife products through information campaigns, for example by convincing people that a potion made of rhinoceros horn will not cure cancer; regulation through mechanisms such as emission trading schemes; and by 'naming and shaming' of corporations that cause environmental damage.

Finally, the increasingly transnational nature of the problems discussed above also has implications for criminology. Green criminology is still a, albeit rapidly, developing field. As Rob White and others have argued, green criminologists should develop an eco-global criminology that focuses on environmental harms and crimes as such, but also on the economic structures and dynamics that underlie these as well as on conflicts and other associated problems that they may cause (White 2010a, 2010b, 2012a; Sollund 2012). Green criminology definitely needs more international and comparative research and theoretical development.

The contributors to this volume address many of the issues raised above. The book is divided into four parts. Part I, 'The Global Context of Environmental Crime and Green Criminology', explores some of the main issues in the field of transnational environmental crime and harm and its containment, as well as some of the challenges for green criminology.

In Chapter 1, Nigel South approaches these questions from the perspective of the 'contested planet' and analyses four dimensions of such contestation, relating to consumption, laws, conflicts and knowledge. All of these propose specific dilemmas. Environmental harms, for example, often follow from normal social and economic behaviour. Defining matters of environmental crime and harm in law and then pursuing processes of enforcement and prosecution is not easy and disputes have often proved unresolvable in courts of law. Environmental problems may be the underlying cause of all sorts of conflict, and resources such as drinking water will be increasingly contested in the near future. Finally, South addresses the contest for evidence for example on climate change, health hazards and harms.

In Chapter 2, Spapens and Huisman discuss the scope of transnational environmental crime and three main strategies to curb the problem: enforcing environmental regulations, reducing general opportunity structures, and putting social pressure on the perpetrators. All three strategies may be successful in specific circumstances, but difficulties often arise. Most importantly, Spapens and Huisman argue that we need a better understanding of the determinants of 'what works' in cases of cross-border environmental crime, and also in the scope of existing theories on situational crime prevention and regulation.

In Chapter 3, Daan van Uhm analyses the global and European scope of trafficking in protected wildlife. Using among other sources empirical data from the EU Trade in Wildlife eXchange database on seizures, he presents an overview of the species involved, and the countries of origin and destination, and analyses the characteristics of the offenders. Furthermore, Van Uhm puts wildlife trade into the perspective of (green) criminological theory by assessing the harms it causes to the world. He concludes that the harms are a global problem that is particularly visible in relatively poor source countries, but very much depending on demand in the richer parts of the world.

Next, James Sheptycki draws attention to the discipline of criminology and examines the implications of the development of green criminology for the paradigmatic boundaries of the field. In the beginning, the objects of criminology were crimes that 'ordinary' criminals commit, such as property crimes, violent crimes, and drug dealing and trafficking. The introduction of the concept of 'white collar crime' by Edwin Sutherland in 1939 first expanded the field of study for criminology to crimes committed by 'respectable' individuals and corporations. William Chambliss in 1989 again set new boundaries for the criminological discipline with his observation that states could also be criminal actors. Here, Sheptycki addresses the question of whether green criminology is yet again substantially expanding the field of study for criminologists.

Part II, 'Law Enforcement Responses to (Transnational) Environmental Crime', addresses aspects of policing and prosecuting these types of crime. To begin with, Carole Gibbs in Chapter 5 describes the results of a process evaluation of one innovative policing effort in which intelligence-led policing was implemented to reduce illegal exports of hazardous waste. This chapter highlights the promise of such strategies for reducing a portion of transnational environmental problems, as well as dimensions of the trade that must be addressed using additional forms of intervention.

In Chapter 6, Grant Pink considers the issue of law enforcement responses to transnational environmental crime with a particular focus on the role of environmental regulatory agencies as well as the range of operational and policy factors which inform and shape their enforcement responses.

Jan Glazewski offers in Chapter 7 a judicial perspective by discussing the problems of prosecuting three suspects who had illegally harvested rock lobster in South African waters and exported them to the United States over a period of 14 years. In this case, the defendants were initially criminally prosecuted under South African and US laws and subsequently subjected to a civil restitution claim under the US Mandatory Victims Restitution Act. The issues raised include the nature of South Africa's property interest, as opposed to a regulatory interest, in living marine resources located in its waters; the quantification of damage caused by loss of natural resources, in this case by theft, over a period of time; and the difficulties that arise in tackling transnational fisheries crime.

Chapter 8 by Rob White examines four problems that environment courts encounter as they take heed of human interests as well as nonhuman interests in their deliberations, and in their efforts to repair environmental harm. These are the problems of victimization – victim status and engagement of the nonhuman in court; of ontology – determining the boundaries of the natural object; of expertise – who is to speak on behalf of nonhuman nature and in what capacity; and, of temporality – dealing with social and ecological change over time and space.

Part III, 'Alternative Methods to Combat (Transnational) Environmental Crime', considers responses outside the scope of law enforcement as well as multi-agency approaches. To begin with, in Chapter 9 Cameron Holley presents the concept of 'new environmental governance' (NEG) which offers an alternative to traditional command and control approaches. NEG aims to tackle environmental problems through cooperation between private, public and non-government actors.

In Chapter 10, Giuseppe Rotolo discusses the similar concept of 'deliberative democracy'. It aims at problems which have a social impact and in which the commitment and participation of the entire community may help to reach a feasible solution. Deliberative democracy involves processes of information, debates about the problems, and deliberations by a random sample of the population. Rotolo examines whether deliberative democracy could also contribute to environmental protection.

Karin van Wingerde in Chapter 11 addresses the question of how to deter corporations from committing environmental crimes. She interviewed representatives of 40 firms in the Dutch waste industry to explore 'what works'. Her findings are that deterrence often fails if sanctions only communicate a threat message. Instead, sanctions that communicate a moral message may contribute to compliance with environmental regulations by emphasizing that the penalized behaviour is condemned and by creating consensus about the blameworthiness of the penalized offence. As a rule, corporations embedded in the Dutch society are particularly responsive to negative publicity, reputational damages and pressures from the local community and therefore 'naming and shaming' could be more effective than traditional law enforcement.

Chapter 12 highlights another alternative approach to environmental issues: the EU Emission Trading Scheme (ETS). However, such a provision cannot function without proper enforcement and Floor Fleurke and Jonathan Verschuuren explore how this is organized in the 31 participating member states. Their conclusion is that this is a continuous, dynamic and complex process. In practice, enforcement strategies, institutional settings and funding differ widely.

Part IV, '(Transnational) Environmental Crime and Criminological Research', offers new ideas on the study of environmental crimes and harms as well as the results of specific case studies. In Chapter 13, Lorraine Elliott presents an analytical framework for the study of criminal networks and black markets in transnational environmental crime. Taking the black markets in ozone depleting substances, smuggled wildlife and trafficked timber as an example, she finds that these are characterized by varying forms of network arrangements that link together poachers, producers, traders, brokers and purchasers to manage illicit chains of custody. Elliott concludes that rather than focusing only on the illegal transaction as the unit of analysis (the enterprise model) or on the compilation of entities and social relations that are central to social network analysis, the two should be brought together to focus on structure as a key element.

Chapter 14 by Lorenzo Natali offers an elaboration of the use of photographic images to gather information and explore environmental harms and crimes. This method can bring together the multiple and complex nature of the experiences of individuals who live in polluted areas, and allow them to describe in detail and from their point of view what they know, think of and feel about the reality in which they find themselves living. In particular, Natali demonstrates the value of visual methods generally, and photo-elicitation specifically, as part of green cultural criminological research.

The final two chapters each present the results of a specific case study. First, in Chapter 15, Pasquale Peluso analyses illegal waste disposal in the Italian region of Campania. Being an endemic problem it involves not just organized crime, but also white-collar crime. Public authorities that do not exert sufficient formal control, and also poor social control in general, are the root causes of the problem.

In Chapter 16, Janine Janssen addresses the question of migration of other than human animals and observes that the political rhetoric is often quite comparable. Migration by other species may also be called 'invasive' and indeed may sometimes have devastating effects on indigenous animal populations. According to Janssen, migration raises fundamental questions about social inclusion and exclusion that trace back to the story of Noah's Ark.

References

Clunan, A. and Trinkunas, H. 2010. *Ungoverned Spaces*. Stanford: Stanford University Press.

Dijk, van J., Huisman, W. and Nieuwbeerta, P. 2014. *Actuele Criminologie*. Den Haag: Sdu uitgevers.

Higgins, P. 2010. *Eradicating Ecocide: Exposing the Corporate and Political Practices Destroying the Planet and Proposing the Laws Needed to Eradicate Ecocide*. London: Shepheard-Walwyn Publishers.

Michalowski, R. and Bitten, K. 2005. 'Transnational Environmental Crime', in *Handbook of Transnational Crime and Justice*, edited by P. Reichel. London: Sage Publications, 139–59.

Peters, M. and Spapens, T. 2015. 'The Potential for Information Exchange in Europe for the Purpose of an Administrative Approach to Crime', in *Administrative Approaches to Crime*, edited by T. Spapens, M. Peters and D. van Daele. The Hague: Eleven International Publising, 615–68.

Sollund, R. 2012. 'Introduction', in *Eco-Global Crimes: Contemporary Problems and Future Challenges*, edited by R. Ellefsen, R. Sollund and G. Larsen. Farnham: Ashgate, 3–14.

Spapens, T. 2011. *Cross-Border Police Cooperation in Tackling Environmental Crime*. Paper presented at the 9th INECE Conference, Whistler, Canada, 18–24 June.

——— 2014. 'Invisible Victims: The Problem of Policing Environmental Crime', in *Environmental Crime and its Victims*, edited by T. Spapens, R. White and M. Kluin. Farnham: Ashgate, 221–36.

White, R. 2010a. 'Globalisation and Environmental Harm', in *Global Environmental Harm*, edited by R. White. Cullompton: Willan Publishing, 3–19.

——— 2010b. 'Transnational Environmental Harm and Eco-Global Criminology', in *International Handbook of Criminology*, edited by S. Shoham, P. Knepper and M. Kett. Boca Raton: CRC Press, 231–57.

——— 2012a. 'The Foundations of Eco-Global Criminology', in *Eco-Global Crimes: Contemporary Problems and Future Challenges*, edited by R. Ellefsen, R. Sollund and G. Larsen. Farnham: Ashgate, 15–31.

——— 2012b. 'NGO Engagement in Environmental Law Enforcement: Critical Reflections', *Australasian Policing: A Journal of Professional Practice and Research* 4(1), 7–12.

Part I

The Global Context of Environmental Crime and Green Criminology

1 The Contested Planet

Global Green Criminology and Environmental Crime in Transnational Context

Nigel South

Introduction

At the beginning of October 2013, a report from the Intergovernmental Panel on Climate Change (IPCC) drew the world's attention to the serious implications of our current lack of concern for the planet: 'Warming of the climate system is unequivocal, and since the 1950s, many of the observed changes are unprecedented . . . The atmosphere and ocean have warmed, the amounts of snow and ice have diminished, sea level has risen, and the concentrations of greenhouse gases have increased' (IPCC 2013). Although this reflects the majority view in world science, this analysis is nonetheless contested. So, coinciding with the IPCC report, a similarly substantial publication from the Non-Governmental International Panel on Climate Change (NIPCC) presented an alternative view. This concluded that: 'the human effect [on the climate] is likely to be small relative to natural variability, and whatever small warming is likely to occur will produce benefits as well as costs' (NIPCC 2013). The NIPCC is sponsored by the Heartland Institute which, as its website makes clear, pursues a mission to 'discover, develop, and promote free-market solutions to social and economic problems'[1] and is funded by tobacco companies, fossil fuel producers and foundations to the right of the political spectrum (Kolbert 2013).

Debate is, of course, to be valued but the matters in dispute in this case are particularly momentous. The social sciences can contribute to discussion about climate change, our use and misuse of the planet, and the challenges we face and possible responses. In this chapter I bring one perspective to bear on these issues – the idea of a global green criminology. This is introduced as a device or method for orienting criminology to the study of global harms and crimes with an environmental and ecological impact. The aim of the chapter is to illustrate the ways in which the planet itself, and claims made upon it and about it, are contested – the definition of which I take to be 'the action or process of disputing or arguing' and related to events 'in which people compete for supremacy in activity'.[2] Four

1 See http://heartland.org/about.
2 Oxford Dictionaries: www.oxforddictionaries.com/definition/english/contest.

dimensions of such contestation are described, relating to consumption, laws, conflicts and knowledge. The chapter concludes with some observations on justice, rights and the prospects for a law of ecocide.

A Global Green Criminology

Bowling (2011, p. 365) has distinguished between criminological approaches of a transnational, international and global orientation but acknowledges that a truly 'global criminology' is 'some way from being fully established'. However, a 'green' criminology already offers much to such a project, demonstrating how forms of local and international environmental victimization are connected; how wildlife, timber and waste are trafficked through transnational commodity chains; and how air and water pollution are circulated globally (Bisschop 2012; South and Brisman 2013; Wyatt 2013; Walters 2013; White 2011). This global or planetary orientation is fundamental to a green criminology and is explicit in White's (2011) proposal for an eco-global criminology, and in any agenda for green criminology that is also concerned with crimes of war and violations of human rights (South 1998, p. 226).

The great global conundrum for the future is how to address energy and resource deficits and address the question of what we mean when we talk of 'sustainability'. A related problem faces us as we become a 'waste society' – how to cope with the unwanted discards of consumer society and mounting waste? Advanced economies continue to consume at a ferocious rate, now rapidly followed by the growth of other major markets and sources of demand. The economic system is ever more interdependent, reproducing its methods and models of production and consumption around the world, generating both benefits and dis-benefits from the flow of trade and exchange in goods, people and ideas. Among the dis-benefits are numerous instances of environmental degradation, resulting from complex trade relationships and consumption trends. These relationships and trends are built upon the idea of 'environment as property', and as a 'resource', that is owned and exploited for the benefit of some but not for the benefit of all. The following sections provide examples.

Contest in the Legal Marketplace: Problems of Consumption and 'Business as Usual'

World poverty and hunger are undeniable facts. According to the UN Food and Agriculture Organization (2012), in 2010–11, nearly 870 million people of the 7.1 billion people in the world (one in eight) lived with chronic undernourishment, almost all doing so in developing nations. There is no doubt that some of those who share our planet do not 'consume' enough at the level of basic nutrition and satisfaction of fundamental needs for water, shelter, security and health, all basic human rights (Pretty 2013; UNEP 2011). One proposition for a sustainable rather than contested planet that follows from this, is that in order for those 'without' to be able to consume more, those with more than they need should consume less (Pretty 2013). But across developed economies, consumption and growth are internalized and internationalized obsessions (Coghlan 2009).

Growth depends on the treadmill of production and the cycle of consumption (Stretesky et al. 2013; Brisman and South 2014). Aside from the purchase of necessities, additional consumerism continues to turn the wheels because we are persuaded to 'buy more', to 'buy new' and to discard the old as soon as new models and fashions appear, while technical built-in obsolescence means electronic goods have a rapid turnover in both domestic and work situations (Ferrell 2013). Consumers in advanced, wealthy economies are links in a 'long global chain' (Polgreen 2008, p. 1), in which 'the richest countries . . . often treat the poorest less as partners in progress than as cheap targets for resource extraction' (Owen 2012, p. 74), a relationship in which we are also contributors to environmental degradation and human rights abuses.

This is a 'global chain' on which Western economies are dependent and these patterns of consumption are accepted as essential to support 'business as usual' (Fussey and South 2012) and a standard of living that must be guaranteed. This could be seen in particularly uncompromising fashion in the political discourses of the Bush Administration, which, as Lynch et al. (2010) demonstrated, aimed to undermine climate change evidence and reassure consumers about the acceptability of carbon-profligate lifestyles. The 'national security' and 'national interest' of the United States provided reasons why the supply chain should win any contest over appeals for restraint.

This reflects the tendency of most (or all) societies to minimize the significance of environmental crime and damage, because 'much of the economy is based on the exploitation of natural resources' and because 'many of the most serious forms of environmental risk come from "normal social practice"' (Skinnider 2013, p. 3). According to Lynch (2013, p. 49), if we were to compare rates of 'ordinary crime' to environmental harms and negative impacts, the latter would significantly outweigh the former. As Skinnider (2013, pp. 2–3) points out, '[c]riminal law generally focuses on individual victims whereas environmental legislation often describes the environmental harm as an offence against public interest'. When one realizes that (1) the damage caused by environmental crime may be difficult to identify because it may not be immediate, (2) identifying the perpetrator of environmental crime and establishing criminal liability can be challenging given lengthy and complex chains of causation, and (3) the victims of environmental crime are not always aware of the fact that they have been victimized and, even if they are, they might not consider themselves to be 'crime victims' (Skinnider 2013, pp. 5–6; White and Heckenberg 2014), it becomes understandable that instances of environmental crime or harm are underestimated, overlooked or disguised, their severity minimized, and life and business continue 'as usual'.

Contested Laws and Environmental Crimes

Environmental crime or harm can be defined in terms of either the destruction and degradation of the earth's resources or as taking advantage of such situations and/or the efforts made (or not made) to regulate or prevent it. Acts formally recognized as crimes will have broken criminal law; harms will be interpreted more broadly and include actions which may be legally and economically acceptable although ecologically undesirable, through to those which are seen as damaging, to be discouraged and governed by forms of civil or administrative law. In some cases, actions and events may be identified as 'harmful' but appear to be permitted under laws relating to property or commerce, or be subject to no form of lawful oversight or intervention at all. As Higgins (2012, p. 15) says, 'Law shapes our societies, our way of thinking, our behaviour. By labelling our world a thing of property, legal systems have legitimised and encouraged the abuse of Earth by humans'. This is the underpinning of legal rights to exploit. Nonetheless, there are systems of law and regulation, as well as normative understandings, that are concerned to prevent or minimize abuse and exploitation. The question is how effective these are or can be?

Defining matters of environmental crime and harm in law and then pursuing processes of enforcement and prosecution is not easy. For example, various populations may be exposed to hazardous waste and emissions but cases attempting to establish liability and responsibility for this may be contested by the accused and have often proved unresolvable in courts of law (Eurojust 2014; Everson 2012, p. 175; Uhlmann 2009). Establishing 'responsibility' may also be difficult in cases where there is denial of a 'problem' or where a problem occurs not because of an intentional or mistaken action but because of actions that were not taken at all. For example, in their study of over 20 examples of environmental crime cases in the Netherlands, Huisman and van Erp (2013) found the phenomenon of 'denial' to be a common running thread. But the behaviour that accompanies 'denial' – 'doing nothing' – was particularly significant: 'most (although not all) of [the] . . . cases of environmental crimes were crimes of omission: crimes that constitute not taking actions prescribed by regulation or, in other words, crimes that consist of doing nothing'. In fact, the authors argue, white-collar crimes might often be better seen as cases where actions that might have been expected are not performed and compliance with rules is overlooked or ignored rather than there being a 'purposeful choice to deviate from the rules by taking an alternative course of action'.

Of course, there are deliberate acts of environmental crime as well and these may involve offenders from both sides of the legal/illegal borderline. Block (2002), for example, uses routine activity theory to examine the involvement of organized crime in illegal waste disposal in New York and Haiti, describing failures of regulation. Szasz (1986) examined the relationships between legal industries that produce toxic waste and the organized crime enterprises employed to dispose of this. Here corporate actors were not ignorant or powerless in the exchange but evidently benefited from their relationship with organized crime. The Naples garbage crisis arose from profitable collaborations primarily between local government and legitimate business, with the support of organized crime groups (Ruggiero and South 2010). Indeed, as Dines (2013) shows, the 2008 'trash emergency' was more a result 'of corporate malpractice and institutional complicity' than stereotypical Mafia activity. All of these examples suggest that normative assumptions about compliance with regulations and laws concerning unmanaged waste disposal and actions damaging to the environment and public health can be contested.

Some targeted crimes are committed because nature can yield commodities for which there may be specific demand in illegal markets. Wildlife are part of such a global trade as 'commodities', with the literature now providing many case studies (Nurse 2013; Wyatt 2013); e.g. elephant poaching, the ivory trade and the effect of CITES agreements (Lemieux and Clarke 2009), trafficking of fur and falcons (Wyatt 2012), trade in parrots and related species decline (Sollund 2011). In these cases it should be recalled that legal and policy frameworks are overwhelmingly anthropocentric, so laws and regulations are already limited in scope and weak in application.

Contest as Conflict: Fighting over Resources and the Future

Abundance of resources may, ironically, be a curse for a nation or community although this is not inevitable. Muffett and Bruch (2011, p. 4) note that 'well-managed resources can help fund reconstruction efforts and help bring order from chaos' while Lujala and Rustad (2011, p. 19) argue that '[h]igh-value natural resources have the potential to promote and consolidate peace' and can 'help to jump-start development, secure sustainable growth, raise living standards, and increase economic equality'. Nonetheless, resource contestation can lead to various kinds of conflict (see Brisman et al. 2015). Late-modern consumption is highly dependent on the exploitation of the mineral, plant and wildlife wealth of developing countries by global capital. Transnational corporations owe little allegiance to any particular nations and establish subsidiaries and operations where conditions offer relaxed taxation and governance arrangements and local populations and resources provide exploitable markets and products. In the developing world their activities lay claim to the 'rights' to indigenous knowledge, patent the genetic or pharmaceutical products of plants of local origin, and pursue the mining of ores and felling of timber to meet the demands of global consumer markets in both advanced as well as emerging economies (South 2007; EIA 2014; Bavinck et al. 2014; Wyatt 2014). As a result of such activity, indigenous peoples have suffered impositions enforced by violence and protestors have been subject to lethal responses (van de Sandt 2009, pp. 14–15; Global Witness 2014).

Historically, conflicts have occurred over the desirable nature of land owned by others, based on ambitions to extend power, to punish or to repatriate and, as part of this process, to gain control over resources that such land – or seas – can bring. So, for example, tensions between China and Japan reflect a long history of rivalry, suspicion and conflict, dating back centuries and exacerbated during and since the Second World War. But if these tensions have historical roots, they also have a forward-looking dimension, spanning the next decade and the rest of this century, anticipating a resource-hungry future in which competition will intensify

(Xu 2014) and a return to conflict may follow. But it is probably the experience of several nations in Africa that illustrate this potential for conflict best, having already suffered wars over or fuelled by resource wealth.

The Democratic Republic of Congo has now experienced decades of 'highly organized and systematic exploitation' (UN 2002, p. 10, para. 52) involving, inter alia, rebels and government forces profiting from the trades in mineral ores (gold, tantalum, tin, tungsten), subjecting civilians to massacres, rape and extortion, and using forced labour and coercing children into the role of soldiers. In Nigeria, as Dorward (2012) shows, 'Despite being rich in oil, the country is overwhelmed by corruption and violence'. Oil production profits are supposed to be distributed among all states to support those in areas that are 'resource-poor' and 'to maintain social services'. However, as Dorward noted, 'successive military strongmen, politicians, corrupt bureaucrats and businessmen swindled much of the money. The people of the oil-producing areas of the Niger Delta, who bore the brunt of ecological degradation by the oil industry and human-rights abuses of the military, eventually took up arms'. A period of hope for change following election of a new civilian government in 1999 did not last, leading to current conflicts between Muslim and non-Muslim groups. This has been inflamed by the granting to the oil-producing regions of the south-east, the 'first call on 13% of locally-derived oil revenue, in addition to their share of revenue'. As Dorward observes, 'While a long-overdue compensation for decades of neglect, this further enraged the poor and unemployed in other parts of Nigeria, especially in the Islamic North'. Beyond the matter of physical conflict, the operations of Shell Oil and its subsidiaries in the Niger Delta have given rise to a range of litigated cases, accusations and controversies concerning environmental pollution and failure to clean up affected land and water, as well as lack of due diligence with regard to environmental sustainability and abuses of human rights (Leader et al. 2012). More recently, Shepherd (2013), writing of anticipated large-scale oil production in Uganda in coming years, notes that the nation has 'been gripped by intense debate' with the example of 'Waste, corruption, environmental catastrophe and conflict in a country like Nigeria' providing a 'stark warning' and where 'The spectre of the "resource curse" looms large'.

Ownership and control of water sources and distribution can also be a source of tension. Water is one of the most fundamentally important resources for life and the planet and its supply is a priority for national governments and local communities. Increasingly though, the delivery of water supply has been privatized and, in some cases, where excessive prices or profits have been consequences, then resistance, protest and conflict have followed. A notable example is the case of Bolivia which, in 1999, leased the public water system of the city of Cochabamba to the Aguas Del Tunari, in which US company Bechtel Group was the majority shareholder. This lease was provided by Bolivia for a small payment, rumoured to be less than US$20,000 (Rieu-Clarke and Loures 2009; Rodwan and Cingranelli 2007, p. 141). The leasing arrangement resulted in the most vulnerable groups being unable to afford water. This led to violent protests resulting in hundreds being injured. More recent examples of water conflicts were the 2014 confrontations in South Africa (BBC News 2014) and Detroit, USA (Burns 2014).

In a future where climate change increases the incidence of drought in some regions then such conflicts could be expected to become more frequent. As Michel (2009) warns:

> Insufficient water supplies can impair agricultural production, endanger public health, strain established settlement patterns, and jeopardize livelihoods and social well-being. Where different countries (e.g., upstream and downstream) or different communities (e.g., rural and urban) share the same river, worsening climate pressures could engender sharpened competition or even violent confrontations to secure an increasingly scarce resource.

Contested Evidence: Denial of Climate Change, Health Hazards and Harms

Agnew (2012, p. 37) has issued a 'dire forecast' about the influence that climate change may have on criminal activity but also warns that corporations and states are 'actively engaged in efforts to ensure that many of the harmful acts that they commit remain legal'. These efforts can include funding publicity campaigns and mounting court cases, using significant financial resources. Climate change is expected to damage infrastructure, making resources scarce and leading to displacement of peoples (Abbott 2008, pp. 6–7; South 2012). In a future world beset by the consequences of climate change there will be implications for legislation and law enforcement, for the security of borders and for the ways in which human communities act. This latter point is easily overlooked but may drive a retrogressive environmental politics of fortress mentalities and right-wing survivalism. Both host and incoming communities may initiate or perceive prejudice, victimization and hate crimes directed against those of different cultures and religions. Such incidents and processes may create insider/outsider boundaries between the dispossessed, over-policed and unwelcome on the one hand and the protected and affluent tourists of cross-border consumption on the other (Fussey and South 2012, p. 35; White 2014).

Yet, particularly in the United States, denial and contestation about the reality of climate change are strongly expressed (Brisman 2012, 2013; Pappas 2014; for views of prominent critics of climate change science in the UK, see: Booker 2015; Ridley 2013). Other environmental concerns face similar objections. For example, although environmental justice investigators and activists have drawn attention to various links between patterns of race and class stratification and the likelihood of victimization by unhealthy exposures to sources of pollution, Brown (2007) shows that evidence of environmental health problems is strongly contested. According to Brown (2007, p. 2), this is because the cases and hazards identified by residents, representatives and scientists are products of processes at the heart of the modern economy: 'When environmental factors are the subject of inquiry, discussions of science are very contested because they lead to potential challenges to the underlying status quo production, distribution, disposal and regulatory practices of our society'. Brown argues that

> corporations and government regulators will be unlikely to accept removal of many chemicals from circulation or to bear the exorbitant costs of extracting these chemicals from the environment . . . corporate interests will likely oppose a research agenda that targets their products rather than individual susceptibilities . . . [and] . . . corporate and government actors will likely oppose strong lay participation because such involvement often stems from an approach that values community over corporate rights and that supports greater democratic participation in science, which in turn invites [other] challenges.

Environmental Justice, Rights and Ecocide

Heckenberg and White (2013) recommend that we adopt a forward-looking and horizon-scanning approach in order to identify the environmental crimes, harms and risks that lie 'over the horizon'. As a related exercise, we should consider the horizon of possible responses to these phenomena.

Environmental Justice and Human Rights

According to Lewis (2012, p. 87) environmental justice can be defined in terms of whether there is 'inequality or unfairness in the distribution of environmental burdens, where there is exclusion from the processes which determine how that distribution will be effected, or where disproportionate distribution is not balanced by sufficient reparation. This extends to potential injustices between developed and developing states, and between present and future generations'. Human rights and environmental justice are tied together in principle and in politics yet can be difficult to bring together in effective response even in very evident cases where both rights and the environment suffer, are violated and destroyed (Ruiz 2011; South and Brisman 2012). This duality of human rights and environmental justice can be seen expressed in international treaties, in some national laws and constitutions, in propositions that environmental rights should be seen as human rights and in cases where human rights regimes explicitly incorporate environmental rights, and in some discourses around the rights of future generations (Hiskes 2008; Gianolla 2013).

But none of this is straightforward. White (2007, p. 35), for example, asks whether environmental rights should be considered 'an extension of human or social rights (e.g. related to the quality of human life, such as provision of clean water)' or indeed whether human rights should 'be seen as merely one component of complex ecosystems that should be preserved for their own sake (i.e. as in the notion of the rights of the environment)?' White (2007, p. 41) also stresses the importance of recognizing our 'interconnectedness and human obligations to the non-human world' and argues that '[e]cological justice demands that how humans interact with their environment be evaluated in relation to potential harms and risks to specific creatures and specific locales as well as the biosphere generally'.

To enact environmental justice on any basis requires action but experience indicates that self-interest and contested evidence (Hulme 2009) disincline many or most from seeking genuine change in their own lives or on a broader scale. So, for example, returning to the theme of consumption and the present global state of inequality in which some have too much and some have too little, we can note the observation of Brown Weiss (2008, p. 216) that 'one cannot expect people to fulfil obligations to future generations if they are not able to satisfy their basic needs'. This is important because it can apply to both the very poorest for whom day-to-day survival provides the main time horizon. But for the more comfortable and well provided, it also serves as the basis for a powerful set of denials about the need for change at both individual and societal levels – 'basic needs' being re-defined by consumer society in quite significant ways.

If appeals to justice and rights will not persuade the unconvinced, then it may be at this level of the politics of consumption in everyday life that campaigns for hearts and minds must be mounted. Hence as spokespersons involved in leading the 2014 IPCC report have argued, rapid action involving a move from use of dirty fossil fuels to clean energy sources would mean 'It doesn't cost the world to save the planet' (Professor Ottmar Edenhofer) and, in fact, 'It is actually affordable to do it and people are not going to have to sacrifice their aspirations about improved standards of living' (Professor Jim Skea) (Carrington 2014). Such messages may be more palatable and perhaps more effective, yet they seem to dilute the importance and urgency of the challenge. However, the need to stress 'importance and urgency' is being expressed in the call for a new international law applying to a crime of ecocide.

Ecocide, Law and Leadership

The 1957 Treaty of Rome was a product of an era when environmental concerns were not high on the international agenda. Subsequently, an increasingly environmentally aware policy context has meant that some legislation directed at environmental protection has been required and in the European Union the basis for this was provided by the 1987 Single European Act (Cardwell et al. 2011, p. 2), strengthened in subsequent revisions to the Treaty. The problem in the EU – and internationally – is one of harmonization: how can the criminal law and tariffs of penalties operating in so many member states in the EU (and those beyond) ever be reconciled? Although there are now many international laws in place, the case against reliance on law alone is that it is so frequently and strongly contested.

On 1 July 2002, following adoption of the Rome Statute in 1998, the International Criminal Court came into operation, covering genocide, war crimes and crimes against humanity as offences that can be subject to court trial. But as Graham (2013) reminds us, while these crimes can involve the trial of those involved in combat and implementation, 'The Rome Statute also contains a fourth crime – an act of aggression. Unlike the others, this is a leadership crime' under which heads of government, cabinet ministers, military chiefs and others can be charged.

In many cases of environmental harm, failure to 'act to prevent', or to provide safeguards, can be commercially motivated or arise from inefficiencies or basic lack of concern. But there are also classes of inaction that are more than simply criminal, cynical or selfish. These may be examples of what could be called crimes of leadership. Leadership is a well-known and crucial issue, considered in relation both to what leaders did and did not do, reflecting fundamental failings of those in positions of leadership and responsibility. The issue is familiar in relation to simple failures to act, as discussed earlier (Huisman and van Erp 2013), as well as more clearly criminal failures of corporations (Johnson 2003) with resulting losses, harms and miseries for victims. It is also central to crimes of genocide, war-making and persecution (Heller 2007) and is relevant to proposals for policy and law designed to promote environmental justice and to cover 'Crimes against Present and Future Generations'. There is now some momentum gathering in support of such proposals, with the Mary Robinson Foundation supporting a 'Climate Justice' campaign to reduce the impacts of climate change on the most vulnerable and marginal (www.mrfcj.org/) and others calling for extensions of international law in ways now needed for the anthropocene twenty-first century. For example, Triffterer (2010, pp. 481–2) has noted that:

> A remarkable initiative has lately been started by the World Future Council. It proposes 'Crimes against future generations of life' but not meaning only generations of human beings. For these crimes the starting point can be any 'act[s] or conduct, when committed with knowledge of their severe consequences on the health, safety, or means of survival of future generations of humans, or of their threat to the survival of entire species or ecosystems'. It is especially mentioned 'military, economic, cultural or scientific activities, or the regulatory approval or authorisation of such activities', when they cause one of the above mentioned consequences or a specific danger to protected values.

Along similar lines, Higgins has been the principal (although not the first, see e.g. Falk 1973; Gray 1996) advocate of an international law of ecocide and has described the case for this in the following way (Higgins 2012, p. 9):

> In 1948 the United Nations created the crime of genocide in response to the mass atrocities which arose out of World War Two. Today we face mass destruction of the planet, but unlike genocide, ecocide is not a crime of intent. Ecocide is a crime of consequence, one that often arises out of the pursuit of profit without imposition of a legal duty of care. Currently there is no crime to address this anomaly during peace-time . . . War Crimes prohibit mass environmental damage, yet there is no law to stop the daily destruction that has become the norm for business. Corporate law dictates that profit determines

> activity, regardless of the consequence to others in the earth community . . . By its very nature, ecocide leads to resource depletion, and where there is escalation of resource depletion, war comes chasing close behind. The capacity of ecocide to be trans-boundary and multi-jurisdictional necessitates legislation of international scope . . . In the event that ecocide is left to flourish, the 21st century will become a century of 'resource' wars.

A proposal for a crime of ecocide would embrace the principle of holding leaders to account, so that human-caused ecocide becomes a responsibility of governments as well as businesses – those who are policy-makers, directors or who are responsible for funding or investment, become legally bound to ensure that any business practice that causes mass damage, destruction or loss of ecosystems is brought to an end (Higgins et al. 2013). Higgins points out that it is not simply a new spirit in national and international law that is required but also a new spirit in national and international leadership, arguing that 'When leaders fail to act or make decisions that lead to mass damage and destruction, that surely can only be called a crime . . . The plight of our time is the abject failure of leadership, the lack of a duty of care' (Higgins 2013).

This proposal resonates with similar calls for extensions of international law (see e.g. DiMento 2003; Kotzé 2012). But it should also be noted that the idea of such extension is not without its critics, even if they are sympathetic to its aims. Thus Gilbert (2014, p. 552) recognizes that 'The reality of global warming has forced the international community to seek various responses, including legal responses' and observes that 'It is undoubtedly possible to criminalize "ecocide"'. However, and referring specifically to 'global warming', he continues by arguing that 'just because it can be made subject to criminal law in no way justifies a comprehensive application of international criminal law to global warming per se'. Gilbert is concerned in particular with climate change-induced displacement of humans, which he acknowledges is 'automatically to have taken an anthropocentric approach to the problem, from protecting the environment per se to protecting human beings dealing with the consequences of climate change'. Gilbert's purpose here is to make the process of criminalization more compatible with domestic and international criminal law in general. Without taking such an approach, his view is that although in 'some circumstances . . . one may be able to prove that those perpetrating acts that give rise to climate change which then forces people to move could be guilty of international crimes set out in the Rome Statute of the International Criminal Court . . . the complexity of those crimes, the issues surrounding necessary *mens rea*, causation and remoteness, suggest that successful prosecutions will be rare'.

'On the other hand', he adds, 'there is nothing to stop the international community or even states with broad extra-territorial jurisdiction from creating new crimes to protect the environment and those affected by changes thereto'. Gilbert's reticence about the proposal is primarily based on scepticism about whether a measure based on international criminal law is an appropriate way of responding to global warming or the specific consequential problem of human displacement.

Gilbert points out that law requires clarity and that complexity or ambiguity can diminish the chances of successful prosecution. On this point, while the call for a law of ecocide is attracting support, its formulation may still need some clarification and it might be anticipated that interpretation 'in practice' might not be what was intended 'in theory'. For example, the proposal refers to 'inhabitants' of a territory. Given there is also explicit reference to 'ecosystems', this term could be interpreted to include non-human species. However, if used within the work of the International Criminal Court, the term 'inhabitants' might conceivably become restricted to 'humanity', reflecting the existing anthropocentrism of law.[3] This though may only mean that further debate and refinement is required and this is to be welcomed.

Conclusion and Hope

It is doubtful that the 'corporate powerful' or the 'consuming individual' really wish to hasten the end of the planet, and governments, corporations and individuals frequently acknowledge that there are limits to resources and that human activity is having an impact on the planet and its systems. Yet the underlying or counter narrative is powerful and involves the articulation of minimization, neutralization and denial – 'it isn't really all that bad', 'the problems will go away', 'science will make things better' (Norgaard 2006; Szasz 2007). But what if it really is that bad, isn't going to 'go away' and 'science' doesn't have a 'magic bullet' solution (Klein 2014)?

Instead of denial, we need renewal of ideas about sustainability, justice, alternatives and hope. For example, drawing on social disorganization theory and responding to the deficits in community life that this highlights, Lynch (2013, p. 54) has proposed re-thinking, localizing and making more environmentally responsible, our living arrangements – not simply in our everyday lives and home but our communities. He proposes an 'eco-cities' model for the integration of living, working, social and circulation spaces and places, and a reliance on local governance and local oversight of natural resources. For Lynch,

> eco-city principles bring a unique sense of community into play . . . an expanded sense of human belongingness and community tied to recognizing human-environment connections. By expanding and tapping into this sense of environmental community, eco-city design strategies can also enhance neighborhood investment in informal social control, a key aspect of social disorganization's explanation of crime and its control.

Such re-thinking is necessary because, as Bovenkerk (2003, p. 36) observes, 'If alternatives are not actively sought, risk displacement will continue to take place

3 I am grateful to Ragnhild Sollund, Geoff Gilbert and Avi Brisman for points made here and elsewhere in this chapter. I also thank the editors for their helpful comments.

and . . . this invariably disadvantages already marginalized groups. For this reason the environmental justice movement argues for a policy of "Not In Anyone's Back Yard" instead of "Not In My Back Yard" – or from NIMBY to NOPE – Not On Planet Earth'.

To the negative 'Nope' we could perhaps also add more positive and hopeful sentiments. This would echo other directions in contemporary criminology such as the ideas and practice of positive criminology and therapeutic jurisprudence that seek to engage with the benign influential experiences that individuals may have (Ronel and Segev 2015). These can help them to turn away from negative attributes such as self-centredness, criminality and disregard for others and instead support social inclusion, individual development and integration of the personal, the social and spiritual (Segev 2015). We also might pursue this in the sense that Currie (2013, pp. 8–9) has invoked with the idea of 'hope'. Acknowledging that this is 'a fairly unusual criminological concept', Currie wishes to remind us of the importance of 'hope' because 'in its absence people can feel as if what they do or don't do doesn't matter' and that it is acceptable to 'focus on short-term personal gain and comfort' – the kind of factors that support inaction in response to environmental harms and climate change. Currie draws on a distinction made by Vaclav Havel (1991) between 'hope' and 'optimism' – the latter being the belief that 'all will work out for the best' but the former being a matter of conviction – that we can identify what the right path is and can strive to make things happen that we believe need to happen. It is this path of hope and conviction that we need to follow.

References

Abbot, C. 2008. *An Uncertain Future: Law Enforcement, National Security and Climate Change*. Oxford: Oxford Research Group.

Agnew, R. 2012. 'Dire Forecast: A Theoretical Model of the Impact of Climate Change on Crime', *Theoretical Criminology* 16(1), 21–42.

Bavinck, M., Pellegrini, L. and Mostert, E. 2014. *Conflicts over Natural Resources in the Global South: Conceptual Approaches*. London: CRC Press.

BBC News 2014. 'South Africa: Four Killed at Protest over Water Shortages'. Available at: www.bbc.com/news/world-africa-25840703 (accessed 20 December 2014).

Bisschop, L. 2012. 'Is it all Going to Waste? Illegal Transports of E-Waste in a European Hub', *Crime, Law and Social Change* 58(3), 221–49.

Block, A. 2002. 'Environmental Crime and Pollution: Wasteful Reflections', *Social Justice* 29(1–2), 61–81.

Booker, C. 2015. 'The Fiddling with Temperature Data is the Biggest Science Scandal Ever', *Telegraph*, 28 March 2015. Available at: www.telegraph.co.uk/news/earth/environment/globalwarming/11395516/The-fiddling-with-temperature-data-is-the-biggest-science-scandal-ever.html (accessed 12 April 2015).

Bovenkerk, B. 2003. 'Is Smog Democratic? Environmental Justice in the Risk Society', *Melbourne Journal of Politics* 29, 24–38.

Bowling, B. 2011. 'Transnational Criminology and the Globalization of Harm Production', in *What is Criminology?* edited by C. Hoyle and M. Bosworth. Oxford: Oxford University Press, 361–79.

Brisman, A. 2012. 'The Cultural Silence of Climate Change Contrarianism', in *Climate Change from a Criminological Perspective*, edited by R. White. New York: Springer, 41–70.

——— 2013. 'Not a Bedtime Story: Climate Change, Neoliberalism, and the Future of the Arctic', *Michigan State International Law Review* 22(1), 241–89.

Brisman, A. and South, N. 2014. *Green Cultural Criminology: Constructions of Environmental Harm, Consumerism, and Resistance to Ecocide*. London and New York: Routledge.

Brisman, A., South, N. and White, R. (eds). 2015. *Environmental Crime and Social Conflict*. Farnham: Ashgate.

Brown, P. 2007. *Toxic Exposures: Contested Illnesses and the Environmental Health Movement*. New York: Columbia University Press.

Brown Weiss, E. 2008. 'Climate Change, Intergenerational Equity and International Law', *Vermont Journal of Environmental Law* 9(3), 615–38.

Burns, R. 2014. 'Now the UN is Intervening in Detroit's Water Conflict: Could Thirsty Cities Riot?', *Guardian*. Available at: www.theguardian.com/cities.2014/oct/17/united-nations-detroit-water-cities-riot.htm (accessed 12 November 2014).

Cardwell, P., French, D. and Hall, M. 2011. 'Tackling Environmental Crime in the European Union: The Case of the Missing Victim?', *Environmental Law and Management* 23(3), 113–21.

Carrington, D. 2014. 'IPCC Climate Change Report – Averting Catastrophe is Eminently Affordable', *Guardian*, 13 April.

Coghlan, A. 2009. 'Consumerism is "Eating the Future" ', *New Scientist*, August.

Currie, E. 2013. 'Consciousness, Solidarity and Hope as Prevention and Rehabilitation', *International Journal for Crime, Justice and Social Democracy* 2(2), 3–11.

DiMento, J. 2003. *The Global Environment and International Law*. Austin: University of Texas Press.

Dines, N. 2013. 'Bad News from an Aberrant City: A Critical Analysis of the British Press's Portrayal of Organised Crime and the Refuse Crisis in Naples', *Modern Italy* 18(4), 409–22.

Dorward, D. 2012. 'Death, Oil and Religion: The Origins of Conflict in Nigeria Run Deep', *The Conversation*, 31 January. Available at: http://theconversation.com/death-oil-and-religion-the-origins-of-conflict-in-nigeria-run-deep-5067 (accessed 12 April 2015).

EIA. 2014. *Permitting Crime: How Palm Oil Extraction Drives Illegal Logging in Indonesia*. London: Environmental Investigation Agency.

Eurojust. 2014. *Strategic Project on Environmental Crime*. The Hague: Eurojust.

Everson, M. 2012. 'A Review of Federal Environmental Legislation and the Federal Environmental Regulatory Structure', in *Environmental Crime*, edited by M. Clifford and T. Edwards. Burlington: Jones and Bartlett, 153–81.

Falk, R. 1973. 'Environmental Warfare and Ecocide: Facts, Appraisals and Proposals', *Bulletin of Peace Proposals* 4, 80–84.

Ferrell, J. 2013. 'Tangled Up in Green: Cultural Criminology and Green Criminology', in *The Routledge International Handbook of Green Criminology*, edited by N. South and A. Brisman. London: Routledge, 349–64.

Fussey, P. and South, N. 2012. 'Heading toward a New Criminogenic Climate: Climate Change, Political Economy and Environmental Security', in *Climate Change from a Criminological Perspective*, edited by R. White. New York: Springer, 27–40.

Gianolla, C. 2013. 'Human Rights and Nature: Intercultural Perspectives and International Aspirations', *Journal of Human Rights and the Environment* 4(1), 58–78.

Gilbert, G. 2014. 'International Criminal Law is Not a Panacea – Why Proposed Climate Change "Crimes" are Just Another Passenger on an Overcrowded Bandwagon', *International Criminal Law Review* 14, 551–87.

Global Witness. 2014. *Peru's Deadly Environment: The Rise in Killings of Environmental and Land Defenders*. London: Global Witness.

Graham, K. 2013. 'Making Aggression a Crime – a Century Late but Better than Never', 26 September. Available at: http://blog.greens.org.nz/2013/09/26/making-aggression-a-crime-a-century-late-but-better-than-never/ (accessed 12 April 2015).

Gray, M. 1996. 'The International Crime of Ecocide', *California Western International Law Journal* 26, 215–71.

Havel, V. 1991. *Disturbing the Peace*. New York: Vintage.

Heckenberg, D. and White, R. 2013. 'Innovative Approaches to Researching Environmental Harm', in *The Routledge International Handbook of Green Criminology*, edited by N. South and A. Brisman. London: Routledge, 85–103.

Heller, K. 2007. 'Retreat from Nuremberg: The Leadership Requirement in the Crime of Aggression', *The European Journal of International Law* 18(3), 477–97.

Higgins, P. 2012. *Earth is Our Business: Changing the Rules of the Game*. London: Shepheard-Walwyn.

——— 2013. 'Leadership and a Law of Ecocide: Polly Higgins at TEDx Tallinn'. Available at: www.youtube.com/watch?v=zoYq7_x41D4 (accessed 12 April 2015).

Higgins, P., Short, D. and South, N. 2013. 'Protecting the Planet: A Proposal for a Law of Ecocide', *Crime, Law and Social Change* 59(3), 251–66.

Hiskes, R.P. 2008. *The Human Right to a Green Future: Environmental Rights and Intergenerational Justice*. Cambridge: Cambridge University Press.

Huisman, W. and Van Erp, J. 2013. 'Opportunities for Environmental Crime: A Test of Situational Crime Prevention Theory', *British Journal of Criminology* 53(6), 1178–200.

Hulme, M. 2009. *Why We Disagree About Climate Change: Understanding Controversy, Inaction and Opportunity*. Cambridge: Cambridge University Press.

Inter-Governmental Panel on Climate Change (IPCC). 2013. *Summary for Policymakers*. Available at: www.climatechange2013.org (accessed 12 April 2015).

Johnson, C. 2003. 'Enron's Ethical Collapse: Lessons for Leadership Educators', *Journal of Leadership Education* 2(1), 45–56.

Klein, N. 2014. *This Changes Everything*. London: Allen Lane.

Kolbert, E. 2013. 'Lost in the Denialosphere: Climate Change and Obamacare', *The New Yorker*, 2 October. Available at: www.newyorker.com/news/daily-comment/lost-in-the-denialosphere-climate-change-and-obamacare (accessed 12 April 2015).

Kotzé, L. 2012. *Global Environmental Governance: Law and Regulation for the 21st Century*. Cheltenham: Edward Elgar.

Leader, S., Ong, D., Van Ho, T., Yilmaz, A., Michalowski, S., Netto, U., Danesi, R. and Wlodarczak, B. 2012. *Corporate Liability in a New Setting: Shell and the Changing Legal Landscape for the Multinational Oil Industry in the Niger Delta*. Colchester: University of Essex, Essex Business and Human Rights Project. Available at: www.essex.ac.uk/ebhr/documents/niger-delta-report.pdf (accessed 12 April 2015).

Lemieux, A. and Clarke, R. 2009. 'The International Ban on Ivory Sales and its Effects on Elephant Poaching in Africa', *British Journal of Criminology* 49(4), 451–71.

Lewis, B. 2012. 'Human Rights and Environmental Wrongs: Achieving Environmental Justice through Human Rights Law', *International Journal for Crime and Justice* 1(1), 86–98.

Lujala, P. and Rustad, S. 2011. 'High-Value Natural Resources: A Blessing or a Curse for Peace?', *Sustainable Development Law and Policy* 12(1), 19–22, 56–7.

Lynch, M.J. 2013. 'Reflections on Green Criminology and its Boundaries: Comparing Environmental and Criminal Victimization and Considering Crime from an Eco-City Perspective', in *The Routledge International Handbook of Green Criminology*, edited by N. South and A. Brisman. London: Routledge, 43–57.

Lynch, M.J., Burns, R.G. and Stretesky, P.B. 2010. 'Global Warming and State-Corporate Crime: the Politicization of Global Warming under the Bush Administration', *Crime, Law and Social Change* 54, 213–39.

Michel, D. 2009. 'A River Runs Through It: Climate Change, Security Challenges, and Shared Water Resources', in *Troubled Waters: Climate Change, Hydropolitics, and Transboundary Resources*, edited by D. Michel and A. Pandya. Washington, DC: The Henry L. Stimson Center, 73–103.

Muffett, C. and Bruch, C. 2011. 'Introductory Comments: The Pervasive, Persistent, and Profound Links Between Conflict and the Environment', *Sustainable Development Law and Policy* 12(1), 4–6.

Non-Governmental International Panel on Climate Change (NIPCC). 2013. *Climate Change Reconsidered II*. Chicago: The Heartland Institute.

Norgaard, K.M. 2006. '"We Don't Really Want to Know": Environmental Justice and Socially Organized Denial of Global Warming in Norway', *Organization and Environment* 19(3), 347–70.

Nurse, A. 2013. *Animal Harm: Perspectives on Why People Harm and Kill Animals*. Farnham: Ashgate.

Owen, D. 2012. 'Dept. of Invention: The Artificial Leaf', *The New Yorker*, 14 May.

Pappas, S. 2014. '"Global Warming" Scarier Than "Climate Change", Survey Finds', *LiveScience/Yahoo!News*, Not in references: please provide full details 27 May. Available at: http://news.yahoo.com/global-warming-scarier-climate-change-surveys-194130900.html (accessed 12 April 2015).

Polgreen, L. 2008. 'Congo's Riches, Looted by Renegade Troops', *New York Times*, 16 November.

Pretty, J. 2013. 'The Consumption of a Finite Planet: Well-Being, Convergence, Divergence, and the Nascent Green Economy', *Environmental Resource Economics* 55(4), 475–99.

Ridley, M. 2013. 'Why Climate Change is Good for the World', *The Spectator*, 19 October. Available at: www.spectator.co.uk/features/9057151/carry-on-warming/ (accessed 12 April 2015).

Rieu-Clarke, A. and Loures, F.R. 2009. 'Still not in Force: Should States Support the 1997 UN Watercourses Convention?' *Review of European Community and International Environmental Law* 18, 185–97.

Rodwan, A.M. and Cingranelli, D. 2007. *Human Rights and Structural Adjustment*. Cambridge: Cambridge University Press.

Ronel, N. and Segev, D. (eds). 2015. *Positive Criminology*. Abingdon: Routledge.

Ruggiero, V. and South, N. 2010. 'Green Criminology and Dirty Collar Crime', *Critical Criminology* 18, 251–62.

Ruiz, D. 2011. 'Ecocide in the Mesopotamian Marshes', in *Social Control of Unconventional Deviance*, edited by G. Mesko, A. Sotlar and J. Winterdyk. Ljubljana: University of Maribor, 139–47.

Segev, D. 2015. 'Positive Criminology and Therapeutic Jurisprudence', in *Positive Criminology*, edited by N. Ronel and D. Segev. Abingdon: Routledge, 98–108.

Shepherd, B. 2013. 'Uganda's Oil: Lessons on Governance and the Resource Curse', *Guardian*, 20 March.

Skinnider, E. 2013. *Effect, Issues and Challenges for Victims of Crimes that have a Significant Impact on the Environment*. Vancouver: International Centre for Criminal Law Reform and Criminal Justice Policy.

Sollund, R. 2011. 'Expressions of Speciesism: The Effects of Keeping Companion Animals on Animal Abuse, Animal Trafficking and Species Decline', *Crime, Law and Social Change* 55(5), 437–51.

South, N. 1998. 'A Green Field for Criminology? A Proposal for a Perspective', *Theoretical Criminology* 2(2), 211–34.

——— 2007. 'The "Corporate Colonisation of Nature": Bio-Prospecting, Bio-Piracy and the Development of Green Criminology', in *Issues in Green Criminology: Confronting Harms against Environments, Humanity and Other Animals*, edited by P. Beirne and N. South. Cullompton: Willan Publishing, 230–47.

——— 2012. 'Climate Change, Environmental (In)Security, Conflict and Crime', in *Criminological and Legal Consequences of Climate Change*, edited by S. Farrall, D. French and T. Ahmed. Oxford: Hart, 97–111.

South, N. and Brisman, A. 2012. 'Critical Green Criminology, Environmental Rights and Crimes of Exploitation', in *New Directions in Crime and Deviance*, edited by S. Winlow and R. Atkinson. London: Routledge, 99–110.

——— (eds). 2013. *Routledge International Handbook of Green Criminology*. London and New York: Routledge.

Stretesky, P.B., Long, M.A. and Lynch, M.J. 2013. *The Treadmill of Crime: Political Economy and Green Criminology*. London: Routledge.

Szasz, A. 1986. 'Corporations, Organized Crime, and the Disposal of Hazardous Waste: An Examination of the Making of a Criminogenic Regulatory Structure', *Criminology* 24, 1–27.

——— 2007. *Shopping Our Way To Safety: How We Changed From Protecting The Environment To Protecting Ourselves*. Minneapolis: University of Minnesota Press.

Triffterer, O. 2010. 'Comment', Catholic Social Doctrine and Human Rights. Pontifical Academy of Social Sciences, Acta 15, Vatican City, 431–83. Available at: www.pass.va/content/dam/scienzesociali/pdf/acta15/acta15-triffterer.pdf (accessed 13 April 2015).

Uhlmann, D. 2009. 'Environmental Crime Comes of Age: The Evolution of Criminal Enforcement in the Environmental Regulatory Scheme', *Utah Law Review* 4, 1223–52.

UN. 2002. *Interim Report of the Panel of Experts on the Illegal Exploitation of Natural Resources and Other Forms of Wealth of the Democratic Republic of the Congo*. United Nations Document S/2002/565/22.

UNEP. 2011. *Towards a Green Economy: Pathways to Sustainable Development and Eradication of Poverty*. Nairobi: United Nations Environment Programme.

United Nations Food and Agriculture Organization. 2012. *FAO Statistical Yearbook 2012*. Rome: United Nations.

Van de Sandt, J. 2009. *Mining Conflicts and Indigenous Peoples in Guatemala*. The Hague: Cordaid.

——— 2013. 'Air Crimes and Atmospheric Justice', in *Routledge International Handbook of Green Criminology*, edited by N. South and A. Brisman. London: Routledge, 134–49.

White, R. 2007. 'Green Criminology and the Pursuit of Social and Ecological Justice', in *Issues in Green Criminology: Confronting Harms against Environments, Humanity and Other Animals*, edited by P. Beirne and N. South. Cullompton: Willan Publishing, 32–54.

——— 2011. *Transnational Environmental Crime: Toward an Eco-Global Criminology*. London and New York: Routledge.

——— 2014. 'Environmental Insecurity and Fortress Mentality', *International Affairs* 90(4), 835–51.

White, R. and Heckenberg, D. 2014. *Green Criminology: An Introduction to the Study of Environmental Harm*. London: Routledge.

Wyatt, T. 2012. *Green Criminology & Wildlife Trafficking: The Illegal Fur and Falcon Trades in Russia Far East*. Saarbrücken: Lambert.

——— 2013. *Wildlife Trafficking: A Deconstruction of the Crime, the Victims and the Offenders*. London: Palgrave.

——— 2014. 'The Russian Far East's Illegal Timber Trade: An Organized Crime?' *Crime Law and Social Change* 61(1), 15–35.

Xu, B. 2014. 'South China Sea Tensions', *Council on Foreign Relations*, 14 May. Available at: www.cfr.org/china/south-china-sea-tensions/p29790 (accessed 12 April 2015).

2 Tackling Cross-Border Environmental Crime

A 'Wicked Problem'

Toine Spapens and Wim Huisman

Introduction

Environmental crime encompasses a broad range of illegal behaviours. The first main category is the pollution of the air, seas and land. Examples are dumping waste or blending it with other goods, and importing and using illicit pesticides. The second main category concerns illegal acts causing direct harm to flora and fauna, for instance illegal deforestation and the poaching of and trading in protected wildlife. To green criminologists, however, the concept of environmental crime is still too narrow because it does not include equally harmful acts to the environment that have not (yet) been criminalized. Instead, they favour the concept of environmental harm, which includes behaviour contributing to global warming and loss of biodiversity, but also legal deforestation and extensive fishing outside territorial waters (White 2010, p. 237).

In many cases, environmental crimes transcend national borders. To begin with, illegal activities may be transnational in their effect, such as air and water pollution. For many years, for example, the Rhine, the Meuse and other European rivers that run through more than one country were heavily polluted with all sorts of waste, a process that started upstream and affected countries downstream.

Second, the logistical chains of environmental criminal acts may be international in scope, such as the trafficking of hazardous waste from one country to another.

Third, criminals may take advantage of differences in national environmental legislation. For example, a certain amount of soil may count as polluted according to the standards set in one country whereas it is not in another country. Thus, a company hired to clean the soil only needs to export it illegally, thereby avoiding a costly cleaning operation (Spapens 2011).

Fourth, the perpetrators may be operating in two or more countries. One example is a ship that during a journey through different countries continuously dumps waste, such as bilge water and slops, instead of offering it to a specialized harbour facility for processing.

Finally, cross-border environmental crime may even take place in cyberspace, for example fraud in emission trading schemes (Walters and Martin 2014).

The past decades have seen the development of an elaborate international legal framework to fight transnational environmental crime, such as the Basel Convention on the Control of Transboundary Movements of Hazardous Wastes and Their Disposal, the Convention on International Trade in Endangered Species of Wild Fauna and Flora (CITES) and the International Convention for the Prevention of Pollution from Ships (MARPOL). Also, the European Union has drafted regulations for the prevention of environmental harm and pollution, such as the European Waste Shipment Regulation (EWSR) (Bisschop 2014). Despite these initiatives, tackling cross-border environmental crimes remains a complex and in many respects 'wicked problem'.[1]

We begin by addressing the problem of cross-border environmental crime and environmental harm in more detail. We then discuss strategies to control both eco-crime and environmental harm by enforcing (cross-border) laws, by reducing general opportunity structures, and by putting social pressure on those who cause harm to the environment and violate environmental laws. Finally, we offer some brief conclusions.

The Problem of Cross-Border Environmental Crime

The impact of environmental crime and environmental harm has become more transnational in recent decades. Two main factors explain this development. The first is that the Western industrialized states have implemented more stringent regulations since the 1970s, causing visible environmental crime to shift to other parts of the world (Pellow 2007). Hazardous waste, for instance, is now trafficked to less affluent regions, to be dumped or treated in ways that harm both people and habitats (Bisschop 2015; Bisschop and Verhagen 2012, p. 294). The second explanation for the internationalization of environmental crime is the increasing level of social and economic globalization and mobility. This has been accompanied by a growing demand for wildlife products in Asia, for example for ivory and rhinoceros horn, and for exotic pets such as tropical birds and reptiles in Western countries.

Environmental criminals often take advantage of situations where government and consequently law enforcement are weak, and they may exploit military conflicts as well. Examples include the offloading of toxic waste in the coastal waters of Somalia, where the state does not have the means to prevent it, and illegal fishing for tuna off the coast of Libya in 2011, after the Gadhafi regime had collapsed and the Libyan coast guard was no longer able to patrol the area (Waldo 2009; BBC 2011; Brisman et al. 2015).

The proceeds of environmental crime are considerable. Wildlife crime is estimated to cost US$7.8–19 billion, illegal fishing US$4.2–23.5 billion, the illegal timber trade US$7–30 billion and illegal waste dumping US$11 billion.

1 The term 'wicked problem' was introduced in 1973 and refers to problems that are difficult to define and solve. See Rittel and Webber (1973).

Combined, these categories of environmental crime come third after counterfeiting (US$540 billion) and illicit drugs (US$323 billion) (UNEP 2012).

A wide range of perpetrators commit environmental crimes. The first category is petty criminals. In an example in the Netherlands, such perpetrators bought obsolete refrigerators and washing machines from dealers who are legally obliged to hand them over to licensed waste collectors. Next, they shipped the waste illegally to West Africa. Although this was a relatively small-scale operation, it still generated a substantial profit (Raad van Korpschefs 2010).

Second, environmental crime may involve organized crime groups. In Italy, for example, mafia groups are involved in trafficking and dumping hazardous waste (Gruppo Abele-Nomos et al. 2003, pp. 17ff.). According to Interpol, a significant proportion of both wildlife and pollution crime is carried out by organized criminal networks that often use the same routes to smuggle wildlife across countries and continents as they do to smuggle weapons, drugs and people (Interpol, n.d.).

Third, companies commit environmental crimes, for instance by not complying with environmental regulations or by violating the requirements of their operating licences. One example is fuel production companies that blend chemical waste with bunker fuel used in ships to avoid the cost of treating the waste (Spapens et al. 2013). Hazardous components, however, do not burn in the ships' engines but are vented into the air, adding substantially to levels of particulate matter (Andersson et al. 2009). Negligence by companies can also result in serious environmental disasters and food safety problems.

Finally, governmental agencies may commit environmental crimes. An example is the pollution as a result of the dumping of nuclear waste at the Hanford site in the United States (Kauzlarich and Kramer 1998, pp. 106–8). Critical criminologists have therefore argued that such events should be viewed as state crimes (Kauzlarich and Kramer 1998).

Tackling the Problem of Cross-Border Environmental Crime

Tackling environmental crime involves many actors, both governmental and non-governmental. Governance is therefore not limited to the state authorities, but basically involves community recognition of principles, laws, rules and procedures that identify standards of acceptable public behaviour and sufficient compliance to produce behavioural regularities (Keohane and Nye 2000, p. 10). Rules and regulations must therefore be legitimized by communities to be accepted and effective. In such circumstances, the enforcement of the law is indeed the *ultimum remedium*: it need only address a small percentage of persons and companies that willingly violate the rules. Prior to enforcement, other paths may be followed to change unwelcome behaviour.

Below, we discuss three different strategies. The first is to use law enforcement to guarantee compliance with environmental law influence. Second, opportunity structures that render specific crimes profitable may be reduced. Finally, communities ranging from the global to the local can put social pressure on perpetrators in order to change their behaviour.

Law Enforcement

Administrative Enforcement versus a Criminal Justice Approach

Most industrialized countries regulate economic activities that may be harmful to the environment. Such businesses require a permit to emit or discharge a pollutant into the air or water or to dispose of hazardous waste. The competent authority, for example the Environmental Protection Agency, regularly inspects to see if the company is complying with the requirements set in the permit. If it does not comply with general environmental laws, the authorities may impose a fine or a provisional order for penalty payment and/or they may order the shutting down of installations for shorter or longer periods and even revoke the permit. In some countries such interventions may be combined with a criminal investigation. Administrative enforcement is usually future oriented. It primarily aims at putting an end to the harms done to the environment and seeks reparation of the damage. By comparison and in general, the criminal justice approach is backward-looking and primarily aimed at punishing those who were responsible for violating the law. However, especially in environmental criminal law, some jurisdictions also include a criminal sanction aimed at reparation. For instance, the Dutch Economic Crimes Act contains reparatory sanctions for environmental offences (Van de Bunt and Huisman 2007). And the New South Wales Land and Environment Court, in its criminal division, combines fines with reparation orders. It is both forward-looking and backward-looking. As a problem-solving court, it aims to sanction and repair at the same time (White 2014). In addition, sentences are also assumed to have preventive effects on (potential) perpetrators. Of course, administrative enforcement only applies to legal entities. A crime group trafficking CITES-protected wildlife from Asia to Europe, for example, can only be tackled by criminal investigation.

The Difficulties of Enforcing Environmental Laws and Regulations

In practice, it is difficult to enforce environmental laws and regulations, for a number of reasons (Alvazzi del Frate et al. 1999; Bisschop 2011). To begin with, the authorities usually have limited resources, whereas the regulations themselves are complex, making it difficult to prove violations. Second, coordination problems may arise due to the many agencies involved in enforcing environmental law. Third, depending upon offence and jurisdiction, it is often hard to establish the liable party in corporate entities (with the exception of strict liability provisions), combined with the legal ambiguity and transnational differences in environmental regulation (Bisschop 2011, 2015).

If enforcement requires transnational cooperation, matters are even more complicated. One example is the enforcement of the EWSR, which aims to prevent illegal export by licensing exporters, traders, dealers and brokers. It only permits the export of second-hand equipment if the applicant submits a test report showing that all the equipment works and can prove that there is a market for the goods in the destination country. Enforcement agencies have great problems enforcing this regulation, of course; how can they prove that there is no market for a certain good in a specific country? They have equal difficulty proving that a foreign company receiving a shipment of waste will actually be unable to process it according to local environmental regulations, verifying that the waste has indeed reached its intended destination.

Environmental inspectorates try to overcome these problems by cooperating closely with other enforcement authorities (Van Erp and Huisman 2010). This is complex, however, because the EWSR is enforced by more than 25 old and new EU member states that often lack the necessary expertise, personnel and means. In response to these problems, the European Union Network for the Implementation and Enforcement of Environmental Law (IMPEL) launched an 'Enforcement Actions' project to share knowledge and expertise and carry out joint inspections. Despite these efforts, large differences in enforcement levels within the EU remain. Some member states still fail to inspect waste shipments on a regular basis or even lack an enforcement infrastructure stipulating the responsibility for waste shipment inspections. Greece, Spain and Italy have large seaports with easy access to African ports but do not participate in the Enforcement Actions project at all. Enforcement of e-waste regulations is still largely a matter of the personal commitment of certain officials (ESWI 2009, p. 68).

Police and Judicial Cooperation

Criminal investigation of cross-border environmental crimes comes with specific problems. The basis for such cooperation is a well-defined system of legal instruments, mostly conventions adopted at different levels varying from global to bilateral. For evidence to be presented to the court, the exchange of written requests for mutual legal assistance (letters rogatory) is required for which the judicial authorities are competent. If the police want to exchange information for investigative purposes only, they may use Interpol as a channel. This also requires them to send a written request and share information through Interpol's national central bureaus. Each of the 190 members of Interpol has a national bureau that operates on a 24/7 basis. In practice, there are three main barriers to cross-border police cooperation.

The first barrier concerns shortcomings in the global legal framework. Conventions on mutual assistance in criminal matters are concluded bilaterally or multilaterally between states, in the context of the Commonwealth of Nations (Harare Scheme), the Council of Europe and the European Union, for example. The most comprehensive in terms of the number of participating countries is the UN Convention on Transnational Organized Crime. This convention is particularly important because environmental crimes such as the trafficking of waste and endangered species of wild flora and fauna, for example, usually involves countries that are not party to other treaties on mutual assistance in criminal matters. However, many environmental crimes do not qualify as organized crime, for example because the maximum penalty is less than the required minimum of four years' imprisonment (Spapens 2011).

The second barrier is that even if a convention applies, cooperation through letters rogatory is usually slow unless it involves a life-and-death situation. A large-scale investigation may require the exchange of dozens of different letters rogatory. Detectives, public prosecutors and investigative magistrates have heavy workloads as it is, and they will not welcome the extra work involved in cross-border cooperation. Consequently, investigations often 'stop at the border'. The reluctance to seek cooperation also increases with the geographical and cultural distance (Spapens 2008).

The third barrier is that it is often necessary to cooperate with law enforcement agencies in countries with weak governments and where corruption is a problem. A lack of trust not only prevents the proactive exchange of information and intelligence, but it may even prevent authorities from seeking mutual legal assistance altogether, for fear that information will be leaked to suspects and thus compromise ongoing investigations.

The problems involved in effective cross-border investigation of environmental crimes are clearly highly complex. Not surprisingly, NGOs can sometimes collect information on the ground where the police are unable to seek cooperation, even though NGOs do not have coercive powers (White 2012a). A NGO might for instance be able to collect DNA samples of flora and fauna and to interview witnesses. Sometimes NGOs even intervene in situations where sovereignty precludes enforcement. As mentioned above, an example of this occurred during the Libyan conflict in 2011, when the Gadhafi regime collapsed. Libya claims an exclusive fishing zone of 62 miles into the Mediterranean Sea, which includes important breeding grounds for blue fin tuna. The fall of the regime left the zone unguarded and fishermen immediately took advantage. In this case, activist organization Sea Shepherd operated in Libyan waters to prevent illegal fishing (Sea Shepherd 2011).

Reducing General Opportunity Structures

The control and prevention of environmental crime depends on an understanding of the processes by which these types of offences are committed. To control and prevent environmental crimes, we must first identify the specific opportunity structure associated with the offence we wish to prevent. That is, we must identify the features of the settings that allow the crime to occur. Ideally, in order to be effective, law enforcement targets these opportunities. An opportunity for crime is 'a potential course of action, made possible by a particular set of social conditions, which has been symbolically incorporated into an actor's repertoire of behavioural possibilities' (Coleman 1987, p. 409). An opportunity structure is a set of conditions or elements that must be in place in order for the offence to be carried out. This opportunity structure varies from one type of offence to another. Different settings naturally create different opportunities that vary in accessibility and attractiveness to offenders. The specific characteristics of the opportunity define the opportunity structure that can be modified to prevent criminal activity in particular settings (Benson et al. 2009). Since we distinguish two main categories of environmental crime – pollution and wildlife crime – we should also focus the analysis of opportunity structures on these forms of environmental crime. Reducing general opportunity structures may be a highly effective way of curbing cross-border crime problems. Making such changes, however, is often difficult because of the international aspects, political barriers and existing balances of power.

Reducing Opportunities for Wildlife Crime

There may be several ways to reduce opportunities for wildlife crime. A first technique would be to reduce the demand for goods derived from endangered species. The increasing demand for exotic animals and animal products and species of tropical timber drives poaching and illegal logging.

A first option to decrease demand is to control the trade by international and other regulations, such as the Convention on International Trade in Endangered Species of Wild Fauna and Flora (CITES), which prohibits the trade of the most endangered species and strictly regulates less endangered species. However, whether bans have positive effects is debated. Moyle reports that the domestic and international ban of the trade in tiger products has not been associated with marked declines in poaching in Asia (Moyle 2009). Indeed, poaching in India following the domestic ban in China is believed to have increased. Lemieux and Clarke (2009) examined the effectiveness of the ban on the international trade in ivory, and found mixed results. In some African nations, the ban effectively disrupted ivory markets. However, unregulated markets continued in other countries, resulting to some extent in the displacement of poaching. Disruption of all African ivory markets would require coordinated action in all domestic markets. This is unrealistic because it would also include countries experiencing high levels of corruption and civil war.

A less radical way of reducing demand is by informing customers and by making moral appeals. In the case of products derived from endangered species, the options are to dissuade customers from buying because of the harm inflicted on animal populations and to debunk certain features attributed to such products. Rhinoceros horn, for example, is still considered a cure for cancer in certain Asian countries, whereas it is composed largely of keratin, just like human fingernails (PBS.org 2010). It may, however, be difficult to lower the demand for animal products and find less harmful alternatives because of their cultural significance and their being considered a status symbol. Shark fin soup, for example, is traditionally served at Chinese celebrations, such as wedding banquets. The quality and beauty of the product, for example of certain types of tropical timber, may also make it problematic to find alternatives. Education campaigns to reduce demand have been proposed. The difficulty here is in identifying the potential consumers. Further, existing black-market consumers may not be receptive to such messages. Moyle asks the rhetorical question: 'If the current consumers of tiger-products are not dissuaded by a US$50,000 price tag, a possible death sentence if caught and the knowledge that tigers are both endangered and threatened by this trade, what new information can an education campaign provide to reduce demand?' (Moyle 2009).

Another option is to decriminalize and regulate the supply of controlled products and services in order to reduce opportunities for crime entrepreneurs (Spapens 2012). In the context of the environment, attempts are being made to regulate the timber trade in order to create a supply of sustainable harvested wood. Theoretically, one could also consider breeding certain species of animals in captivity, such as birds and reptiles. Before international pressure forced China to put in place a domestic ban on the trade in tiger parts, China had been experimenting with tiger farming to meet the domestic demand for tiger products. The two licensed farms had about half of China's captive tiger population, which is estimated at 4,000–5,000 animals (Moyle 2009). In any case, such regulatory systems also require effective controls and enforcement to function properly.

Pires and Clarke (2012) studied parrot poaching in Bolivia and found that it is mostly the work of local farmers with easy access to parrot nests. To prevent the problem, Pires and Clarke suggest the use of nets and other physical barriers, CCTV surveillance of open areas and installation of nesting boxes out of reach of poachers. Although CCTV cameras are indeed used to prevent the killing of endangered species, such as tigers in Indonesia, poachers often destroy them. In the case of poaching, opportunity-reducing approaches will only succeed if local communities see their wildlife as a resource worth protecting and are able to generate an alternative income, for instance by developing ecotourism and regulated trade, and by employing former poachers as rangers (Pires and Clarke 2012; Wellsmith 2011).

Reducing Opportunities for Pollution

Opportunities for pollution arise from the extra costs that may result from requirements to manufacture goods or dispose of waste using processes that minimize harm to the environment. Here, the main driver for perpetrators is to operate more cost-effectively and increase profits by failing to comply with environmental rules and regulations. Green criminologists relate this type of opportunity structure to the general characteristics of the capitalist system and its focus on continuous economic growth (White 2012b).

Corporate non-compliance with environmental law to reduce costs can take two forms: crimes of commission and crimes of omission. Non-compliance in regard to waste dumping for instance is a purposeful action. However, environmental crime, especially in a corporate setting, can also be purposeful non-action. Such crime constitutes a violation of business regulations, requiring corporations to take certain action, in order to prevent environmental harm (Slapper and Tombs 1999). Entrepreneurs might be of the opinion that complying with such regulations costs extra time and money and complicates business processes, whereas non-compliance saves money and effort. In other words, violations can be the result of not taking action, rather than the outcome of purposeful criminal activity. Such violations are crimes of *omission*: crimes constitute of *not taking* actions prescribed by regulation or in other words crimes that consist of *doing nothing* (Huisman and Van Erp 2013).

This distinction between action and non-action is relevant for designing strategies to reduce opportunity structures. Opportunities for the export of waste are attached to the negative value of waste and transnational price asymmetries, which serves as an incentive to illegally dump waste (Passas 1999). Various regulations have attempted to create stimuli for preventing waste to be produced and for recycling of waste, such as the European Waste Electric and Electronic Equipment Directive. However, these have not yet been successful. Additional instruments to regulatory enforcement are necessary but because these are not alternatives, enforcement will remain necessary (Gibbs et al. 2010).

Prevention of crimes of omission might involve making it easier for companies to comply with environmental regulations. Stimulating the development and the dissemination of cost-effective techniques for treatment or even prevention of polluting by-products of industrial production might be more effective than increased law enforcement. Others have suggested introducing 'reputation rewards' that give environmentally friendly products a better market position. Research has indicated that firms' relationship with their stakeholders is a more powerful incentive for compliance than the threat of legal sanctions (Kagan et al. 2011).

Finally, globalization is often seen as providing opportunities for environmental criminals (White 2011). Many environmental crimes are inherently transnational, linked to globalization and global trade (Beirne and South 2007). For instance, globalization has made it possible to transport toxic waste to third world countries where it can be disposed of at a fraction of the cost and with little threat of apprehension and prosecution. The fragmentation of enterprises and transactions in multiple countries produces illicit opportunities. Price asymmetries are an incentive to move hazardous waste to other countries. Without international regulatory bodies, it is virtually impossible to exercise global governance of transnational flows and multinational corporations. In addition, regulatory asymmetries make it possible to cut the cost of environmental management and labour conditions by outsourcing the risk, whereas law enforcement asymmetries weaken social controls (Van Erp and Huisman 2010).

Social Pressure

Putting social pressure on persons or companies that fail to comply with environmental regulations may be a powerful incentive for them to change specific behaviour (Van Wingerde 2012). Such 'third party regulation' is now an integral part of any contemporary model of business regulation (Gunningham and Grabosky 1998; Braithwaite 2008). Local groups and individuals may initiate such pressure, but so can national groups and non-governmental environmental organizations (NGOs) operating globally, such as Greenpeace and the Environmental Investigation Agency (EIA), or combinations of local and other groups. Of course, media attention plays a crucial role, as it increases public pressure and invokes political reactions, which in turn may be the upshot to law enforcement interventions and additional legislation. It must be noted that not all environmental problems lead to the same degree of public outcry, and thus attract different levels of media attention. Some segments of the population also have easier access to the media and politicians than others.

NGOs have put pressure on electronics producers to reduce the use of toxic materials in their products. Greenpeace's 'Guide to Greener Electronics' in 2010 ranked the 18 top manufacturers of personal computers, mobile phones, televisions and games consoles according to their policies on toxic chemicals, recycling and climate change. Nokia and Ericsson are ranked near the top of this list, whereas Dell, Microsoft and Nintendo rank low (Greenpeace n.d.). Interestingly, companies such as Microsoft and Dell have since adopted the Code of Conduct of the Electronic Industry Citizenship Coalition. However, the effect of such a code, which the industry initiated as a self-regulatory instrument, may be limited because non-compliance is rarely sanctioned. Self-regulation may therefore be mere window-dressing aimed at preventing the government from imposing additional regulation (Van Erp and Huisman 2010).

Third-party enforcement derives its strength from the fact that companies fear the loss of prestige and public humiliation resulting from negative publicity (Fisse and Braithwaite 1983). Collecting and disseminating this type of information is important because it enables consumers to include it in their product choices and, thus, to become active 'co-producers' of market regulation (Gunningham and Grabosky 1998). The aggregate pressure from consumers' individual actions can result in consumers 'punishing' offending companies and 'rewarding' firms that do comply (Bardach and Kagan 1982). As mentioned above, a condition is of course that consumers do care. Research by Karpoff et al. (2005), however, shows that such market sanctions of corporate environmental misconduct are not self-evident.

Apart from consumers and interest groups, direct victims may exert social pressure. They may also file civil lawsuits against companies to demand compensation for damage inflicted on the local environment and living conditions. Nigerian farmers and fishermen successfully filed a lawsuit against the Dutch-British oil company Shell demanding compensation for the loss of livelihood inflicted by pollution (Sekularac and Deutsch 2013).

In some cases, social pressure may change behaviour that is harmful to the environment but not punishable as a criminal offence. One example concerns the protests initiated by Greenpeace in 1995 against the disposal of the Brent Spar, an obsolete storage and tanker-loading buoy that Shell had operated, by sinking it into the Atlantic Ocean. According to Greenpeace, the Brent Spar still contained oil and chemicals harmful to marine life. It launched a successful media campaign that sparked public and political opposition in Europe, as well as a partial boycott of Shell service stations in some countries. Fearing damage to its reputation, the company decided to abandon its plans and agreed to dismantle the Brent Spar on shore.[2]

2 The case is controversial because it later emerged that Greenpeace had grossly exaggerated the amount of oil and other waste products still present in the Brent Spar.

The principal 'targets' of social pressure are the perpetrators and the authorities responsible for establishing and upholding the law. Not all of these, however, may be receptive to actions by pressure groups and individual citizens. To begin with, we may assume that ordinary criminals will be less concerned about their reputation, and therefore less responsive to the community. There may be further differences. Petty criminals such as poachers, who belong to the same community victimized by their behaviour, may be more receptive to correction by social exclusion mechanisms than organized crime groups or itinerant gangs (Obioha and Isiugo 2013).

Similar differences may be found even when the perpetrators are companies. Companies that are deeply embedded in a community may feel more incentive to change behaviour that is harmful to their surroundings, whereas a multinational company may be less receptive. A notorious example is Trafigura, a leading international commodities trading and logistics company that is for tax reasons registered in the Netherland, but operates from London and Lucerne. The company became involved in an environmental scandal in 2006, when chemical waste was found to have been dumped in Ivory Coast. The waste had been produced by upgrading low quality oil on the *Probo Koala*, a vessel that was chartered by Trafigura. Trafigura had planned to offload the waste in the harbour of Amsterdam, but when confronted with high processing costs due to the level of toxicity, the company ordered it to be pumped back into the ship and tried to find a cheaper solution. This attempt was apparently successful several weeks later because the *Probo Koala* then delivered the waste to a company in Ivory Coast. However, instead of processing the waste the Ivorian company had it dumped in and around the capital of Abidjan, allegedly causing environmental damage and health problems to the local population. Trafigura not only vehemently denied responsibility for the dumping, but it also continued upgrading low-grade oil products at sea, thereby producing similar highly toxic waste (Spapens et al. 2013).

Instead of the perpetrators themselves, pressure groups may also target authorities to take action. Whether they are responsive to social pressure once again depends on a number of variables. To begin with, the governments of non-democratic nations that suffer high levels of corruption will usually be less sensitive to social pressure. Furthermore, community action or operations by NGOs may not be without risk in such countries. Nigerian police forces brutally suppressed protests against the environmental pollution caused by oil production in Nigeria, with protestors being tortured and killed and villages burned (Huisman 2010). It is easier for pressure groups to operate in democratic societies, although the authorities may regard the economic aspects, such as jobs and the international competitiveness of specific industries, as more important than the damage certain activities cause to the immediate environment. One example is the Dutch custom of blending bunker fuel with chemical waste, which was identified as a problem in the 1980s and discussed regularly by the Dutch parliament from 1994. Still, the respective governments insisted that the problem be addressed in the context of the International Maritime Organization, to avoid placing Dutch producers of bunker fuel at a competitive disadvantage (Spapens et al. 2013). The authorities may also be slow to respond because it is usually very difficult to prove the nature and the extent of the damage, particularly when adverse effects to people's health are concerned (Jarrell and Ozymy 2014).

Conclusions

Based on this brief analysis of environmental crime interventions, and the cross-border varieties in particular, we may conclude that it is indeed a difficult, 'wicked' problem to control environmental crimes and harms. To begin with, there is little chance of reducing general opportunity structures for transnational environmental crime. It would be difficult to decrease demand in the short term, for instance because of cultural aspects and sometimes ignorance. Partial decriminalization coupled with a regulated alternative to such criminal behaviour as poaching and illegal logging is problematic because it would seriously endanger certain species.

Second, social pressure may be a powerful tool in forcing perpetrators to comply with environmental laws. There have been successful examples of this in recent decades. There are also parties less receptive to social pressure, however, including multinational companies, organized crime groups and weak and failed states (when the onus is on government to take action).

Third, the authorities and other parties may take preventive measures to tackle environmental crimes. Such interventions are predominantly aimed at the local level and although they can be highly effective, they have only a secondary effect on cross-border environmental crime. Situational crime prevention, aimed at reducing opportunities for environmental crime, will need to be developed further before it can encompass both illegal actions and illegal non-actions.

Finally, law enforcement is complex and even more problematic when it comes to cross-border investigations of environmental crime. Despite calls by international organizations and NGOs for stricter law enforcement, most empirical studies agree that enforcement is fragmented and lacks effectiveness as well as efficiency and professionalism. Furthermore, criminal investigations of cross-border environmental crimes are often hampered by the lack of an applicable legal framework for mutual legal assistance, by slow and time-consuming procedures, and by the need to cooperate with nations where government and law enforcement are weak.

We still know very little about what type of intervention is most effective in specific circumstances. It is clear that deterrence alone will not suffice (Simpson 2002; Thornton et al. 2005; Stretesky 2006; Stretesky and Gabriel 2005; Stretesky and Lynch 2009). New and more sophisticated models have evolved based on the principles of responsive regulation while including third parties as surrogate regulators (Ayres and Braithwaite 1992). Smart regulation encourages governments to facilitate and mobilize other network members to intervene. However, it also requires public authorities to empower third parties to this end (Gunningham and Grabosky 1998). Because it has proved difficult to influence behaviour by imposing legal penalties, contemporary regulators have also fixed their hopes on trying to 'name and shame' companies (Van Erp 2009). However, all these alternatives and other potentially more sophisticated compliance models require further empirical testing.

References

Alvazzi del Frate, A., Benjamin, A., Heine, G., Norberry, J., and Prabhu, M. 1999. 'Environmental Protection at National and International Levels: Potentials and Limits of Criminal Justice. An Overview of the Empirical Study', in *Environmental Protection: Potentials and Limits of Criminal Justice. Evaluation of Legal Structures*, edited by G. Heine, M. Prabhu and A. Alvazzi del Frate. Freiburg im Breisgau: United Nations Interregional Crime and Justice Research Institute (UNICRI), 19–57.

Andersson, C., Bergström, R. and Johansson, C. 2009. 'Population Exposure and Mortality due to Regional Background PM in Europe – Long-Term Simulations of Source Region and Shipping Contributions', *Atmospheric Environment* July, 3614–20.

Ayres, I. and Braithwaite, J. 1992. *Responsive Regulation: Transcending the Deregulation Debate*. New York: Oxford University Press.

Bardach, E. and Kagan R. 1982. *Going by the Book: The Problem of Regulatory Unreasonableness*. Philadelphia: Temple University Press.

BBC. 2011. 'Tuna Fished Illegally During Libya Conflict', 7 November. Available at: www.bbc.co.uk/news/science-environment-15597675 (accessed 11 April 2015).

Beirne, P. and South, N. 2007. 'Introduction: Approaching Green Criminology', in *Issues in Green Criminology*, edited by P. Beirne and N. South. Cullompton: Willan Publishing, xiii–xxii.

Benson, M., Eck, J. and Madensen, T. 2009. 'White-Collar Crime from an Opportunity Perspective', in *Criminology of White-Collar Crime*, edited by S. Simpson and D. Weisburd. New York: Springer, 175–93.

Bisschop, L. 2011. 'Transnational Environmental Crime: Exploring (Un)charted Territory', in *EU Criminal Justice, Financial & Economic Crime: New Perspectives, Governance of Security Research Papers, Volume 5*, edited by M. Cools, B. de Ruyver, M. Easton, L. Pauwels, P. Ponsaers, T. Vander Beken, F. Vander Laenen, G. Vande Walle, A. Verhage, G. Vermeulen and G. Vynckier. Antwerpen: Maklu, 155–83.

——— 2014. 'Illegal E-Waste Transports: Exploring their Harmfulness, Scale, Social Organization and Governance', in *Environmental Crime and its Victims: Perspectives within Green Criminology*, edited by T. Spapens, R. White and M. Kluin. Farnham: Ashgate, 171–84.

——— 2015. *Governance of the Illegal Trade in E-Waste and Tropical Timber: Case Studies on Transnational Environmental Crime*. Farnham: Ashgate.

Bisschop, L. and Verhagen, A. 2012. 'The Complex(ity) of Policing Dirty Crime', *Cahiers Politiestudies* 4, 289–306.

Braithwaite, J. 2008. *Regulatory Capitalism*. Cheltenham: Edward Elgar.

Brisman, A., South, N. and White, R. (eds). 2015. *Environmental Crime and Social Conflict: Contemporary and Emerging Issues*. Farnham: Ashgate.

Coleman, W. 1987. 'Toward an Integrated Theory of White-Collar Crime', *American Journal of Sociology* 93(2), 406–39.

ESWI. 2009. *IMPEL-TFS Enforcement Actions II, Enforcement of EU Waste Shipment Regulation 'Learning by Doing'*. Munich: ESWI Consortium.

Fisse, B. and Braithwaite, J. 1983. *The Impact of Publicity on Corporate Offenders*. Albany: State University of New York Press.

Gibbs, C., McGarrell, E.F. and Axelrod, M. 2010. 'Transnational White-Collar Crime and Risk: Lessons from the Global Trade in Electronic Waste', *Criminology & Public Policy* 9(3), 543–60.

Greenpeace. n.d. *Greenpeace Guide to Greener Electronics*. Available at: www.greenpeace.org/international/en/campaigns/climate-change/cool-it/Campaign-analysis/Guide-to-Greener-Electronics/ (accessed 11 April 2015).

Gruppo Abele-Nomos, Legambiente and GEPEC. 2003. *The Illegal Trafficking in Hazardous Waste in Italy and Spain*. Rome.

Gunningham, N. and Grabosky, P. 1998. *Smart Regulation: Designing Environmental Policy*. Oxford: Oxford University Press.

Huisman, W. 2010. *Business as Usual? Corporate Involvement in International Crimes*. The Hague: Eleven International Publishing.

Huisman, W. and Van Erp, J. 2013. 'Opportunities for Environmental Crime: A Test of Situational Crime Prevention Theory', *British Journal of Criminology* 53(6), 1178–200.

Interpol. n.d. *Environmental Crime*. Available at: www.interpol.int/Crime-areas/Environmental-crime/Environmental-crime (accessed 11 April 2015).

Jarrell, M. and Ozymy, J. 2014. 'Communities as Victims of Environmental Crime: Lessons from the Field', in *Environmental Crime and its Victims: Perspectives within Green Criminology*, edited by T. Spapens, R. White and M. Kluin. Farnham: Ashgate, 249–62.

Kagan, R., Gunningham, N. and Thornton, D. 2011. 'Fear, Duty and Regulatory Compliance: Lessons from Three Research Projects', in *Explaining Compliance: Business Responses to Regulation*, edited by C. Parker and V. Lehmann Nielsen. Cheltenham: Edward Elgar, 37–58.

Karpoff, J., Lott, J.R. and Wehrly, E. 2005. 'The Reputational Penalties for Environmental Violations: Empirical Evidence', *Journal of Law and Economics* 68, 653–75.

Kauzlarich, D. and Kramer, R. 1998. *Crimes of the Nuclear State: At Home and Abroad*. Boston: Northeastern University Press.

Keohane, R. and Nye, S. 2000. 'Globalization: What's New? What's Not? (And so What?)', *Foreign Policy* Spring, 104–19.

Lemieux, M. and Clarke, R. 2009. 'The International Ban on Ivory Sales and its Effects on Elephant Poaching in Africa', *British Journal of Criminology* 49, 451–71.

Moyle, B. 2009. 'The Black Market in China for Tiger Products', *Global Crime* 10, 124–43.

Obioha, E. and Isiugo, P. 2013. *Indigenous Law Enforcement Mechanisms and Enforcement of Wildlife Protection Laws in a Nigerian National Park*. Paper presented at the 50th Conference of the Academy of Criminal Justice Sciences, Dallas, 19–23 March.

Passas, N. 1999. 'Globalization, "Criminogenic Asymmetries and Economic Crime"', *European Journal of Law Reform* 1, 399–423.

PBS.org. 2010. 'Rhinoceros', 20 August. Available at: www.pbs.org/wnet/nature/episodes/rhinoceros/rhino-horn-use-fact-vs-fiction/1178 (accessed 11 April 2015).

Pellow, D. 2007. *Resisting Global Toxics: Transnational Movements for Environmental Justice*. Cambridge, MA: MIT Press.

Pires, S. and Clarke, R. 2012. 'Are Parrots Craved? An Analysis of Parrot Poaching in Mexico', *Journal of Research in Crime and Delinquency* 49, 122–46.

Raad van Korpschefs. 2010. *Witboek Milieucriminaliteit*. The Hague: Politie Nederland.

Rittel, H. and Webber, M. 1973. 'Dilemmas in a General Theory of Planning', *Policy Sciences* 4, 155–69.

Sea Shepherd. 2011. *Sea Shepherd Ships to Patrol Libyan War Zone for Poachers*. Available at: www.seashepherd.org/news-and-media/2011/05/13/sea-shepherd-ships-to-patrol-libyan-war-zone-for-poachers-18 (accessed 11 April 2015).

Sekularac, I. and Deutsch, A. 2013. 'Dutch Court says Shell Responsible for Nigeria Spills', 30 January. Available at: www.reuters.com/article/2013/01/30/us-shell-nigeria-lawsuit-idUSBRE90S16X20130130 (accessed 11 April 2015).

Simpson, S. 2002. *Corporate Crime, Law and Social Control*. Cambridge: Cambridge University Press.

Slapper, G. and Tombs, S. 1999. *Corporate Crime*. London: Longman.

Spapens, T. 2008. 'Policing a European Border Region: The Case of the Meuse-Rhine Euroregion', in *Security versus Justice, Police and Judicial Cooperation in the European Union*, edited by E. Guild and F. Geyer. Aldershot: Ashgate, 225–41.

——— 2011. *Cross-Border Police Cooperation in Tackling Environmental Crime*. Paper presented at the 9th INECE Conference, Whistler, 18–24 June.

——— 2012. 'The Question of Regulating Illegal Markets', *GSTF Journal of Law and Social Sciences* 1, 30–37.

Spapens, T., Bruinsma, M., Van Hout, L. and De Jong, J. 2013. *Vuile Olie*. The Hague: Boom Lemma uitgevers.

Stretesky, P. 2006. 'Corporate Self-Policing and the Environment', *Criminology* 44 (3), 671–708.

Stretesky, P. and Gabriel, J. 2005. 'Self-Policing and the Environment: Predicting Self-Disclosure of Clean Air Act Violations under the US Environmental Protection Agency's Audit Policy', *Society and Natural Resources* 18(10), 871–87.

Stretesky, P. and Lynch, M. 2009. 'Does Self-Policing Reduce Chemical Emissions? A Further Test of the EPA Self Audit Policy', *Social Science Research* 38(1), 239–50.

Thornton, D., Gunningham, N. and Kagan, R. 2005. 'General Deterrence and Corporate Environmental Behavior', *Law & Policy* 2, 262–88.

UNEP. 2012. *Transnational Environmental Crime: A Common Crime in Need of Better Enforcement*. January. Available at: http://na.unep.net/geas/getUNEPPageWithArticleIDScript.php?article_id=95 (accessed 11 April 2015).

Van de Bunt, H.G. and Huisman, W. 2007. 'Organizational Crime in the Netherlands', *Crime & Justice: A Review of Research* 35, 217–60.

Van Erp, J. 2009. *Naming and Shaming in het marktoezicht*. The Hague: Boom Juridische uitgevers.

Van Erp, J. and Huisman W. 2010. 'Smart Regulation and Enforcement of Illegal Disposal of Electronic Waste', *Criminology & Public Policy* 3, 579–90.

Van Wingerde, K. 2012. *De afschrikking voorbij. Een empirische studie naar afschrikking, generale preventie en regelnaleving in de Nederlandse afvalbranche*. Nijmegen: Wolf Legal Publishers.

Waldo, M. 2009. 'The Two Piracies in Somalia: Why the World Ignores the Other?' wardheernews.com. Available at: http://wardheernews.com/Articles_09/Jan/Waldo/08_The_two_piracies_in_Somalia.html (accessed 11 April 2015).

Walters, R. and Martin, P. 2014. 'Trade in Dirty Air: Carbon Crime and the Politics of Pollution', in *Environmental Crime and its Victims: Perspectives within Green Criminology*, edited by T. Spapens, R. White and M. Kluin. Farnham: Ashgate, 121–31.

Wellsmith, M. 2011. 'Wildlife Crime: The Problems of Enforcement', *European Journal on Criminal Policy and Research* 2, 125–48.

White, R. 2010. 'Transnational Environmental Harm and Eco-Global Criminology', in *International Handbook of Criminology*, edited by S. Shoham, P. Knepper and M. Kett. Boca Raton: CRC Press, 231–57.

——— 2011. *Transnational Environmental Crime: Towards an Eco-Global Criminology*. London and New York: Routledge.

——— 2012a. 'NGO Engagement in Environmental Law Enforcement: Critical Reflections', *Australasian Policing: A Journal of Professional Practice and Research* 4(1), 7–12.

——— 2012b. 'The Foundations of Eco-Global Criminology', in *Eco-Global Crimes*, edited by R. Ellefsen, R. Sollund and G. Larsen. Farnham: Ashgate, 15–31.

——— 2014. 'Eco-Justice and Problem-Solving Approaches to Environmental Crime and Victimisation', in *Environmental Crime and its Victims: Perspectives within Green Criminology*, edited by T. Spapens, R. White and M. Kluin. Farnham: Ashgate, 87–103.

3 Illegal Wildlife Trade to the EU and Harms to the World*

Daan van Uhm

Introduction

On 4 October 2014, protests all over the world called for a stop to the poaching of elephants and rhinos. 'We are protesting against the political leaders of the world, who do not have the guts and political will to make changes in their laws'. According to the activists, every 9–11 hours a rhino is slaughtered for its horn and one elephant is killed every 15 minutes. An immediate end to the ivory and rhino horn trade was demanded to avoid extinction within 10 years.

Wildlife trade has always existed, in part because it was commonly believed that natural resources were inexhaustible (Worster 1988). During the last century, however, the negative impact of such trade became more transparent. From around 1900 onwards, several organizations around the world, including the Sierra Club in North America, the National Trust in England and the Dutch Society for the Preservation of Nature, emerged with the mission of conserving species and nature (Heijden 2004). Not long after, the first environment protection agreements were also developed to reduce environmental degradation and control overhunting and poaching in the first half of the twentieth century (Roe 2002).

Public awareness of these issues increased dramatically in the 1960s and 1970s due to the international wave of environmental protest movements. These were strengthened by authoritative groups (e.g. Club of Rome) that warned about the impact economic growth would have on the environment. Campaigns against whaling, the fur trade and animal cruelty were developed and media increasingly started to focus on non-human victims (Benton 1998). To protect species from extinction, the trade in endangered species became internationally regulated by the Convention on International Trade in Endangered Species of Wild Fauna and Flora (CITES) in 1975. Species were listed in three appendices based on the degree of extinction; commercial trade in Appendix I species has been banned and trade in CITES II and III species requires appropriate permits (European Commission

* The research results are based on my doctoral research 'Uncovering the Illegal Wildlife Trade: Inside the World of Poachers, Smugglers and Traders' at the Utrecht University.

2010).[1] In 1992 the Convention on Biological Diversity (CBD) came into force to protect the diversity of species and genetic materials.

After the five mass extinctions on earth that were caused by meteorite impacts, volcanism and large-scale climate change, several scientists predict that we are currently at the beginning of a sixth mass extinction (e.g. Leakey and Lewin 1995; Butchart et al. 2010). According to Barnosky et al. (2011) in this scenario it is humankind that is causing the mass extinction by for instance killing species, introducing non-native species, fragmenting habitats, spreading pathogens, co-opting resources and changing global climate. In the last hundred years, the level of species extinction has increased by as much as a 1,000 times (Millennium Ecosystem Assessment 2005). According to Leakey and Lewin (1995), between 17,000 and 100,000 species vanish from our planet each year. Proportions as high as 26 per cent of mammals, 17 per cent of birds, 38 per cent of chameleons, 31 per cent of sharks and rays, and 41 per cent of amphibians are said to be at risk (IUCN 2014). Higgins (2010, 2012) has argued that such *ecocide* ought to be considered as a fifth International Crime Against Peace.

While habitat loss and degradation is the main threat, illegal trade is the second most damaging hazard to wildlife species (Zimmerman 2003). The illegal wildlife trade is a green crime that involves illegal trade, smuggling, abduction, capture or collection of wildlife or products thereof (Sollund 2013). It is said to be in the financial top three illegal enterprises worldwide, along with the global drug trade and the trade in illegal arms (ECOSOC 2002, 2003; UNODC 2012). According to several reports, the trade in wildlife has expanded dramatically in recent decades because of the globalization of the world's economy with the reduction of borders and because of improved infrastructures including farther reaching air transportation (Commission for Environmental Cooperation 2005; Haken 2011).

Although the illegal wildlife trade is getting more public attention, and criminologists have started to focus on environmental issues (e.g. South and Beirne 1998; Beirne and South 2007; Sollund 2008; Herbig and Joubert 2006; White 2008, 2011; Walters 2010), including the illegal trade in wildlife (e.g. Schneider 2008; Sollund 2013; Wyatt 2013), insight into this type of crime has been relatively limited. For example, while the European Union appears to be one of the foremost demand markets for wildlife (Europol 2011), the global focus has tended to be on source countries in Africa, Asia and Latin America. In this chapter, the nature of the illegal wildlife trade in relation to the EU is approached by analyses of wildlife confiscations in the EU over a 10-year period. The chapter considers the diversity and transnational characteristics of the trade, by asking what kind of wildlife is illegally traded, what are the source and destination countries, and who

1 Appendix I includes species threatened with extinction. Trade in Appendix I specimens is permitted only in exceptional circumstances. Appendix II includes species not necessarily threatened with extinction, but controlled in order to avoid utilization incompatible with their survival. Appendix III are protected in at least one country, which has asked other CITES parties for assistance in controlling the trade.

are the offenders? The chapter concludes with a green criminological consideration of the global harms to the world caused by overexploitation of wildlife.

Method

To get an overview of the illegal trade to the EU, data on confiscations in the EU were obtained from the European Union Trade in Wildlife Information eXchange database (EU-TWIX), a database of information on wildlife seizures in the EU. The data includes more than 20,000 shipments (N=22,204) of animals and animal products seized in the EU between 2001 and 2010. The illegal shipments originated from 207 different countries all over the world, with a marked concentration in Africa (5,219 shipments) and Southeast Asia (3,964 shipments). The confiscations were analysed by animal groups, source and destination countries and offenders. The six groups of animals included for this analysis were mammals, birds, reptiles, fish, coral and molluscs. These six animal groups were chosen for the focus of this study because they represent 93 per cent of all incidents.

The reliability of the data is entirely dependent on the accuracy at which EU member states report these data (Blundell and Mascia 2005). Moreover, the confiscations reflect only a fraction of the illegal trade as a large part of the trade is unreported or undiscovered, the so-called dark figure of crime (Coleman and Moynihan 1996). Law enforcement experts estimate that no more than 10 per cent of all contraband wildlife is seized (Stiles et al. 2013). After analysing the data by sub-category there will be a practical exploration of how these data can be addressed and approached from a green criminological harm perspective.

Species

While several studies have been conducted on individual cases of illegal trade in wildlife (e.g. Wyatt 2009, 2011; Herbig 2010; Lindsey et al. 2012; Pires 2012; Petrossian and Clarke 2014), it remains unclear as to what kind of major flows there are in relation to animal species traded illegally. To gain more insight, Figure 3.1 presents the common animal groups confiscated during seizures in the EU between 2001 and 2010. The wildlife confiscations were analysed by the animal groups: mammals, birds, reptiles, fish, coral and molluscs.[2] Although much attention is given to illegal trade in mammal species (e.g. elephants, rhinos, tigers), it is reptiles that dominate the figures with one-third of the total wildlife confiscations, followed by coral and mammals.[3] Not live animals but

2 Seventy per cent of the seizures were related to CITES II species, compared to 27 per cent CITES I and 3 per cent CITES III species.

3 The 22,204 confiscations consist of 33 per cent (7,303) reptile-, 20 per cent (4,385) coral-, 17 per cent (3,814) mammal, 13 per cent (2,809) mollusc-, 9 per cent (1,883) fish- and 7 per cent (1,490) bird-related seizures. Around 2.5 per cent of the seizures consists of other animal groups (e.g. *Amphibia, Arachnida, Insecta*) and were not included.

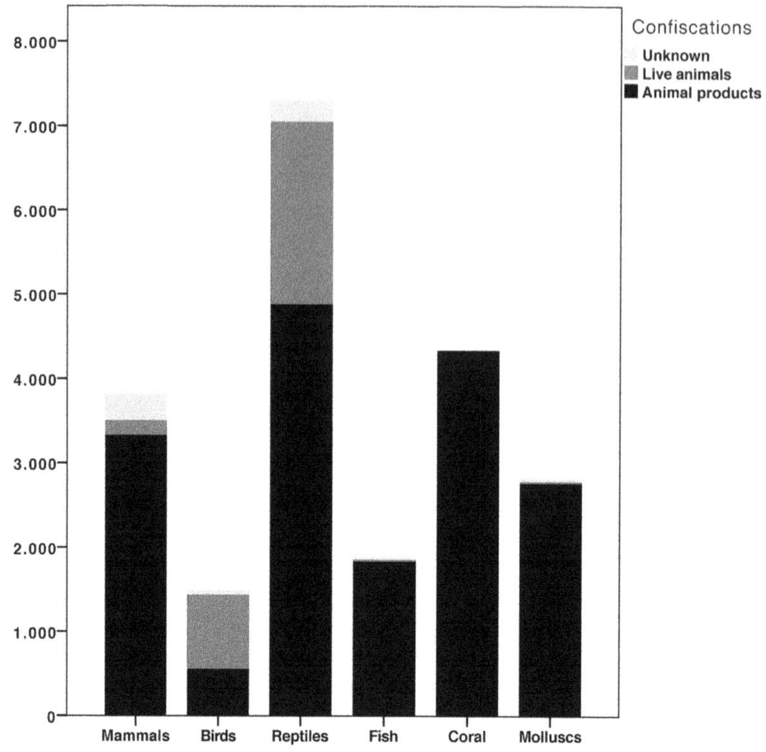

Figure 3.1 Illegal wildlife groups

Source: Personal analysis of the EU-TWIX database, 2001–10.

animal products make up the majority of seizures (82 per cent), compared to 15 per cent of the seizures involving live animals.[4]

Mammal Products

As mentioned in the introduction the illegal trade in ivory has reached extremely high levels, indeed, the seizures with illegal mammal products consist mainly of ivory of elephants followed by various animal products used for traditional Chinese

4 The 3,405 confiscations of *live* animals consist of 64 per cent reptile-, 26 per cent bird- and 5 per cent mammal-related seizures. Only 1 per cent of confiscations consists of live amphibians, including poison dart frogs and salamanders (59 per cent *Dendrobatidae* and 21 per cent *Ambystomatidae*). It is possible that the reptile trade will increase given the growing number of large-scale reptile fairs all over Europe.

medicine.[5] The international illegal trade in ivory seems to have increased since the CITES Standing Committee approved a sale of African government-owned ivory stocks to China and Japan in 2008.[6] Legal ivory on the market provided opportunities to launder illegal ivory (Gabriel et al. 2012; Underwood et al. 2013; EIA 2013).[7] Medicine, dominated by traditional Chinese medicines (TCM), is the largest category across categories in terms of quantity of mammal products, which include big cat, musk deer, bear, saiga antelope, pangolin and rhinoceros products.[8] The impact of this trade is demonstrated by the extinction of the Javan rhino in Vietnam; the last one was left to die with its horn sawed off in 2010 (Van Uhm 2014).

Live Birds

In contrast to other species groups, live birds dominate bird-related seizures, consisting mostly of parrots and falcons.[9] Already in the early 2000s, the EU became the main *legal* importer of birds; between 2000 and 2003 the EU imported 2.8 million wild CITES birds, representing 93 per cent of imports registered worldwide (FAO 2011). From 2006, wild birds are hardly legally imported, because of a European import ban and protection measures in response to the growing threat of avian influenza (2005/94/E.G.; Cooney and Jepson 2006; Nijman 2010). It is believed that crime groups immediately filled the gap with illegally traded birds (Van Uhm 2012b).

Live Reptiles

The largest group of live species consists of seizures of live reptiles, including tortoises, followed by chameleons and turtles.[10] More than 30,000 live reptiles were confiscated between 2001 and 2010 in the EU, with 3,180 spur-thighed tortoises, mainly from Morocco, at the top of the list.[11] Morocco traditionally supplies the EU with reptiles. Certain populations of spur-thighed tortoises have suffered over 90 per cent decline in Morocco (van Dijk et al. 2014). Moreover, native European

5 The 3,814 confiscations of mammal products consist of 42 per cent *Elephantidae*, 16 per cent *Felidae*, 9 per cent *Ursidae*, 8 per cent *Moschidae* and 4 per cent *Bovidae*.

6 Fifty tons of ivory from Botswana, Namibia, and Zimbabwe were sold to Japan in 1999 and 108 tons of ivory from Botswana, Namibia, South Africa and Zimbabwe were sold to Japan and China in 2008.

7 Ivory in Asia is related to status and due to increased economic prosperity more people can afford this luxury. One example is the so-called *Hanko* (family stamp carved from ivory), described as a 'must have item' for each family. The *Hanko* is often painted to deceive customs officials.

8 The confiscations of more than 50,000 medicines include 7,200 big cat products, 4,600 musk deer products, 3,100 bear products, 1,900 saiga antelope products and 1,000 rhino products.

9 The 877 confiscations of live birds consist of 61 per cent *Psittacidae* and 6 per cent *Falconidae*.

10 The 2,171 confiscations of live reptiles consist of 63 per cent *Testudinidae*, 9 per cent *Chamaeleonidae* and 9 per cent *Emydidae*.

11 Little seems to have changed since Interpol mentioned in the internal report 'Noah' (1996) that Europe is highly involved in the illegal trade in spur-thighed tortoises.

pond turtles are threatened by the illegal trade because when the commonly confiscated red-eared sliders are released into the wild they compete for food and basking spaces (Silva et al. 2009).

Reptile Products

The EU is well known to be world's largest importer by value of reptile skins (Engler and Parry-Jones 2007).[12] Indeed, a significant amount of seizures of reptile products were related to leather products from pythons, snakes and crocodiles.[13] According to Liddick (2011) more than 10 million reptiles are killed for the leather industry each year, which is largely unregulated. Commercial enterprises change the number of skins, origin or use illegal wild skins and launder them through legal farms (Liddick 2011; UN 2012).

Fish

Seizures of fish products were clearly dominated by caviar from sturgeons.[14] The European Union seems to be one of the main destination markets of illegal caviar with more than 16 tonnes of seized caviar between 2000 and 2010.[15] The price for original wild caviar is fuelled by declines in the total amounts available for smuggled caviar from the Caspian Sea to the EU.[16] Since the sturgeon population has substantially decreased, prices for caviar have reached extraordinary heights, with up to €20,000 per kilo for wild Beluga caviar (Siegel and Van Uhm 2014).

Coral

Rarely mentioned, coral seizures are the second most frequently seized wildlife group, comprised of mainly stony star or hard corals related seizures.[17] According to Jones (2008) the EU is, besides the United States, the major importer of hard corals and the trade is mainly linked to the collection of coral for aquaria. The main targets are often the rare, slow-growing and long-lived corals. Each year, tonnes of coral are confiscated in the EU from major export countries such as Indonesia and the Philippines. As corals play an important role in the marine ecosystem, the effects of their decimation could be substantial (NOAA 2010).

12 The value has been estimated at over €100 million based on imports of reptile skins in 2005.

13 The 4,883 confiscations of reptile products consist of 22 per cent *Pythonidae*, 14 per cent *Elapidae*, 9 per cent *Boidae* and 8 per cent *Crocodylidae*.

14 The 1,835 confiscations of fish products consist of 85 per cent *Acipenseridae* and 12 per cent *Syngnathidae*.

15 According to the EU-TWIX database 16.5 tons of caviar was seized between 2000 and 2010.

16 The Caspian Sea was the source of 90 per cent of the global caviar trade last century.

17 The confiscations of corals consist of 90 per cent *Scleractinia* – most seizures were not specified in families: 80 per cent unknown, 4 per cent *Faviidae* and 4 per cent *Acroporidae*.

Molluscs

Even less mentioned are true conchs and giant clams, which dominate the confiscations of molluscs.[18] Despite fishing bans and regulations, significant amounts of (queen) conchs and giant clams are still fished illegally for tourism and aquaria (CITES 2003; DeBoer and Barber 2010). While large numbers of incidents involving one or two molluscs may be associated with tourists, abalones appear to be currently threatened by illegal commercial crime groups (Tailby and Gant 2002; Goga 2014).

Within the EU a large market exists for extraordinary and rare species (e.g. caviar, exotic animals, coral) and critically endangered species are at the top of the list, since they generate extremely high prices (Engler and Parry-Jones 2007). An exclusive pair of parrots can be sold for more than €50,000,[19] while the price of a kilo of rhino horn exceeds the price of a kilo of gold (Van Uhm 2012a). The EU demand market is influenced by popular fads (e.g. after the movie *Harry Potter* an increased demand for snowy owls) and the development of relatively new markets (e.g. popularity of alternative Chinese medicine). While traditional well-known wildlife demand markets were identified in the EU (e.g. ivory, reptile leather products, caviar, live reptiles and birds), the analysis of seizures demonstrates relatively lesser-known flows in corals, shells and incidentally live mammals.[20] Due to the relatively high economic prosperity level of EU citizens, it is plausible that currently more people can afford these luxury products. The impact is clearly visible, as a large variety of species in the illegal trade are on the brink of extinction.

Countries of Origin and Destination

Origin

Generally, the source countries of wildlife trade include some of the poorest countries with the richest sources of biodiversity. The flow of wildlife trade appears to be from developing to developed countries (Roe 2002). In several studies African and Southeast Asian countries have been identified as the main source countries of illegal wildlife (Rosen and Smith 2010; UNODC 2010; World Bank 2008; Lawson and Vines 2014). This is confirmed in the confiscation data of the EU where illegal shipments originated mainly from Africa and Southeast Asia (Figure 3.2).[21]

18 The 2,809 confiscations of molluscs consist of 63 per cent *Strombidae* and 37 per cent *Tridacnidae*.

19 EU-TWIX directory of prices, 2013.

20 Old world monkeys (e.g. macaques and vervet monkeys) were mainly found in the seizures of live mammals (45 per cent of the seizures were *Cercopithecidae*). During the 2000s there was a substantial illegal trade in Barbary macaques from Morocco into the EU. This is confirmed in the seizures of live mammals between 2001 and 2010; the most confiscated endangered mammal in the EU is the Barbary macaque.

21 A marked concentration in Africa with 5,219 seizures and Southeast Asia with 3,964 seizures has been identified.

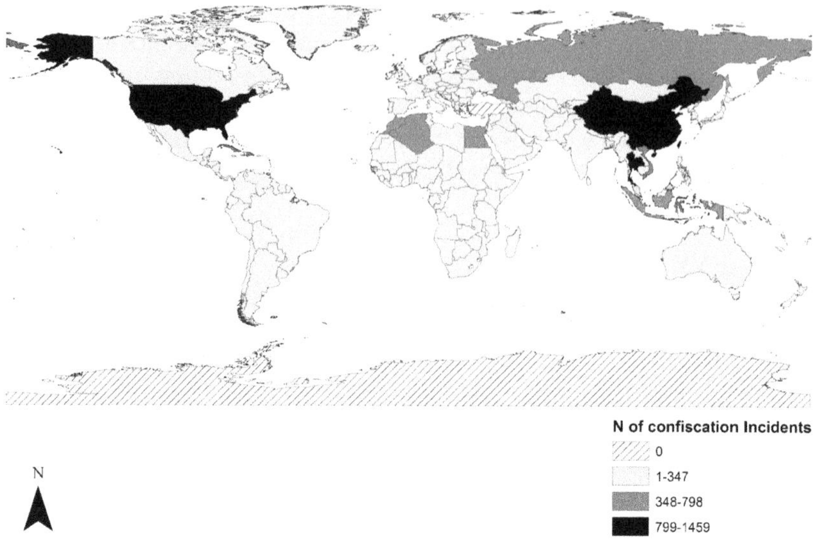

Figure 3.2 Export countries of illegal wildlife

Source: Personal analysis of the EU-TWIX database, 2001–10.

The main African countries of origin are Morocco, Egypt, Algeria, South Africa and Nigeria.[22] North African countries seem to play an important role in the illegal wildlife trade to the EU because of their geographical advantages, since the southern coastline of Europe could easily be used to smuggle wildlife over the sea into the EU. For instance the Strait of Gibraltar is well known as the main port between Africa and the EU for the illegal drug trade (cocaine, heroin, cannabis and synthetic drug precursors) and migration (UNODC 2006; Europol 2011; Carpenter 2012), as well as the illegal wildlife trade (Highfield and Bayley 1996; Cowdrey 2002). The illegal wildlife from Morocco and Algeria is mainly smuggled through the Strait of Gibraltar and consists mostly of live animals, such as spur-thighed tortoises, chameleons and Barbary macaques.[23] The illegal trade from Egypt includes mostly small numbers of coral probably from tourists who, consciously or not, bring them back home. South Africa and Nigeria are well known countries of origin of ivory (Lemieux and Clarke 2009; Nowell 2012; UNEP 2013), which is clearly confirmed by a substantial amount of seized tusks and ivory.[24]

22 The confiscations from Africa consist of 612 seizures from Morocco, 531 seizures from Egypt, 446 seizures from Algeria, 315 seizures from South Africa and 310 seizures from Nigeria.

23 The confiscations of *live* animals from Morocco and Algeria include 2,414 *Testudo graeca*, 65 *Chamaeleo chamaeleon* and 37 *Macaca sylvanus*.

24 The confiscations of ivory from South Africa and Nigeria include thousands of tusks and carvings.

Southeast Asia is home to a unique variety of animals threatened with extinction and identified as major hub of wildlife trade. Even Singapore, which is a highly urbanized country, has a reputation as being an active trader in wildlife (Sodhi et al. 2004). The top illegal exporters of wildlife from Southeast Asia are Thailand, China, Vietnam, Indonesia and the Philippines.[25] The Southeast Asian countries seem to be more specialized in illegal trade in animal products, such as medicine, leather products, corals and molluscs. The demand for TCM has spread worldwide as a result of globalization and the expansion of Chinese diasporas around the world as seen in the increasing TCM export from China every year (Engler and Parry-Jones 2007; Xueyan 2007). According to Felbab-Brown (2011) China ranks as the number one market for illegal wildlife. However, based on confiscations, Thailand and Vietnam also appear to be major exporters of illegal TCM, the main trade from these countries involving leather products from reptiles to the EU.[26] Skins of snakes, lizards and crocodilians consist of a substantial part of the trade from Southeast Asia with the EU as major importer (Nijman 2010). For instance, Indonesia, with biodiversity hotspot Borneo, is one of the main source countries for wild pythons in the skin trade (Kasterine et al. 2012). According to Wood et al. (2012) Indonesia is also the main supplier of trade in live corals,[27] and together with the Philippines, these countries are the main exporters of molluscs (Venkatesan 2010). As confirmed by the confiscations, these countries seem to be specialized in illegal exports of corals and shells to the EU.[28]

Although most illegal shipments come from African and Southeast Asian countries, the United States and Russia are noteworthy (Figure 3.2); the top six countries of illegal exporters consist of the United States, Thailand, China, Russia, Vietnam and Morocco.[29] However, illegal wildlife coming from the United States and Russia is not regularly mentioned. The confiscated illegal trade from the United States consists mainly of leather products from pythons, alligators and crocodiles.[30] Reptile skins are imported, processed, re-exported for manufacture, and imported in the EU, passing through different transit countries in order to launder illegally caught reptiles (Cowdrey 2002; Engler and Parry-Jones 2007). Russia is famous in the illegal wildlife trade as the source country for caviar: over

25 The confiscations from Southeast Asia consist of 1,263 seizures from Thailand, 845 seizures from China, 688 seizures from Vietnam, 434 seizures from Indonesia and 172 seizures from the Philippines.

26 The confiscations from Thailand and Vietnam consist of 1,051 reptile seizures, including 454 Indian cobra (*Naja naja*) and 77 reticulated python (*Python reticulatus*) seizures.

27 In the past decade, Indonesia has provided an average of 70 per cent of trade in live corals.

28 The confiscations from Indonesia and the Philippines consist of 301 coral seizures and 140 mollusc seizures.

29 Top export countries of seized illegal shipments to the EU: United States (1,457 seizures), Thailand (1,263 seizures), China (845 seizures), Russia (798 seizures), Vietnam (688 seizures) and Morocco (612 seizures).

30 The confiscations from the United States consist of 805 reptile-related seizures, including 278 seizures with large leather products and 269 seizures with small leather products (429 seizures from *Crocodylia* and 233 seizures from *Serpentes*).

40 per cent of all EU seizures of caviar (more than 3.5 tons) originate from Russia. The annual value of exported caviar by top exporter Russia is estimated between US$40 and 100 million, while the illegal Russian export of caviar is estimated to be no less than US$250–400 million (Pikitch et al. 2005; Schneider 2012). Although Turkey is a well-known transit country for Caspian caviar to the EU, no confiscations from Turkey are recorded, probably due to insufficient seizure information from Greece and Bulgaria. In addition, it is remarkable that Brazil, home to the world's biodiversity hotspot the Amazon, and the Republic of the Congo with the Congo basin are respectively 22nd and 19th on the list of exporters of illegal wildlife to the EU.

Destination

The EU is an important destination and transit market of trade in wildlife. While according to Engler and Parry-Jones (2007) the EU ranks as top importer by value of wildlife, Europol (2013a) indicates that the EU is simultaneously one of the most important markets of *illegal* trade in endangered species. Large European airports (e.g. Schiphol, Frankfurt, Heathrow) and major harbours (e.g. Antwerp, Hamburg, Rotterdam) appear to play an important role as main entry points to enter the EU for the demand market or in transit. For instance, the EU functions as transit points for illegal wildlife trade, such as ivory and rhino horn, from Africa to Asia and the Middle and Far East (IFAW 2013; European Commission 2014).

Criminogenic asymmetries with structural discrepancies, mismatches and inequalities in the realms of the economy, law, politics and culture (Passas 1999) may offer opportunities for illegal wildlife trade in the EU with its different regulation and enforcement cultures. Moreover, the free trade agreement between European countries provides unhindered trade and suitable transhipment locations for illegal wildlife trade within the Schengen area (Cowdrey 2002).[31] While the EU appears to have an important demand market for illegal wildlife, certain countries seem to have a more prominent role in the illegal trade, since more than half of all confiscations were seized in Germany and the Netherlands (Figure 3.3).[32] While seizures could also reflect efforts of enforcement, both countries are well-known as main transit countries of illegal wildlife (Zembla 2001).

Germany became since the late 1990s famous as the largest black market centre for birds of prey. The birds are smuggled from Germany to the Middle East where there is substantial demand for these birds (Holden 1998). Second, Germany is well-known as the main importer in the EU of caviar and imported almost 250 tons of wild caviar between 1998 and 2006 (Engler and Knapp 2008). Besides

31 The Schengen area consists of 26 members with 10,000 km land borders, 50,000 km sea borders and 2,000 official crossing points.

32 Top import countries of seized illegal shipments to the EU: Germany (7,266 seizures), the Netherlands (2,590), Poland (1,599), France (1,229) and Italy (1,037).

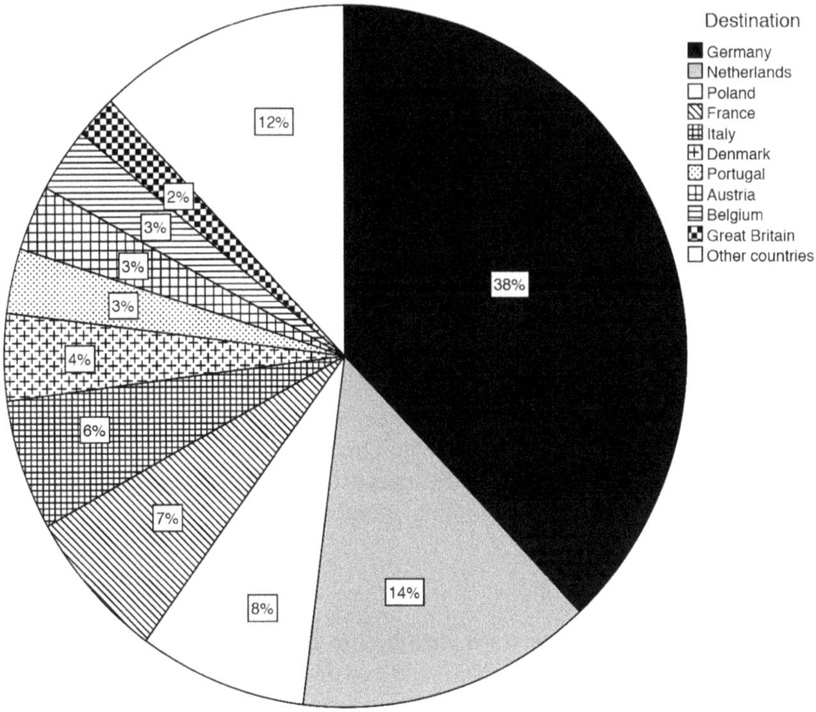

Figure 3.3 EU destination countries of illegal wildlife

Source: Personal analysis of the EU-TWIX database, 2001–10.

birds and caviar, the seizures in Germany consist mainly of reptile leather products, corals, shells and live reptiles.[33]

The role of the Netherlands is also important; since the early 1990s, several reports, including internal police reports, have mentioned the Netherlands as a major player in the international illegal wildlife trade (e.g. CRI 1992; RRD 1995; Interpol 1996; Holden 1998; Cowdrey 2002; KLPD 2005; Van Uhm 2009; Kemner 2010; Liddick 2011). Huge numbers of parrots and falcons are smuggled into the Netherlands via the Czech Republic and Germany. These birds are 'laundered' by forged identification rings to suggest a captive-bred origin, while the birds are in reality from the wild (KLPD 2005). According to internal report 'Noah' from Interpol (1996), a handful of Dutch persons are identified as key

33 The confiscations in Germany include 1,909 seizures with corals, 1,093 seizures with shells, 717 seizures with small leather products, 713 seizures with caviar and 483 seizures with live animals (mainly reptiles and birds).

actors in the illegal wildlife trade that involves reptiles as well as exotic birds. These perpetrators not only operate from the Netherlands, but also from countries such as Indonesia, Madagascar, Nicaragua and Spain. Besides the fact that the Netherlands has been identified internationally as a hub for the illegal reptile and bird trade around the world, the illegal TCM within the EU seem to be mainly imported and distributed by the Netherlands (Holden 1998; LNV 2000; Kemner 2010). A substantial part of the seizures consists indeed of TCM, live birds and reptiles, and leather reptile products and corals are also present.[34]

A possible explanation for the role of both countries in the international illegal wildlife trade could be the geographically central location of Germany and the Netherlands in Western Europe. Second, the national economic and logistic infrastructure that include major airports (Schiphol and Frankfurt) and main harbours (Rotterdam and Hamburg). Third, the strong historical trading position in Europe and strong ties with former colonies in Africa, Southeast Asia and Latin America. Although the EU advocates environmental governance and sustainable use, the substantial demand market for wildlife appears to be a stimulator of illegal trade, threatening species and ecosystems (Engler and Parry-Jones 2007).

Offenders

Different types of perpetrators are identified in the illegal wildlife trade, from individual operating actors to highly organized networks that control some or all facets of trade. According to Wyatt (2013), some offenders might be considered to be 'blameless' (e.g. poor local people who kill endangered species for food), while others oversee the whole process and make high profits (e.g. transnational crime groups). A range of perpetrators could be involved along the illicit chain of the wildlife trade, from local poachers, smugglers and middlemen to corrupt officials and state or private corporations (Kazmar 2000; Zimmermann 2003; Wyatt 2013; Sollund 2014). According to a study on the enforcement of the EU wildlife trade regulations (European Commission 2006), there seem to be three main types of illegal traders:

1 small-scale illegal traders;
2 legal traders involved in illegal trade;
3 criminal organizations.

Based on the confiscations of wildlife, incidents vary from one single product to huge amounts of illegal wildlife in cargo. Although tourists may unknowingly bring illegal souvenirs (e.g. shells, coral) or small-scale illegal traders may smuggle relatively little wildlife, legal enterprises and crime groups seem to be

34 The confiscations in the Netherlands include 2,695 medicines and 1,904 live animals (mainly birds and reptiles), 5,502 corals and 3,079 leather products.

Table 3.1 Job and main trade of perpetrators

Job	*%*	*Main trade*	*%*
Animal trader	14.2	Live reptiles and birds	46.8
Businessman	11.4	Caviar	33.6
Liberal profession	7.2	Ivory carvings and derivatives	31.0
Unemployed	6.9	Live reptiles	32.4
Zoo/wildlife park owner	6.5	Live birds and mammals	73.4
Pensioner/retired	5.9	Live reptiles and reptile products	43.1
Public service administrative professionals	4.8	Ivory carvings, derivatives and coral	37.5
Student	4.5	Live reptiles	37.8
Armed forces	4.4	Reptile products and coral	72.1
Antique dealer	4.3	Ivory carvings	27.9

Source: Personal analysis of the EU-TWIX database, 2001–10.

involved in the trade of substantial amounts of highly profitable wildlife across the borders of the EU (Traffic 2014).

There were 911 cases of the EU seizures in which the job of the perpetrator was referred to; these consisted mainly of animal traders, businessmen, liberal professionals, unemployed, and zoo or wildlife park owners. In general, animal traders deal illegally in live birds and reptiles, businessmen in the caviar business, and liberal professionals are trading in ivory carvings and derivatives (see Table 3.1).

Not incidental, legally registered companies operate illegally and commit environmental crimes. Ruggiero and South (2010) used the term 'dirty collar crime' to demonstrated that in most European countries corporate entrepreneurs benefit from legal structures to mismatch quantities or falsify certification of waste. In the wildlife trade the interrelation between legality and illegality is not uncommon, as many investigations presented the involvement of legal enterprises in the illegal wildlife trade (e.g. Cook et al. 2002; KLPD 2005; Lyons and Natusch 2011). The backgrounds of the perpetrators of these 'green collar crimes' seem to confirm this assumption: a large proportion of offenders (>30 per cent) trade legally in wildlife.[35] For example, they include animal traders, zoo or wildlife park owners, antique dealers, fashion trading companies and breeders.[36] Besides these, illegal wildlife is smuggled for legitimate business such as reptile meat and caviar for restaurants, big cats for circuses and primates and bears for, ironically, wildlife film producers. According to Naylor (2004) the illegal wildlife trade always has been run by the same actors who operate the legal one with the same infrastructure.

35 In an analysis of perpetrators in the Netherlands (KLPD 2005), half of the studied perpetrators were professional legal wildlife traders.

36 Confiscations from animal traders (14.2 per cent), zoo or wildlife park owners (6.5 per cent), antique dealers (4.3 per cent) fashion trading companies (2.9 per cent) and breeders (1.4 per cent).

While the previous examples demonstrate the interrelation between the legal and illegal trade in wildlife, anecdotal evidence about the illegal wildlife trade and organized criminal groups has been forwarded as well. In the early 2000s, several UN reports suggested the heavy involvement of Chinese, Japanese, Italian and Russian organized crime groups in the illegal wildlife trade. The Wo Shing Wo group and 14K were linked to smuggling ivory, rhino horn and shark fin. The Neapolitan Mafia was said to be behind illegal trading in endangered parrots and Russian organized crime groups seemed to be involved in the illegal caviar trade as well as poaching of tigers and bears (ECOSOC 2002, 2003; Wyler and Sheikh 2008). More recent reports indicate the involvement of Chinese organized crime groups in Hong Kong in traditional Chinese medicine with derivatives of endangered species to several companies across the EU (Europol 2011), an Irish mobile organized crime group (the Rathkeale Rovers) active in robbing more than 100 rhino horns from European museums and selling the horns to Southeast Asian dealers (Ayling 2013; Van Uhm 2012b) and crime groups involved in high-level drugs trafficking in Brazil, Colombia and Mexico who illegally supply endangered species to the EU (Europol 2011). According to Europol (2013b), the role of organized criminal groups in wildlife trafficking within the EU is increasing which is reflected in a direct threat to the stability of the society. The major organized criminal groups participate in the wildlife trade because of the high profits, the low risk with which smugglers can bring wildlife into a country and the ability to incorporate this type of trade with other types of contraband (Zimmermann 2003).[37]

Harms to the World

This chapter has presented an overview of species, countries and offenders involved in the illegal wildlife trade in the EU in order to understand the transnational character, complex diversity and global effects of the market. It has become clear that the trade in wildlife is a global affair with involvement of a diversity of source and destination countries, different species and both small-scale traders and large criminal organizations. To demonstrate the impact of wildlife trade and the interconnection between species, geographic locations and offenders, this last section will approach the harms from different green criminological frameworks.

From a critical criminological perspective it is important to explore the intentional and unintentional harms of the illegal *and* legal wildlife trade. Social and moral norms change societies together with the continual re-examination of laws and criminalization. According to Hulsman (1986) crime has no ontological reality; crime is not the object but the product of criminal policy. In the field of wildlife trade, many activities are not criminalized but may cause harm. According to Passas and Goodwin (2004) these kind of *delinquencies* are 'lawful but awful'.

37 Several reports indicate that the same routes established for other types of illegal commodities are used to transfer illegal wildlife.

The basic proposition here is that something or someone has suffered harm (Halsey and White 1998; White 2011; Wyatt 2013). For example, it may not be illegal to trade in non-protected animals or animals from vulnerable populations with export documents, yet there may very well be significant injury to the population. Actually the majority of wildlife trade is perfectly legal, but is nonetheless seriously harmful (Wyatt 2013). By allowing trade in general based on export quotas alone, populations may become threatened with extinction. Indeed, Hutton and Dickson (2000) state that there is a trend for species to move up on the CITES gradation from less threatened to more seriously threatened.

From an anthropocentric perspective, based on the notion of the superiority of humankind in relation to all other (non-human) species on earth, trade in wildlife is justifiable for human benefit. Yet intentional harms include human victims, such as rangers or soldiers who are killed during an attack on poachers. For instance, in early 2012 in Cameroon, hundreds of elephants were slaughtered for their ivory by heavily armed criminal gangs from Chad and Sudan. Intervention of local authorities resulted in soldiers from Chad getting killed. Dozens of rangers were killed during similar types of confrontations (Wyler and Sheikh 2013). Additional unintentional harms to humans include side effects of (illegal) wildlife trade, such as outbreaks of life-threatening zoonotic diseases. The outbreak in 2003 of Severe Acute Respiratory Syndrome (SARS) coronavirus was traced back to the small carnivore and bat trade (Bell et al. 2004; Lau et al. 2005). Another striking example is the avian influenza virus (H5N1) that partly through (illegal) trade in wildlife has gained ground (Yee et al. 2009). In addition, rainforests are inhabited by millions of people who are dependent on the natural resources of the rainforest, which partly disappear as result of the wildlife trade (Boekhout van Solinge 2010). Furthermore, with the global disappearance of species a culturally and emotionally poorer world is left for future generations (Herbig 2010).

From a green criminological perspective, the harm principle can be extended with species and ecosystems as victims of (human) actions (South 2008; White 2008). Humans can be seen as part of a complex ecosystem and no longer as central actors. According to Herbig (2010), the existence of human and non-human species depends on the biodiversity of the earth. From an ecocentric perspective, this relationship is based on the ecological principles: 'everything is related to everything else' (Benton 1998). For instance, the disappearance of keystone species would have a disastrous impact on perennial species and their ecosystems (Wilson and Kellert 1993; Mills et al. 1993; Power et al. 1996). For example, as a result of reduction in sea star populations, mussel populations will explode and extrude most other species (Paine 1966) and vice versa the reintroduction of grey wolves in Yellowstone National Park has led to the recovery of the entire ecosystem from vegetation to beavers and bison (Ripple and Beschta 2012). At the same time, the (re)introduction or release of non-native animals could have serious negative effects on the stability of an ecosystem. Although several exotic species have been introduced for the purposes of benefiting agri- or aquaculture, side effects of these introductions include loss of native species and changes in ecosystem functions and services (Mooney and Hobbs 2000). From this perspective, ecosystems may become unbalanced or could even collapse as a result of the wildlife trade due to the strong symbiosis between species in ecosystems (Lindsey et al. 2012; Myers et al. 2007).

While humankind seems to understand more than ever before the complexity of social and mental lives of animals and their interdependence with humans (evolutionary, spiritually and ecologically), animals are still emphasized as instruments instead of non-human species with rights and an inherent and intrinsic value (Benton 1998; Sollund 2014). According to White (2007), non-human animals are perceived as inferior to human species in a similar way that sexism and racism involve prejudice and discrimination against 'other' people. From a biocentric perspective all species are equal and all species should be treated equally. From this point of view the quality of their individual lives and well-being is important (Singer 1975; Regan 1983; Cazaux 2007). Most non-human animals in the trade are killed for manufacturing or placed outside of their ecosystem (Wyatt 2013). According to Gonzales (2003), up to 75–90 per cent of illegally traded parrots will die during transit. According to Wyatt (2013) the victimization is continuous. If the non-human animals survive the transport they are kept in cages or held in captivity their whole lives. From a biocentric perspective this would be unacceptable.

Applying the harm principle may vary in different stages of the wildlife trade. Not only are harms interconnected in several ways, environmental harms are partly determined by transnational transference (e.g. avian influenza, SARS, Ebola) (Heckenberg 2010). Due to the variety of different forms of wildlife trade (e.g. species, purposes) and geographical dispersion, it has become clear that wildlife trade involving the EU can result in various intentional and unintentional harms. The degree and form of these harms appears to be dependent on type of species, geographic location and offenders.

First of all, trade in endangered species can be extremely harmful for the remaining population. A shining example of this impact is the illegal trade in critically endangered tortoises such that together they now make up more than 20 per cent of the total wild population in the EU (Perälä 2003). It is significant, therefore, that 1,569 Egyptian tortoises were confiscated in the EU between 2001 and 2010, given that the wild population of Egyptian tortoises is estimated to be 7,470 animals. As shown by the trade in caviar the more a species is threatened with extinction, the higher its value will be on the black market. More severe in terms of harm is the disappearance of keystone species, which may disturb the stability of the whole ecosystem and subsequently other species may also disappear. This may in turn have significant consequences for the local communities in terms of lack of natural resources, and humanity in general if potential medicines will be lost.[38]

38 Biodiversity is a large collection of genetic material supplies that can be used for the development of new drugs. One in every four drugs originates from the tropical rainforest and every year new animals and plants are discovered by science that may have medicinal properties.

Second, harms are dependent on the geographic location. According to Hall (2013), environmental harm is unequally distributed. Relatively poor countries in Africa and Southeast Asia own nature-rich areas, which are being overexploited. In addition, the vulnerability of a species is often related to some areas where only a few specimens remain in the wild (e.g. the Javan rhino in Vietnam). Transference of harms may arise during the (illegal) transportation of wildlife from abroad to the EU. The dispersion of zoonotic viruses is evidently connected to the wildlife trade. For instance two eagles infected with avian influenza were hidden in pipes and illegally imported into Brussels from Thailand (Yee et al. 2009). As mentioned earlier, wildlife entering the EU and released in the wild can lead to ecosystem degradation.

Third, harms are dependent on the offenders. The incidental removal of animals by local communities who are dependent on natural resources differs significantly from commercial companies or organized crime groups which structurally weed out species. An excellent example is the impact of poaching on sturgeon. Besides the fact that since the early 2000s sturgeons themselves are threatened by well-equipped professional hunters sent by the *caviar mafia*, it is also the case that confrontations with human victims are not uncommon. Kidnappings, bombings of apartments of officials, and the use of weapons such as Kalashnikovs increase potential human harms and threaten state security (Siegel and Van Uhm 2014).

Simultaneously, with the increasing degradation of species, the diversity and unequal distribution of harms to humans, non-human species and ecosystems has become more clearly visible. Insofar as the demand markets of wildlife manifest in the EU, the harm is mainly visible in the relatively poor source countries in Africa and Southeast Asia. Not only human victims in the wildlife trade, but also degraded ecosystems, loss of natural resources, the emergence of zoonotic diseases, loss of potential medicines and billions of non-human victims characterize the harms of the wildlife trade. Green criminologists argue against the anthropocentric perspective of harm and are in favour of a more ecocentric and biocentric perspective, where ecosystems and non-human animals can be seen as victims. To appreciate the value of non-human animals and the natural environment is paramount in itself, rather than simply the value that they may have for humans (Beirne and South 2007; Lynch and Stretesky 2007).

Conclusion

To support future studies in the field of wildlife trade, this chapter has given an overview of the nature of the wildlife trade to one of world's largest demand markets, the European Union. There is European demand for TCM, exclusive wild caviar and exotic animals as pets as well as relatively lesser-known collector markets for corals and shells. The demand market is mainly fuelled by flows from African and Southeast Asian countries involving small-scale illegal traders, legal traders who in one or more cases go beyond the limits of the law, and criminal organizations. The diversity of the illegal wildlife trade is reflected in a variety of harms to the world.

Green criminologists argue that the harm principle should be extended to non-human species and ecosystems as victims of (human) actions. We may well be on the brink of the sixth mass extinction, but this time one caused by humankind. The disappearance of species is reflected in unbalanced ecosystems and loss of habitat. While the demand markets of wildlife manifest themselves in Western countries, the harm is mainly visible in relatively poor source countries in Africa and Southeast Asia. Nevertheless, wildlife trade is not a dismissible third world problem but a global one. The demand market is fuelled by flows from different geographic locations by a large diversity of perpetrators reflected in an overwhelming variety of unequal distributed harms to the world. While humankind clearly seems to understand the interconnectedness in nature and the global side effects of the wildlife trade, it will be a challenge to prevent the rapid extinction of many species.

References

Ayling, J. 2013. 'What Sustains Wildlife Crime? Rhino Horn Trading and the Resilience of Criminal Networks', *Journal of International Wildlife Law & Policy* 16(1), 57–80.

Barnosky, A.D., Matzke, N., Tomiya, S., Wogan, G.O., Swartz, B., Quental, T.B. and Ferrer, E.A. 2011. 'Has the Earth's Sixth Mass Extinction Already Arrived?', *Nature* 47(7336), 51–7.

Beirne, P. and South, N. (eds). 2007. *Issues in Green Criminology: Confronting Harms against Environments, Humanity and Other Animals*. Cullompton: Willan Publishing.

Bell, D., Roberton, S. and Hunter, P.R. 2004. 'Animal Origins of SARS Coronavirus: Possible Links with the International Trade in Small Carnivores', *Philosophical Transactions of the Royal Society of London. Series B: Biological Sciences* 359(1447), 1107–14.

Benton, T. 1998. 'Rights and Justice on a Shared Planet: More Rights or New Relations?', *Theoretical Criminology* 2(2), 149–75.

Blundell, A.G. and Mascia, M.B. 2005. 'Discrepancies in Reported Levels of International Wildlife Trade', *Conservation Biology* 19(6), 2020–25.

Boekhout van Solinge, T. 2012. 'Ontbossing en criminologie', *Justitiële verkenningen* 38(2), 9–28.

Butchart, S.H., Walpole, M., Collen, B., van Strien, A., Scharlemann, J.P., Almond, R.E. and Watson, R. 2010. 'Global Biodiversity: Indicators of Recent Declines', *Science* 328(5982), 1164–8.

Carpenter, A. 2012. *Security and Europe's Sea Ports: Threats and Issues Facing Maritime Gateways to Europe*. Paper presented at the Policing and European Studies research conference, 30 March, University of Abertay, Dundee.

Cazaux, G. 2007. 'Labelling Animals: Non-Speciesist Criminology and Techniques to Identify Other Animals', in *Issues in Green Criminology*, edited by P. Beirne and N. South. Cullompton: Willan Publishing, 87–113.

CITES. 2003. *Review of Significant Trade in Specimens of Appendix-II Species* (Resolution Conf. 12.8 and Decision 12.75).

Coleman, C. and Moynihan, J. 1996. *Understanding Crime Data: Haunted by the Dark Figure*. Buckingham: Open University Press.

Commission for Environmental Cooperation. 2005. *Illegal Trade in Wildlife: A North American Perspective*. Montreal: Commission for Environmental Cooperation.

Cook, D., Roberts, M. and Lowther, J. 2002. *The International Wildlife Trade and Organised Crime: A Review of the Evidence and the Role of the UK*. University of Wolverhampton.

Cooney, R. and Jepson, P. 2006. 'The International Wild Bird Trade: What's Wrong with Blanket Bans?', *Oryx* 40(1), 18–23.

Cowdrey, D. 2002. *Switching Channels: Wildlife Trade Routes into Europe and the UK*. Wolverhampton: University of Wolverhampton.

CRI. 1992. *Milieuhandhaving en natuurbescherming; criminaliteitsbeeld van en om de handel in bedreigde plant en diersoorten*. The Hague: Centrale Recherche Informatiedienst.

DeBoer, T.S. and Barber, P.H. 2010. 'Isolation and Characterization of 9 Polymorphic Microsatellite Markers for the Endangered Boring Giant Clam (Tridacna crocea) and Cross-Priming Testing in Three Other Tridacnid Species', *Conservation Genetics Resources* 2(1), 353–6.

Dijk, van P.P., Corti, C., Mellado, V.P. and Cheylan, M. 2004. *Testudo graeca. The IUCN Red List of Threatened Species*. Version 2014.2.

Economic and Social Council United Nations (ECOSOC). 2002. *Progress Made in the Implementation of Economic and Social Council Resolution 2001/12 on Illicit Trafficking in Protected Species of Wild Flora and Fauna*. Report of the Secretary-General, 9–12.

——— 2003. *Illicit Trafficking in Protected Species of Wild Flora and Fauna and Illicit Access to Genetic Resources*. Report of the Secretary-General (E/CN.15/2003/8).

EIA. 2013. *Blood Ivory: Exposing the Myth of a Regulated Market*. London: EIA.

Engler, M. and Knapp, A. 2008. *Briefing on the Evolution of the Caviar Trade and Range State Implementation of Resolution Conf. 12.7 (Rev. CoP14)*. Brussels: Traffic.

Engler, M. and Parry-Jones, R. 2007. *Opportunity or Threat: The Role of the European Union in Global Wildlife Trade*. Brussels: Traffic Europe.

European Commission. 2006. *Study on the Enforcement of the EU Wildlife Trade Regulations in the EU-25*. Brussels: European Commission.

——— 2010. *Wildlife Trade Regulations in the European Union: An Introduction to CITES and its Implementation in the European Union*. Luxembourg: European Commission.

——— 2014. *Communication from the Commission to the Council and the European Parliament on the EU Approach against Wildlife Trafficking*. Brussels, 7 February, COM (2014) 64 final.

Europol. 2011. *Organised Crime Threat Assessment (OCTA)*. The Hague: Europol.

——— 2013a. *Serious and Organised Crime Threat Assessment (SOCTA)*. The Hague: Europol.

——— 2013b. *Threat Assessment 2013: Environmental Crime in the EU*. The Hague: Europol.

FAO. 2011. 'International Trade in Wild Birds, and Related Bird Movements, in Latin America and the Caribbean', *Animal Production and Health Paper No. 166*. Rome: FAO.

Felbab-Brown, V. 2011. *The Disappearing Act: The Illicit Trade in Wildlife in Asia*. Washington, DC: The Brookings Institution.

Gabriel, G., Hua, N. and Wang, J. 2012. *Making a Killing: A 2011 Survey of Ivory Markets in China*. Yarmouth Port: IFAW.

Goga, K. 2014. *The Illegal Abalone Trade in the Western Cape*. Institute for Security Studies Papers (261).

Gonzales, J.A. 2003. 'Harvesting, Local Trade, and Conservation of Parrots in the Northeastern Peruvian Amazon', *Biological Conservation* 114, 437–46.

Haken, J. 2011. *Transnational Crime in the Developing World*. Washington, DC: Global Financial Integrity.

Hall, M. 2013. *Victims of Environmental Harm: Rights, Recognition and Redress under National and International Law*. London: Routledge.

Halsey, M. and White, R. 1998. 'Crime, Ecophilosophy and Environmental Harm', *Theoretical Criminology* 2(3), 345–71.

Heckenberg, D. 2010. 'The Global Transference of Toxic Harms', in *Global Environmental Harm: Criminological Perspectives*, edited by R. White. Cullompton: Willan Publishing.

Heijden, van der, H.A. 2004. 'De milieubeweging in de twintigste eeuw', *Belgisch Tijdschrift voor Nieuwe Geschiedenis* 32(3), 4.

Herbig, F.J.W. and Joubert, S.J. 2006. 'Criminological Semantics: Conservation Criminology – Vision or Vagary?', *Acta Criminologica* 19, 88–103.

Herbig, J. 2010. 'The Illegal Reptile Trade as a Form of Conservation Crime: A South African Criminological Investigation', in *Global Environmental Harm: Criminological Perspectives* edited by R. White. Cullompton: Willan Publishing, 110–31.

Higgins, P. 2010. *Eradicating Ecocide: Laws and Governance to Prevent the Destruction of Our Planet*. London: Shepheard-Walwyn Publishers.

Higgins, P. et al. 2012. *Ecocide is the Missing 5th Crime against Peace*. Human Rights Consortium. School of Advanced Study, University of London.

Highfield, A.C. and Bayley, J.R. 1996. 'The Trade in Tortoise-Derived Souvenir Products in Morocco', *Traffic Bulletin* 16(1), 33–5.

Holden, J. 1998. *By Hook or by Crook: A Reference Manual on Illegal Wildlife Trade and Prosecutions in the United Kingdom*. Sandy: Royal Society for the Protection of Birds.

Hulsman, L.H. 1986. 'Critical Criminology and the Concept of Crime', *Crime, Law and Social Change* 10(1), 63–80.

Hutton, J. and Dickson, B. (eds) 2000. *Endangered Species, Threatened Convention: The Past, Present, and Future of CITES, the Convention on International Trade in Endangered Species of Wild Fauna and Flora*. London: Earthscan.

IFAW. 2013. *Criminal Nature: The Global Security Implications of the Illegal Wildlife Trade*. Brussels: IFAW.

Interpol. 1996. *Internal Report: Noah*. Lyon: Interpol.

IUCN. 2014. *The IUCN Red List of Threatened Species. 2014.3*. Gland: IUCN.

Jones, R. 2008. 'CITES, Corals and Customs: The International Trade in Wild Coral. Advances in Coral Husbandry in Public Aquariums', *Public Aquarium Husbandry Series*, 351–61.

Kasterine, A., Arbeid, R., Caillabet, O. and Natusch, D. 2012. *The Trade in South-East Asian Python Skins*. Geneva: International Trade Centre (ITC).

Kazmar, J. 2000. 'The International Illegal Plant and Wildlife Trade: Biological Suicide', *U.C. Davis Journal of International Law and Policy* 6(105), 105–29.

Kemner, J. 2010. *Illegale handel in exotische diersoorten uitgestorven?* Amsterdam: Bureau Milieu Criminaliteit.

KLPD. 2005. *Analyse CITES-criminaliteit. Een analyse van de illegale handel in CITES-soorten*. Zoetermeer: KLPD.

Lau, S.K.P., Woo, P.C.Y., Li, K.S.M., Huang, Y., Tsoi, H., Wong, B.H.L., Wong, S.S.Y., Leung, S.Y., Chan, K.H. and Yuen, K.Y. 2005. 'Severe Acute Respiratory Syndrome Coranavirus-Like Virus in Chinese Horseshoe Bats', *Proceedings of the National Academy of Sciences of the United States* 102, 14040–45.

Lawson, K. and Vines, A. 2014. *Global Impact of the Illegal Wildlife Trade: The Costs of Crime, Insecurity and Institutional Erosion*. London: Chatham House.

Leakey, R.E. and Lewin, R. 1995. *The Sixth Extinction: Patterns of Life and the Future of Humankind*. New York: Doubleday.

Lemieux, A.M. and Clarke, R.V. 2009. 'The International Ban on Ivory Sales and its Effects on Elephant Poaching in Africa', *British Journal of Criminology* 49(4), 451–71.

Liddick, D.R. 2011. *Crimes against Nature: Illegal Industries and the Global Environment*. Oxford: Praeger Publishers.

Lindsey, P., Balme, G., Becker, M., Begg, C., Bento, C., Bocchino, C., Dickman, A., Diggle, R., Eves, H., Henschel, P., Lewis, D., Marnewick, K., Mattheus, J., McNutt, J.W., McRobb, R., Midlane, N., Milanzi, J., Morley, R., Murphree, M., Nyoni, P., Opyene, V., Phadima, J., Purchase, N., Rentsch, D., Roche, C., Shaw, J., van der Westhuizen, H., Van Vliet, N. and Zisadza, P. 2012. *Illegal Hunting and the Bush-Meat Trade in Savanna Africa: Drivers, Impacts and Solutions to Address the Problem*. New York: Wildlife Conservation Society report.

LNV. 2000. *Voortgangsrapportage CITES*. The Hague: LNV.

Lynch, M.J. and Stretesky, P.B. 2007. 'Green Criminology in the United States', in *Issues in Green Criminology: Confronting Harms against Environments, Humanity and Other Animals*, edited by P. Beirne and N. South. Cullompton: Willan Publishing, 248–69.

Lyons, J.A. and Natusch, J.D. 2011. 'Wildlife Laundering through Breeding Farms: Illegal Harvest, Population Declines and a Means of Regulating the Trade of Green Pythons (Morelia viridis) from Indonesia', *Biological Conservation* 144, 3073–81.

Millennium Ecosystem Assessment. 2005. *Ecosystems and Human Well-Being: Desertification Synthesis*. Washington, DC: World Resources Institute.

Mills, L.S., Soulé, M.E. and Doak, D.F. 1993. 'The Keystone-Species Concept in Ecology and Conservation', *BioScience*, 219–24.

Mooney, H.A. and Hobbs, R.J. (eds). 2000. *Invasive Species in a Changing World*. Washington, DC: Island Press.

Myers, R.A., Baum, J.K., Shepherd, T.D., Powers, S.P. and Peterson, C.H. 2007. 'Cascading Effects of the Loss of Apex Predatory Sharks from a Coastal Ocean', *Science* 315, 1846–50.

Naylor, R.T. 2004. 'The Underworld of Ivory', *Crime, Law and Social Change* 42, 261–95.

Nijman, V. 2010. 'An Overview of International Wildlife Trade from Southeast Asia', *Biodiversity and Conservation* 19(4), 1101–14.

NOAA. 2010. *Strategic Plan for Deep-Sea Coral and Sponge Ecosystems: Research, Management, and International Cooperation*. Silver Spring, MD: NOAA Coral Reef Conservation Program.

Nowell, K. 2012. *Wildlife Crime Scorecard: Assessing Compliance with and Enforcement of CITES Commitments for Tigers, Rhinos and Elephants*. World Wildlife Fund.

Paine, R.T. 1966. 'Food Web Complexity and Species Diversity', *American Naturalist*, 65–75.

Passas, N. 1999. 'Globalization, Criminogenic Asymmetries and Economic Crime', *European Journal of Law Reform* 1(4), 399–423.

Passas, N. and Goodwin, N.R. (eds). 2004. *It's Legal but It Ain't Right: Harmful Social Consequences of Legal Industries*. Ann Arbor: University of Michigan Press.

Perälä, J. 2003. 'Testudo kleinmanni', in *IUCN 2012. IUCN Red List of Threatened Species*. Version 2012.2.

Petrossian, G.A. and Clarke, R.V. 2013. 'Explaining and Controlling Illegal Commercial Fishing: An Application of the CRAVED Theft Model', *British Journal of Criminology* 54(1), 73–90.

Pikitch, E.K., Doukakis, P., Lauck, L., Chakrabarty, P. and Erickson, D.L. 2005. 'Status, Trends and Management of Sturgeon and Paddlefish Fisheries', *Fish and Fisheries* 6(3), 233–65.

Pires, S.F. 2012. 'The Illegal Parrot Trade: A Literature Review', *Global Crime* 13(3), 176–90.

Power, M.E., Tilman, D., Estes, J.A., Menge, B.A., Bond, W.J., Mills, L.S., Daily, G. Castilla, J., Lubchenco, J. and Paine, R.T. 1996. 'Challenges in the Quest for Keystones', *BioScience* 46(8), 609–20.

Regan, T. 1983. *The Case for Animal Rights*. Oakland: University of California Press.

Regionale Recherche Dienst Rotterdam (RRD). 1995. *Eindrapportage Team HID. Project Wildlife Criminaliteit*. Rotterdam: RRD.

Ripple, W.J. and Beschta, R.L. 2012. 'Trophic Cascades in Yellowstone: The First 15 Years after Wolf Reintroduction', *Biological Conservation* 145(1), 205–13.

Roe, D. 2002. *Making a Killing or Making a Living: Wildlife Trade, Trade Controls, and Rural Livelihoods*. Stevenage: IIED/Traffic.

Rosen, G.E. and Smith, K.F. 2010. 'Summarizing the Evidence on the International Trade in Illegal Wildlife', *EcoHealth* 7(1), 24–32.

Ruggiero, V. and South, N. 2010. 'Green Criminology and Dirty Collar Crime', *Critical Criminology* 18(4), 251–62.

Schneider, J.L. 2008. 'Reducing the Illicit Trade in Endangered Wildlife: The Market Reduction Approach', *Journal of Contemporary Criminal Justice* 24(3), 274–95.

——— 2012. *Sold into Extinction: The Global Trade in Endangered Species*. Santa Barbara: ABC-CLIO.

Siegel, D. and Van Uhm, D.P. 2014. 'Zwarte kaviaar. Criminele netwerken, illegale handel en de bedreiging van de steur', *Justitiële verkenningen* 30(2), 54–70.

Silva, J.P., Toland, J., Jones, W., Eldridge, J., Hudson, T. and O'Hara, E. 2009. *Life and Europe's Reptiles and Amphibians: Conservation in Practice*. Luxembourg: European Communities.

Singer, P. 1975. *Animal Liberation: A New Ethics for Our Treatment of Animals*. New York: Discus.

Sodhi, N.S., Koh, L.P., Brook, B.W. and Ng, P.K. 2004. 'Southeast Asian Biodiversity: An Impending Disaster', *Trends in Ecology & Evolution* 19(12), 654–60.

Sollund, R.A. 2008. *Global Harms: Ecological Crime and Speciesism*. Hauppauge: Nova Science Publishers.

——— 2013. 'Animal Trafficking and Trade: Abuse and Species Injustice', in *Emerging Issues in Green Criminology: Exploring Power, Justice and Harm*, edited by R. Walters, D.S. Westerhuis and T. Wyatt. New York: Palgrave Macmillan, 72–92.

——— 2014. 'Crimes Against Animal Life', in *Encyclopedia of Criminology and Criminal Justice*, edited by G. Bruinsma and D. Weisburd. New York: Springer, 759–69.

South, N. 2008. 'Nature, Difference and the Rejection of Harm: Expanding the Agenda for Green Criminology', in *Global Harm: Ecological Crime and Speciesism*, edited by R.A. Sollund. Hauppauge: Nova Science Publishers, 191–3.

South, N. and Beirne, P. (eds). 1998. 'For a Green Criminology'. Special issue of *Theoretical Criminology* 2(2).

Stiles, D., Redmond, I., Cress, D., Nellemann, C. and Formo, R.K. 2013. *Stolen Apes – The Illicit Trade in Chimpanzees, Gorillas, Bonobos, and Orangutans: A Rapid Response Assessment*. Arendal: United Nations Environment Programme/ GRID-Arendal.

Tailby, R. and Gant, F. 2002. *The Illegal Market in Australian Abalone*. Canberra: Australian Institute of Criminology.
Traffic. 2014. *Wildlife Trade in the European Union. Traffic Briefing*. Brussels: Traffic.
Underwood, F.M., Burn, R.W. and Milliken, T. 2013. 'Dissecting the Illegal Ivory Trade: An Analysis of Ivory Seizures Data', *PloS one* 8(10). Available at: http://journals.plos.org/plosone/article?id=10.1371/journal.pone.0076539 (accessed 4 April 2015).
UNEP. 2013. *Elephants in the Dust–The African Elephant Crisis. A Rapid Response Assessment*. Nairobi: United Nations Environment Programme.
United Nations. 2012. *Improving International Systems for Trade in Reptile Skins based on Sustainable Use*. Geneva: United Nations.
UNODC. 2006. *Organized Crime and Irregular Migration from Africa to Europe*. Vienna: United Nations Office on Drugs and Crime.
——— 2010. *The Globalization of Crime: A Transnational Organized Crime Threat Assessment*. Vienna: United Nations Office on Drugs and Crime.
——— 2012. *Wildlife and Forest Crime Analytic Toolkit*. Vienna: UNODC.
Van Uhm, D.P. 2009. *Illegale dierenhandel en de rol van Nederland. Masterthesis Criminology*. Utrecht: Universiteit Utrecht, Willem Pompe Institute for Criminal Law and Criminology.
——— 2012a. 'De illegale handel in beschermde diersoorten', *Justitiële verkenningen* 28(2), 91–100.
——— 2012b. 'Organised Crime in the Wildlife Trade', *Centre for Information and Research on Organised Crime Newsletter* 10(2), 2–4.
——— 2014. 'Criminaliteit en traditionele Chinese medicijnen', *Proces* 93(2), 130–43.
Venkatesan, V. 2010. 'Marine Ornamental Molluscs', *National Training Programme on Marine Ornamental Fish Culture*, 27–32.
Walters, R. 2010. *Eco Crime and Genetically Modified Food*. Abingdon: Routledge.
White, R. 2007. 'Green Criminology and the Pursuit of Social and Ecological Justice', in *Issues in Green Criminology: Confronting Harms against Environments, Other Animals, and Humanity*, edited by N. South and P. Beirne. Cullompton: Willan Publishing, 32–54.
——— 2008. *Crimes Against Nature: Environmental Criminology and Ecological Justice*. Cullompton: Willan Publishing.
——— 2011. *Transnational Environmental Crime: Toward an Eco-Global Criminology*. London: Routledge.
Wilson, E.O. and Kellert, S.R. (eds). 1993. *The Biophilia Hypothesis*. Washington, DC: Island Press.
Wood, E.M., Malsch, K. and Miller, J. 2012. 'International Trade in Hard Corals: Review of Management, Sustainability and Trends', in *Proceedings of the 12th International Coral Reef Symposium, Cairns, Australia*, 9–13.
World Bank. 2008. *What's Driving the Wildlife Trade?* Washington, DC: World Bank.
Worster, D. (ed.). 1988. *The Ends of the Earth: Perspectives on Modern Environmental History*. New York: Cambridge University Press.
Wyatt, T. 2009. 'Exploring the Organization of Russia Far East's Illegal Wildlife Trade: Two Case Studies of the Illegal Fur and Illegal Falcon Trades', *Global Crime* 10(1–2), 144–54.
——— 2011. 'The Illegal Trade of Raptors in the Russian Federation', *Contemporary Justice Review* 14(2), 103–23.
——— 2013. *Wildlife Trafficking: A Deconstruction of the Crime, the Victims, and the Offenders*. Basingstoke: Palgrave Macmillan.

Wyler, L.S. and Sheikh, P.A. 2008. *International Illegal Trade in Wildlife: Threats and US Policy*. Washington, DC: Library of Congress Washington Congressional Research Service.

——— 2013. *International Illegal Trade in Wildlife: Threats and US Policy*. Washington, DC: Library of Congress Washington Congressional Research Service.

Xueyan, L. 2007. 'Promoting Sustainable Use of Chinese Traditional Medicines', in *The State of Wildlife Trade in China: Information on the Trade in Wild Animals and Plants in China*. Beijing: Traffic.

Yee, K.S., Carpenter, T.E. and Cardona, C.J. 2009. 'Epidemiology of H5N1 Avian Influenza', *Comparative Immunology, Microbiology and Infectious Diseases* 32(4), 325–40.

Zembla. 2001. *De Madagascar-connectie*. Documentary. Available at: http://zembla.vara.nl/seizoenen/2001/afleveringen/24-05-2001 (accessed 4 April 2015).

Zimmerman, M.E. 2003. 'Black Market for Wildlife: Combating Transnational Organized Crime in the Illegal Wildlife Trade', *The Vanderbilt Journal of Transnational Law* 36, 1657–66.

4 Is Green Criminology Paradigm-Breaking?

Some Reflections on Hydrocarbon and Resource Extraction, Crime and Criminological Thinking

James Sheptycki

Introduction

Crime is inherently a political category, as Stanley Cohen repeatedly argued (1985, 1988, 1996; Downes et al. 2007) and thus, when confronted with a development like 'green criminology' (Beirne and South 2007; Spapens et al. 2014), criminologists are again compelled to examine the limits of the field. Criminology is not a settled discipline, its perceptual boundaries are contested, the field has long been fragmented and its futures plural (Nelken 1994). Actually and despite what most introductory textbooks say, criminology only became an academic subject in the twentieth century. Even the date of inception is contested, but the publication of Edwin Sutherland's first edition of *Principles of Criminology* in 1924 is arguably the most robust contender. Fittingly, Sutherland was the first President of the American Society of Criminology which was, again arguably, the first really academic, university-based organization representing a collective intellectual enterprise that could be called criminological (Sheptycki 2010).[1]

As Mary McIntosh (1975) explained it long ago, the roots of criminological thinking lie in originating sociological questions about why some people stray from the straight and narrow path and gradually extended in the slow accretion of a broadly sociological understanding of crime, crime definition and corresponding social reactions. Sutherland himself was perhaps the first to radically

1 Conventional textbooks generally begin the story of criminological ideas by reference to eighteenth- and nineteenth-century thinkers such as Cesare Beccaria, Jeremy Bentham, Adolphe Quetlet, Cesare Lombroso, Gabrielle Tarde and the like. While there can no disputing that these thinkers provide essential stepping-stones in the history of criminological ideas, criminological thinking did not coalesce into a recognized university subject for teaching purposes until the 1920s, at which time sociological approaches were ascendant. The Foucauldian insistence that criminology is merely a reflection of penological power has already lost sight of the real historical development of criminological language when it remains focused on nineteenth-century precursors to its institutionalization as an academic subject taught in universities on a widespread basis (cf. Garland 1992). It is simply an historical mistake to conclude that the paradigmatic contours of criminology were in any way firmly established before the twentieth century and any critique of criminology that fails to take account of fundamental developments in the field of criminological thought in the 1920s through to the 1960s falls well short of the mark.

challenge the conceptual boundaries of criminological thinking when he began to write about so-called white-collar crime in the 1940s (Gaylord and Galliher 1988). He began this paradigm-busting attempt in his Presidential Address to the American Society of Sociology in 1939 – an event that was captured as front page news (Laub 2006). The details of this chapter in the history of criminological ideas are complex. In this context it is suffice to say that Sutherland tried to sweep away the presumption that crime was somehow the preserve of the economically less well-off and show that criminality was a feature of the highest echelons of the social order. This is perhaps not paradigm-breaking in and of itself, but in arguing that criminological thinking should not be confined to narrow parameters defined by criminal law, that it should explain all forms of law violation (not just criminal law violation) and should take into account the effects of harmful behaviour he certainly stretched theoretical boundaries. However, after some initial enthusiasm, academic criminology gradually drifted back to the comfortable confines of more limited thinking, seeking an understanding of individuals' pathways to crime (cf. Sellin and Wolfgang 1964).

It was not long before William Chambliss' presidential address to the American Society of Criminology again challenged the field (Chambliss 1989). Chambliss' questions about 'state-organized crime' not only challenged narrow criminological thinking about individual causes and pathways to crime – instead locating an understanding of criminality in basic social-structural conditions – they also, much like Sutherland's questions about white-collar crime, focused the criminological gaze on crimes of the powerful. In arguing that understanding the role of professional, elected, politicians and senior level state bureaucrats in the social structure of organized crime was to say, in effect, that 'the State' itself is an organized crime racket (cf. Tilly 1985). Chambliss undoubtedly stretched the boundaries of criminological thinking. He raised these testing questions primarily during the decade of the 1980s, when the activities of people at the highest levels of American government were brought under the criminological microscope – notably in the Iran-Contra scandal. But these ideas were largely subsumed and smothered by the disciplinary corpus and most academic criminology continued to reflect more traditional assumptions.

The history of criminological ideas reveals the field to be one in which the parameters of thinking have been repeatedly stretched, challenged and questioned as the interrelated issues of power, justice and harm rub up against one another in the context of trying to understand particular and highly variable manifestations of socially condemnable conduct. Myriad examples of this arose from the 1970s onwards and include the rise to prominence of 'critical', 'radical', 'feminist' and other 'new criminologies'. In the history of criminological ideas there are currents of thinking that allow the continuing emergence, sometimes to positions of prominence, of thinkers who break rules and challenge assumptions about the parameters of its thinking. As Cohen (e.g. 1988) often argued, real, questioning, academic criminology reveals intractable problems in the concept of crime because the concept is political. The over-arching question for this chapter is how to understand the implications of 'green criminology' in this ongoing history of criminological ideas.

Green Criminology: Precepts and Pitfalls

When James Lovelock conceived of the Gaia Principle in the 1970s, he did so partly because of a new image of the earth made possible when the astronauts aboard Apollo 17 captured and transmitted the famous 'blue marble' picture, which was the first full-view photograph of our planet from the perspective of outer space (Wuebbles 2012). As is by now well known, the Gaia Principle suggests that the earth itself is a living organism and its plant life and bestiary are akin to the flora and fauna of the human digestive system. Gaia is a life form. Mother Earth is one. This view of the earth ultimately made possible the criminological concept of 'ecocide', that the earth could be the victim of crime and that the environment itself had rights to exist (Brisman and South 2014). Indeed, subsequent the realizations of the 1970s, numerous crimes against the environment have been named: wildlife crime, illicit trafficking in endangered species and the products made from them, illegal logging and the illicit trade in timber products and toxic waste dumping are just some of them. This criminological vocabulary reflects the institutional thinking of an emerging global policing architecture (Bowling and Sheptycki 2012). For example, when Interpol formed an environmental crime working-group in the early 1990s, it harnessed concerns about environmental degradation to its own institutional form, semantically entangling the Gaia Principle in police institutional red tape.

As yet unanswered questions arise about how police statistics might be used to measure the successes in suppressing environment crime. Pursuit of environmental crimes has a symbolic dimension. When Hillary Clinton, in her capacity as US Secretary of State, made 'wildlife crime' and trafficking in endangered species a 'national security matter' in 2012, it was welcomed by conservation and environmental societies (Goldenberg 2012). Cristián Samper, President of the Wildlife Conservation Society, for example, stated that the 'important thing is linking this [wildlife crime] with security issues and acknowledging that this is an international crime', while Crawford Allan of the World Wildlife Fund commented that 'regardless of whether Secretary Clinton stays at the State Department or not, there is no going back now. She has let the genie out of the bottle' (Goldenberg 2012).

Clinton has closely associated herself with efforts to 'save the elephants' (Goldenberg 2013a). Crimes against charismatic mega-fauna such as elephants, rhinoceros, orangutans and gorillas offer emotive environmental victimage which in turn provide justification for Interpol and other involved transnational policing organizations to continue and expand their security-control practices. Wildlife crime is an especially emotive area and the symbolic stakes are high. This is perhaps best exemplified by observing the brouhaha in 2006–7 over Royal Dutch Shell Petroleum's high-profile sponsorship of the Wildlife Photographer of the Year awards; environmental activists labelled it 'greenwashing' and pointed out that the company had a long track record of environmental harm (Goldenberg 2013a). Images of polar bears featured prominently in this episode.

An interesting, if unremarked, antithesis of these developments has been the emergence of the 'eco-terrorist', a process whereby ecological activists seeking to emphasize the influence of elites in ongoing environmental harm have been branded as 'security threats'. When Greenpeace activists scaled Mount Rushmore in 2009 protesting against environmental degradation and climate change they risked running afoul of eco-terrorism laws enforced by the FBI (Ruskin 2013). The FBI defines eco-terrorism broadly as:

> The use or intended use of violence of a criminal nature against innocent victims or property by an environmentally oriented sub-national group for environmental-political reasons or aimed at an audience beyond the target, often of a symbolic nature.

Richard Fadden, the Director of the Canadian Security Intelligence Service, told a parliamentary committee that 'it is the new normal for Canada's security agencies to watch the activities of environmental organizations', adding that more than half of the Canada's security monitoring efforts were aimed at domestic targets. According to Jeffrey Monaghan, a researcher at the Surveillance Studies Centre at Queen's University, in Kingston, Ontario, Canadian security agencies had a particular 'fixation' with Greenpeace, which had been described in Threat Assessments as 'potentially violent' (Leahy 2013; see also Walby and Monaghan 2011). Looking at crime control as an industry and observing the emerging language concerning crimes against the environment reveals a contradiction. On the one hand is a victimological picture which plays the politics of affect. Images of vulnerable animal victims provide justification for increasing crime control measures – for example using drone technology to police the wildlife of the African savannah – which has the effect of legitimating those control practices more generally. On the other hand, the shifting sands between environmental activism and so-called eco-terrorism also provide justification for the bolstering of control methods on a global scale. Perhaps the arrival of concerns about crimes against the environment has not been paradigm-busting for criminology. On this reckoning, the addition to the criminological lexicon of these new crime categories has only provided further structural material for bolstering the already existing security and crime control apparatus emerging in the global system.

And yet, 'it oughta be a crime'. This commonly spoke aphorism has been applied to ecocide. Just as there was no law pertaining to genocide until after 1945, there is not yet a globally enforceable law against ecocide. Such a law was mooted at the International Institute for Sustainable Development's World Congress on Justice, Governance and Law for Sustainability in June of 2012, but as yet no such legal tool has been brought into force (Dyer 2012). David Suzuki, Canada's foremost science broadcaster and environmental activist, presented his legal reasoning on how crimino-legal thinking could be handled in the case of massive global crimes against the environment in a lecture titled *Imagining a Sustainable Future; Foresight over Hindsight*:

> There is in Canada a legal category where people can be sued and thrown in the slammer, called willful blindness. If people in positions of power

> deliberately suppress or ignore information that is vital to the decisions they're making, that is willful blindness. I call it more than willful blindness. I call it criminal negligence because it's a crime against future generations, to avoid facing the reality.
>
> (Suzuki 2013)

So the context for green criminology is that the legal tool pertaining to possibly the most serious criminal charge has not yet been forged, but there are strong pressures to do so and these follow a common sense legal reasoning. To many people the general category of 'crimes against the environment' makes sense and thus arise expectations about how such would be policed. Following Suzuki's logic, such policing would be undertaken on the basis of preventing future harm. As it happens, this expectation is in accord with broad contemporary currents in criminological thinking which highlight efforts at pre-emptive action against measurable risk in order to suppress harm (Zedner 2007).

Despite the inherent difficulties and the ever-present possibility of unintended consequences (such as successful greenwashing propaganda and the legitimation of transnational crime-control agendas and practices) green criminology ideas are here to stay. The next section seeks to understand this a bit better by taking a close look at a particular example.

Petroleum Resource Extraction and Green Criminology in Canada: A Study in Contrasts

Facts are sometimes elusive and it is never easy to measure things with reliable precision so, depending on how one reckons things, the largest or second largest dam in the world is the Tailings Pond in Fort McMurray, Alberta – a gigantic slough of poisoned water. Partly because of its scale, the tar sands mining complex operating in the area around Fort McMurray presents a useful environmental case study for green criminology. However, at the outset it ought to be emphasized that this particular example is not the end of the story for green criminology in Canada. For example, the problems of heavy oil do not end at the extraction site, since 'up-stream', en-route to the refineries, there are hazards, risks and threats. The people of Lac-Megantic, Quebec learned this in July of 2013 when a runaway train with 72 carloads of highly volatile petroleum condensate crashed and exploded killing 47 people and injuring and traumatizing many more (AP 2013). Then too, the extraction of other minerals also provides sources of risk, as residents of British Columbia learned in August of 2014, when the tailings pond at the Mount Polley mine was breached releasing 4.5 million cubic metres of toxic sludge into the Hazeltine Creek, Polley Lake and Quesnel Lake waterway (Moskowitz 2014). Environmental activists in Canada might also point to other issue areas – such as clear-cut logging and over-fishing – as relevant examples of the broad panorama of green criminology in Canada (Amos et al. 2011).

In 2007 Mike Hudema, speaking on behalf of Greenpeace Canada, argued that tar sands extraction was 'the biggest global warming crime ever seen' (Milmo

2007). Hudema explained that 'it takes about 29kg of CO2 to produce a barrel of oil conventionally. That figure can be as much as 125kg for tar sands oil. It also has the potential to kill off or damage the vast forest wilderness, greater than the size of England and Wales, which forms part of the world's biggest carbon sinks' (Milmo 2007). By inference, tar sands extraction causes significant ecological harm worthy of criminalization. The risk that the Greenpeace representative focuses on in focusing his criminalization rhetoric is so-called global warming. However, the ecological impact of open-pit petroleum mining in the Athabasca region is not restricted to greenhouse gas emissions. Actually, oil extraction from the tar sands is an expensive business and it only really becomes profitable when oil rises above the $100-per-barrel mark, in current currency conditions.[2]

One of the un-costed costs is water. Tar sands extraction currently requires approximately 3.5 to 5 million barrels of water annually in order to facilitate extraction, a resource which is drawn off the river system at no cost to the extraction operation. Another cost is an energy since it takes 1,000 cubic feet of natural gas in the extraction of every barrel of heavy oil. The gas is burned in order to heat the water that is used to dislodge unwanted elements from the heavy oil, which can then be shipped by train or pipeline to further points on the production and refinement line. In essence, tar sands mining extracts oil by heating massive amounts of water with natural gas. This process accounts for an estimated 8 per cent of Canada's annual carbon emissions. Only a percentage of the water extracted from the Athabasca waterway can be returned to nature. The remainder, which is probably most of it, must be stored in tailings ponds. These ponds contain the leftovers – a mixture of salts, heavy metals, sulfur naphthenic acids and more – that are highly toxic. Were the dyke to be breached, the consequences would be enormous, perhaps destroying the entire Athabasca watershed. Already millions of litres of polluted liquid have leached into the groundwater. Downstream from the tailings ponds, over 300,000 indigenous people live and public health providers claim to have observed increased incidents of auto-immune diseases, diabetes, renal failure, hypertension, cancer (including rare types) in unusually high numbers.

Not all of these public health risk indicators are attributable to the toxins in the tailings ponds upriver, but it is not unreasonable to assume that some of them are. First Nations people in Canada have recognized the impact of toxic pollutants in lakes and rivers for a long time. In 2012, an English language report was published concerning the results of a study first begun in 1975 following the discovery that 10 tonnes of mercury, a dangerous neurotoxin, has been leaked into the

2 During the research, conception and writing of this chapter the price of oil fell precipitously on world markets (*The Economist* 2014, 2015). This caused consternation among those involved in heavy oil production in Canada, because this is relatively expensive oil to produce. To date this price fall has yet to significantly curtail infrastructure development for heavy oil production in Canada. As of this writing, prices are expected to stay relatively low – in the $50–60 range. All eyes are on Saudi Arabia and the Arab Gulf States who have opened the spigots and flooded world oil markets and many people hope that this move will signal the end of heavy oil extraction in Canada.

Wabigoo River system in northern Ontario between 1962 and 1970. That study revealed the considerable long-term impact of mercury poisoning – Minamata disease – on people dependent on natural sources of drinking water (McQuigge 2012). The immediate harmful impact of tar sands oil extraction is enormous, the long-term consequences are incalculable. The toxic lakes annually accumulating behind the dykes near Fort McMurray have nowhere to go, so potential future harm is a roll of the dice every day into an ever receding future until one day they come up snake-eyes. In effect, they are a time-bomb waiting to go off.

Accompanying this set of phenomena is another one in the realm of symbolic politics. As already noted, crime is a political category and the symbolic politics of crime control in Canada can turn environmental activists into eco-terrorists. This is partly achieved by manipulating scientific evidence and public understanding (Turner 2012). It is also partly about turning the whistle-blower into a potential risk. This has to be taken seriously, as the case of Weibow Ludwig, who was found guilty in a court of law on several counts involving sabotage of oil-field production facilities, shows. Ludwig engaged in this direct action against oil company property after repeatedly complaining about the effects of sour gas development near his community near Trickle Creek, Alberta. In 2012 details from a Canadian Security Intelligence Service Threat Assessment emerged, and one quote received especially wide publicity:

> Eco-extremists, Aboriginal Extremists and other issue-motivated groups in Canada, though very small in number, can encourage, threaten and support serious acts of violence. In certain cases, issues which provoke a sense of urgency and frustration – such as perceived policy failures or the belief that capitalism has a dehumanizing effect on society – may increase the likelihood that certain individuals or groups could adopt a more violent and destructive strategy to achieve their desired results.
>
> (McCarthy 2012)

The conflation of environmental activism and political extremism by the Canadian security establishment coalesced around the potential for disorder in connection with the so-called Northern Gateway pipeline project and a number of other pipeline projects intended to facilitate the movement of tar sands oil to the seaboard for overseas shipment by tanker. In Canada, the blurring of threat and risk categories in official discourse inverts understanding which means that a wide diversity of actions are being governed through surveillance and criminal law, but the original source of the environmental harm (the process of hydrocarbon extraction itself) is not one of them.

Green Criminology's Global Horizon

The issue of tar sands exploitation is global news. Celebrities including Neil Young, Oliver Stone, Leonardo DiCaprio and Daryl Hannah make it so. It is a relatively high value symbolic target in the politics of green criminology in Canada and internationally. There is something simplistic about the symbolism however, which obscures a more complex reality. Rob White and Diane Heckenberg (2011) grapple with this complexity, arguing that the visible event horizon for green criminology involves an array of rights infringements and harms and complicated causal relations. Eco-crime can affect human rights by threatening the safety of the environment and thinking in this domain has extended human rights to the environment itself by granting that ecosystems have an integrity worthy of legal protection. The trouble is, when it comes to hydrocarbon crime, the production of harm is systemic not particularistic.

The scaration of land at Fort McMurray is visible on Google Maps, but it is not the epicentre of the problem. The gigantic accumulations of automobiles and associated detritus – rubber tires, batteries, hub caps and wing mirrors – together with the smog polluting city atmospheres from Beijing, to Tehran, to Los Angeles and Oklahoma City – and the forest fires in southern California, and New South Wales, Australia, the acidification of the oceans, and acid rain are all effects of the systemic dependence of the global system on hydrocarbon-based energy. As with other issue areas that confront green criminology, the conceptualization of harm and its causation reach far beyond conventional criminological understandings. Complex systemic causal chains – not least transportation supply chains, but also physio-chemical chain-reactions, emergency chain-of-events, chains of financial obligation, etc. – form part of the global system which encompasses the entire field of human activity. Most humans alive today participate in some way or another in the perpetuation of the hydrocarbon-based energy economy and therefore, when it comes to hydrocarbon crime, we have met the enemy and it is us.

Academic criminology looks on all this complexity from a number of vantage points (White 2009). It problematizes the boundary between illegality and legality in the enforcement of criminal law, for example, casting light on the interrelations between the illicit and the licit trade in a number of commodities, notably timber and fish (White 2009, pp. 231–3). Although academic criminologists have not yet studied the phenomenon, it is known that there is a significant illicit market in hydrocarbon products, including oil and coal, and that this has a transnational dimension and this could become a matter of concern for green criminology. In the early 2000s UK Customs and Excise released figures suggesting that it was losing between 3 and 4 per cent of customs revenue on oil duties due to fraud and smuggling (Report by the Comptroller and Auditor General 2002). There is considerable, yet scattered, evidence internationally about illegal coal mining in places as far apart at Ukraine, India and China.[3] The consumption of these illicit fuels adds to the sum total of global CO_2 emissions and the incentive to move these products through illicit markets will only increase if governments attempt to control carbon emissions by adopting a 'carbon tax', thus creating an emerging

3 Scanning the environmental literature available online searching for the term 'illegal coal mining', one finds many entries but, to my knowledge, there has yet to be a systematic study of this phenomenon.

issue area for criminologists. Regulation creates ladders of criminal opportunity and, as regulators look to shape hydrocarbon consumption by shifting boundaries between licit and illicit trade and consumption and by 'pulling fiscal levers', criminologists will be on the lookout for criminogenic results.

The criminological gaze can be cast across the horizon of ecological issues and topics from a number of different perspectives (White 2009). It can be *comparative*, for example looking at the control responses to cases of Minamata disease in different national jurisdictions. It can be *transnational*, by for example looking at the cross-border financial interconnections and transnational commodity chains that constitute illicit transnational trade. It can be *international*, by looking specifically at crimes constituted in international criminal law, for example in the widespread use of depleted uranium by so-called Coalition Forces in the conduct of the Iraq wars. It can be *global* in perspective, for example by looking at how global institutions provide the necessary criminal opportunity structures in order for criminal environmental harm to occur. This can be exemplified through consideration of the global banking and financial system, which allows multinational corporations to shield revenue from tax authorities. Corporations themselves are global institutions which may seek to avoid regulation and, insofar as they are successful in doing so in the realm of environmental, health and safety issues, this can result in considerable harm, as the Deepwater Horizon disaster painfully revealed. Lastly, criminologists might adopt a *supranational* point of view, by looking for examples of how supranational judicial bodies like the International Criminal Court and supranational police agencies like Interpol might interdict in matters involving environmental harm.

Because academic criminology is an interdisciplinary empirical social science, the criminological vantage point emphasizes practical methodological knowledge about what constitutes good data and how it is best analysed. For example, in considering the effects of different regulatory regimes over time, the interpretation of trend data concerning licit management and illicit dumping of toxic waste in more than one jurisdiction, requires attention to detail. Consider the estimated two million tons per annum of oil products that end up in international waters every year as the residue from bilge tanks is routinely flushed out. An estimated 3,000 cases of illegal dumping of hydrocarbons occur in European waters annually (Oceana 2003). Criminologists studying these phenomena need to make sense of data from the 'environmental forensic toolbox' (e.g. DNA testing, satellite surveillance, CCTV monitoring, chemical audits, etc.) and alternative sources of data (e.g. oral history, focus group studies in marginal communities, whistle-blower evidence, etc.), as well as governmental sources and information from campaigning organizations, but they also need a critical academic perspective on the measurement, definition and interpretation of risks, threats and harms in order to make sense of the myriad of sometimes overlapping, sometimes competing truth claims. In bringing these and other considerations to bear, green criminology has a purpose, 'namely to help us address issues of pressing concern that are destroying environments, non-human species and human lives in the here and now' (Oceana 2003, p. 245).

More Hydrocarbon Flashpoints

A flashpoint is the lowest temperature at which a volatile material is likely to combust. Sociologically speaking, a flashpoint signals the convergence in space and time of trouble such that violence or anger flares up. Criminologists interested to study the policing of public order introduced the idea of 'flashpoints' to describe the moment at which disorder breaks out and rioting begins (Waddington 1989). *Flashpoint* is also the name of a popular Canadian police drama that aired over five seasons from 2008–12. Metaphorically speaking, there are a number of convergences – flashpoints – which bear on all of these linguistic connections when considering contemporary hydrocarbon politics and this is particularly evident in Canada.

On the banks of the Detroit River in the years 2012–13 a gigantic black mountain grew, a mountain of petroleum coke, the detritus from the refining process of heavy tar sands oil which is a mixture of pure carbon, sulfur and heavy metals such as nickel, vanadium and selenium, as well as polycyclic aromatic hydrocarbons (PAHs) which are believed to be highly carcinogenic (Gordon 2012; Goldenberg 2013b). Since every barrel of tar sands oil leaves between 60 and 130 pounds (approx. 25–60 kg), Canada had already stockpiled some 80 million tons of these nearly useless hazardous materials by then and a 'little bit of Alberta' (Austen 2013) – a mountain approximately as tall as a three-storey building with a base area of one city block – had accumulated there attracting widespread attention (Goldenberg 2013b).

The fuel cannot, at present, be burned in the United States or Canada, due to environmental regulations, but is being shipped in large quantities to China, Brazil, Mexico and Eastern Europe where it is used as an energy source. When it is burned petroleum coke puts enormous quantities of pollutants into the atmosphere and when it is stockpiled, as it is in Chicago and Detroit and many other places in North America, it is blown on the wind as fine black dust that gets everywhere (Goldenberg 2013b). The BP refinery in Chicago was estimated to produce over two million tons of the stuff in 2014 while US exports were in the region of 11 million.

Petroleum coke is shipped to export markets to be burned on an industrial scale in the manufacture of other products, notably cement and aluminium. The ships that transport it burn Heavy Fuel Oil, sometimes known as bunker fuel, which is the heaviest grade of fuel oil, thicker than molasses on a cool autumn morning. Also known as residual fuel oil, bunker fuel is the lowest grade of liquid petroleum left at the end of the refining process; it amounts to about 10 per cent of the total volume of a barrel of tar sands oil, once that has been manufactured by removing the sand, coke and other heavy materials. One barrel of crude oil is approximately 45 per cent gasoline and 9 per cent diesel, with the remainder made up of approximately equal percentages of very light (e.g. naphtha gas) and very heavy materials (Lattanzio 2014).

Ships are backed up at Vancouver, the only commercial harbour on Canada's Pacific coast. Trade is booming, especially exports of coal, grain and oil. In 2013, close to 40 million tons of coal, about 35 per cent of the port exports, was shipped to the Far East. About 50 oil tankers were loaded in that year as well, but if the expansion of the Trans Mountain pipeline development from Alberta proceeds that will soar to an estimated 400 per annum. In December of 2012 a coal ship rammed a loading trestle at the Vancouver terminal which further contributed to the backlog; ships waiting to load, sometimes for more than two months, were anchored up and down the coast in some of the most picturesque settings of British Columbia (McCulloch 2013).

In 2013, with grain harvests at record levels, the port could not handle the traffic – more than 22 million tons – and because oil shipping by rail had increased by about 33 per cent over the previous year to about 400,000 barrels per day – the backlog of ships in the harbour stood at 14 or 15 at any one time. According to official reports, plans to increase pipeline capacity to ship heavy oil to the West Coast will increase the likelihood of major spills to 'very high' and smaller ones would likely become common and the southern tip of Vancouver Island was identified as being one of the most probable areas for a major spill. The heavy oil being shipped from Alberta is particularly difficult to clean up – the bitumen either sinks to the bottom or coagulates into floating tar balls – as a 3.5-million-litre spill of the stuff into the Kalamazoo River in 2010 demonstrated.

As of this date, the Kalamazoo spill cost an estimated $1.2 billion to clean up, and the job is still incomplete, while the existing Trans Mountain pipeline from Alberta to Vancouver had already leaked more than double that amount in a series of leaks (mostly at or near land-based oil facilities) over a 10-year period (Prystupa 2014a). Controversial plans have been put forward to develop the so-called Northern Gateway pipeline to bring heavy oil from Fort McMurray to Kitimat British Columbia – an Enbridge project (Enbridge being the same company responsible for the Kalamazoo spill; Ebner and Iltan 2010). Aboriginal groups maintain that pipelines crossing their territorial claims are a risk to their land and environmental groups also protest about the impact of the pipelines themselves. When it was revealed that Enbridge's spill detection technology would not set off any alarms for leaks of less than 200,000 litres per 12-hour period, it only confirmed the doubts, despite the vaunted '209 conditions' imposed if the proposed pipeline were to be built (Prystupa 2014b).

According to the Calgary-based Pembina Institute, the Northern Gateway pipeline was indeed at risk for leaks and spills, as was the proposed terminal at Kitimat (Polczer 2010). Ironically, Kitimat was already being developed to export liquid natural gas from interior British Columbia at the same time that the oil pipeline project has been held up on environmental concerns (Hunter 2012; Jang 2014). The Pembina Institute report emphasized that the production of heavy oil from Fort McMurray would consume the same amount of natural gas as 1,300,000 Canadian households and would produce 25 million barrels of toxic waste, which would inevitably allow for some leakage, estimated to be equivalent to 182 Olympic-sized swimming pools.

When the Canadian federal government accepted the recommendation of the National Energy Board and approved the Northern Gateway heavy oil pipeline project, subject to '209 conditions' for environmental safety and security standards, it left Enbridge (the pipeline builders and operators) pondering the economics of the project and indigenous and environmental groups vowing to pursue matters through the courts (Lewis and Canadian Press 2014). The government's position was that the projected cost of the project – $7.9 billion – would be offset by compelling economics with unspecified 'billions in revenues and GDP at stake' (Lewis and Canadian Press 2014).

The regulatory conditions enforced on the safety of the pipeline will affect production costs, but there is significant scepticism among influential media opinion leaders that regulation will really protect the environment. Add to the mix concerns about so-called direct-action protest in the event that construction commences at some future date and it is easy to see that the politics of the '209 conditions' is a Canadian flashpoint in the hydrocarbon-criminalization debate. Here the legality–illegality boundary so interesting to criminologists is clearly manifest in a sort of paradox since security-practice is exercised against groups who aim to minimize environmental harm, which deflects understanding away from the underlying concerns and re-orients formal social control (White 2009). When it comes to the political-economy of hydrocarbon – in Canada and around the world – the concepts of criminalization and environmental harm have a complex relation to each other.

Green Criminology as a Paradigm Buster?

Criminology is a contested field and it is difficult to generalize about its essential characteristics. However, when the subject came to be widely taught in universities during the twentieth century it tended to have a broadly sociological view concerning the criminality of individuals. Still, the parameters of the paradigm were continually challenged, notably by Sutherland and Chambliss. These two major criminological thinkers brought to light the phenomena of elite crime, both in the state and corporate sectors, but despite the radical implications of their inquiries, academic criminology overall retained a basic theoretical focus. Green criminology is another would-be paradigm buster in an elastic field of human enquiry (Lynch and Stretesky 2014) and the general question raised here is the extent to which it is a harbinger of fundamental change in the language game of criminology.

Some argue that green criminology is a radical re-write of criminological thinking on the grounds that the conceptual category of 'ecocide' grants Gaia – or Mother Earth, our planet – the same rights to exist as those generally granted to people. Regardless of the specific issue area of interest to individual green criminologists, this idea alone makes the turn to green a radical one. Add *criminalization* to concerns about environmentalism and criminological discourse changes how? It is supposed that it is radical to grant ecosystem rights. However, as the experience of Ecuador shows, passing a law to enshrine ecosystem rights does not make for straightforward results. In Ecuador's case, in 2011 laws were created to 'protect the ecosystem', including the right of nature 'to not be affected by mega-infrastructure and development projects that affect the balance of ecosystems and the local inhabitant communities' (Vidal 2011).

In 2014, a major political conflict between government on the one side and indigenous and environmental activist groups on the other was manifest over the issue of oil exploration, drilling and production in the Tasuni Biosphere Reserve – the heart of the western Amazon and of the earth's most biodiverse, complex and fragile, eco-regions (Vidal 2014). Ecuadorian President Correa argued on the basis of economic logic that the country could not be a 'beggar sitting on a sack of gold', that 'minor sacrifices' needed to be made in order for the betterment of society. In mid-2013 protests met with stern police response, and although these events did not achieve media attention, Manuela Picq argues that the criminalization of anti-extraction protest in Ecuador is at the political cutting-edge of the extractive frontier (Picq 2013, p. 29).

Criminological inquiry concerning hydrocarbon extraction reveals the politics of crime, crime definition and crime control, but I do not think that this is the revolution in thought that some would-be green criminologists might conclude. At the frontiers of the legal and illegal, where the political pressure to criminalize is being felt, there are obvious harms – to the water, landscape and air, among other things – that some opinion leaders would criminalize. Conventionally speaking, criminalization requires state action, but in the political-economy of resource extraction, states are always already predisposed to industry. Environmental activists are instead made the target of criminal labelling, in a classic psychological inversion. The problem was revealed by earlier generations of paradigm-busting criminologists. Since 'the State' *qua* State is the source of criminal law, it can evade its own laws. The paradoxes of criminalization serve only to make the expanded field of inquiry marked out by green criminologists all the more fertile.

Except that is not where it ends, with the image of green criminologists in a fertile garden of inquiry. When it comes to hydrocarbon extraction, transportation, refining and consumption we have, I think, arrived at a topic that is pretty central to planetary wellbeing. Because green criminology traces its philosophical roots back to the Gaia Theory and subsequent predictions about the limits to capitalist growth and global climate change, there is a predicted timeline to ecocide and it is largely fuelled by hydrocarbon. Current predictions of a global temperature rise of more than two degrees Celsius before the middle of this century, coupled with other trends in, human population growth and consumption patterns suggest some kind of planetary end-point.

According to Naomi Klein (2013), ecological science is unequivocal and the evidence demands revolutionary change to the existing political and economic hegemony. Accordingly, this scientific knowledge creates the basis for political upheaval. Metaphorically, Klein and others say, this political and social resistance can be likened to antibodies in the human global system rising up to fight the planet's spiking fever. Criminology excels as the dismal science and the unhappy calculus is that significant climate change, coupled with food, water and energy shortages, might well spark massive political revolt and world-wide cataclysm.

Therefore criminological thinking may, or may not, change and thereby affect the overall prognosis, and green criminology is, perhaps, but one more way that human society has of anxiously responding to the looming crisis.

References

Amos, W., Lammey, J., Cairns, M. and Turan, C. 2011. *Getting Tough on Environmental Crime? Holding the Government of Canada to Account on Environmental Enforcement.* Vancouver: Ecojustice.

AP – Associated Press in Toronto. 2013. 'Canadian Runaway Train Disaster Firm Faces Criminal Charges', *Guardian*, 13 May.

Austen, I. 2013. 'A Black Mountain of Canadian Oil Waste Is Rising Over Detroit', *New York Times*, 17 May.

Beirne, P. and South, N. 2007. *Issues in Green Criminology: Confronting Harms Against Environments, Humanity and Other Animals*. Cullompton: Willan Publishing.

Bowling, B. and Sheptycki, J. 2012. *Global Policing*. London: Sage.

Brisman, A. and South, N. 2014. *Green Cultural Criminology: Constructions of Environmental Harm, Consumerism and Resistance to Ecocide*. London: Routledge.

Chambliss, W.J. 1989. 'State-Organized Crime – the American Society of Criminology 1988 Presidential Address', *Criminology* 27(2), 183–208.

Cohen, S. 1985. *Visions of Social Control: Crime, Punishment and Classification*. Cambridge: Polity.

——— 1988. *Against Criminology*. New Brunswick: Transaction Publishers.

——— 1996. 'Crime and Politics: Spot the Difference', *British Journal of Sociology* 47(1), 1–21.

Downes, D., Rock, P., Chinkin, C. and Gearty, C. 2007. *Crime, Social Control and Human Rights: From Moral Panics to States of Denial. Essay in Honour of Stanley Cohen.* London: Routledge.

Dyer, G. 2012. 'It Oughta be a Crime – and Will be; an Ecocide Law Will Come But Rio+20 Shows it Will be Too Late', *The Hamilton Spectator*, 26 June.

Ebner, D. and Iltan, C. 2010. 'Spill Halted and Enbridges Reputation Sullied', *Globe and Mail*, 29 July.

The Economist. 2014. 'The Economist Explains Why the Oil Price is Falling', *The Economist Magazine*, 8 December, 69.

——— 2015. 'The Saudi Project – Part 2', *The Economist Magazine*, 21 February, 42.

Garland, D. 1992. 'Criminological Knowledge and Its Relation to Power', *British Journal of Criminology* 32(4), 403–22.

Gaylord, M. and Galliher, J.F. 1988. *The Criminology of Edwin Sutherland*. London: Transaction Books.

Goldenberg, S. 2012. 'US Intelligence Teams to Track Wildlife Poachers in Africa and Asia', *Guardian*, 8 November.

——— 2013a. 'Hilary and Chelsea Clinton Unveil $80 Million Effort to Fight Illegal Ivory Trade', *Guardian*, 26 September.

——— 2013b. 'Detroit's Mountains of Petroleum Coke are "Dirtier than the Dirtiest Fuel" ', *Guardian*, 7 June.

Gordon, D. 2012. *Understanding Unconventional Oil*. Washington, DC: Carnegie Endowment for International Peace

Hunter, J. 2012. 'Kitimat Weighs up the Risks of Oil and Gas', *The Globe and Mail*, 12 January.

Jang, B. 2014, 'TransCanada to Build $19-billion Pipeline Link for Kitimat LNG Project', *The Globe and Mail*, 14 June.

Klein, N. 2013. 'How Science is Telling us all to Revolt', *New Statesman*, 29 October.

Lattanzio, R.K. 2014. *Canadian Oil Sands: Life-Cycle Assessments of Greenhouse Gas Emissions*. Washington, DC: Congressional Research Service Report R42537.

Laub, J.H. 2006. 'Edwin Sutherland and the Michael-Adler Report: Searching for the Soul of Criminology Seventy Years Later', *Criminology* 44(2), 235–57.

Leahy, S. 2013. 'Canada's Environmental Activists seen as a "Threat to National Security"; Police and Security Agencies Describe Green Groups' Protests and Petitions as "Forms of Attack", Documents Reveal', *Guardian*, 14 February.

Lewis, J. and Canadian Press. 2014. 'Northern Gateway Pipeline Approved by Federal Government with Conditions', *The Financial Post*, 17 June.

Lynch, M.J. and Stretesky, P.B. 2014. *Exploring Green Criminology*. Farnham: Ashgate.

McCarthy, S. 2012. 'Security Services Deem Environmental and Animals-Rights Activist Groups "Extremist" Threats', *The Globe and Mail*, 16 February.

McCulloch, S. 2013. 'Coal-Ship Backlog Clutters Cowichan Bay', *Times Colonist*, 15 January.

McIntosh, M. 1975. *The Social Organization of Crime*. London: Macmillan.

McQuigge, M. 2012. 'Two Ontario First Nations Still Plagued by Mercury Poisoning: Report', *The Globe and Mail*, 4 June.

Milmo, C. 2007. 'The Biggest Environmental Crime in History', *Independent*, 10 September.

Moskowitz, P. 2014. 'Mount Polley Mine Spill: A Hazard of Canada's Industry-Friendly Attitude?', *Guardian*, 13 August.

Nelken, D. (ed.). 1994. *The Futures of Criminology*. London: Sage.

Oceana. 2003. *The Dumping of Hydrocarbons from Ships into the Seas and Oceans of Europe; the Other Side of Oil Slicks*. Brussels: Oceana.

Picq, M. 2013. 'Self-Determination as Anti-Extractivism: How Indigenous Resistance Challenges World Politics', in *Restoring Indigenous Self-Determination*, edited by M. Woons. Leuven and Bristol: KU Leuven/E-International Relations, 26–33.

Polczer, S. 2010. 'Pembina Report Faults Pipeline to West Coast', *The Calgary Herald*, 19 January.

Prystupa, M. 2014a. 'Kinder Morgan's Historic Oil Spills are Double the Kalamazoo Disaster', *The Vancouver Observer*, 16 May.

——— 2014b. 'Northern Gateway President Cross-Examined on Oil Spill Risk on Eve of Kitimat Vote', *The Vancouver Observer*, 2 April.

Report by the Comptroller and Auditor General. 2002. *HM Customs and Excise: The Misuse and Smuggling of Hydrocarbon Oils*. London: House of Commons Stationary Office, HC 614 Session 2001–2002, 15 February.

Ruskin, G. 2013. *Spooky Business: Corporate Espionage Against Non-Profit Organizations*. Washington, DC: Centre for Corporate Policy.

Sellin, T. and Wolfgang, M. 1964. *The Measurement of Delinquency*. New York: John Wiley and Sons.

Sheptycki, J. 2010. 'Edwin Sutherland', in *Fifty Key Thinkers in Criminology*, edited by K. Hayward, S. Maruna and J. Mooney. London: Routledge, 63–71.

Spapens, T., White, R. and Kluin, M. 2014. *Environmental Crime and Its Victims: Perspectives within Green Criminology*. Aldershot: Ashgate.

Suzuki, D. 2013. *The 2013 Jack Beale Lecture on the Global Environment*. University of New South Wales, 21 September.

Tilly, C. 1985. 'War Making and State Making as Organized Crime', in *Bringing the State Back In*, edited by P.B. Evans, D. Rueschemeer and T. Skocpol. Cambridge: Cambridge University Press, 169–90.

Turner, C. 2012. *The War on Science: Muzzled Scientists and Wilful Blindness in Stephen Harper's Canada*. Toronto: Greystone Books.

Vidal, J. 2011. 'Bolivia Enshrines Natural World's Rights with Equal Status for Mother Earth', *Guardian*, 10 April.

——— 2014. 'Yasuni Campaigners Claim Oil Drilling Petition Results are Being Manipulated', *Guardian*, 30 April.

Waddington, D. 1989. *Flashpoints: Studies in Disorder*. London: Routledge.

Walby, K. and Monaghan, J. 2011. 'Private Eyes and Public Order: Policing and Surveillance in the Suppression of Animal Rights Activists in Canada', *Social Movement Studies* 10(1), 21–37.

White, R. 2009 'Researching Transnational Environmental Harm: Toward an Eco-Global Criminology', *International Journal of Comparative and Applied Criminal Justice* 33(2), 229–48.

White, R. and Heckenberg, D. 2011. 'Environmental Horizon Scanning and Criminological Theory and Practice', *European Journal of Criminal Policy and Research* 17(2), 87–100.

Wuebbles, D.J. 2012. 'Celebrating the Blue Marble', *Eos* 93(4), 509–10.

Zedner, L. 2007. 'Pre-Crime and Post-Criminology?', *Theoretical Criminology* 11(2), 261–81.

Part II

Law Enforcement Responses to (Transnational) Environmental Crime

5 Addressing Transnational Environmental Crime

The Role of Intelligence-Led Policing

Carole Gibbs

Introduction

Business transactions frequently cross national borders and are increasingly global. As a result, opportunities for the externalization of risks and harms have also risen. Globalization allows people (and nations) to pass off risks and harms to others while themselves remaining insulated from negative impacts associated with these transactions (Gibbs, McGarrell, and Axelrod 2010; Passas 2002). Some of this externalization occurs through legal transactions, but illegal opportunities have also soared.

Crime is increasingly transnational, meaning that it has its "origin, execution, and impact in two or more nations" (Dammer, Reichel, and He 2005, p. 37) or "offenders or victims are located in or operate through more than one country" (Passas 1999, p. 401). This trend, due in part to the profitability of these forms of crime, is also apparent in the environmental arena. Transnational environmental crimes (TEC) are often described as trafficking in natural resources (e.g., timber), pollutants (e.g., ozone depleting substances) and protected species across borders, in violation of domestic law or international environmental treaties (Elliott 2012; Wright 2011). Some types of TEC are estimated to be more profitable than drug trafficking (Graycar and Felson 2010; Schmidt 2004).

The characteristics of TEC present a number of challenges for intervention. Transnational crimes often occur via informal networks that intersect until a specific transaction is complete and then disband, making them difficult to track (Williams 2001; Wright 2011). The movement of illegal goods across borders also occurs via multiple smaller crimes, posing challenges for disentangling the sequence of events (Hill 2005). The use of technology to move illegal goods and services across borders also presents difficulties for intervention due to the increased speed and anonymity of the criminal activities (Felsen and Kalaitzidis 2005; Passas 2002; Shover and Hochstetler 2006). The volume of goods moving through ports also makes detection problematic.

Like other forms of cross-border crime, TEC are also completed through large-scale, complex transactions (Elliott 2009; Wright 2011). But, these forms of crime pose some additional challenges for intervention. The generally cooperative nature of regulatory agencies may reduce the threat of strong penalties for illegal shipments (Pink 2013). In addition, in traditional criminal justice agencies, environmental crimes are often low on the priority list in comparison to other import or export issues (Elliott 2009; Wright 2011). As previously stated, some form of trade in natural resources and hazardous substances is legal, making it difficult to distinguish the illegal transactions or products (Gibbs, McGarrell, and Axelrod 2010; Graycar and Felson 2010; Wright 2011).

The externalization of environmental risks and harms from legal transactions are also a significant problem, leading many critical scholars to reject legalistic definitions of TEC in favor of broader conceptualizations. These broader definitions of TEC include cross-border environmental impacts that are not necessarily regulated. For example, Michalowski and Kramer (2014) define TEC as "any action that causes environmental harm outside its country of its origin, whether or not its victim or some other entity have been given legal standing to punish wrongdoers or seek redress for damages" (p. 190).

It is important to consider legalistic and broader frameworks when formulating policies to reduce cross-border environmental impacts. Addressing only TEC (or only transnational environmental harms) is unlikely to effectively reduce the damage to wildlife, natural resources and ecosystems that occurs via international transactions, as well as the associated impacts on human health. Significant improvements will require interventions that reduce environmental harms that result from legal *and* illegal activity.

The Conservation Criminology framework (Gibbs et al. 2010) indicates the need to examine and address environmental crimes *and* environmental risks that simultaneously pose threats to the environment and human health. In this chapter I draw upon this perspective to illustrate the need to address legal transactions and TEC in order to reduce cross-border environmental impacts. Specifically, I argue that drawing upon recent innovations in policing and environmental policy can help advance efforts to address both the legal and illegal dimensions of these problems. As such, I integrate and apply theory and research on intelligence-led policing, Smart Regulation (Gunningham and Grabosky 1998) and the New Environmental Governance (Holley, Gunningham, and Shearing 2011) to demonstrate the potential utility of moving beyond a single form of government response (Gunningham and Grabosky 1998) and including decentralized and cooperative components to create solutions to complex problems (Holley, Gunningham, and Shearing 2011).

I use the global trade in electronic waste (E-waste) as an example to demonstrate these policy perspectives. I begin by describing the problem of E-waste to provide a concrete example of a transnational environmental issue that includes both legal and illegal transactions that create challenges for interventions. I next describe one innovative policing effort to address the regulated components of the trade, known as the Securing Compliant Waste Exports project. The Environment Agency of England (EA) developed a special project to implement intelligence-led policing (ILP) to reduce the illegal export of hazardous waste, including E-waste. Thus, I provide an overview of the EA's efforts to implement this program. I then frame these efforts within the larger context of transnational environmental problems. Namely, I use E-waste as an example to discuss how ILP must be coupled with broader interventions to fully prevent and reduce these complex environmental issues.

Transnational Environmental Problems: An E-Waste Example

The global trade in electronic waste (E-waste) represents an example of a complex transnational environmental problem. Electronics is the world's fastest growing industry (Grossman 2006; Puckett et al. 2002) and many products quickly become obsolete. Estimates of the volume of obsolete electronics discarded each year range from 7 to 40 million tons (Grossman 2006; Schluep et al. 2009). In fact, electronics now comprise the fastest-growing segment of the waste stream (Ladou and Lovegrove 2008) and the rate of obsolescence exceeds the rate of production (Kang and Schoenung 2005). In addition to being disposed of in landfills and incinerators, discarded electronics are often exported from developed to developing nations (U.S. EPA 2007; Gibbs, McGarrell, and Axelrod 2010; Gibbs et al. 2011).

The legal status of this trade varies significantly from country to country. Thus, there is no single definition that distinguishes illegal E-waste from legal exports of electronics. Conceptual definitions include "televisions, computers and monitors, laptops, printers, cell phones, VCRs, DVD layers, copiers, fax machines, stereos, and video gaming systems" that are broken, obsolete or irreparable (Luther 2007, p. 1). However, these types of electronics can be legally exported from many countries, such as the United States (Gibbs et al. 2011).

Whether exported legally or illegally, the E-waste trade poses problems. Alleged recycling facilities in developing countries often do not possess the capability to dismantle and recycle old electronics (Pellow 2007). In addition, many electronics sent for reuse are actually broken and irreparable (INTERPOL 2009; Ladou and Lovegrove 2008). Rather than being recycled or reused, E-waste is frequently dumped in local villages in countries such as Nigeria, Ghana, China, the Philippines, Indonesia, Pakistan and India (Greenpeace 2008; Iles 2004). Dumpsites present a number of threats to environmental protection and human health. Electronics contain substances such as lead, mercury, hexavalent chromium, and polybrominated flame retardants (Jackson, Shuman, and Dayaneni 2006; Pellow 2007). Exposure occurs when electronics are improperly dismantled and recycled, often by burning component parts to extract the metals in demand in developing countries. In addition to groundwater contamination and ozone depletion, these activities can cause organ damage and cancer (Grossman 2006; Huo et al. 2007; Jackson, Shuman, and Dayaneni 2006; Silicon Valley Toxics Coalition 2004).

Despite these threats, this issue is referred to as "trade" because much of the global movement of E-waste is legal. As with other forms of TEC, the specific nature of illegal transactions varies by country, depending on regulatory requirements (Gibbs et al. 2011). These regulatory requirements are quite technical, making it difficult for regulators to verify the legality of shipments of electronics.

For example, in the United States, most electronics are exempt or excluded from the Resource Conservation and Recovery Act's (1976) definitions of hazardous waste. Rather than waste, they are classified as products or commodities and therefore unregulated (Tonnetti 2007a). Electronics are only considered hazardous waste if they are generated in large volume by non-households, are exported for disposal, and have a hazardous waste characteristic, but EPA has not assessed most electronics for this characteristic. Thus, if enforcement officials intercept a potentially illegal shipment, they must conduct a significant amount of intensive testing to determine whether the electronics are hazardous (Tonnetti 2007; Luther 2007). Only a few electronics, such as Cathode Ray Tubes (CRTs) have been previously tested and determined to be hazardous. However, CRTs may still be exported for recycling or reuse, provided that specific paperwork requirements are followed (Tonetti 2007). If intercepting CRTs, regulatory officials would have to assess how electronics will ultimately be used at their destination and assess paperwork to determine whether the E-waste shipment is legal. Therefore, it is extremely difficult to distinguish illegal from legal E-waste exports from the U.S.

Other countries have electronics legislation that is more conducive to assessing the legality of shipments. For example, used electronics exported from England for reuse must be in working condition, meaning they must be packaged appropriately for transit and operate when plugged in. However, the electronics export regulations are still complex. While England prohibits the export of all hazardous wastes destined for disposal, it only limits the export of electric and electrical equipment destined for other purposes, such as reuse (ESA 2007; SEPA 2009). Therefore, regulators must still determine whether working electronics meet an intricate set of regulatory requirements when intercepting shipments of electronic and electrical equipment.

In addition to the challenge of determining the legality of transactions, disentangling those involved presents an additional difficulty that is similar to other forms of transnational crime/harm. A variety of actors are involved in the illegal trade, using a complex set of transactions masked by technology to complete the trades. For example, illegitimate business enterprises are involved, as well as individuals. Studies conducted in the United Kingdom have indicated that unlicensed waste management sites are used to gather E-waste for illegal exports. In addition, individuals known as "waste tourists" travel from developing to developed countries to illegally export E-waste to family in their home country. Unlicensed carriers and brokers are also complicit in illegal transactions (INTERPOL 2009). The Internet is often used to facilitate illicit E-waste transactions. For example, the U.S. Government Accountability Office (GAO) monitored E-waste trading websites to document the export of U.S. E-waste to developing countries. The GAO also posed as a fictitious broker to assess whether U.S. companies would respond to e-mail requests to purchase illegal E-waste. Forty-three companies indicated a willingness to do so (GAO 2008).

Many entities are involved in legal trades as well. Legitimate companies engage in E-waste trades, sometimes moving E-waste across the globe from one company facility to another. Small businesses are also involved, often shipping E-waste to a consignee in the destination country (Gibbs, McGarrell, and Axelrod 2010). Efforts to address illegal transactions will have no impact on these legal shipments even though they too can end up in uncontrolled E-waste dumpsites.

Discussions of those involved in the trade draw our attention to the end of the system, but it is also important to recognize a larger set of actors involved in the E-waste problem. Additional stakeholders create the large volume of (illegally and legally) discarded electronics in the first place. Electronics are a huge global industry because of consumer demand (Grossman 2006). In addition, producers heavily market (and consumers purchase) new electronics that provide minimal updates and upgrades. This is reflected in the Basel Action Network's open letters to electronics producers encouraging them to delink innovation and obsolescence (Basel Action Network 2007). Producers have also been slow to remove toxins from the production process (Robinson and Sadik 2009; Ladou and Lovegrove 2008).

Thus, like other complex transnational environmental problems, E-waste will require creative interventions to significantly reduce the criminal and legal trades. In the following section, I discuss one effort to improve policing and enforcement in the TEC arena, including the E-waste trade. I then describe the need for additional interventions to address legal E-waste transactions.

Intelligence-Led Policing: Addressing TEC

Discussions of transnational crime highlight the need for innovative policing and enforcement strategies. In fact, Hill (2005) has argued that intelligence analysis is *required* to disentangle the activities of interconnected individuals and organizations involved in transnational crime. Proactive, long term intelligence programs provide a mechanism for information sharing and cooperation among multiple state agencies to uncover transactions and shipment details (Mandel 2011). Elliott (2009) has also argued that "joined up" collaborative enforcement efforts are needed to address similarly linked TEC offenders.

Through research conducted on behalf of the INTERPOL Environmental Crimes Committee (INTERPOL 2009), my colleagues and I learned of the Environment Agency of England's efforts to implement intelligence-led policing to reduce illegal exports of hazardous waste, with E-waste being one area of emphasis (i.e., the Securing Compliant Waste Exports project). As a result of our connection to INTERPOL, we were able to collaborate with the EA team to conduct a process evaluation of their work (for additional details on the process evaluation, see Gibbs, McGarrell and Sullivan 2014). We used triangulation as our research methodology, which involves comparing multiple pieces of data to assess whether findings converge (Campbell and Fiske 1959; Denzin 1978). Specifically, we compared qualitative and quantitative data to examine how the program achieved (or did not achieve) its goals. These data sources consisted of five in-depth interviews with the leadership of the EA team, quantitative data on the intelligence cycle (e.g., amount of incoming data; number of field actions issued, site visits and inspections, intelligence logs and noncompliant organizations identified), observational data (e.g., an in-house demonstration of the intelligence system and processes) and a review of team presentations and documents. At the time of our data collection, the team was approximately two years into a three-year project period.

Our goal in this process evaluation was to examine the EA team's adherence to the National Intelligence Model (National Center for Policing Excellence 2005), an innovation in policing originally developed and now widely practiced in the United Kingdom (Carter 2009; Global Intelligence Working Group 2003; International Association of Chiefs of Police 2002; National Center for Policing Excellence 2005; Ratcliffe 2008). There is no one definition of ILP, but there is some agreement on the general concept. ILP is not merely a set of tools, but rather a shift from reactive to proactive ways of addressing crime problems. It involves collecting and analyzing information about crime patterns to create intelligence products to assess potential problems (e.g., offenders, victims, contexts) and target resources to disrupt the most serious offenses and offenders (Carter 2009; Ratcliffe 2008). Thus, rather than relying on random inspections or only issuing penalties after a TEC has been discovered, ILP involves proactively gathering and analyzing information on potential transnational environmental criminals or export routes to understand priority locations, subjects, crime series and potential preventative measures, as well as problem and target profiles for further intervention. These interventions may range from providing compliance assistance to low-level violators to initiating an investigation to target the most serious and organized criminal activity for prosecution.

Overall, our qualitative and quantitative data converged regarding the EA team's level of implementation. Our data demonstrated that the EA team was able to implement an intelligence-led policing program consistent with the National Intelligence Model, but designed to address TEC. The team established "Direction" (i.e., step 1 in the intelligence cycle) for the strategic and tactical assessment, including an overview of the priority waste streams and organizations involved, by drawing on existing sources of data (e.g., agency databases, experienced employees). For example, agency databases were used to construct a universe of permitted facilities that had some relevance to electronics dismantling or recycling. Experienced employees were interviewed for information on previous experiences with these sites and potentially suspicious activity, as well as insights into how illegal transactions occurred. This step provided an overview of the market, including key players and methodologies used in the trade. Team members also worked to build relationships with the shipping sector to gather additional information on exports to fill knowledge gaps. This primarily came in the form of information regarding containers that had been exported on a monthly basis. This information provided a detailed record of exports' volume, customs codes and container descriptions. This new information source fed into the second step of the intelligence cycle, "Collection and Collation," in addition to regular data collection from internal EA databases, other regulatory and enforcement agencies and site visits.

All incoming information was assessed for quality, source and the handling code for security, consistent with the "Evaluation" stage of the intelligence cycle. After this process of converting information into intelligence, "Analysis" (i.e., the fourth step in the intelligence cycle) was conducted. Shipping line data were assessed for patterns that could indicate illegal waste activity, such as container descriptions inconsistent with the business conducted at the loading site or large volume shipments from new companies. Organizations thought to be or previously involved in illegal hazardous waste exports were identified and ranked according to risk. Intelligence products were then created for the "Dissemination" phase of the intelligence cycle. These might take the form of graphical representations of cradle to grave waste streams or relationships between multiple parties suspected of illegal exports. Tactical assessments were provided to management every six weeks for decisions regarding the appropriate intervention. The expertise developed through each round of analysis then fed back into the direction phase of the next cycle. Suspected cases of illegal exports were then prioritized to target high-level problems. For example, in cases in which small-scale exporters seemed to misunderstand proper export protocol, compliance assistance was provided. However, cases that reflected intentional, large-scale and organized exports were prioritized for investigation to prepare for prosecution.

Although we did not conduct an outcome evaluation, the results of our process evaluation are promising for the viability of using ILP to address TEC. The convergence between the quantitative and qualitative data suggested a high level of implementation, meaning that an ILP program can be established to address TEC. In establishing the steps in the NIM, the EA team was able to gather information to create actionable intelligence and produce intelligence products regarding illegal hazardous waste shipments. In the case of E-waste, for example, analysts identified cargo descriptions commonly used by certain types of organizations to disguise illegal exports. Analysts were also able to map waste streams from cradle to grave to assess where illegal activity occurred in the chain to provide direction for further investigation to build cases for prosecution. For example, volumes of E-waste accepted by legitimate recycling facilities were compared to those reported as outputs. Discrepancies suggested that illegal electronics were being diverted elsewhere rather than through the domestic recycling process. Thus, in one of the first efforts of its kind, the team was able to implement ILP to address illegal exports of hazardous waste in England, including E-waste.

The generalizability of this program for other countries, however, remains to be seen. For example, it is unclear whether access to shipping line data sources would result in an effective ILP program in other nations. England is a small country in comparison to exporters such as the United States and Australia. It therefore has a relatively small number of shipping lines, producing data that is likely more manageable than shipping information that would have to be collected for ILP programs in larger exporting nations. In addition, the EA team noted that the specific form of implementation of ILP would miss exports that fall outside of the domain of analysis. For example, a focus on ports means that projects will miss illegal exports that do not go out on a ship. England is an island. Therefore, a focus on ports may not overlook a large volume of exports. Countries such as the United States, however, would need methods to detect and address the movement of illegal hazardous substances across land borders in addition to hazardous waste exports from ports.

Beyond issues of generalizability, team members were also careful to mention that ILP should not be viewed as a panacea for preventing illegal shipments. ILP practices will likely return many individuals and companies to compliance, but it may also create some amount of displacement. For example, the EA team had already observed a shift in exports to evenings and weekends, non-working hours during which regulatory employees could not intervene. Some illegal exporters had also moved shipping container loading sites to areas that were not on the EA radar screen (e.g., unpermitted sites).

Furthermore, the EA team noted that even with complete resources ILP would not prevent every illegal shipment due to a number of uncontrollable factors. For example, when the global market and therefore shipping rates drop, the number of exports of illegal waste is likely to increase because costs are so low. It may be difficult for ILP teams to address the sudden surge in illegal exports. In addition to favorable shipping prices, there are financial incentives for receiving countries to take illegal hazardous waste like E-waste. The profits made from extracting metals from electronic waste during the dismantling process may be greater than the incentive to work with exporting nations to stop the illegal trade.

The notion that ILP is not a panacea extends further when the characteristics of transnational environmental problems are considered. Recall that much of the global trade in electronic waste, for example, is legal. In addition to illegal exports, one must consider the role of legal exporters, producers and consumers to fully address the impacts of E-waste.

Current environmental policy discussions are consistent with these perspectives. Collectively, the policy literature suggests that enforcement is an important component of efforts to address environmental issues, but must be coupled with broader interventions and strategies (Gunningham and Grabosky 1994; 2004; Holley, Gunningham, and Shearing 2011). Multi-faceted efforts are likely needed to address transnational environmental trade problems.

Expanding Intervention Efforts: Addressing Transnational Environmental Harms

In the environmental arena, a growing body of scholarship indicates the need to broaden environmental policy beyond a single form of government response, such as enforcement or market alternatives (Gunningham and Grabosky 1998; 2004; Holley, Gunningham and Shearing 2011). Smart Regulation highlights the importance of combining multiple instruments (e.g., command-and-control regulation, economic incentives, certifications) and multiple "regulators" (e.g., third parties, self-regulation) with government intervention. Single interventions are unlikely to succeed, as each type of policy has weaknesses. Instead, complementary methods of addressing problems must be used concurrently such that one instrument compensates for the weaknesses of another (and vice-versa). Smart Regulation requires flexibility, as solutions must be tailored to address the specific problem at hand (Gunningham and Grabosky 1998).

The New Environmental Governance (NEG) offers strategies for producing this type of governance system (Holley, Gunningham and Shearing 2011). The NEG also advocates the use of broader policy response, focusing primarily on methods to draw upon third parties to facilitate collective responses to environmental problems. This framework advocates a set of principles designed to bring regulated entities (or stakeholders involved in a non-regulated issue) together with the general public to develop and implement creative policy interventions. These private, public and non-government stakeholders are involved in a participatory process in which dialogue and deliberation are used to construct flexible, inclusive and transparent solutions through consensus building (Holley, Gunningham and Shearing 2011). "This enterprise involves collaboration between a diversity of private, public and non-government stakeholders who, acting together towards commonly agreed (or mutually negotiated) goals, hope to achieve far more collectively, than individually" (Gunningham 2009, p. 203). Further, although NEG typically seeks to incorporate local expertise and context into local solutions, discussions of integrating governance between different scales to address larger-scale problems are underway. For example, many local decision-making groups may operate as an interdependent system (Holley, Gunningham and Shearing 2011).

These frameworks can also be used to advance discussions of specific interventions to address legal forms of E-waste that enter domestic landfills and cause environmental impacts in developing countries. Many countries have begun to implement producer responsibility programs to require producers to help address the E-waste problem. The EU's Waste Electronics and Electronic Equipment Directive's "extended producer responsibility" provisions, for example, allow consumers to return electronics to producers for appropriate recycling and disposal (Selin and VanDeever 2006). Similar programs are operating in Switzerland (Khetriwal, Kraeuchi and Widmer 2009). Smart Regulation provides some ideas regarding mechanisms that might be used to implement these types of programs. Legislative, command-and-control requirements provide one avenue, but economic incentives to encourage producers to participate may also represent a viable option. Deposit refund systems may be used to increase consumer participation (see also Kahhat et al. 2008). Certification programs could be explored as a way to reward producers that voluntarily develop successful return programs by drawing consumers' attention to these efforts (for a fuller discussion of these instruments, see Gunningham and Grabosky 1998).

Certification programs for recyclers that conduct legitimate business within a developed country could also be explored. Some certification programs exist. The R2 Responsible Recycling Certification Program, for example, is an independent certification (issued by SERI, a non-profit organization) recognized by the United States Environmental Protection Agency. It has been criticized for failing to go far enough to reduce the E-waste problem (Basel Action Network 2013). However, more stringent programs also exist. The Basel Action Network established one such program. Recycling facilities (and other organizations involved in the electronics trade) can be certified as "E-Stewards" if they meet several requirements. Certified companies can export fully functional electronics that are tested, as well as non-toxic steel, aluminum and plastic, but they must agree to follow the standards set in the Basel Convention and refrain from exporting hazardous electronic waste from developed to developing countries. Companies must also implement a specific environmental management program (for further details, see http://e-stewards.org/). Using the NEG approach may provide an approach to develop certification standards that are more acceptable to various stakeholders in the E-waste trade.

The inclusion of citizens is an important component of attempts to address E-waste, as the general public's purchasing practices play a significant role in creating the E-waste problem. Consumers and governments, have extensive purchasing power that could be used to influence the production and marketing practices of large corporate producers. Many argue that signals sent by large bodies of prospective consumers can influence the market (Grabosky 1994), creating third-party regulators to help control the accumulation of E-waste. Efforts to harness citizen purchasing power may be supported by education and information instruments, such as information disclosure programs. These types of instruments seek to improve the ability of the community to help address environmental problems (Gunningham and Grabosky 1998). Education and training efforts may also help overcome the seeming lack of political will in countries such as the United States.

Reducing the risks associated with E-waste that will continue to be produced is also important. For example, the European Union's Restriction on Hazardous Substances (RoHS) Directive limits the use of toxic substances in many categories of waste electrical equipment (Selin and VanDeever 2006). Absent these legislative requirements, certification programs and standards could also be used to direct consumers to more environmentally friendly products. For example, Greenpeace's (2010) "Guide to Greener Electronics" ranks electronics manufacturers based on toxic chemical, recycling and energy policies.

Interventions to address E-waste problems in developing countries are also likely needed. Pollutants comprise only a small portion of waste electronics (Widmer et al. 2005). Thus, promoting recycling coupled with proper disposal of pollutants (rather than uncontrolled burning) can decrease the risks associated with the E-waste trade. The United Nations Environment Program (UNEP) suggests funneling legal E-waste to developing countries that have the necessary recycling, legal, economic and social infrastructure to properly recycle it (Schluep et al. 2009). Some countries, such as Chile and Malaysia have invested extensively to develop E-waste recycling capacity (Prochile magazine 2007; Australian Federal Reister 2008). Some of these countries fought against international bans on the E-waste trade due to concerns about declining revenues (Lepawsky and McNabb 2010; Prochile Magazine 2007). Technology transfer from developed to developing countries can also help develop this infrastructure and increase the economic benefits of E-waste for developing countries and local populations working in this trade (Schluep et al. 2009).

Developing national recycling infrastructure in countries such as the United States will be an important base component of efforts to reduce the impacts and risks of E-waste, as most U.S. E-waste is discarded in domestic landfills and incinerators (U.S. EPA 2007). The U.S. currently lacks a national recycling infrastructure. Although some states have developed recycling systems, further efforts are impeded by a lack of national strategy (Kang and Schoenung 2006). Analysis of E-waste management systems in other countries may be used to construct a system more likely to succeed within the political structure and social context of the U.S. (Kahhat et al. 2008).

Overall, addressing the E-waste problem will require more holistic and integrated approach that tackles illegal exports as well as legal trade (Gibbs et al. 2010; Gibbs et al. 2011). Existing research indicates that intelligence-led policing is a promising approach to reducing illegal hazardous waste exports. Environmental policy discussions offer many options for coupling enforcement efforts with broader interventions that address additional components of complex environmental problems like E-waste, as well as encouraging third-party involvement in constructing solutions.

Ultimately, the viability of these strategies for addressing E-waste is an empirical question. Assessments of broader policy initiatives for E-waste are lacking. Further questions remain regarding the generalizability of these strategies for other forms of TEC. In the following section, I extend the discussion of this multi-strategy approach to TEC more generally.

Implications for TEC

TEC's and cross-border environmental transactions are complex. Many entities are involved in the movement of pollutants and natural resources across the globe. The use of technology to conduct these transactions makes them difficult to track. Distinguishing legal from illegal trade is also challenging.

Existing discussions of environmental governance indicate the need for an equally complex set of responses to address these types of problems. In addition to innovative policing strategies, such as ILP and cooperative programs between multiple countries (Elliott 2009), broader policy responses will be required. Drawing on multiple instruments and types of "regulators," and using cooperative and inclusive decision-making strategies may be needed to reduce cross-border environmental impacts. In the current article, I apply these ideas to the problem of E-waste to illustrate these policy discussions and discuss potential methods of implementation. However, despite some shared characteristics among various forms of TEC, each form has unique dimensions. Thus, in addition to further analysis of E-waste interventions, the generalizability of this approach to environmental governance of TEC more generally is also an important question for future research.

The viability of ILP for other forms of TEC is unclear. For example, TEC scholars have expressed concern with whether information that can be converted into intelligence will be available for TEC given the lack of attention paid by regulatory officials to most of these forms of crime (Elliott 2009). In this case, the EA team was able to establish the initial direction for the ILP program by gathering information from existing agency databases and personnel because at least some portion of the hazardous waste exporters had EA permits. This may not necessarily be the case when attempting to address illegal trade in endangered species or timber.

The lack of or inadequate legislation may also be a roadblock in other attempts to implement ILP. Legislation that defines some exports as illegal must exist. It must also be written in such a way that allows for the reasonable identification of illegal environmental goods. For example, U.S. legislation that requires intensive testing to establish the hazardous characteristics of many forms of electronics places undue burden on regulators even if they are able to detect potentially illegal shipments. However, export legislation in the UK requires that electronics operate when plugged in, providing a much simpler test of the legality of intercepted shipments. As previously stated, legal exports may continue to create environmental risks and must be addressed through alternative policy strategies (e.g., national recycling infrastructure to reduce the need for export). Absent these broader policy interventions, legal exports will continue to shift into the illegal market after export. But, this type of legislative requirement can at least enable regulators to effectively address illegal exports within their country. Implementation of ILP within regulatory agencies may further help with this point, as the ILP and broader policy interventions could be housed within the same agency to create a holistic approach.

An additional point of discussion for considering ILP and broader policy interventions is the direction of the global movement of E-waste. Electronic waste is primarily generated in developed nations and exported to developing countries. In other words, it moves from the Global North to Global South. As such, much of the efforts to reduce E-waste impacts would be implemented in developed countries.

Other forms of TEC, such as timber trafficking and additional types of natural resource extraction, move in the opposite direction from the Global South to the Global North. The primary area of intervention, therefore, may need to be developing countries. However, many of these environmental policy ideas have been generated in developed nations. As previously noted, it is important to consider political structures and social context when constructing policy rather than assuming that what works in one location will work in another (Kahhat et al. 2008). It is unclear whether these broader policy interventions will translate to developing countries. If they can be implemented, issues with the digital divide (Sheptycki 2004) and corruption (Mandel 2011; Schreier 2009) may impede success. Additional research is clearly needed to fully understand the viability of ILP and broader policy interventions for addressing TEC.

References

Australian Federal Register. 2008. *Hazardous Waste (Regulation of Exports and Imports) Regulation: 1996. Statutory Rules 1996 No. 284*: http://www.comlaw.gov.au/ComLaw/Legislation/LegislativeInstrumentCompilation1.nsf/0/2081D85BE050FEF8CA2575150020A39E/$file/HazWasteRegExpImp96.pdf (accessed 24 October 2014)

Basel Action Network. 2007. 'Open Letter to Microsoft', *Ban.org*: http://ban.org/library/Microsoft_Letter.pdf (accessed 24 October 2014).

Basel Action Network. 2013. 'Five Fundamental Flaws: A Concise Critique of the R2:2013 Standard', *Ban.org*: http://ban.org/Library/FiveFundamentalFlawFinal.pdf (accessed 24 October 2014).

Campbell, D.T. and Fiske, D.W. 1959. 'Convergent and Discriminant Validation by the Multitrait-Multimethod Matrix', *Psychological Bulletin* 56, 81–105.

Carter, D.L. 2009. 'Law Enforcement Intelligence: A Guide for State, Local, and Tribal Law Enforcement Agencies, Second Edition', *Office of Community Oriented Policing Services, U.S. Department of Justice*: http://fas.org/irp/agency/doj/lei.pdf (accessed 24 October 2014).

Dammer, H.R., Reichel, P.L. and H., N. 2014. 'Comparing Crime and Justice', In The *Handbook of Transnational Crime and Justice* (2nd edition) edited by P. Reichel and J. Albanese. Thousand Oaks, CA: Sage Publications, 20–42.

Denzin, N.K. 1978. *The Research Act* (2nd edition). New York, NY: McGraw-Hill.

Elliott, L. 2009. 'Combating Transnational Environmental Crime: 'Joined Up' Thinking About Transnational Networks', in *Eco-Crime and Justice: Essays on Environmental Crime* edited by K. Kangaspunta and I. Haen-Marshall. Turin, Italy: Public Information Department, United Nations Interregional Crime and Justice Research Institute, 55–77.

Elliott, L. 2012. 'Fighting Transnational Environmental Crime', *Journal of International Affairs* 66 (1), 87–104.

Environmental Services Association (ESA). 2007. 'The Environment Agency's Priorities for Enforcing the TFS Regulations', *Environmental Services Association*: http://www.esauk.org/enforcement_1818563.pdf (accessed 24 October 2014).

Scottish Environmental Protection Agency (SEPA). 2009. 'WEEE Amendment Regulations Factsheet': www.sepa.org.uk/waste/waste_regulation/producer_responsibility/weee/uk_weee_regulations.aspx (accessed 24 October 2014).

Felsen, D., and Kalaitzidis, A. 2005. 'A Historical Overview of Transnational Crime', in *Handbook of Transnational Crime and Justice* edited by P. Reichel. Thousand Oaks, CA: Sage, 3–19.

Gibbs, C., McGarrell, E. and Axelrod, M. 2010. 'Transnational White-Collar Crime and Risk: Lessons from the Global Trade in Electronic Waste', *Criminology and Public Policy* 9, 543–560.

Gibbs, C., McGarrell, E., Axelrod, M. and Rivers, L. 2011. 'Conservation Criminology and the Global Trade in Electronic Waste: Applying a Multi-Disciplinary Research Framework', *International Journal of Comparative and Applied Criminal Justice* 35 (4), 327–346.

Gibbs, C., Gore, M., McGarrell, E., and Rivers, L. 2010. 'Introducing Conservation Criminology: Toward Interdisciplinary Scholarship on Environmental Crimes and Risks', *British Journal of Criminology* 50, 124–144.

Gibbs, C., McGarrell, E. and Sullivan, B. 2014. 'Intelligence-Led Policing and Transnational Environmental Crime: A Process Evaluation', *European Journal of Criminology* 12(2), 242–259.

Global Intelligence Working Group. 2003. 'The National Criminal Intelligence Sharing Plan', *Global Justice Information Sharing Initiative, U.S. Department of Justice*: https://it.ojp.gov/documents/National_Criminal_Intelligence_Sharing_Plan.pdf (accessed 24 October 2014).

Government Accountability Office (GAO). 2008. 'Electronic Waste: EPA Needs to Better Control Harmful U.S. Exports through Stronger Enforcement and More Comprehensive Legislation': http://www.gao.gov/assets/280/279792.pdf (accessed 24 October 2014).

Grabosky, P. 1994. 'Green Markets: Environmental Regulation by the Private Sector', *Law and Policy* 16, 420–448.

Grabosky, P. 2009. 'Globalization and White-Collar Crime', in *The Criminology of White-Collar Crime*, edited by S. Simpson and D. Weisburd. New York, NY: Springer, 129–151.

Graycar, A., and Felson, M. 2010. 'Situational Prevention of Organised Timber Theft and Related Corruption', in *Situational Prevention of Organised Crimes*, edited by K. Bullock, R.V. Clarke and N. Tilley. Portland, OR: Willan, 81–92.

Greenpeace. 2008. 'Poisoning the Poor: Electronic Waste in Ghana', *Greenpeace.org*: http://www.greenpeace.org/international/en/news/features/poisoning-the-poor-electroni/ (accessed 24 October 2014).

Greenpeace. 2010. 'Guide to Greener Electronics', *Greenpeace.org*: http://www.greenpeace.org/international/en/campaigns/climate-change/cool-it/Campaign-analysis/Guide-to-Greener-Electronics/ (accessed 24 October 2014).

Grossman, E. 2006. *High Tech Trash: Digital Devices, Hidden Toxics, and Human Health*. Washington, DC: Island Press/Shearwater Books.

Gunningham, N. and Grabosky, P. 1998. *Smart Regulation: Designing Environmental Policy*. Oxford, UK: Oxford University Press.

Gunningham, N. 2009. 'Environmental Law, Regulation and Governance: Shifting Architectures', *Environmental Law* 21(2), 179–212.

Hill, C. 2005. 'Measuring Transnational Crime', in *Handbook of Transnational Crime and Justice*, edited by P. Reichel. Thousand Oaks, CA: Sage, 47–65.

Holly, C., Gunningham, N. and Shearing, C. 2011. *The New Environmental Governance*. New York, New York: Earthscan Publications.

Huo, X., Peng, L., Xu, X., Zheng, L., Qui, B., Qi, Z., Zhang, B., Han, D. and Piao, Z. 2007. 'Elevated Blood Lead Levels of Children in Guiyu, an Electronic Waste Recycling Town in China', *Environmental Health Perspective* 115, 1113–1117.

Iles, A. 2004. 'Mapping Environmental Justice in Technology Flows: Computer Waste Impacts in Asia', *Global Environmental Politics* 4, 76–107.

International Association of Chiefs of Police. 2002. 'Criminal Intelligence Sharing: A National Plan for Intelligence-Led Policing at the Local, State and Federal Levels', *Office of Community Oriented Policing Services, U.S. Department of Justice*: http://epic.org/privacy/fusion/intelsharerpt.pdf (accessed 24 October 2014).

INTERPOL. 2009. *Electronic Waste and Organised Crime: Assessing the Links*. Lyon: Interpol.

Jackson, A.S., Shuman, A. and Dayaneni, G. 2006. 'Toxic Sweatshops: How UNICOR Prison Recycling Harms Workers, Communities, the Environment, and the Recycling Industry', *Report by the Center for Environmental Health, Prison Activist Resource Center, Silicon Valley Toxics Coalition and the Computer TakeBack Campaign*: http://www.ceh.org/legacy/storage/documents/toxicsweatshops.pdf (accessed 24 October 2014).

Kahhat, R., Junbeum Kim, J., Xu, M., Allenby, B., Williams, E., and Zhang, P. 2008. 'Exploring E-waste Management Systems in the United States', *Resources, Conservation and Recycling* 52 (7), 955–964.

Kang, H.Y. and Schoenung, J.M. 2005. 'Electronic Waste Recycling: A Review of U.S. Infrastructure and Technology Options', *Resources, Conservation and Recycling* 45 (4), 368–400.

Khetriwal, D.S., Kraeuchi, P. and Widmer, R. 2009. 'Producer Responsibility for E-waste Management: Key Issues for Consideration—Learning from the Swiss Experience', *Journal of Environment Management* 90, 153–165.

Ladou, J. and Lovegrove, S. 2008. 'Export of Electronics Equipment Waste', *International Journal of Occupational and Environmental Health* 14, 1–10.

Lepawsky, J. and McNabb, C. 2010. 'Mapping International Flows of Electronic Waste', *The Canadian Geographer* 54 (2), 177–195.

Luther, L. 2007. 'Managing Electronic Waste: An Analysis of State E-waste Legislation', *Congressional Research Service Report for Congress*: http://assets.opencrs.com/rpts/R40850_20091007.pdf (accessed 24 October 2014).

Mandel, R. 2011. *Dark Logic: Transnational Criminal Tactics and Global Security*. Stanford, CA: Stanford University Press.

Michalowski, R., and Britten, K. 2005. 'Transnational Environmental Crime', in *Handbook of Transnational Crime and Justice*, edited by Philip Reichel. Thousand Oaks, CA: Sage, 189–212.

National Centre for Policing Excellence. 2005. *Guidance on the National Intelligence Model*: https://whereismydata.files.wordpress.com/2009/01/national-intelligence-model-20051.pdf (accessed 24 October 2014).

Passas, N. 1999. 'Globalization, Criminogenic Asymmetries, and Economic Crime', *European Journal of Legal Reform* 1, 399–423.

Passas, N. 2002. 'Cross Border Crime and the Interface Between Legal and Illegal Actors', in *Upperworld and Underworld in Cross-Border Crime*, edited by P.C. van Duyne, K. von Lampe and N. Passas. Nijmegen: Wolf Legal Publishers, 11–42.

Pellow, D.N. 2007. *Resisting Global Toxics: Transnational Movements for Environmental Justice*. Cambridge, MA: MIT Press.

Pink, G. 2013. 'Law Enforcement Responses to Transnational Environmental Crime: Choices, Challenges, and Culture', *Transnational Environmental Crime Project Working Paper*: http://ips.cap.anu.edu.au/sites/default/files/IPS/IR/TEC/PINK_%20Visiting_Fellow_Research_TEC_Research_Project_Workshop_Presentation_13FEB2012.pdf (accessed 24 October 2014).

Prochile Magazine. 2007. 'Waste that Doesn't Go to Waste': http://www.residuoselectronicos.net/archivos/documentos/ProChile0607english.pdf (accessed 24 October 2014).

Puckett, J., Byster, L., Westervelt, S., Gutierrez, R., Davis, S., Hussain, A. and Dutta, M. 2002. 'Exporting Harm: The High-Tech Trashing of Asia'. *Ban.org*: http://www.ban.org/E-waste/technotrashfinalcomp.pdf (accessed 24 October 2014).

Ratcliffe, J. 2008. *Intelligence-Led Policing*. Portland, OR: Willan.

Robinson, P. and Sadik, P. 2009. *The Economic Downturn May be a Fortuitous Speedbump on the Road to the E-waste Landfill*: http://www.davidsuzuki.org/media/news/2009/03/the-economic-downturn-may-be-a-fortuitous-speed-bump-on-the-road-to-the-e-waste/ (accessed 24 October 2014).

Silicon Valley Toxics Coalition (SVTC). 2004. 'Poison PCs and Toxic TVs: California's Biggest Environmental Crisis that You've Never Heard Of', *Svtc.org*: http://svtc.org/wp-content/uploads/ppc-ttv1.pdf (accessed 24 October 2014).

Schmidt, C.W. 2004. 'Environmental Crimes: Profiting at the Earth's Expense', *Environmental Health Perspectives* 112(2), 96–103.

Schluep, M., Hagelueken, C., Kuehr, R., Magalini, F., Maurer, C., Meskers, C., Mueller, E. and Wang, F. 2009. 'Recycling—From E-waste to Resources'. *United Nations*

Environmental Programme: http://www.unep.org/pdf/Recycling_From_e-waste_to_resources.pdf (accessed 24 October 2014).

Schreier, F. 2009. 'Human Trafficking, Organised Crime, and Intelligence', in *Strategies Against Human Trafficking: The Role of the Security Sector*, edited by C. Friesendorf. Vienna: National Defense Academy and Austrian Ministry of Defence and Sports, 213–259.

Selin, H. 2010. *Global Governance of Hazardous Chemicals: Challenges of Multilevel Management*. Cambridge, MA: MIT Press.

Selin, H. and VanDeever, S. 2006. 'Raising Global Standards: Hazardous Substances and E-waste Management in the European Union', *Environment* 48 (10), 6–18.

Sheptycki, J. 2004. 'Organizational Pathologies in Police Intelligence Systems: Some Contributions to the Lexicon of Intelligence-Led Policing', *European Journal of Criminology* 1 (3), 307–332.

Shover, N., and Hochstetler, A. 2006. *Choosing White-Collar Crime*. New York, NY: Cambridge University Press.

Tonetti, R. 2007. 'EPA's Regulatory Program for 'E-waste', *Epa.gov*: http://www.epa.gov/osw/conserve/materials/ecycling/docs/e-wasteregs.pdf (accessed 24 October 2014).

United States Environmental Protection Agency (U.S. EPA). 2007. 'Management of Electronic Waste in the United States', *U.S. Environmental Protection Agency*: http://www.epa.gov/waste/conserve/materials/ecycling/docs/fact7–08.pdf (accessed 24 October 2014).

Widmer, R., Oswald-Krapf, H., Sinha-Khetriwal, D., Schnellmann, M. and Boni, H. 2005. 'Global Perspectives on E-waste', *Environmental Impact Assessment Review* 25 (5), 436–458.

Williams, P. 2001. 'Transnational Criminal Networks', in *Networks and Netwars: The Future of Terror, Crime and Militancy*, edited by J. Arquilla and D. Ronfeldt. Santa Monica, CA: RAND, 61–97.

Wright, G. 2011. 'Conceptualising and Combating Transnational Environmental Crime', *Trends in Organized Crime* 14 (4), 332–346.

6 Regulatory Responses to Transnational Environmental Crime

An Overview of Choices, Challenges and Culture

Grant Pink

Introduction

This chapter considers the issue of law enforcement responses (LERs) to transnational environmental crime (TEC) with a particular focus on the role of environmental regulatory agencies as well as the range of operational and policy factors which inform and shape their enforcement responses.[1] The operational context involves a range of activities and responses which include the practical application of law enforcement and regulatory powers (or authorities) by government bodies. These are activities and responses that mainstream law enforcement agencies and environmental regulatory agencies associate with formal investigations undertaken as part of assessing allegations of criminal wrongdoing and serious non-compliance respectively. Policy includes the 'suite of documents, plans, programs, regulatory schemes, and strategies that provide for a coordinated, coherent response to, and support for' combating transnational environmental crime (Horne 2013, p. 1).[2]

The aim of this chapter is to furnish environmental regulatory agencies with information, options, and strategies to more effectively detect, deter, and disrupt TEC. This research has particular relevance for environmental regulatory agencies, because, like all public service agencies, they seek efficiencies and effectiveness. This extends to and includes staff involved in environmental compliance and enforcement.

1 Any views or opinions expressed in this paper are those of the author and not those of the Australian Government's Department of Environment, or the University of New England. A longer version of this chapter was first published as "Law Enforcement Responses to Transnational Environmental Crime: Choices, Challenges, and Culture", Transnational Environmental Crime Project Working Paper 4/2013 (Canberra: Department of International Relations, Australian National University, 2013). It was part of an Australian Research Council funded project on Transnational Environmental Crime at the Australian National University.

2 For a more comprehensive consideration of the policy aspects associated with transnational environmental crime, see Horne (2013).

Environmental Enforcement: The Regulatory Context

The operating environment for environmental regulatory agencies is a challenging one. There are many factors which make this so. Most relate broadly to complexity and culture.

The challenges associated with undertaking enforcement activities in general (Pink 2008; Van der Schraaf 2008; Farmer 2007) are even more complex for environmental enforcement (Clifford and Edwards 2012; White 2008; Wijbenga et al. 2008). This position is confirmed by a number of international organisations. The United Nations Office on Drugs and Crime (UNODC), which focuses on more traditional crime types, suggests that 'since crime has gone global, purely national responses are inadequate' (UNODC 2010, p. ii). This is a point reinforced with respect to TEC by Interpol's Environmental Crime Programme and the United Nations Environment Programme (UNEP). In March 2012, these two agencies combined to convene the inaugural International Chiefs of Environmental Compliance and Enforcement Summit to bring together and better coordinate the role of environmental regulatory agencies as they partner with police agencies and customs and port agencies. The Summit Report notes that:

> [e]nvironmental law enforcement is not always the responsibility of one national agency, but rather, is multi-disciplinary in nature due to the complexity and diversity of crime type which can encompass disciplines such as wildlife, pollution, fisheries, forestry, natural resources and climate change, with reaching effect into other areas of crime.
>
> (Interpol 2012, p. 5)

Cultural challenges manifest in the tension between expectation and reality regarding the role and function of public service agencies/departments. This tension occurs principally for those agencies/departments originally established to assist the general public and that function with a customer service approach, many of which have tended to adopt what is referred to as a 'client' oriented approach. Alford and Speed warn against a strong 'client' focus as a regulatory agency, or hybrid agency carrying out regulatory responsibilities, suggesting it can complicate effective action (2006, p. 325). This is especially so in circumstances where regulators are attempting to achieve high levels of 'voluntary compliance' or 'contingent compliance' with the latter from time to time requiring the use of coercive powers. The challenge for regulating 'clients' is how to effectively combine punishment with persuasion (John Braithwaite, cited in Alford and Speed 2006, p. 325). Similarly, White observes that very often the preference on the part of state authorities is for education, promotion and self-regulation rather than imposition of directive legislation and active enforcement and prosecution (2008, pp. 212–214). These viewpoints are supported by Bricknell (2010, p. 114) who states that 'agencies who only recently adopted the mantle of regulator are still negotiating the regulatory culture', indicating the reticence evident when moving from a service to an enforcement culture.

Environmental Enforcement: The Global Operating Environment

The Three Core Agencies and Transnational Environmental Crime

In global terms, most enforcement action taken in terms of transnational environment crime is initiated by three core agencies. Known by various titles, hereafter they are referred to as environmental regulatory agencies (ERAs), customs/port authorities (CPAs) and police agencies (PAs). These agencies relate with one another either bilaterally or trilaterally as they partner to combat transnational environmental crime.

Each joint investigation or enforcement activity will usually have a designated lead agency. Lead and key support agencies will, where necessary, be further supported by other agencies through a variety of multilateral arrangements.[3]

The three core agencies also link to other international organisations and entities to further coordinate their efforts. These organisational arrangements and support bodies, tend to be based upon discipline, commodity, and crime type. See Table 6.1 for the primary examples.

The three core agencies – what Clifford and Edwards (2012) call 'control agents' – bring different approaches to combating TEC. Situ and Emmons (2000, p. 140) suggest that 'the single most important requirement for effective environmental law enforcement is co-operation between regulatory agencies and traditional law enforcement officials'. However, as Sparrow (2008, pp. 53–54) notes, 'battles' can and often do occur between agencies especially in the face of 'overlapping jurisdictions, [or] where two or more agencies share responsibility for control of certain harms, but have sharply differing views on how best to proceed'. These differences can be amplified given the nature of TEC and organisational variations between

Table 6.1 Agency type, international institutions and their intersecting interests in transnational environmental crime

Core agency	*International organization*
ERAs	Secretariats of the various Multilateral Environment Agreements (MEAs)
	International Network for Environmental Compliance and Enforcement (INECE)
	International Consortium Combating Wildlife Crime (ICCWC)
CPAs	World Customs Organisation (WCO)
PAs	International Criminal Policing Organisation (ICPO or Interpol)
	European Law Enforcement Agency (EUROPOL)

3 In the case of TEC agencies such as Quarantine, Tax and Immigration are often involved due to the interrelationship with disease risk (associated with animal and plant products), money laundering and proceeds of crime, and the involvement of illegal people smuggling routes and organisations respectively.

the three core agencies. Such organisational variations reflect the relative position of the three core agencies on the regulatory and enforcement spectrum which, in turn, can shape their preference for, if not predilection towards, particular types of LERs (Ayres and Braithewaite 1992; Grabosky and Braithewaite 1986).

ERAs tend to be the more traditional 'customer service focused' public service agencies at one end of the spectrum with PAs (as mainstream law enforcement agencies) at the other end. CPAs (which have hybrid characteristics of public service agencies and mainstream law enforcement agencies) span and fluctuate between the two extremes. Their precise position can prove dependent on which of these other two agencies they happen to be partnering with.[4] Researchers from the Australian Institute of Criminology highlighted the fact that:

> there remain a number of significant challenges that will need to be addressed by regulatory and law enforcement agencies if longer term gains are to be made. In particular, there is currently no nationally structured approach or framework for addressing environmental crime in Australia, which makes it almost impossible to determine (among other things) the precise responsibilities and activities of each agency and where any overlaps in function may lie, as well as understanding if agency activities are coordinated and [are] actually effective.
>
> (Willis and Bricknell 2012, p. 6)

The Three Main Types of Law Enforcement Responses and Transnational Environmental Crime

Despite the different legislative arrangements and nomenclature used throughout the world, there are three broad categories of law enforcement responses, each of which is informed by different legal principles and systems of law – administrative, civil, and criminal. The corresponding law enforcement responses include those that involve 'direct command control on the part of the State' through to responses that involve 'voluntary compliance on the part of companies and individuals' (White 2008, p. 211).These responses are different in nature, have different legal meanings, and are not (generally speaking) all available to each of the three core agencies, see Table 6.2 for an overview.

Administrative (Also Known as an Administrative Sanction or Response)[5]

Commonly used for minor or technical breaches, or breaches that are able to be attended to by the regulator exercising its statutory authority without referral to

4 In most countries, CPAs are considered to be and operate as mainstream law enforcement agencies, irrespective of whether or not they are a public service agency.

5 Some scholars refer to administrative responses as being part of 'regulatory enforcement' (Clifford and Edwards 2012, p. 110).

Table 6.2 The three core agencies: use of the three main types of law enforcement responses

Agency Type	*Administrative LER*	*Civil LER*	*Criminal LER*
ERAs	Used Extensively	Used Frequently	Used Infrequently
CPAs	Used Frequently	Used Occasionally	Used Frequently
Pas	Used Infrequently (in limited circumstances)	Not available	Used Extensively (predominantly)

a court (Freiberg 2010, p. 34; Lynott and Cullinane 2010). Responses can take the form of warnings, cautions, fines, or varying, suspending or revoking an environmental authorisation (licence/permit) (DoE 2012a; Freiberg 2010).

- perceived advantages: the use of administrative responses is within the mandate and control of the regulator (EPA Ireland 2009b). They can resolve matters quickly and keep relatively low-level and uncontested matters from 'clogging' the courts.
- perceived disadvantages: they can be seen as a 'soft option' when applied without full consideration of other options, especially when the alleged wrongdoer is a repeat offender and/or the breach is one that is worthy of an escalated response.
- perceived efficacy: their use is considered appropriate and timely for the majority of minor and technical breaches of environmental law and is an especially useful tool when regulators have frequent and ongoing contact with a regulated entity (Ayres and Braithwaite 1992; Black 2002).
- common or frequent criticism: relates to overuse of this response when coupled with a repeated failure or lack of willingness by regulators to escalate their responses to include civil or criminal options.
- usage by the three core agencies: as a general rule this is extensively used by ERAs, frequently used by CPAs and used infrequently in limited situations by PAs (see Table 6.2).[6]

Civil (Also Known as a Civil Penalty or Remedy)

Commonly used for instances where the regulator is keen to have the court impose some form of monetary or other order (not permitted/accessible through either the administrative or criminal responses). Responses can take the form of enforceable

6 Minor breaches of; traffic laws, operating licensed (liquor) premises, and residential noise complaints are possible examples where this response may be used.

undertakings and remediation determinations (DoE 2012; Freiberg 2010; Macrory 2006, 2010).

- perceived advantages: actions need only satisfy the civil burden of proof ('balance of probabilities') which is lower than the criminal burden (White 2009; Freiberg 2010). This option is also considered to be more flexible (Macrory 2006) and enables greater use of innovative (non-prosecutorial) 'outcomes' (Baird 2011) than is the case for criminal responses, but at the same time has more 'teeth' than administrative responses (Macrory 2010).
- perceived disadvantages: generally outcomes are achieved within a shorter timeframe when compared to pursuing and finalising a criminal action. However, they can be as lengthy if not longer, and this form of litigation can be substantially more expensive compared with the litigation costs of a criminal prosecution[7] which is usually undertaken by a government prosecuting authority.[8] It is underpinned by fewer legal safeguards and processes than is the case in the criminal response (Freiberg 2010).
- perceived efficacy: use is appropriate for those breaches which are not minor or technical in nature (EPA Ireland 2009b; Macrory 2006, 2010).
- common or frequent criticism: can be seen as a 'soft' or 'easy' option taken by regulators who are not prepared to escalate their non-compliance responses (Lipman 2010) and 'test their arm' in a criminal prosecution.
- usage by the three core agencies: this is frequently (and increasingly) used by ERAs, occasionally used by CPAs, and is not available to PAs (see Table 6.2).[9]

Criminal (Also Known as a Criminal Prosecution or Action)

Commonly used for more serious breaches of legislation and where there is a clear public expectation of punishment (Clifford and Edwards 2012, p. 174; Stuart Bell and Donald McGillivray cited in White 2011a, p. 135; Situ and Emmons 2000, p. 21). Take the form of criminal prosecutions.

- perceived advantages: criminal LERs are authoritative and provide legal precedent; they are also underpinned by legal safeguards and processes (DoE 2012; Freiberg 2010; Macrory 2006; Macrory 2010).
- perceived disadvantages: can involve lengthy and costly litigation (DoE 2012; Freiberg 2010; OEE 2009). Any action is predicated upon satisfying

7 This depends on a range of factors such as whether or not the agency initiating the action has access to in-house legal staff, whether such staff are able to attend court and practice case work, and whether external legal counsel has to be used, which then incurs commercial rates (typically charged in six minute increments) and can amount to tens if not hundreds of thousands of dollars.

8 Such as the Office of the Director of Public Prosecutions in Australia.

9 The mandates of international and national police organisations such as Interpol and the Australian Federal Police expressly preclude them from initiating civil actions.

the criminal burden of proof ('beyond a reasonable doubt'). This burden of proof requires proving fault elements (Clifford and Edwards 2012, pp. 107–8) which can result in an 'all or nothing' outcome for regulators (DoE 2012).

- perceived efficacy: some practitioners and academic commentators consider criminal sanctions central to underpinning the effectiveness of legal and regulatory regimes. Criminal sanctions also achieve specific and general deterrence (Ayres and Braithwaite 1992; see also Simpson et al. 2014).[10]
- common or frequent criticism: seen as being 'too harsh' a response as it treats environmental crime the same as real crime which conflicts with 'prevailing attitudes and perceptions within the criminal justice system . . . [and the fact that] environmental crime frequently embodies a certain ambiguity' (White 2011a, pp. 134–5).
- usage by the three core agencies: as a general rule criminal LERs are used infrequently by ERAs (depending on jurisdiction), frequently used by CPAs, and almost exclusively by PAs (see Table 6.2).[11]

As Brickey notes:

> [a]lthough criminal penalties for environmental crimes exist in the statutes, the more severe criminal penalties are rarely used, and the majority of environmental violations are addressed through regulatory [administrative] or civil remedies.
>
> (cited in Clifford and Edwards 2012, p. 111)

Before leaving the three broad categories of law enforcement responses, it is important to note that some countries have developed hybrid forms of laws and responses (usually combining aspects of administrative/civil and civil/criminal) relating to enforcement of environmental law.

Key Definitions and Terminology

A number of key definitions are particularly relevant, as they influence the enforcement approaches of the three core agencies generally and specifically in terms of TEC. If misapplied, or if their context (agency and cultural) is not fully appreciated or entirely understood, these terms can further complicate and exacerbate the existing differences between agencies in respect to their ability to use LER (whether individually or in concert with co-regulators) in the field of TEC.

10 The recent meta-valuation study by Simpson et al. (2014), focusing on corporate crime deterrence, suggests that older studies show higher levels of deterrence value than those that are newer.

11 Their predominant responses result in some form of court action which typically attracts custodial or non-custodial sentences, and fines and convictions being recorded against individuals.

The following definitions are also important in terms of their potential operational and policy impacts for each of the three core agencies.[12] Simply put, these definitions (based upon their interpretation and application) influence the ability of agencies not only to be actively involved in combating TEC but also to determine the relative priority and importance afforded to TEC.[13]

Crime

Crime is seen or considered as 'an act (or sometimes a failure to act) that is deemed by statute or by the common law to be a public role and is therefore punishable by the State in criminal proceedings' (Gooch and Williams 2007, p. 94).

Traditional Crime

Traditional (or real) crime is investigated and dealt with by the police or mainstream law enforcement agencies and it includes offences against the person and offences against property. Traditional crimes are more readily associated with having actual and readily identifiable victims (Willis and Bricknell 2012; Moore 2012, p. 184; Epstein 1998, p. 145). Such crimes are dealt with through the criminal justice system.

Environmental Crime

Clifford and Edwards (2012, p. 111) query 'whether all environmental violations should be considered environmental crimes or where the environmental crimes are restricted to activities for which criminal remedies are sought is an open question'. The definition of 'environmental crime' is influenced by a range of concepts and factors introduced by society, organisations, or entities. White and Habibis (2005, p. 10) argue that 'environmental crime is socially constructed, both through definitional processes, and by the ways in which environmental law enforcement is carried out in practice'.[14]

12 The majority of definitions that follow are either legal definitions or ones adapted from legal definitions. There are also sociological definitions of crime and environmental crime worthy of considering as part of a broader analysis, see Hayes and Prenzler (2012) and White and Heckenberg (2014).

13 It is worth noting, depending on the sector and industry, that environmental crime is committed by corporations as well as by natural persons. While beyond the scope of this chapter, and depending on their operating environment, some readers may find that corporate crime and associated issues are worthy of additional consideration (Simpson et al. 2013).

14 A central issue relating to definitions, which goes beyond the scope of this paper, is whether or not a violation or a environmental harm be a defining criteria, see White and Heckenberg (2014); South and Brisman (2013); and South and Beirne (2006).

Transnational Environmental Crime

There is no settled definition for TEC. Elliott (2009, p. 59) suggests that, 'transnational environment crime involves the trading and smuggling of plants, animals, resources and pollutants in violation of prohibition or regulation regimes established by multilateral environmental agreements and/or in contravention of domestic law'.

Organized Crime

Organized crime under Article 2 of the United Nations Convention against Transnational Organised Crime is further defined by definitions relating to '. . . (a) Organised criminal group . . . (b) Serious crime . . . [and] (c) Structured group . . .'.

Serious and Organized Crime

Australia for example, under the *Australian Crime Commission Act 2002*, defines serious and organised crime as 'an offence that involves two or more offenders, substantial planning and organisation and the use of sophisticated methods and techniques; which is committed in conjunction with other serious offences punishable by imprisonment for a period of three years or more'.[15] This definition covers a broad range of serious offences, most of which are now recognised as either cross-over crimes[16] or predicate crimes associated with TEC (Interpol 2012, p. 5; UNODC 2008).

Transnational Organized Crime

Under the 2000 United Nations Convention against Transnational Organised Crime, transnational organised crime is defined as, 'any serious transnational offence undertaken by three or more people with the aim of material gain' (UNODC 2010, p. 1). The preceding discussion highlights that not all environmental crime is transnational environmental crime and that not all TEC is transnational organised crime.

Law Enforcement Responses and the Influence of Literature

This section examines how mainstream law enforcement agencies (such as police and customs), enforcement agencies (such as tax and child protection agencies),

15 Many other countries have developed their respective national definitions based upon the definitions of 'organized criminal group' and 'serious crime' as contained within the *United Nations Convention against Transnational Organized Crime* (2000).

16 Cross-over crimes include corruption, fraud, tax evasion, money laundering, and murder. See Interpol (no date, p. 3).

and other agencies (such as environmental regulatory agencies) have approached the task of responding to alleged breaches of legislation. It considers law, policy, compliance and enforcement operations, as well as organisational capacity, capability, and culture.

There are various and often competing factors that combine 'all the sources of authority with which the regulator acts', sometimes referred to as the regulator's 'authorising environment' (Fels 2003, pp. 5–6). The 'authorising environment' enables and determines the nature of the exercise of regulatory power, influencing and shaping the operational and policy responses to TEC by ERAs. The concepts that have most influenced the operational and policy responses of environmental regulatory and enforcement agencies have been clustered into five categories: *responsive regulation*, *problem solving*, *sanctions*, *enforcement tools*, and *risk management*.

Consideration is now given to the *influence* such ideas have had on how governmental regulators approach their roles and responsibilities, the *demonstrable effects* measured in terms of regulatory outcomes, and the *impact* upon the law enforcement responses of governmental regulators.

Responsive Regulation

Responsive regulation relates to engagement and responses and the resultant relationships of and for interaction between the regulator and the regulated. Ayres and Braithwaite (1992, p. 5) consider that, '[f]or the responsive regulator, there are no optimal or best regulatory solutions, just solutions that respond better than others to the plural configurations of support and opposition that exist at any particular moment in history'. The enforcement pyramid developed by Ayres and Braithwaite has had a significant and enduring influence on the enforcement approaches and associated strategies of governmental regulators. This is evidenced, for example, by its prevalence in compliance and enforcement polices and strategies of Australian regulators (ANAO 2014; DAFF 2012; TGA 2012; OGTR 2007).

The enforcement pyramid is complemented by the enforcement strategies pyramid which contains a range of corresponding enforcement strategies. These strategies loosely align with the steps in the enforcement pyramid and reflect the preferred approach and parameters of an agency's response.

Ayres and Braithwaite argue that '[r]egulators will do best by indicating a willingness to escalate intervention up those pyramids or to deregulate down the pyramids in response to the industry's performance in securing regulatory objectives'. Furthermore, they:

> argued that the greater the heights of tough enforcement to which the agency can escalate (at the apex of its enforcement pyramid), the more effective the agency will be at securing compliance and less likely that it will have to resort to tough enforcement. Regulatory agencies will be able to speak more softly when they are perceived as carrying big sticks.
>
> (Ayres and Braithwaite 1992, p. 6)

Problem Solving

Sparrow has highlighted operating and cultural differences between mainstream law enforcement agencies, government agencies with regulatory functions, and those government agencies without regulatory functions. He explained that:

> [s]ome government agencies exist primarily to deliver obligations at one time or another, rather than services, to citizens. These agencies are often thought of as "enforcement and regulatory" agencies – a label that focuses attention on the necessarily coercive aspects of their work. An alternative formulation of their function – "procuring compliance"– reminds us that government acts on behalf of citizens, not against them, even when its agencies take actions which are coercive or adversarial.
>
> (1994, p. ix)

Sparrow's later work continues with the theme of *problem solving* from the perspective of unravelling complex and cross-cutting problems including environmental regulation. It focuses on operational responses and outlines the challenges law enforcement and regulatory agencies face when developing 'intervention strategies' to stop a variety of crime types. It details the multi-layered thinking involved in developing, deciding upon and executing (tactical, operational, and strategic) law enforcement responses.[17] Choosing the 'right response' is made more difficult when it requires interaction with one or more different agencies (irrespective of whether operational or policy in nature). Sparrow observes that the most obvious clashes occur in two situations which involve issues associated with organisational culture and complexities and challenges concerning jurisdiction. Firstly, in terms of organisational culture, he suggests that:

> organisational mergers, where constituent pieces arrived with differing traditions and self-images. [That] [p]erhaps one of the merged departments comes as a traditional regulator, heavily reliant on enforcement. Another comes with a tradition of providing technical consulting to industry, and with staff who view themselves as service-providers and advisers. Two such groups may well have trouble appreciating each other; they represent different theories of operation.
>
> (2008, p. 53)

Secondly, the situation arises due to 'overlapping jurisdictions, where two or more agencies share responsibility for control of certain harms, but have sharply differing views on how best to proceed' (Sparrow 2008, pp. 53–54).

17 In this context, 'tactical' means one case or suspect, 'operational' might relate to one gang or crime syndicate in a geographic area such as a suburb, whilst 'strategic' would relate to taking a whole of jurisdiction zero tolerance approach to a particular crime type.

Sanctions

There is a correlation between this section on *sanctions* and the next on *enforcement tools*. Sparrow (2000, p. 2) argues that 'the nature and quality of regulatory practice hinges on which laws regulators choose to enforce, and when; on how they focus their efforts and structure their uses of discretion; [and] on the choice of methods for procuring compliance'. The issue of choice emerges because, as Freiberg (2010, p. 215) suggests, 'the line between criminal, civil and administrative . . . is unclear and has become blurred over time'.

Horne (2013) also considers that the influence of the policy setting and context should not be overlooked. He suggests that appropriate penalties are an important aspect of multifaceted policy responses, in what is an overall suite of complimentary policy instruments, which collectively aim to address one overall problem.

The works of Hampton (2005), Macrory (2006; 2010), and Farmer (2007) consider sanctions generally and specifically in the environmental context, influencing the approaches taken by governmental regulators to 'identify ways in which the administrative burden of regulation on businesses can be reduced, while maintaining or improving regulatory outcomes'(Hampton 2005, p. 3). In relation to sanctions Hampton (2005, p. 6) noted that:

> [b]usinesses and regulators have an interest in proper sanctions against illegal activity in order to prevent businesses operating outside the law from gaining a competitive advantage. At present, regulatory penalties do not take the economic value of a breach into consideration and it is quite often in a business's interest to pay the fine rather than comply.

This reinforces the notion that sanctions can be seen and considered by some regulated entities as a cost of doing business (Macrory 2006). This is a point of frustration frequently raised by regulators (Pink 2013). Equally, it highlights concerns about the lack of 'a level playing field' for regulated entities. Hampton considered this to be exacerbated by the fact that '[p]enalty regimes are also slow and comparatively weak . . . because penalties are low absolutely, but more worryingly because penalties imposed often do not reflect the commercial advantage a business has gained from non-compliance'(2005, p. 26).

One of the recommendations therefore stated that '[t]he few businesses that persistently break regulations should be identified quickly, and face proportionate and meaningful sanctions' (Hampton 2005, p. 7).

Building on Hampton's work, Macrory (2006, 2010) focused on the effectiveness of sanctions. He made a number of observations on criminal sanctions, and considered that whilst there was a 'heavy reliance on criminal sanctions' (2006, p. 15) by regulators, it should be noted that:

- criminal sanctions currently are often an insufficient deterrent to the 'truly' criminal or rogue operators, since the financial sanctions imposed in some criminal cases are not considered to be a sufficient deterrent . . .

- regulators may not have any alternative available to them in their toolkit and so must prosecute, even where a different type of sanction may be more effective . . .
- Heavy reliance on criminal sanctions leads to some non-compliance not being addressed at all. Criminal sanctions are costly and time-consuming for both businesses and regulators. In many instances, although non-compliance has occurred, the cost or expense of bringing criminal proceedings deters regulators from using their limited resources to take action. This creates what has become known as a compliance deficit;
- Criminal convictions for regulatory non-compliance have lost their stigma . . . being prosecuted is regarded as part of the business cycle . . . strict liability offences committed by legitimate business, and the deliberate flouting of the law by rogues is prosecuted in the same manner with little differentiation between these two types of offender; and
- Since the focus of criminal proceedings is on the offence and the offender, the wider impact of the offence on the victim [or the environment] may not be fully explored.

(2006, pp. 15–16)

Conversely, Clifford and Edwards (2012, pp. 110–111) noted that, '[a]lthough criminal penalties for environment crimes exist in the statutes, the more severe criminal penalties are rarely used, and the majority of environmental violations are addressed through regulatory [administrative] or civil remedies'. Another factor raised by White (2008, p. 191) which highlights a general move away from command and control regulation and its predominant use of criminal sanction is that '[o]ne of the major stumbling blocks in using the "big stick", much less other instruments in the law enforcement tool box, has been the difficulty in establishing liability in certain types of [environmental] cases'.

Macrory's work on sanctions culminated in the development of a set of 'penalty principles' and 'regulator characteristics', following empirical research of 524 regulatory bodies[18] in the United Kingdom (2006, p. 6).

The Six Penalties Principles suggest a sanction should:

1. Aim to change the behaviour of the offender;
2. Aim to eliminate any financial gain or benefit from a non-compliance;
3. Be responsive and consider what is appropriate for the particular offender and regulatory issue, which can include punishment and the public stigma that should be associated with a criminal conviction;
4. Be proportionate to the nature of the offence and the harm caused;

18 Specifically the research involved 56 national regulators and 468 local authorities.

5 Aim to restore the harm caused by regulatory non-compliance, where appropriate; and
6 Aim to deter future non-compliance.

The Seven Characteristics suggest regulators should:

1 Publish an enforcement policy;
2 Measure outcomes not just outputs;
3 Justify their choice of enforcement actions year on year to stakeholders, Ministers and Parliament;
4 Follow-up enforcement actions where appropriate;
5 Enforce in a transparent manner;
6 Be transparent in the way in which they apply and determine administrative penalties; and
7 Avoid perverse incentives that might influence the choice of sanctioning response.

(2006, p. 10)

Farmer's (2007, p. 138) work, informed by the work of Hampton and Macrory, looks at sanctions from the perspective of operationalising them in such a way that the primary objective relates to protecting the environment. In terms of 'putting the sanctions into practice', Farmer outlines nine issues that should be taken into account in determining an appropriate enforcement response. These are:

> nature of the offence . . . financial issues [specifically financial benefits arising from the offending] . . . impact on the environment and on others . . . deterrent effect of the enforcement action . . . intent of the offender . . . previous compliance history . . . attitude of the offender . . . predictability . . . [and] financial issues [referring to the financial resources required by the regulator to take forward an enforcement action].
>
> (Farmer 2007, p. 140)

Enforcement Tools

The various *enforcement tools* available for use by regulators can be contained within singular families or can span the three broad types of law enforcement responses, namely administrative, civil, and criminal.

Freiberg (2010, p. 84) outlines six broad ranges of tools: economic, transactional, authorisation, structural, informational, and legal. To date it has been the legal aspects which have received the most attention from regulators. Freiberg cautions against this, urging regulators to take a more holistic approach. He notes that:

> regulators may well have relied too heavily on some tools while under-utilising others that may have been more effective or efficient. The lack of a

> broad framework within which regulatory decisions can be made, and regulatory tools chosen, has inhibited regulators and policymakers from being more creative in their response to social, environmental and economic harms.
> (Freiberg 2010, p. v)

Freiberg (2010, p. vi) acknowledges that the selection and application of regulatory tools is a complex task as it:

> requires a clear understanding of many elements: the range and nature of regulatory methods; the timing of the regulatory interventions; the number, nature and motivations of the people or organisations to be regulated; the resources available; the cost of each tool; the order or combination in which the regulatory tools can or should be used; their efficiency and suitability for use in the particular environment; their legal and political legitimacy; their efficacy; and their transparency and accountability.

Freiberg (2010, pp. 205–257) provides some advice, assistance, and guidance to regulators in terms of the application of the legal tools which span the three main types of law enforcement responses. The advice covers a raft of issues including, but not limited to, risk, deterrence and implementation. All of which in combination highlight that the application of sanctions across administrative, civil, and criminal matters requires a nuanced approach.

Risk Management

Risk management has emerged in government administration as a cross-cutting and ubiquitous issue (variously influencing decision-making, prioritization, and resource allocation) which is used both as a means of identifying and addressing risk factors. While risk management might be viewed as a subset of *problem solving*, its historical emergence from project management, and financial oversight and care, give it particular standing given the culture of 'risk' within public sector agencies. Many public sector agencies now have chief financial officers and chief risk officers with responsibility for the financial and operational aspects of organisations. Similarly, risk management is recognised as a relevant consideration and trigger in relation to regulation, compliance and enforcement activities undertaken by ERAs.

ERAs have developed a number of continual improvement practices, which have been informed by risk principles, relating to environmental: licensing and permitting (Environment Agency 2014; NSW EPA 2014), inspection and monitoring (Nicol et al. 2014; IMPEL 2012), and investigations (INTERPOL 2014).[19]

19 See also Gouldson, Morton and Pollard 2009, which looks at broader risk-based decision-making to inform better environmental regulation, and Hutter, 2005, which considers the imperative for regulators to adopt risk-based strategies and tools.

When focusing on administrative burdens and the efficiency of regulatory and enforcement inspections, Hampton repeatedly emphasises the benefits of risk management, principally through the use of risk assessments:

> though widely recognised as fundamental to effectiveness – is not implemented as thoroughly and comprehensively as it should be. Risk assessment should be comprehensive, and should be the basis for all regulators' enforcement programmes. Proper analysis of risk directs regulators' efforts at areas where it is most needed, and should enable them to reduce the administrative burden of regulation, while maintaining or even improving regulatory outcomes.
>
> (Hampton 2005, p. 1)

Hampton makes a number of recommendations relating to the implementation of risk management practices and usage, including that:

- comprehensive risk assessment should be the foundation of all regulators' enforcement programmes;
- there should be no inspections without a reason, and data requirements for less risky businesses should be lower than for riskier businesses;
- resources released from unnecessary inspections should be redirected towards advice to improve compliance.

(Hampton 2005, p. 1)

Hampton (2005: 28) was also of the view that:

> [u]nless risk assessment is carried through into resource allocations and regulatory practice, it is wasted effort. Risk assessment needs to be comprehensive, and inform all aspects of the regulatory lifecycle from the selection and development of appropriate regulatory and policy instruments through to the regulators work including data collection, inspection and prosecution.

In this schema, risk assessment becomes a tool for the proper allocation of resources to achieve maximal compliance results within set limitations. Sparrow (1994, p. xxv) noted:

> [a]gencies begin asking what is feasible, what is most important, and what presents the greatest risks. They have to define some analytic framework within which risks can be assessed and evaluated. Then they have to develop criteria for selection, and begin allocating organisational resources according to agreed priorities. Resource allocation becomes more fluid, more analytical, more intelligent.

Environmental Enforcement Networks: Capacity Building Role

The increasing capacity-building role played by dedicated environmental enforcement networks and other enforcement networks (with environmental aspects) is evident in the literature (Pink 2014; Stas 2011; White 2011b; Bricknell 2010; Tomkins 2009; Sparrow 2008; Farmer 2007; Blindell 2006).

Faure, De Smedt and Stas (2015), Zaelke, Kaniaru and Kružíková (2005), Slaughter (2004) and Raustiala (2002) consider the role and importance of enforcement networks. Specifically, Faure, De Smedt and Stas (2015) observe that throughout the world:

> 'those engaged in enforcement of environmental laws have recognised that creating environmental enforcement networks is of importance'. Adding that '[t]he mere fact that many different environmental enforcement networks exist, shows that those networks apparently respond to a particular demand in practice and that hence enforcers feel that the creation of those networks can add to the effectiveness of enforcement efforts.
>
> (2015, p. 510)

Zaelke, Kaniaru and Kružíková suggest that:

> [t]he lack of meaningful enforcement and compliance has often been seen as one of the greatest weaknesses of international law, and international environmental law in particular, but new models of cooperation present great promise for effective international action.
>
> (2005, p. 383)

Raustiala (2002), working from a policy and strategic perspective, suggests that networks enhance activities associated with multilateral environmental agreements (MEAs), fill gaps where there are no MEAs, and facilitate negotiations for future MEAs.

Conversely, Slaughter (2004), suggests that given that organised crime operates through 'global networks' it is appropriate that governments similarly coordinate their efforts when it comes to global enforcement efforts with such an approach having benefits for tactical and operational enforcement. Slaughter (2004, p. 19) suggests that '[e]nforcement networks typically spring up due to the inability of government officials in one country to enforce that country's laws'. These 'weaknesses' in enforcement systems both within and across countries was a key finding of the report of Akella and Cannon (2004). An inability or less than optimal ability in one county is of great concern when considering an issue such as law enforcement responses to transnational environmental crime.

There has been a discernible increase in society's expectations in relation to the enforcement of environmental issues (Bricknell 2010; Wijbenga et al. 2008). Macrory (2010, p. 353) is of the view that '[p]ublic concern and governmental interest in environmental issues has reached new peaks in the last few years'. Furthermore, responding to environmental issues is further compounded by the fact that the public is less tolerant of actual or artificial border demarcation issues (whether sub-national, regional, or international) and they expect a seamless whole-of-government, regional, or even global response as is appropriate (Pink and Lehane 2012).

Research also shows that enforcement bodies and various enforcement networks are increasingly combining with one another to maximise the effectiveness of their law enforcement responses (White 2011a, 2011b; Pink and Lehane 2011; Pink 2011; Farmer 2007, pp. 249–62; Taschereau and Bolger 2007; Gerardu and Zaelke 2005).

White (2011a, p. 138) also suggests that '[n]etworking provides a practicable basis for intervention in areas that are by their nature complex and multifaceted'. Several practical examples across the three types of core agency functions include Interpol and UNODC[20] (for mainstream policing and law enforcement agencies); the World Customs Organisation[21] (for customs and port authorities); and the International Network for Environmental Compliance and Enforcement (INECE)[22] and the Australasian Environmental Law Enforcement and Regulators neTwork (AELERT) (for environmental regulatory agencies).

The last two decades has seen a proliferation of environmental enforcement networks (Pink 2015; Pink 2011) as well as an increase in the partnering between international organisations (combining to combat various cross-cutting environmental, enforcement, and economic issues). This is consistent with the view of Achim Steiner, executive director of UNEP, who considers that 'global problems need global partnerships . . . [and that] enforcement networking is one small example of the benefit of such cooperation' (UNEP 2007, p. 2).

Conclusion

Barbara Young, former chief executive of the Environment Agency in the UK, suggested that '[m]odern regulation aims to find the right balance – a proportionate, risk based response, that will drive environmental improvements, reward good performance, but still provide the ultimate reassurance that tough action will be taken on those who fail to meet acceptable standards' (Environment Agency 2003, p. 1). The challenges associated with determining and applying appropriate, effective, and efficient law enforcement responses are many and varied, and span a range of legal fields. As Sparrow (2000, p. 17) points out, '[r]egulators, [are] under unprecedented pressure, face a range of demands, [which are] often contradictory in nature'. Similarly, Gemmell and Scott note that '[i]t is also often the regulator's challenge to deal with inconsistencies and misalignments between instruments' (2013, p. 125).

A review of the literature relating to environmental regulation, compliance, and enforcement generally, and the transnational environmental crime specifically, recognises the challenges and competing interests informing that literature and its

20 Environmental crime is considered a subject worthy of special consideration. See UNODC (2010).

21 The World Customs Organisation has developed an environment programme in terms of controlling MEAs, especially those that are trade related. See www.wcoomd.org/en/topics/enforcement-and-compliance/activities-and-programmes/ep_environmental_crime.aspx.

22 INECE brings together a range of experts from government, non-government, civil society, and academia. See INECE (no date).

ongoing development and accumulation. It needs also to be noted that the body of literature developed to address this intersection between fields remains fundamentally practical, rather than purely theoretical in its scope and aims.

This chapter has highlighted some of the difficulties arsing due to the interaction between the different types of agencies undertaking environmental regulation and enforcement. Some difficulties present as a result of agency identity and preferences. Notable among these preferences are regulatory responses, all of which can usually be found, singly and in combination, in environmental regulatory regimes. The result of the diversity across agency types and available responses is a need for nuanced and adaptive approaches to achieve regulatory and environmental outcomes. This chapter recommends an evidence and harms-based responsive and adaptive approach with clearly determined and pursued outcomes. Achieving this requires building and combining capability within and across environmental regulatory agencies and response agencies of all types. Networks provide forums for participation, as well as the sharing of resources, knowledge and experiences. Central to facilitating and maximising the benefits of such exchanges is the understanding that agencies of each type have their reasons for their differences and that it is precisely those differences that can be harnessed to bring better protection to the environment.

References

Akella, A.S. and Cannon, J.B. 2004. *Strengthening the Weakest Links: Strategies for Improving the Enforcement of Environmental Laws Globally.* Washington, DC: Center for Conservation and Governance, Conservation International.

Alford, J. and Speed, R. 2006. 'Client Focus in Regulatory Agencies: Oxymoron or Opportunity', *Public Management Review* 8(2), 313–331.

ANAO (Australian National Audit Office) 2014. *Administering Regulation: Achieving the Right Balance — Better Practice Guide.* Canberra: ANAO.

Ayres, I. and Braithwaite, J. 1992. *Responsive Regulation: Transcending the Deregulation Debate.* New York: Oxford University Press.

Baird, R. 2011. 'Big Sticks, Carrots and Enforceable Undertakings under the Environment Protection and Biodiversity Conservation Act 1999', *Environmental and Planning Law Journal* 28, 3–8.

Black, J. 2002. 'Critical Reflections on Regulation', *Australian Journal of Legal Philosophy* 27, 1–46.

Blindell, J. 2006. *21st Century Policing: The Role of Police in the Detection, Investigation and Prosecution of Environmental Crime.* Adelaide: Australasian Centre for Policing Research, ACPR Issues 2.

Bricknell, S. 2010. *Environmental Crime in Australia.* Canberra: Australian Institute of Criminology, AIC Reports: Research and public policy series 109.

Clifford, M. and Edwards, T. 2012. *Environmental Crime,* 2nd edition. Burlington, MA: Jones & Bartlett Learning.

DAFF (Department of Agriculture, Fisheries and Forestry) 2012. *Biosecurity Compliance Strategy: A plan for managing compliance and enforcement in Australia.* Canberra: Commonwealth of Australia.

DoE (Department of Sustainability, Environment, Water, Population and Communities) 2012. *Annual Report: 2011–2012.* Canberra: Commonwealth of Australia.

Elliott, L. 2009. 'Combating Transnational Environmental Crime: "Joined Up" Thinking About Transnational Networks', in *Eco-Crime and Justice: Essays on Environmental Crime* edited by K. Kangaspunta and I.H. Marshall. Turin: UNICRI, 55–77.

Environment Agency 2014. *Environmental Permitting Regulations Operational Risk Appraisal (Opra for EPR) version 3, 9 April 2014.* Bristol: Environment Agency.

Environment Agency 2003. *Delivering for the Environment: A 21st Century Approach To Regulation.* Bristol: Environment Agency.

EPA (Environmental Protection Agency) Ireland 2009a. *Focus on Environmental Enforcement in Ireland: A Report for the Years 2006–2008.* Wexford: Environmental Protection Agency.

EPA (Environmental Protection Agency) Ireland 2009b. *A Study on the Use of Administrative Sanctions for Environmental Offences in Other Comparable Countries and Assessment of Their Possible Use in Ireland.* Wexford: Environmental Protection Agency.

Epstein, J. 1998. 'State and Local Environmental Enforcement', in *Environmental Crime: Enforcement, Policy and Social Responsibility* edited by M. Clifford. Gaithersburg, MD: Aspen Publishers, 145–168.

Farmer, A. 2007. *Handbook of Environmental Protection and Enforcement: Principles and Practice.* London: Earthscan.

Faure, M., De Smedt, P. and Stas, A. 2015. 'Concluding and Comparative Remarks', in *Environmental Enforcement Networks: Concepts, Implementation and Effectiveness* edited by M. Faure, A. Stas and P. De Smedt. Cheltenham, UK: Edward Elgar, 510–524.

Fels, A. 2003. 'The Role of the Privacy Regulator in an Era of Transparency', Speech, 25th *International Conference of Data Protection and Privacy Commissioners*, Sydney, September 10, 2003.

Freiberg, A. 2010. *The Tools of Regulation.* Sydney: Federation Press.

Gemmell, J.C. and Scott, E.M. 2013, 'Environmental regulation, sustainability and risk', *Sustainability Accounting, Management and Policy Journal, Vol. 4, Issue 2,* 120–144.

Gerardu, J.J.A. and Zaelke, D. 2005. 'The Importance of International Environmental Enforcement Networks', *Environmental Law Network International* 2, 3–7.

Gooch, G. and Williams, M. 2007. *Dictionary of Law Enforcement.* Oxford: Oxford University Press.

Gouldson, A., Morton, A., and Pollard. S.J.T. 2009. 'Better Environmental Regulation; Contributions from Risk-Based Decision-Making', *Science of The Total Environment* 407(19), 5283–5288.

Grabosky, P., and Braithwaite, J. 1986. *Of Manners Gentle: Enforcement Strategies of Australian Business Regulatory Agencies.* Melbourne: Oxford University Press.

Hampton, P., 2005. *Reducing Administrative Burdens: Effective Inspection and Enforcement.* London: HM Treasury.

Hayes, H., and Prenzler, T. (eds) 2012. *An Introduction to Crime and Criminology*, 3rd edition. Frenchs Forest, NSW: Pearson.

Horne, D. 2013. *Policy Responses to Transnational Wildlife Crime in the Asia-Pacific Region – Part 1: Global and Regional Policy Context and a Potential Framework for Optimal National Policy.* Transnational Environmental Crime Project Working Paper 1/2013, Canberra: Department of International Relations, Australian National University.

Hutter, B.M., 2005. *The Attractions of Risk-based Regulation: Accounting for the Emergence of Risk Ideas in Regulation.* Discussion Paper 33, CARR Discussion Paper Series,

Economic & Social Research Council (ESRC) – Centre for Analysis of Risk and Regulation (CARR), London: ESRC.

IMPEL (European Network for the Implementation and Enforcement of Environmental Law) 2012. *EasyTools – Risk Assessment Guidance Book.* Brussels: IMPEL.

INECE (International Network for Environmental Compliance and Enforcement), no date. *Raising Awareness, Developing Networks, Strengthening Capacity*, Brochure.

INTERPOL (International Criminal Policing Organization) 2014. *Pollution Crime Forensic Investigation Manual Volume I of II.* Lyon: INTERPOL.

INTERPOL (International Criminal Policing Organization) 2012, *1st International Chiefs of Environmental Compliance and Enforcement Summit* [Summit Report]. Lyon: INTERPOL.

Lipman, Z., 2010. 'An Evaluation of Compliance and Enforcement Mechanisms in the Environment Protection and Biodiversity Conservation Act 1999(Cth) and their Application by the Commonwealth', *Environmental and Planning Law Journal* 27, 98–112.

Lynott, J.D. and Cullinane, R. 2010. 'Administrative Sanctions', *Irish Planning and Environmental Law Journal*, 17(1), 12–21.

Macrory, R. 2006. *Regulatory Justice: Making Sanctions Effective – Final Report, November 2006.* London: Cabinet Office.

Macrory, R. 2010. *Regulation, Enforcement and Governance in Environmental Law.* Oxford and Oregon: Hart Publishing.

Moore, D. 2012. 'State and Local Environmental Enforcement', in *Environmental Crime*, 2nd edition, edited by M. Clifford and T.D. Edwards. Louisville: Jones & Bartlett Learning, 183–214.

New South Wales Environment Protection Authority (NSW EPA) 2014. *Risk-Based Licensing: Improving Environmental Regulation in NSW.* Sydney: Environment Protection Authority.

Nicol S., Evans M., Chadės I., Whitten S., Wolfe, N. and Rough, T. 2014. *Developing a Risk-Based Approach to Environmental Compliance and Monitoring.* Canberra: CSIRO.

OEE (Office of Environmental Enforcement) 2009. *A Study on the Use of Administrative Sanctions for Environmental Offences in Other Comparable Countries and Assessment of Their Possible Use in Ireland.* Ireland: Environmental Protection Agency.

OGTR (Office of the Gene Technology Regulator) 2007. *Monitoring and Compliance Framework; In accordance with the Gene Technology Act 2000.* Canberra: Commonwealth of Australia.

Pink, G., 2008. 'Building Regulatory Capacity in Environmental Agencies: Through Tailored Training', *INECE 8th International Conference on Environmental Compliance and Enforcement: 5–11 April 2008 Cape Town, South Africa, Proceedings.* London: Cameron May, 225–233.

Pink, G. 2011. 'Assessing the Utility of Environmental Enforcement Networks: In an Attempt to Maximise Benefits to Members', in *INECE 9th International Conference on Environmental Compliance And Enforcement: 20–24 June 2011 Whistler, British Columbia, Canada, Proceedings.* Washington, DC: International Network for Environmental Compliance and Enforcement, 797–804.

Pink, G. 2013. *Law Enforcement Responses to Transnational Environmental Crime: Practical Considerations and Suggested Improvements Arising from an International Analysis.* Transnational Environmental Crime Project Working Paper, Canberra: Department of International Relations, Australian National University.

Pink, G. 2015. 'Environmental Enforcement Networks: Theory, Practice and Potential', in *Environmental Enforcement Networks: Concepts, Implementation and Effectiveness*, edited by M. Faure, P. De Smedt and A. Stas. Cheltenham, UK: Edward Elgar, 13–36.

Pink, G. and Lehane, J. 2011. 'Environmental Enforcement Networks: Development of a Network Evaluation Matrix', in *INECE 9th International Conference on Environmental Compliance and Enforcement, Conference Proceedings, 20–24 June 2011, Whistler, British Columbia, Canada, Proceedings.* Washington, DC: International Network for Environmental Compliance and Enforcement, 805–821.

Pink, G. and Lehane, J. 2012. 'Environmental Enforcement Networks: Their Role in Climate Change Enforcement', in *Climate Change From a Criminological Perspective*, edited by R. White. New York: Springer, 109–133.

Raustiala, K. 2002. 'The Architecture of International Cooperation: Transgovernmental Networks and the Future of International Law', *Virginia Journal of International Law* 43(1), 1–92.

Simpson, S., Rorie, M., Alper, M.E., Schell-Busey, N., Laufer, W., and Craig Smith, N. 2014. *Corporate Crime Deterrence: A Systematic Review*. Oslo: The Campbell Collaboration.

Simpson, S., Gibbs, C., Rorie, M., Slocum, L.A., Cohen, M., and Vandenbergh, M. 2013. 'An Empirical Assessment of Corporate Environmental Crime-Control Strategies', *Journal of Criminal Law and Criminology* 103(1), 231–278.

Situ, Y. and Emmons, D. 2000. *Environmental Crime: The Criminal Justice System's Role in Protecting the Environment.* Thousand Oaks, CA: Sage.

Slaughter, A-M. 2004. *A New World Order.* New Jersey: Princeton University Press.

South, N. and Beirne, P. (eds) 2006. *Green Criminology*. Aldershot: Ashgate.

South, N., and Brisman, A. (eds) 2013. *Routledge International Handbook of Green Criminology*, London: Routledge.

Sparrow, M. 1994. *Imposing Duties: Government's Changing Approach to Compliance.* Westport, CT: Praeger.

Sparrow, M. 2000. *The Regulatory Craft: Controlling Risks, Solving Problems, and Managing Compliance.* Washington, DC: Brookings Institute Press.

Sparrow, M. 2008. *The Character of Harms: Operational Challenges in Control.* New York: Cambridge University Press.

Stas, A. 2011. 'The Flemish High Council of Environmental Enforcement – A Coordinated Environmental Enforcement Policy', *in INECE, 9th International Conference on Environmental Compliance and Enforcement: 24 June 2011, Whistler, British Columbia, Canada: Proceedings*. Washington, DC: International Network for Environmental Compliance and Enforcement, 822–833.

Taschereau, S. and Bolger, J. 2007. *Networks and Capacity*. Discussion Paper 58C, Maastricht: European Centre for Development Policy Management.

TGA (Therapeutic Goods Administration) 2012. *TGA regulatory framework.* Canberra: TGA.

Tomkins, K. 2009. 'Police, Law Enforcement and the Environment', in *Environmental Crime: A Reader*, edited by R. White. Cullompton: Willan Publishing, 515–27.

United Nations, 2000. *United Nations Convention against Transnational Organized Crime*.

UNEP (United Nations Environment Programme) 2007. *Networking Counts: Combating illegal trade in ozone depleting substances*. Paris: United Nations Environment Programme.

UNODC (United Nations Office on Drugs and Crime) 2008. *Building Capacity to Counter Trafficking in Illegal Timber and Timber Products in East Asia and the Pacific Region*, draft concept. Bangkok: UNODC.

UNODC (United Nations Office on Drugs and Crime) 2010. *The Globalization of Crime: A Transnational Organized Crime Threat Assessment.* Vienna: UNODC.

Van der Schraaf, A. 2008. 'Capacity Building in the Dutch Inspectorate: Bridging the Gap', in *INECE 8th International Conference on Environmental Compliance and Enforcement: 5–11 April 2008 Cape Town, South Africa, Proceedings*. London: Cameron May, 243–51.

White, R. 2008. *Crimes Against Nature: Environmental Criminology and Ecological Justice*. Cullompton: Willan Publishing.

White, R. (ed.), 2009. *Environmental Crime: A Reader*. Cullompton: Willan Publishing.

White, R. 2011a. *Transnational Environmental Crime: Toward an Eco-Global Criminology*. Abingdon, Oxon: Routledge.

White, R. 2011b. 'Environmental Law Enforcement: The Importance of Global Networks and Collaborative Practices', *Australasian Policing: A Journal of Professional Practice and Research* 3(1), 16–22.

White, R. and Habibis, D. 2005. *Crime and Society*. Melbourne: Oxford University Press.

White, R. and Heckenberg, D. (eds) 2014. *Green Criminology: An Introduction to the Study of Environmental Harm*. London: Routledge.

Wijbenga, B., Ruessink, H., De Wit, A., and Kapitein P. 2008. 'Environmental Policing in the 21st Century – Background, Organisation and Experience in the Netherlands', in *INECE 8th International Conference on Environmental Compliance And Enforcement, 5–11 April 2008 Cape Town, South Africa, Proceedings*. London: Cameron May, 323–33.

Willis, K. and Bricknell, B. 2012. *The Elephant in the Room: Measuring the Harm that Environmental Crime Causes*. Unpublished paper, Canberra: Australian Institute of Criminology.

Zaelke, D., Kaniaru, D. and Kružíková, E. (eds) 2005. *Making Law Work: Environmental Compliance and Sustainable Development*, Volume 2. London: Cameron May.

7 Transboundary International Fisheries Crime and Restitution for South Africa

The Case of *United States v. Bengis*, 2013

Jan Glazewski[*]

Introduction

The seventeenth-century Roman Dutch jurist Grotius, whose seminal work *Mare Liberum* laid the foundations of contemporary International Law of the Sea, in particular the various high seas freedoms including freedom of fishing,[1] expressed the view that the resources of the sea were inexhaustible (Grotius 1916).

Phenomena such as climate change, land degradation, pollution and its consequences for community health, and natural resource depletion including overfishing were largely unknown to the Roman and Dutch jurists who laid the foundations of the South African common law. The Roman law jurists, and later their Roman Dutch law counterparts, fashioned a sophisticated classification system for classifying things. Relevant to wildlife law are the categories of *res publicae*, *res omnium communes* and *res nullius*, which are still of fundamental relevance and importance in contemporary South African environmental law as this case study will show. In South African common law, wild animals including fish in the sea are classified as *res nullius*, meaning that they are owned by nobody but fall into the category of objects which can be owned (*res intra commercium*). This contrasts with *res extra commercium*, which are things incapable of private ownership, such as the sea and seashore, which were regarded as *res omnium communes*, being things owned by nobody, but enjoyed by all. Finally *res publicae* were things owned by the emperor (today the state) but on behalf of the people, such as sacred grave sites (today parks and reserves would be an arguable example).

The *Bengis* case, described below, raises a number of broad-ranging issues from questions of criminology, such as the nature of fisheries crime, to the nature

* I am indebted to the Pescadolus (www.pescadolus.org) steering committee for their support and asssitance in compiling this chapter. Responsibility for its contents reamins my own.

1 The other traditional high seas freedom was freedom of navigation and now further freedoms have been added: see Article 87 of 1982 UN Convention on Law of the Sea (UNCLOS) (21 ILM 1261 (1982)).

of who is the 'victim' of fisheries crime to hard law questions such the nature of the South African government's property interest in fish (*res nullius*) located in the country's 200 nautical mile Exclusive Economic Zone (EEZ) as well in the areas beyond national jurisdiction where complex questions of international and national enforcement jurisdiction arise.[2]

This chapter outlines the contemporary issue of the nature of fisheries crime, particularly the question of who is the victim of such crime against the backdrop of the nature of *res publicae* or the doctrine of the public trust as it is known in the United States. This was the central issue in the *Bengis* case.

Bengis[3] Case Study

During 2001 three defendants, then Cape Town based businessmen, Arnold Bengis, his son David, and business associate, Jeffrey Noll, were apprehended by South African authorities on suspicion of grossly exceeding their quota for the harvest of South African west coast and south coast rock lobster, as well as other species, and illegally smuggling their take abroad, including to the United States.[4] Their South African registered company, Hout Bay Fishing Industries (Pty) Ltd, of which they were directors, held legitimate fishing rights and quotas under the South African Marine Living Resources Act of 1998 (MLRA)[5] but when the South African authorities opened a container in a warehouse in Cape Town harbour, authorized to contain 3,600 pounds of rock lobster, they found a container that actually contained some 38,000 pounds.[6] This amount exceeded the defendants' permitted quota by over 1,000 per cent and was the first concrete evidence of a much greater criminal scheme which later investigations and court proceedings were to reveal.[7] Relevant to the question of 'victimhood' which is central to this chapter is the fact that Bengis and company were not the only perpetrators of this sophisticated transboundary fisheries crime, which commenced in South African waters and ended up in the South African and New York courts. The US Court papers identify a number of other perpetrators, including a number of South African fishery inspectors who had been bribed by Bengis and company to look the other way, as well as workers who left South Africa for the United States, who falsely posed as tourists but were actually employed by the perpetrators to process the illicitly exported resource and were also party to the sophisticated scheme.

2 See for example Witbooi (2014).

3 Case 43 ELR 20133 (No. 1–03-cf.-00308, (S.D.N.Y., 06/14/2013) (Kaplan, J.)).

4 The US Court limited its action to rock lobster captured in the South African 200 nautical mile EEZ for practical reasons, but the Court papers indicate that not only lobster but also other marine resources were illegally harvested from waters beyond South African jurisdiction.

5 Act No. 18 of 1998.

6 South Africa uses a metric system, kilograms in this case, but these figures in pounds are from US Court papers.

7 The US Court papers – discussed below. See also Glazewski (2014).

On discovery of the illegal catch, the South African authorities brought proceedings during 2002 against Hout Bay Fishing Industries (Pty) Ltd, which at the time was the largest privately registered fishing company in South Africa. The defendants' company was initially prosecuted under the South African MLRA, as well as the Customs and Excise Act 1964.[8] The three defendants had by that time left South Africa and were resident in the United States. However Arnold Bengis returned on behalf of the company to enter a plea of guilty to several charges under the South African MLRA in relation to the smuggling scheme. They were subsequently prosecuted under the US Lacey Act 1900, before being subjected to a civil restitution claim under the Mandatory Victims Restitution Act 1996 (MVRA).[9] The question of restitution was not considered by the South African courts but enjoyed a long and protracted journey through two hearings in the New York District Court, eventually culminating in the US Appeal Court which issued the restitution order described below.

As regards the South African prosecution, the company paid a fine of South African Rand 12m (approximately US$1.2 million) and forfeited two vessels, as well as the container seized by the government. This was a paltry sanction in relation to the magnitude of the criminal scheme, as outlined below. As regards the US criminal action and later a civil claim, the US Southern District Court for New York handed down a restitution order in favour of South Africa in an amount of over US$29 million for the illegal harvest of tons of rock lobster after a long and drawn out battle in both the criminal and civil courts as described below.[10] This has been described as the biggest wildlife crime prosecuted under the US Lacey Act[11] (Asner 2013) with the order representing the culmination of a lengthy legal process spanning the South African and US courts.

The case raises a broad-ranging set of questions from 'hard' law issues such as the South African government's property interest in a natural resource which is classified as *res nullius* in the country's common law for purposes of a restitution claim, to economic issues relating to the quantification of damage of common property resources and related marine ecosystems, to organized crime pertaining to a transboundary natural resource, to various issues in criminology touching on attitudes to fisheries related crime. The main issue discussed below focuses on 'victimhood' in the case of *res nullius.* Before doing so the relevant South African and US legislation is outlined partly to explain how a departure was made from the general rule that criminal prosecutions and accompanying restitution claims cannot be brought extra-territorially.

8 Act No. 91 of 1964, s 84(1).

9 18 U.S. Code § 3663A.

10 Westlaw citation: 2013 WL 2922292. The exact amount was $29,495,800, but the Court reduced the amount of restitution by $7,49,080, the latter being the amount that the defendants had already paid South Africa in respect of the criminal proceedings.

11 16 USC §§ 3377–3378.

The Nature of Fisheries Crime

In one of the court proceedings referred to below, the US Appeal Court referred to a judgment in the lower New York District Court,[12] in the following terms:

> In ruling, Judge Kaplan remarked on Arnold Bengis's 'astonishing display of the arrogance of wealth and power. Among other things, Judge Kaplan pointed to the facts, undisputed by the defendants, that Arnold Bengis, during the course of the United States investigation, had: (i) withheld documents responsive to grand jury subpoenas; (ii) shredded important documents to keep them from the hands of U.S. law enforcement; and (iii) even hired a private investigator to follow the United States agents during their investigation'.[13]

The classic utilitarian model of crime generally developed by Becker (1968) from the work of Bentham (1907 [1789]) and others is that an individual commits a crime if the expected utility from committing the crime exceeds the utility from engaging in the legitimate activity.[14] In the *Bengis* case the perpetrators came from a wide spectrum of economic actors and included not only the three named corporate directors of Hout Bay Fishing (Pty) Ltd, but also the company itself as well as government officials who were bribed as well as workers who were flown from South Africa to the United States posing as 'tourists' to circumvent immigration control but who were actually employed as fish processors. In the course of the legal proceeding Arnold Bengis stated that his activities promoted the economy by developing the hitherto underdeveloped South African rock lobster market. This raises an interesting series of questions regarding whether the maximizing utility theory can be applied evenly to different sectors of societal actors, as clearly the other perpetrators were driven by different motivations.

These questions are not pursued here. Rather this chapter develops the theme of environmental crime and its victims (Spapens et al. 2014) by focusing on the question of who is the 'victim' in the case of illegal capture of *res nullius* (fish in the sea), in the case of Bengis, and second, how the victim is compensated, how that compensation is calculated in the case of a common property resource, and how much constitutes adequate compensation?

South African Legislation

The South African MLRA includes standard provisions, which make it an offence to harvest, process or possess fish without a permit, as well as to breach permit conditions as was done in this matter, in that quota allocations were exceeded by

12 2007 WL 2669315 (S.D.N.Y.).

13 United States Court of Appeals for the Second Circuit, Docket No 07–4895-cr. The US Court of Appeals judgment is outlined below.

14 Becker (1968 at p. 176 referring to Bentham 1789). See also Kuperan and Sutinen (1998).

a significant amount for a period of over a decade.[15] Significantly, the opening sections of the MLRA include a set of objectives and principles which are relevant to the question of the role of the state in acting as custodian of the nation's fish resources and damage to ecosystems. The following provisions are relevant in that they provide statutory guidelines on how the minister and his or her officials are to exercise discretion under the Act:

a. The need to achieve optimum utilisation and ecologically sustainable development of marine living resources;
b. the need to conserve marine living resources for both present and future generations;
c. the need to apply precautionary approaches in respect of the management and development of marine living resources;
d. the need to utilise marine living resources to achieve economic growth, human resource development, capacity building within fisheries and mariculture branches, employment creation and a sound ecological balance consistent with the development objectives of the national government;
e. the need to protect the ecosystem as a whole, including species which are not targeted for exploitation;
f. the need to preserve marine biodiversity.[16]

These provisions point to the possible '*res publicae*' or trustee role that the state plays in safeguarding the nation's natural resources. This point is included as one of the national environmental management principles of the framework National Environmental Management Act of 1998 (NEMA[17]) in the following terms: 'The environment is held in trust for the people, the beneficial use of environmental resources must serve the public interest and the environment must be protected as the people's common heritage'.[18]

Of further relevance is a provision headed 'Compensation and Restitution' in the Criminal Procedure Act of 1977[19] which provides that a 'court may award compensation where an offence causes damage to or loss of property'.[20] This section grants the court a discretion, following the conviction of an offence, to order compensation for damages at the instance of the victim or the prosecutor subject to certain conditions. To the best of the writer's knowledge this section has never

15 Ss 13(1), 58(1)(a)(i); and the applicable regulations (*Government Gazette 19205Government Notice R1111 in, dated 2 September 1998* as amended), namely ss 27(1)(c) and (f), 44(1) and 54, which relate to permit offences; and s 85(2), which makes it an offence to transfer at sea any fish without supervision of a fishery control officer.

16 S 2.

17 Act No.73 of 1998.

18 NEMA, s 2(4)(o).

19 Act No. 51 of 1977.

20 S 300(1).

been evoked subsequent to the successful prosecution of an environmental crime in South Africa. The issue of restitution is taken up below.[21]

US Legislation

The cornerstone of the US based litigation was the Lacey Act. The Act is the United States' oldest wildlife protection law having been enacted over a century ago in 1900.[22] Its stated purpose is: '[to protect] those species of fish and wildlife whose continued existence is presently threatened' by 'gradually drying up the international market for endangered species', thus 'reducing the poaching of any such species in the country where it is found'.[23]

The original objective of the over-100-year-old statute was to address issues including the interstate shipment of unlawfully killed game, the introduction of harmful invasive species, and the killing of birds for the feather trade. The Act has been amended a number of times and broadened to combat trafficking in illegal wildlife, fish and, more recently, to combat illegal trade in plants and plant products. An initial question is on what basis could the perpetrators of a crime committed in South Africa be prosecuted in the United States? A crucial section in the Lacey Act states:

> It is unlawful for any person –
>
> (2) to import, export, transport, sell, receive, acquire, or purchase in interstate or foreign commerce (A) any fish or wildlife taken, possessed, transported, or sold in violation of any law or regulation of any State or *in violation of any foreign law*. [own emphasis][24]

It is thus evident that the emphasized phrase 'in violation of any foreign law' results in the US courts having extra-territorial jurisdiction where the listed wildlife crimes are committed beyond US territory and are the subject of 'foreign commerce'. More specifically the Lacey Act provides the opportunity to prosecute transgressions of foreign law within the United States itself. Congressman Lacey envisioned a three-fold purpose when he introduced it at the beginning of the twentieth century and they were: (1) to authorize the introduction and preservation of game, song and insectivorous wild birds; (2) to prevent the 'unwise' introduction of foreign birds and animals; and (3) to supplement state laws for the protection of game and birds. But it has been considerably modified and amended since its inception (Anderson 1995, p. 6).

Today the Lacey Act has taken on a different hue. As noted by the lead Counsel in the *Bengis* case, who pointed out in subsequent testimony before the US House

21 See Fourie (2009, pp. 93–127).

22 For a thorough survey of the Lacey Act see Anderson (1995, p. 85).

23 *United States* v. *Bernal*, 90 F.3d 465, 467 (11th Cir.1996).

24 16 U.S.C. § 3372(a)(2)(A).

of Representatives 'the Lacey Act is an important tool for law enforcement in the on-going effort to combat sophisticated criminal organisations and to protect legitimate businesses and US consumers. Lacey Act prosecutions have been used to disrupt large-scale criminal organizations with illegal behaviour extending beyond fish, wildlife, and plant violations'. He pointed out that when he was a prosecutor, he experienced first-hand how the Lacey Act can be used as a tool to: (1) dismantle criminal operations and deter illegal activities that are having economic and environmental impacts; (2) protect US interests; and (3) protect the victims of environmental crimes (Asner 2013).

It has been noted that while Congressman John Lacey has not received such wide acclaim as other historic US conservationists such as John Muir and Aldo Leopold, 'his legacy remains vibrant and effective today in the form of a law that is arguably our nation's most effective tool in the fight against an illegal wildlife trade whose size, profitability, and threat to global biodiversity Lacey could probably not have imagined' (Anderson 1995, pp. 36–7).

Apart from the Lacey Act, a further key US law in this matter is the MVRA. This statute, which applies to criminal prosecutions generally and not only to wildlife crime, makes restitution a mandatory part of sentencing for a specific set of property interest crimes and related crimes to commit conspiracy including under the Lacey Act.[25] Under the MVRA, restitution is mandatory in all cases involving 'an offense against *property* under this title [Title 18] . . . including any offense committed by fraud and deceit',[26] 'in which an identifiable victim or victims has suffered a . . . pecuniary loss'.[27]

The key issue is the question of who is the identifiable victim or victims in the *Bengis* case; more particularly whether the South African government, on whose behalf the United States claimed restitution, can be regarded as such. The MVRA defines the term 'victim' as:

> a person directly and proximately harmed as a result of the commission of an offense for which restitution may be ordered including, in the case of an offense that involves as an element a scheme, conspiracy, or pattern of criminal activity, any person directly harmed by the defendant's criminal conduct in the course of the scheme, conspiracy, or pattern.[28]

Under the MVRA, restitution is mandatory rather than discretionary for defendants convicted of certain offences, including offences against property committed by fraud or deceit.[29] Specifically the MVRA reads: 'Notwithstanding any other provision of law, when sentencing a defendant convicted of an offence described

25 S 3663A.
26 § 3663A(c)(1)(A)(ii) (emphasis added).
27 § 3663A(c)(1)(B).
28 18 U.S.C. s 3663A(a)(2).
29 18 U.S.C. § 3663A(a)(1) (1996).

in subsection (c), the court *shall order* . . . that the defendant make restitution to the victim of the offence or, if the victim is deceased to victim's estate' [own emphasis].[30]

A related and further relevant US statue is the Voluntary Witness Protection Act (VWPA),[31] and under which the United States also pursued restitution for losses suffered by South Africa. This act empowers district courts to order restitution to 'victims'.[32] The MVRA and VWPA are similar in that the MVRA was enacted in 1996 and amended the VWPA. While similar, the MVRA contains some notable differences from the previous Act.[33] The VWPA previously held that 'the court, when sentencing a defendant convicted of an offence under this title . . . *may* order . . . that the defendant make restitution to any victim of such offence' [own emphasis].[34] In addition, and in contrast to the VWPA, the US district courts do not consider a defendant's financial circumstances when determining the amount of restitution to be paid. The MVRA states, 'In each order of restitution, the courts shall order restitution to each victim in the full amount of each victim's losses as determined by the court and without consideration of the economic circumstances of the defendant'.[35] By making restitution mandatory rather than discretionary for defendants convicted of certain offences, the MVRA is viewed as the more 'pro-victim' law.[36] Further, by disregarding the defendant's financial means when calculating restitution, the MVRA creates more opportunities for victim self-help.

The Lacey Act thus provided the opportunity to prosecute transgressions of foreign law within the United States itself. In this instance, the relevant foreign law transgression to which the statue refers was a contravention by the defendants of South Africa's Customs and Excise Act,[37] and the applicable permitting scheme required by the MLRA together with its regulations.[38] The MVRA and VWPA on the other hand provide the opportunity to claim restitution under US law for

30 18 U.S.C. § 3663A(c)(1)(ii) (1996).

31 18 U.S.C. s 3663.

32 Section 3663(a)(1)(A), which provides that '[t]he court, when sentencing a defendant convicted under this title [Title 18,] may order . . . that the defendant make restitution to any victim of such offense'. Importantly, this statute defines 'victim' as being 'a person directly and proximately harmed as a result of the commission of an offense for which restitution may be ordered including, in the case of an offense that involves as an element a scheme, conspiracy, or pattern of criminal activity, any person directly harmed by the defendant's criminal conduct in the course of the scheme, conspiracy, or pattern'. 18 U.S.C. § 3663(a)(2).

33 *United States* v. *Szarwark*, 168 F.3d 993 (7th Cir. 1999).

34 18 U.S.C. § 3663(a)(1) (1995).

35 18 U.S.C. § 3664(f)(1)(A) (1996).

36 *United States* v. *Perry* v. *Hossler* 360 F.3d 519 (6th Cir. 2004).

37 Act No. 91 of 1964 s 84(1).

38 Act 18 of 1998 ss 13(1), 58(1)(a)(i) (which together make it an offence to harvest, process or possess fish without a permit); and the applicable regulations (*Government Gazette 19205Government Notice R1111 in, dated 2 September 1998* as amended), namely ss 27(1)(c) and (f); 44(1); 54; which relate to permit offences and s 85(2) which makes it an offence to transfer at sea any fish without supervision of a fishery control officer.

environmental crimes committed outside that country if the proceeds of the crime find their way to the United States.

Of indirect relevance and not relevant in the *Bengis* case directly is the European Union Directive 2012/29/EU of 25 October 2012, establishing minimum standards on the rights, support and protection of victims of crime.[39] It defines 'victim' as meaning: 'a natural person who has suffered harm, including physical, mental or emotional harm or economic loss which was directly caused by a criminal offence; family members of a person whose death was directly caused by a criminal offence and who have suffered harm as a result of that person's death' (Definitions Article 2 (1) (a)).

Clearly this definition is unhelpful in the case of environmental crime particularly where the object of the crime is a *res nullius* and there is no readily identifiable victim, alternatively a number of different categories of victim. Potential victims in the *Bengis* matter included: other quota holders whose legitimate Total Allowable Catch (TAC) could not be met because of the excessive take by Bengis and company; employees of other legitimate quota holders and arguably the marine environment itself as Bengis' excessive catch undoubtedly resulted in disturbance of the ecosystem balance. These questions are pertinent to the issue of how the restitution amount of US$29 million will be allocated, a matter which has not been resolved at the time of writing (November 2015) as among other things Bengis launched counter proceedings against the South African government and other parties during 2015.

The above outline of the relevant legislation leads to the key issue whether the South African government, on whose behalf the United States brought a restitution claim, can be regarded as a 'victim' in the *Bengis* matter. More specifically the question is whether the state can be regarded as a victim insofar as it may be regarded as having a custodian or trusteeship role in fisheries resources generally in its 200 nautical mile EEZ. In line with the above classification of things the question is whether the fish stock as whole, as opposed to individual fish, can be regarded as *res publicae* (held by the state on behalf of the people) in South African law or whether the doctrine of the public trust, a related US notion, can be of assistance in determining questions of 'victimhood'. A related question considered by the US courts as outlined below is whether the South African government has a property interest in a *res nullius* resource.

The Doctrine of the Public Trust

The United States

The public trust doctrine refers to a state's duty to manage, preserve and protect certain resources for the benefit of its citizens (Kanner 2005, p. 62). It provides that certain natural resources are held by the sovereign in trust and on behalf of

39 *Official Journal of the European Union* L 315/57 dated 14 November 2012.

the public because of their unique characteristics and central importance (Kameri-Mbote 2007, p. 197). Simply defined, it provides that these resources belong to the public as a whole and that private owners may not deprive the public of access and enjoyment of these resources; the state, as public trustee, being enjoined to ensure this. Of relevance is that the state has a legal authority and in fact bears a duty, to seek damages and interdictory relief against those who cause harm to these resources (Kanner 2005, p. 62).

The notion of a public trust doctrine played a central role in the heyday of the US environmental movement during the 1970s, largely due to the ideas propounded by Joseph Sax (Sax 1970, p. 471).[40] The doctrine is encapsulated in the nineteenth-century case of *Illinois Central Railroad Company*,[41] which concerned the validity of a grant by the State of Illinois of a portion of shorefront land on Lake Michigan. In holding the grant invalid, the Court held: '[w]hen a state holds a resource which is available for the free use of the general public, a court will look with considerable skepticism upon any government conduct which is calculated either to reallocate that resource to more restricted uses or to subject public uses to the self-interest of private parties'.[42] In the United States, the doctrine traditionally applied only to tidelands and waters used in navigation, water-related commerce and fisheries. It has, however, been extended to also apply to national parks, inland lakes and wildlife (Buck 2006).

The doctrine seems to resemble the Roman law which classified certain property as not being capable of private ownership (*res extra commercium*) and suggested that certain property belonged to the people and was referred to as *res universitas* (Lee 1956). In Roman law, categories of *res extra commercium* included *res publicae* and *res omnium communes* (things that belong to no one but are enjoyed by all, for example, the air that we breathe). Although it is an ancient concept, it is currently topical, having been discussed in the context of the Rio+20 conference (Turnipseed et al. 2012).

South Africa

The question whether the South African government has a property interest in the lobster resource in its 200 nautical mile EEZ, as opposed to a mere regulatory one, arose in both the US courts. The argument that was presented on behalf of South Africa was that although individual fish in the sea may be *res nullius* under South African common law, the stocks as a whole could be regarded as *res publicae*, implying that the South African government acts as custodian of the fish on behalf of the people of South Africa. This form of property interest is akin to that of a custodian or trustee. As pointed out above this is echoed in one of the principles in the NEMA of 1998, which states: '[t]he environment is

40 See also Delgado (1991, p. 1209).

41 146 US 387 (1892).

42 146 US 387 (1892) at 422.

held in public trust for the people, the beneficial use of environmental resources must serve the public interest and the environment must be protected as the people's common heritage'.[43] It was pointed out that under South African common law, which has its roots in the Roman Dutch law, fish in the sea or wild animals roaming in the open field are classified as *res nullius*, meaning they are owned by nobody but are subject to capture by anybody. This is in contrast to *res publicae*, which are objects owned by the state (the emperor in Roman law times) on behalf of and for the enjoyment of the general populace. The common law has been modified by statute law; in this case the MLRA makes it a criminal offence to take part in activities of the sort in which the defendants were involved. However, it was argued by the defendants that South Africa was exercising its regulatory powers and that this did not have a bearing on the question whether the country had a property interest in fish occurring in its EEZ. The District Court upheld this argument, noting that 'South Africa did not own the fish in question'.[44]

However this was reversed by the Court of Appeals, which did not find it necessary to delve into the nature of 'property' in South African law, but found that South Africa, having been deprived of revenues that it was due, did have a property interest in the resource.[45] The Court thus concluded that the defendants' conduct in depriving South Africa of that revenue is an offence against property and that it does have a property interest in the resource, although it did not literally own the lobster resource.[46]

It is this writer's view that the US Court of Appeals came to the correct conclusion as regards South Africa's property interest in the marine resources in its EEZ. However, it is suggested that it could have better grounded its argument by relying on the similarities between the US notion of the public trust and the South African common law notion of *res publicae*. It could be added that since the advent of 200 nautical mile EEZs, coastal states enjoy sovereign rights over natural resources in 'their' 200 nautical mile zones, further adding a trusteeship flavour to the states' interest in fish stocks in coastal states' EEZs.

As pointed out by Van der Schyff, the principles behind this doctrine can be commonly found across many jurisdictions (Van der Schyff 2010, pp. 125–39). In France, for example, a clear distinction is made between *le domain public* and *propiété* (private ownership), similarly in Germany there is the concept that a 'certain category of property can be removed from the sphere of private property altogether' (Van der Schyff 2010, p. 123). or where 'a certain category of property rights can be transformed into public-law rights for the sake of more effective control' (Van der Schyff 2010, pp. 123–4). The United States, which coined the

43 NEMA s 2(4)(o).

44 *United States of America* v. *Bengis et al* 2007 WL 2669315.

45 Case 43 ELR 20133, (No. 1–03-cf.-00308, (S.D.N.Y., 06/14/2013) (Kaplan, J.)), discussion at pp. 5–7

46 Case 43 ELR 20133, (No. 1–03-cf.-00308, (S.D.N.Y., 06/14/2013) (Kaplan, J.)), pp. 5–7.

phrase of the public trust doctrine, has the most jurisprudence on this concept and accordingly the analysis focuses on its development within this jurisdiction.

The US Courts

Pursuant to the guilty pleas and finalization of the criminal proceedings, the United States sought restitution on South Africa's behalf under the MVRA for damage that the criminal activity caused to South Africa.[47] As seen above the MVRA stipulates that restitution is mandatory in all cases involving 'an offense against *property* . . . including any offense committed by fraud and deceit',[48] 'in which an identifiable victim or victims has suffered a . . . pecuniary loss'.[49] The New York District Court relied on the VWPA,[50] under which the United States pursued restitution for losses suffered by South Africa which provided the opportunity to claim restitution under US law for environmental crimes committed outside that country if the proceeds of the crime find their way to the United States.[51]

It is striking that despite acknowledging that South Africa has a regulatory interest in the marine resources of its coastal waters, the Court held that such an interest was equivalent to an interest which had no financial value and that the public trust doctrine was insufficient to warrant South Africa's interest in the fish to be treated as a form of property. It held that had South Africa sold fishing rights at a cost, then perhaps the finding would be different, however, that not being the case it was difficult to see how South Africa had incurred any financial loss in the circumstances.[52] It also relied on evidence that the TAC[53] of rock lobster had (at the time of judgment) begun to increase and that perhaps, if anyone, it was Hout Bay Fisheries' competitors who had suffered a financial loss and who may have been entitled to claim as outlined by a report commissioned by the Court (Peck Report I 2006).[54] The Court also rejected the argument made by the defendants that the applicants had vacillated on whether it was the people of South Africa or the government which owned the resource, finding it a point of mere semantics. It was held that whichever way it was framed neither the people nor their government enjoyed title to claim. This raises the question of whether South Africa's financial interest in its wild natural resources is too 'remote' in the legal sense to

47 18 USC §3663A.

48 § 3663A(c)(1)(A)(ii).

49 § 3663A(c)(1)(B) (emphasis added).

50 18 USC § 3663.

51 *Pasquantino* v. *United States* 544 US 349 (2005), 365.

52 Ibid.

53 The total allocated number of rock lobster per year from which fishing permits and rights may be issued.

54 *United States* v. *Bengis* 2006 WL 3735654 (SDNY, Dec. 19, 2006) (Peck, M.J.) (Peck Report I 2006') as adopted by Kaplan DJ in *United States* v. *Bengis*, 2007 WL 241370 (SDNY, Jan. 29, 2007).

warrant a legal entitlement. Does its role as trustee of the nation's environmental resources render its interest as merely regulatory and insufficient to claim damages to ensure the sustainability and viability of the resource? The matter raises an interesting question of whether wild animals which have not been captured, at least in terms of South African law, amount to property, and if so what type of interest does the state hold in it before it is captured?

Be that as it may, after the first hearing in the New York District Court, it recommended that the United States' request for restitution be denied on two grounds (Peck Report I 2006). The judge noted that the United States sought restitution primarily under the MVRA, which makes restitution a mandatory component of sentencing only for specific types of crime. Under the MVRA, restitution is mandatory in all cases involving 'an offense against *property* under this title [Title 18] . . . including any offense committed by fraud and deceit',[55] 'in which an identifiable victim or victims has suffered a . . . pecuniary loss'.[56] The MVRA defines the term 'victim' as: 'a person directly and proximately harmed as a result of the commission of an offense for which restitution may be ordered including, in the case of an offense that involves as an element a scheme, conspiracy, or pattern of criminal activity, any person directly harmed by the defendant's criminal conduct in the course of the scheme, conspiracy, or pattern'.[57]

The judge found that the Republic of South Africa did not suffer any independent pecuniary loss and therefore was not entitled to restitution (Peck Report I 2006, p. 8). More specifically, the South African government had no property interest in the lobster resource in its EEZ, only a regulatory one. In the judge's words:

> Defendants' actual taking of the fish from South African waters was not an offence against property against the Government's designated victim, South Africa, because under South African law, South Africa does not own the wildlife in its waters and therefore had none of its 'property' taken by defendants.
> (Peck Report I 2006, p. 6)

It went on to state:

> An appropriate analogy is to compare South Africa's MLRA to regulation of air emissions from smokestacks. While a government has regulatory power over the amount of noxious emissions that smokestacks can emit, a government clearly has no ownership or property interest in the air in the atmosphere or the emissions from a smokestack. Similarly, while South Africa clearly has regulatory power over how fishing companies operate in South

55 § 3663A(c)(1)(A)(ii).

56 § 3663A(c)(1)(B) (emphasis added).

57 18 USC § 3663A(a)(2).

> African waters, under its own laws it has no ownership or property interest in the wildlife that lives in those waters.
>
> (Peck Report I 2006, p. 7)

However, this, as well as South Africa's property interest in the resource, was to come up on appeal as outlined below.

The United States Court of Appeals,[58] heard argument on two questions: first, whether the District Court erred in concluding that South Africa has no property interest in the overharvested lobsters; and second, whether the District Court erred in concluding that South Africa was not properly considered a 'victim' under the MVRA and VWPA. As regards the question of South Africa's property interest in the illegally harvested rock lobsters, it found that the defendants':

> conspiracy to conceal their illegal trade in lobster deprived South Africa of money it was due. Had the defendants not undertaken efforts to conceal their overharvesting, including off-loading overharvested lobsters at night and under-reporting the amounts of their catch to South African authorities, those lobsters caught in excess of the legal limits would have been seized and sold by the government. As a consequence, the defendants' conduct deprived South Africa of proceeds from the sale of the illegally harvested lobsters.[59]

On the second point, the Court found that the District Court's decision to reject restitution under the MVRA and VWPA was premised on an overly narrow interpretation of the term 'property'. This 'property interest' question is elaborated on below. The Court also ruled that South Africa was entitled to damages, but specifically refused to express an opinion on the difficult task of calculating the *quantum* of damage and referred the issue back to the District Court to quantify. This latter issue is not pursued here.

Conclusions

The above survey illustrates some of the issues in dealing with transnational fisheries crime, in particular the question of identifying who is the victim; whether the State is a 'victim' given its potential role as custodian of the nation's resources and the possible *res publicae* nature of fish stocks as a whole in South Africa's EEZ as opposed to individual fish in the sea which are indisputably *res nullius* in South African common law. If the state is indeed a victim and entitled to restitution then the further question is what is the state's role in distributing the compensation received among other varied classes of victims and how they are to be identified. Many questions remain in this regard.

58 631 F.3d 33, 35–37 (2d Cir. 2011).

59 Case 43 ELR 20133, (No. 1–03-cf.-00308, (S.D.N.Y., 06/14/2013) (Kaplan, J.)), p. 6.

References

Anderson, R.S. 1995. 'The Lacey Act: America's Premier Weapon in the Fight against Unlawful Wildlife Trafficking', *Public Land Law Review* 16, 27–63.

Asner, M. 2013. Testimony before the US House of Representatives Committee on Natural Resources Sub-Committee on Fisheries, Wildlife, Oceans and Insular Affairs: Oversight Hearings on the 2008 Lacey Act Amendments, 16 May.

Becker, G. 1968. 'Crime and Punishment: An Economic Approach', *Journal of Political Economy* 76(2), 169–217.

Bentham, J. 1907 [1789]. *An Introduction to the Principles of Morals and Legislation*. Oxford: Clarendon Press.

Buck, S. 2006. *Understanding Environmental Law and Administration*, third edition. Washington, DC: Island Press.

Delgado, R. 1991. 'Our Better Natures: A Revisionist View of Joseph Sax's Public Trust Theory of Environmental Protection, and Some Dark Thoughts on the Possibility of Law Reform', *Vanderbilt Law Review* 44, 1209–26.

Fourie, M. 2009. 'How Civil and Administrative Penalties can Change the Face of Environmental Compliance in South Africa', *South African Journal of Environmental Law and Policy* 16(2), 93–127.

Glazewski, J. 2014. 'United States v. Bengis: A Victory for Wildlife Law and Lessons for International Fisheries Crime', *The International Journal of Marine and Coastal Law*, 173–83.

Grotius, H. 1916. *The Freedom of the Seas* (trans. D. Von Mogoffin). New York: Oxford University Press.

Kameri-Mbote, P. 2007. 'The Use of the Public Trust Doctrine in Environmental Law', *Law, Environment and Development Journal* 3(2), 195–202.

Kanner, A. 2005. 'The Public Trust Doctrine; Parens Patriae, and the Attorney General as the Guardian of the State's Natural Resources', *Duke Environmental Law and Policy* 16, 57–116.

Kuperan, K. and Sutinen, J.G. 1998. 'Blue Water Crime: Deterrence, Legitimacy, and Compliance', *Fisheries Law & Society Review* 32(2), 309–38.

Lee, R.W. 1956. *The Elements of Roman Law*, fourth edition. London: Sweet & Maxwell.

Peck Report. 2006/2007. Cited in United States v. Bengis, 03 Cr. 0308, 2007 WL 241370 (S.D.N.Y. Jan. 29, 2007) (Kaplan, D.J.), adopting 2006 WL 3735654 (S.D.N.Y. Dec. 19, 2006) (Peck MJ).

Sax, J. 1970. 'The Public Trust Doctrine in Natural Resource Law: Effective Judicial Intervention', *Michigan Law Review* 68, 471–566.

Spapens, T., White, R. and Kluin, M. (eds). 2014. *Environmental Crime and its Victims: Perspectives within Green Criminology*. Farnham: Ashgate.

Turnipseed, M., Berkman, J., Blumm, M., Crowder, L., Currie, D., Gjerde, K., Longest, R., Osherenko, G., Parenteau, P., Roady, S., Sagarin, R., Sand, P. and Wood, M. 2012. *The Public Trust Doctrine and Rio+20*. Available at: www.e-joussour.net/files/The%20Public%20Trust%20Doctrine%20and%20Rio%20+20_0.pdf (accessed 25 March 2015).

Van der Schyff, E. 2010. 'Unpacking the Public Trust Doctrine: A Journey into Foreign Territory', *PER/PELJ* 13(5), 121–89.

Witbooi, E. 2014. 'Illegal, Unreported and Unregulated Fishing on the High Seas: The Port States Measures Agreement in Context', *International Journal of Marine and Coastal Law* 17(3), 290–320.

8 Four Problems for Specialist Courts in Dealing with Nonhuman Environmental Victims

Rob White

Introduction

A perennial issue within green criminology is the perception that the formal institutions of criminal justice do not take environmental crime seriously enough. Whilst there is plenty of evidence to substantiate this claim (*Cf.* South and Brisman 2013; White and Heckenberg 2014), there are also important exceptions to this general rule (see for example, Walters and Westerhuis 2013; White 2013a). The reasons why range from social and legal ambiguities over definitions of harm, through to the inadequate operational knowledge of courts in responding to specific offences and/or in assigning suitable penalties for environmental offenders.

As the central fulcrum upon which justice hinges, the dynamics and nature of the court have a major bearing on what occurs prior to a case, what happens during a case, and what happens after a case has been officially processed. Environmental crime has typically been assigned low value by magistrates and judges, as reflected objectively in sentencing outcomes (i.e., sentencing patterns over time in relation to various environmental offences) (see de Prez 2000a; de Prez 2000b; Fogel and Lipovsek 2013), although this is due to a variety of definitional, investigatory, evidentiary and social reasons (Bell and McGillivray 2008; White 2011), and there is some indication that this is changing (Walters and Westerhuis 2013).

Revisiting these critiques is not the concern of this chapter. As indicated, these issues are now being addressed in several different ways, including through the development of specialist environmental knowledge within legal forums. Rather, the intention is to delve more deeply into the jurisprudential quagmire faced by courts as they attempt to unpack and respond to environmental harm. For sake of illustration, this chapter presumes that specialist courts can and do have greater insight into the nature of environmental offences. Such institutions represent a significant step-up when it comes to both comprehending the extent and nature of environmental harm and in providing remedies that best match the offence in question. For these courts, taking environmental crime seriously is their express mandate. Therefore, the concern is less about urging these courts to be more proactive, punitive and/or pragmatic in dealing with environmental crime, than with understanding some of the basic challenges they face in dealing with highly complex technical and philosophical matters.

The specific topic of nonhuman environmental victims is raised here as a substantive matter for deliberation by environment courts in particular. This is of interest to green criminologists since it pertains to eco-justice issues and how these are dealt with institutionally. Green criminology broadly deals with matters pertaining to environmental justice (in which humans are the victims), ecological justice (in which specific eco-systems are the victims) and species justice (in which nonhuman animals are the victims) (White 2013b). Nonhuman environmental victims include natural objects such as rivers, mountains and oceans, as well as flora (plant life) and fauna (animal life). Consideration of the nonhuman environmental victim incorporates discussion of individual landscape features and specific living entities, through to particular eco-systems. Any particular eco-system is made up of both abiotic components (air, water, soil, atoms and molecules) and biotic components (plants, animals, bacteria and fungi) (Merchant 2005). Global processes that affect the biotic and abiotic around the world, such as climate change, are very pertinent to any discussion of the nonhuman environmental victim.

This chapter describes the difficulties associated with legal proceedings involving nonhuman environmental victims in terms of four key socio-legal problems. These include: the problem of victimisation, the problem of ontology, the problem of expertise, and the problem of temporality. In outlining these problems the intention is to provide a platform for later in-depth examination of the practical complexities facing environment courts in responding to the plight of nonhuman environmental victims.

Harm and Environmental Courts

The overall aim of criminal law is to prevent certain kinds of behaviour regarded as harmful or potentially harmful. The purpose of criminal law varies, and involves a constant weighing up of moral wrongness, individual autonomy, and community welfare (Findlay et al. 1994). What falls within the ambit of criminal law (and what does not) is the outcome of a social process that is ongoing and inherently political, since it embodies basic principles and visions of the kind of society people prefer to live in, and differential capacities to exert power and persuasion in the making of key decisions.

A primary task of criminal law is to stipulate the degree of seriousness of criminal conduct. This involves assessing such factors as the physical impact on the victim, psychological trauma, the monetary value of property crimes and so forth. Social scientists argue that it is 'harm' that needs to be measured and assessed, but in doing so, the study of crime must go beyond existing legal definitions and criteria (Hillyard et al. 2004; Hillyard and Tombs 2007; Matthews and Kauzlarich 2007; Pemberton 2015).

When it comes to environmental victimisation, there are extra-legal concepts and factors to consider if the nature of environmental harm is to be fully captured; this requires a different framing of the issues. For example, an ecology-based analysis of activity provides quite a different picture of 'harm' than an economic-based analysis. What is defined as criminal harm, and the measure of the seriousness of that harm, are contingent upon the social interests bound up with the definitional process (White 2013a; White 2013b).

Most fundamentally, the basis for environmental harm often incorporates contradictory and at times opposing social, legal and economic principles and practices. Environmental crime is typically defined on a continuum ranging from strict legal definitions through to broad harm perspectives (White and Heckenberg 2014).

The matter of legality – the separation between legal and illegal – is far from trivial when it comes to environmental harm. This is not simply a question of distinguishing 'harm' from 'legality' as such, and critiquing certain types of ecologically harmful, but legal, practices such as clear-felling forests. From a criminal justice perspective, the issue goes much deeper, to the heart of why environmental crime itself is consistently under-valued in law:

> Of note is the consistent use of the preface 'illegal' in the listed activities constituting environmental crime, a preface not regularly employed when describing other categories of crime. This reflects the fact that some component or level of these activities is still condoned and that it only becomes illegal once a set boundary has been passed. The tipping point of illegality contrasts environmental crimes with other established criminal offences.
>
> (Bricknell 2010, p. 4)

Cutting down trees and pulling species out of the ocean are thus NOT intrinsically criminal or 'bad' activities from the point of view of the law. It is the context that makes something allowable or problematic. Assessment of potential harm is based upon evaluation of uncertainty and estimates of probability. Assessment of cost-benefit is driven by expediency and threshold acceptance of a level of paradoxical harm, that is, harm that is consciously induced and intended for the (presumed) sake of a greater good. In other words, when dealing with environmental matters a court ideally, has to take into account various and diverse calculations of harm, risk and utility.

The ambiguities and complex harms generated by and associated with environmental crime demand responses that are flexible and multi-dimensional. From the point of view of jurisprudence and the operation of the court, specialist environmental courts that operate on the basis of problem-solving methods would seem to be the most likely to succeed in achieving the mission of eco-justice. At the very least, specialist expertise and knowledge is required to adjudicate and respond to cases involving non-human environmental victims.

Specialist Expertise and Environment Courts

The notion of 'special expertise' in dealing with environmental harms and crimes does not rest solely in the establishment of specific and separate environmental courts (White 2013a). This is especially undesirable in jurisdictions which have experienced the recent consolidation of a wide range of criminal matters (including environmental) into generalist courts (as opposed to the development of crime-specific and client-specific specialist tribunals, courts and agencies). What is more vital is the development and growth of specific expertise around environmental matters, specialist knowledge that is able to assess the value of the harm, degree of seriousness, and extent and nature of victimisation, and to propose remedies suited to the nature of the crime and its perpetrator(s). Analysing instances where such expertise has been institutionalised within criminal justice – as in the case of specialist environmental courts –can provide an evidence-based insight into the types of expertise and understanding of the processes of deliberation now required in this area of law. This type of analysis would build upon existing studies of courts which have been directed at assessing the seriousness of environmental offences, determining sentencing criteria for environmental offences, and working through specific types of cases (see de Prez 2000a, de Prez 2000b; White 2011; Fogel and Lipovsek 2013; White and Heckenberg 2014).

From a legal perspective, the value attributed to environmental harm is linked to the seriousness of the offence. Assessing the seriousness of environmental offences usually involves criteria such as the immediate and direct impact of the environmental crime; its wider effects in environmental, social and economic terms; human fatality, injury or ill health; the health of flora and fauna; the offence pattern, especially for serial offenders; and so on (see Magistrates Association 2009). Criminal law is normally reserved for the punishment of socially unacceptable behaviour. Yet harm to the environment is, in many situations, considered to be acceptable (for example in certain circumstances pollution is allowed under license or authorization) because such harm is an inherent consequence of many industrial activities which provide significant economic and social benefits. This rationale underpins a system of regulation which defines the framework for determining whether such benefits outweigh the harm caused. The criminal law is not suited to such a balancing process, and thus is mainly used to address clearly unacceptable behaviour or to reinforce the regulatory system (Bell and McGillivary 2008, p. 281).

The concept of environmental harm is built into various statutes and guidelines pertaining to environmental crime and justice. In general, distinctions are made on the basis of seriousness, material environmental harm, and level of nuisance (Bricknell 2011; Mandiberg 2009). It has been demonstrated that greater consistency in approach and outcome can be achieved by specialist agencies that deal with environmental crimes, harms and issues on a regular basis (Pring and Pring 2009). Among the building blocks for an effective environmental court or tribunal is the mobilisation of scientific and technical expertise and the competence of judges and decision-makers. A defined environment court provides an established forum for the development of specialist expertise aided by the availability of technical experts within the court itself (see Preston 2011a; Westerhuis 2013; Walters and Westerhuis 2013). Moreover, such courts and tribunals provide a ready platform for the further extension of environmental jurisprudence and coherent sanctioning processes.

Importantly, recent surveys of environment courts point in the direction of *problem-solving*, rather than punishment per se, as a key objective in how they are dealing with environmental harm (Walters and Westerhuis 2013; White 2013a; Pring and Pring 2009). Institutionalisation of specialist expertise thus reinforces and furthers the development of innovative practice and practical implementation of the law. This gives content and shape to what have often formerly been simply abstract declarations of principle and emergent rights with little applied substance.

The nonhuman environmental victim is assessed here from the point of view of their status as victims of harm within the environment court. Not all courts deal with environmental crime per se, nor are all harms perpetrated against nonhuman objects considered to be criminal in nature. For present purposes, the primary focus is on criminal harm as defined in relevant legislation.

Nonhuman Environmental Victims and Environment Courts

Presented below are four problems that have major implications for how environment courts deal with cases featuring nonhuman environmental subjects. They provide a suggested 'framing' of the kinds of theoretical, practical and philosophical issues facing environment courts as they grapple with how best to respond to environmental harm perpetrated against non-human victims.

The Problem of Victimisation

Here the central issues relate to court recognition of *nonhuman interests* (e.g., intrinsic rights, value and status of the nonhuman in court proceedings) and *nonhuman agency* (e.g., active role of the nonhuman victim in legal processes). In addressing this problem, it is important to critically evaluate matters pertaining to animal laws (e.g., animal welfare, animals as property) and to specific environments (plant and nature conservation/preservation).

Chief Justice Brian Preston of the New South Wales Land and Environment Court in Australia describes how responding to environmental harm is an intergenerational concern and how non-human biota may be considered victims:

> Environmental harm may require remediation over generations and hence the burden and the cost of remediation is transferred to future generations. Remediation of contaminated land and restoration of habitat of species, populations and ecological communities are examples of intergenerational burdens passed from the present generation to future generations. Where intergenerational inequity is caused by the commission of an environmental offence, the victims include future generations. . . . The biosphere and non-human biota have intrinsic value independent of their utilitarian or instrumental value for humans. When harmed by environmental crime, the biosphere and non-human biota also are victims. The harm is able to be assessed from an ecological perspective; it need not be anthropocentric.
>
> (Preston 2011b, p. 143)

Identifying the victims is only part of the process however. Just as the human victim has a voice in the courts, similarly the voice of the non-human victim needs to be heard as part of justice proceedings. Among the issues for consideration are:

- 'victimisation' as something that pertains to the nonhuman as well as the human, and as not reducible to human interests
- 'legal standing' that be granted in some circumstances to the nonhuman
- 'surrogate victims' as a means of acknowledging active nonhuman participation

The literature to date has also tended to focus on humans as victims rather than other species or particular environments (see for example, Williams 1996; Jarrell and Ozymy 2012; Hall 2013). This is starting to change. An example of changes in thinking about who/what constitutes an environmental victim, is the notion of eco-justice where the active concern is with both the human and the nonhuman (White 2013b). More expansive definitions of rights and justice are extending the definition of 'victim' to include the non-human in the moral equation. This means that animals and eco-systems are, under certain circumstances, considered 'victims', too.

- *Environment justice* – **the victim is human**

  environmental rights are seen as an extension of human or social rights so as to enhance the quality of human life now and into the future

- *Ecological justice* – **the victim is a specific environment**

  human beings are merely one component of complex ecosystems that should be preserved for their own sake

- *Species justice* – **the victim is an animal or plant**

  animals have an intrinsic right not to suffer abuse, and plants not to suffer degradation of their habitat to the extent that threatens biodiversity loss (White 2013b).

Acknowledgement of 'victim' status is crucial to understanding how environmental harm affects both human and nonhuman. This means locating creatures and environments within their unique ecological niche and context. It also means examining events and contemporary human practices from the vantage point of history and geography, and extrapolating this knowledge to consider near and over the horizon harms.

Analysing the problem of victimisation must also acknowledge the divergent interests that cut across legal discussion of specific harms. For example, from the point of view of a stream, the stress may be on the rights of the stream itself and any damage caused to its functioning in and through human activity. This involves a 'preservationist' logic that insists upon viewing the stream in terms of its intrinsic value. Conversely, from the point of view of human and riparian rights, the issue may be one of conflicting interests between upstream and downstream rights holders. This involves a 'conservationist' logic based upon the value of the stream to humans.

The Problem of Ontology

Here the issues revolve around identifying those *justice principles* that ought to guide assessment of nonhuman victimhood – such as distribution, recognition, participation, and capability – and the problems associated with working out a 'legal ontology' of natural objects. This refers to the nonhuman in law and problems in defining the *boundaries of the 'natural object'* (Stone 1972). Adjudication needs to consider issues such as how 'harm' and 'rights' are calculated in general, in law, in quantum, and in orientation through consideration of the new jurisprudence of Earth Rights (see Cullinan 2003). Schlosberg (2007) considers nonhuman rights from the point of view of various conceptions of justice:

- *Distribution*: justice as fairness/equality (need, desert, entitlement)
- *Recognition*: justice as acknowledgement (subordination, non-recognition, disrespect)
- *Participation*: justice as engagement (decision-making procedures, protecting interests)
- *Capacities*: justice as functionings (opportunities to 'do' and to 'be')

In a discussion of the subject status of a natural object, such as a river or tree, Stone (1972) argues that some authoritative body needs to review the actions and processes of those who threaten it, but to make this count (i.e., to have it legally recognised worth and dignity in its own right), it is necessary:

- that the natural object can institute legal actions *at its behest*
- that in determining the granting of legal relief, the court must take *injury to it* into account
- that relief must run to the *benefit* of it (Stone 1972).

Central to this problem of ontology are questions of essence and essentialism. Cullinan (2003), for example, points out that a fundamental river right (i.e. the riverine equivalent of a human right) would be the right to flow. If a water body couldn't flow it wouldn't be a river, and so the capacity to flow (given sufficient water) is essential to the existence of a river. Therefore, 'from the perspective of the river, building so many dams across it and extracting so much water from it that it ceased to flow into the sea, would be an abuse of its Earth rights' (Cullinan 2003, p. 118). But what constitutes 'essence' can and does change over time. For instance, domesticated animals such as dogs and cats have a contemporary 'way of life' and 'way of being' that reflects thousands of years of evolution and human relationships and engagement. To be and to do for dogs is immediately contextualised by their role and status relative to their human counterparts, and what they have been bred and trained to be and do over time (e.g., animal companions, racing dogs, hunting dogs). Their 'essence', as with the essence of humans, is a social and historical product, and as such is continuously revised and reconstructed with the passage of time.

The Problem of Expertise

This problem focuses on issues of evidence and *expertise* from the point of view of identifying *who speaks for and on behalf of whom*. It deals with the question of 'whose voices' are or should be heard in court; how this is, ought or might occur; and specifically, how and to whom does non-human nature communicate its needs. The idea here is that *problem-solving* is not only about Alternative Dispute Resolution and devising suitable incorporation of 'experts' (e.g., single court appointed, single experts agreed upon by parties, 'hot tubbing'). Problem-solving also demands attention to defining the substantive or empirical nature of nonhuman environmental subjects, and hence, developing baseline standards and environmental qualities There are also issues surrounding *guardianship* and *stewardship*.

The law does allow for a modicum of protection for the nonhuman as well as the human. This is reflected in legislation pertaining to endangered species (e.g., particular animals such as tigers) and to conservation more generally (e.g., in the form of national parks). Harm is central to these forms of social regulation, however, whether 'harm to the environment' is of consequence *unless* it is measured with reference to human values (e.g., economic, aesthetic, cultural) is of ongoing concern in legal decision-making (see Lin 2006). In essence, natural objects (such as trees and forests) lack legal rights (and agency or volition) and so must rely upon humans to bring actions to protect them. Some argue that the inherent interests of 'natural objects' ought to be protected through legal actions by the objects themselves, with humans serving as their guardians or trustees (see Stone 1972; Lin 2006).

If the nonhuman is to be acknowledged in law as a 'victim' then the nonhuman must be able to convey, in some way, the nature of their victimisation. In other words, the non-human victim needs a human translator to speak on their behalf about the nature and consequences of the harms suffered. In practice, this means advocates must give voice to the concerns of those who cannot articulate what is happening to them such as trees, soil, bees, orchids, rivers, and lakes (see Schlosberg 2007; Preston 2011b; Besthorn 2004, 2012). Increasingly, including within environmental courts, it is acknowledged that there is much to learn by bringing the nonhuman into the dialogue about ecological health and wellbeing that affects all.

To date, most judicial and legal attention has been on humans as environmental victims, however this definition of 'victim' is evolving and expanding. For example, public interest law has been invoked to give standing to human representatives of non-human entities such as rivers and trees. In New

Zealand, a river was represented at a restorative justice conference, by the chairperson of the Waikato River Enhancement Society (see Preston 2011b; and also Morris and Ruru 2010), and the Whanganui River became a legal entity with a legal voice in 2012 (Shuttleworth 2012; Findlayson 2012). For the purpose of the restorative process, 'surrogate victims' are being recognised as representing the affected community, including harms to particular biotic groups and abiotic environs. Public trust and public interest law have been used to establish future generations as victims of environmental crime (Preston 2011b; Mehta 2009) including human as well as the environment and non-human biota, where surrogates (such as parents or NGOs) have provided representation. Who speaks for whom or what is nevertheless still controversial, especially when it comes to non-human victims such as trees, rivers and specific eco-systems.

The question of expert evidence is particularly important in defining the 'subject' of the law (e.g., 'river', 'riparian zone') and thus identifying the nature of 'victimisation', and hence the scope of what needs to be done to 'repair the harm'. For example, a 'river' may be defined in spiritual and cultural terms by an Indigenous community (Morris and Ruru 2010), be viewed primarily in terms of water flow according to the narrow Eurocentric conceptions common in Australian courts (Davies et al. 2011; Taylor and Stokes 2007), be seen as being constituted by its channel banks and channel bed according to the science of geomorphology (Taylor and Stokes 2007), and conceptualised as inclusive of consideration of riparian zones, which relate to the observed influence of the river on the biota within and adjacent to the river, from an ecological perspective (Davies et al. 2011). Thus there are quite different associations with and types of expertise pertaining to rivers.

The problem of expertise raises questions around how evidence is assessed and responded to in court. They include matters such as:

- defining the 'victim' and implications of this for assessments of perpetrators, harms and remedies
- addressing how the link of ontology and definition of 'entity' via legal means implies a need for expertise, but expertise also varies (for example, Geomorphology versus Ecological science)
- asking why these particular speakers are most suitable: issues of standing, legitimacy, specific types of roles
- making appointments from a pool that may include diverse and opposing speakers for the voiceless (e.g., Royal Society for the Prevention of Cruelty to Animals [RSPCA] versus Animal Liberation)

Inevitably the court will have to weigh up and deal with substantive contests over knowledge, evidence, thresholds, and concepts of harm. The problem of expertise is basically one of how and to whom does nonhuman nature communicate its 'needs'; and how is the court to make resolutions when knowledge and expertise is partial, skewed and/or ideological (see White and Heckenberg 2014).

The Problem of Temporality

Public trust and public interest law have been used selectively worldwide to establish future generations as victims of environmental crime. A vital concept, especially in regards to human interests, is the notion of *intergenerational equity*. What are the implications of such concepts in regards to the notion of Earth Rights and addressing the needs of the nonhuman environmental victim? Here the problem once again rests upon both what are considered the essential attributes of this sort of victim, and over what time period.

The reverence for and privileging of nonhuman nature sometimes translates into a concern for the 'righteous management' of nature, and manifests in an agenda that advocates for the mass preservation of wilderness, protection of endangered nonhuman species and restoration of disturbed areas towards a *pristine nature* or pristine condition (Devalle and Sessions 1985). There are two immediate problems with this view. First, it implies a separation of humanity and nature as if this was and always has, empirically, been the case. The notion of 'pristine nature' implies precisely this kind of rigid separation, yet historical and cross-cultural study indicates exactly the opposite – namely, constant and continuous living in nature by humans (Plumwood 2004; Merchant 2005; Tsing 2005), including within the most inhospitable environments possible from a human perspective (Robyn 2002).

Secondly, the notion of 'pristine nature' implies immutable or unchanging conditions. Yet, nature is inherently changeable. If we re-cast the issue into the language of 'harm', then it becomes even more complicated. To protect against intrinsic harm to the environment requires an understanding of what the environment is and how it can be harmed. If 'environment' refers to the natural world, and if the source of value in the natural world is its self-maintaining sustaining properties, then harm to the environment involves setbacks to these self-maintaining properties. Harm to the environment, in other words, might be defined as a change from the environment's 'natural', self-maintaining state. The problem with this view is that the environment is not in static equilibrium; rather, it is a dynamic entity undergoing constant change. Preserving the environment in its natural state is likely an impossible, and perhaps undesirable, mission (Lin 2006, p. 981).

For an environment court, relevant issues include:

- defining and describing the 'original' state before harm was perpetrated and examining how closely, if at all, reclamation efforts might be able to return the disturbed vegetation and/or animal species to this state;
- determining whether or not appropriate 'off-sets' are available, such that destruction or damage to one geographical area can be mitigated by preservation of another geographical area with similar flora and fauna;
- ensuring that the areas and eco-systems within which nonhuman environmental victimisation has occurred are restored, in ways that maximise the robustness and diversity of said areas and eco-systems.

From the perspective of nonhuman environmental victims, the initial difficulty is ascertaining when a 'natural state' exists or what a 'natural state' is, given that life is transient and in a constant state of flux. Such considerations are especially important in relation to matters of repairing the harm, one of the core tasks expressed through and by a specialist environment court.

As courts move closer to determinations of environmental harm, the issues become even more complicated. Consider, for example, the issue of 'scale'. A recent court case in New South Wales, Australia, provides a case example of an approach to considering the impact of the environmental harm (in this case illegal land clearing) at several different levels (see Box 1).Where one draws the line in terms of scale is highly relevant not only to determining and assessing harm, but also, as indicated in Box 1, to the possibilities of remediation.

Box 1 Assessments of environmental harm according to local or landscape scale

Local scale

The native vegetation cleared from the Land was in good condition because:

a. It contained a diversity of native plant species in four strata;
b. It was of uneven age and contained mature trees;
c. It contained recruitment trees and senescent trees; and
d. Did not contain exotic plants (weeds) (Heffernan at [para. 47]):

(Heffernan at para.8. The conservation value of the native vegetation at the local scale was high and the clearing may have caused significant impacts on vegetation and fauna at this scale.

Landscape scale

(Heffernan at [para. 51, 52]. Conservation value of native vegetation considered low at the landscape level, and its clearing unlikely to have caused significant impacts on the vegetation, fauna habitats or habitat connectivity at landscape scale, because (Heffernan at [para. 52]):

a. The vegetation communities on the land consist of three vegetation communities that are well represented in South-East Australia including within conservation reserves;
b. The clearing of the vegetation has impacted small areas of the vegetation communities that are well represented at a landscape level;
c. Affected vegetation appears to lie at the north edge of the Nullica State Forest, which occupies about 6,700 hectares of forested land; and
d. Previous disturbances to vegetation communities to the northern part of the Land have already compromised any habitat interconnections.

Considerations of scale are also relevant to the *possibilities for remediation.* (Heffernan at [para. 54]) The remaining vegetation on the Subject Areas has moderate to good potential to recover in the medium to long-term because:

a. The retention throughout the Subject Areas of mature canopy trees;
b. The developed root systems of these trees will assist with soil stabilisation;
c. The canopies of the retained mature trees will moderate temperature and moisture conditions at the soil's surface
d. A good source of seeds is expected in the soil and the mature trees will provide a further source of seeds;
e. Fruit and flowers from the mature trees will assist pollen and seed transfer in the regenerating strata;
f. The stacks of cleared vegetation provide a source of mulch and a further seed source for regenerating areas;
g. The soil has not been subjected to significant disturbance or compaction from the clearing works that would affect the regeneration of vegetation; and
h. Following the clearing, a sterile annual cover crop was sown over bare soil in the Subject Areas. The cover crop has stabilised the topsoil and will assist the regeneration of native plants from the seed bank contained within the soil and from vegetative underground root structures.

Source: *Director-General, Department of Environment Climate Change and Water v Vin Heffernan Pty Ltd* [2010] NSWLEC 200

The four problems outlined above provide a framing of the conundrums associated with translating lofty ideals pertaining to nonhuman environmental victims into suitable practice within forums such as specialist environment courts. The issues are not only of a legal nature in the sense that courts have to interpret legislation is particular ways and be guided and bound by both statute and precedent. They also increasingly demand considerable technical knowledge which relies upon the judiciary as well as outside professionals having adequate expertise in regards to ecological and zoological phenomena. Again, this reinforces the importance of having specialist courts and appropriately educated judiciary, to deal with environmental crimes and to understand the implications of these for human as well as non-human victims.

Conclusion

This chapter has laid some initial foundations for subsequent research and scholarship in how specialist environment courts deal with matters pertaining to the non-human environmental victim. The four problems outlined constitute important legal and philosophical dilemmas associated with trying to impose human evaluations on matters that involve the fate and wellbeing of nonhuman environmental victims.

Questions of justice, fairness and appropriateness, as well as those of expertise, responsibility and stewardship will inevitably feature in such discussions. So, too, will issues pertaining to conflicts of interest – between human and nonhuman, between divergent views about who/what constitutes a nonhuman environmental victim (e.g., protecting animals versus protecting plants), and between system needs and individual rights and interests (e.g., eco-systems versus specific natural objects or specific creatures). This is just the beginning of a much wider conversation about environmental victimisation. There is much yet to consider, and much more to learn.

Cases

Director-General, Department of Environment Climate Change and Water v Vin Heffernan Pty Ltd [2010] NSWLEC 200

References

Bell, S. and McGillivray, D. 2008. *Environmental Law*, 7th edition. London: Oxford University Press.

Besthorn, F.H. 2004. 'Restorative Justice in Environmental Restoration – The Twin Pillars of a Just Global Environmental Policy: Hearing the Voice of the Victim', *Journal of Societal and Social Policy* 3(2), 33–48.

Besthorn, F.H. 2012. 'Speaking Earth: Environmental Restoration and Restorative Justice', in *Restorative Justice Today: Practical Applications* edited by K. Wormer and L. Walker. Los Angeles: Sage, 233–244.

Bricknell, S. 2010. *Environmental Crime in Australia*. AIC Reports Research and Public Policy Series 109. Canberra: Australian Institute of Criminology.

Cullinan, C. 2003. *Wild Law: A Manifesto for Earth Justice*. London: Green Books in association with The Gaia Foundation.

Davies, P., Ives, C., Findlay, S. and Taylor, M. 2011. 'Urban Rivers and Riparian Systems – Directions and Recommendations for Legislators, Policy Makers, Developers and Community Users', *Environmental Planning and Law Journal* 28, 313–331.

Devalle, B. and Sessions, G. 1985. *Deep Ecology: Living as if Nature Mattered*. Layton, UT: Gibbs Smith.

Findlay, M., Odgers, S. and Yeo, S. 1994. *Australian Criminal Justice*. Melbourne: Oxford University Press.

Finlayson, C. 2012. 'Whanganui River Agreement Signed', beehive.govt.nz: The Official Website of the New Zealand Government, August 30, 2012: beehive.govt.nz – Whanganui River Agreement signed (Accessed April 6, 2015).

Fogel, C. and Lipovsek, J. 2013. 'Green Crime in the Canadian Courts'. *Journal of Politics and Law* 6(2), 48–52.

Hall, M. 2013. *Victims of Environmental Harm: Rights, Recognition and Redress Under National and International Law*. London: Routledge.

Hillyard, P. and Tombs, S. 2007. 'From "Crime" to Social Harm?', *Crime, Law and Social Change* 48, 9–25.

Hillyard, P., Pantazis, C., Tombs, S. and Gordon, D. (eds) 2004. *Beyond Criminology? Taking Harm Seriously*. London: Pluto Press.

Jarrell, M. and Ozymy, J. 2012. 'Real Crime, Real Victims: Environmental Crime Victims and the Crime Victims' Rights Act (CVRA)', *Crime, Law and Social Change* 58(4), 373–389.

Lin, A. 2006. 'The Unifying Role of Harm in Environmental Law', *Wisconsin Law Review* 3, 898–985.

Magistrates' Association (UK) 2009. *Costing the Earth: Guidance for Sentencers*. London: Magistrates' Association.

Mandiberg, S. 2009. 'Locating the Environmental Harm in Environmental Crimes', *Utah Law Review* 4, 1177–1222.

Matthews, R. and Kauzlarich, D. 2007. 'State Crimes and State Harms: A Tale of Two Definitional Frameworks', *Crime, Law and Social Change* 48, 43–55.

Mehta, M. 2009. *In the Public Interest: Landmark Judgement and Orders Of The Supreme Court of India on Environment and Human Rights*, Vols. 1–3. New Delhi: Prakriti Publications.

Merchant, C. 2005. *Radical Ecology: The Search for a Livable World*. New York: Routledge.

Morris, J. and Ruru, J. 2010. 'Giving Voice to Rivers: Legal Personality as a Vehicle for Recognising Indigenous Peoples' Relationships to Water?', *Australian Indigenous Law Review* 14(2), 49–62.

Pemberton, S. 2015. *Harmful Societies: Understanding Social Harm*. Bristol: Policy Press.

Plumwood, V. 2004. 'Gender, Eco-Feminism and the Environment', in *Controversies in Environmental Sociology*, edited by R. White. Melbourne: Cambridge University Press.

Preston, B. 2011a. 'Operating an Environment Court: The Experience of the Land and Environment Court of New South Wales and 12 Benefits of Judicial Specialisation in Environmental Law', Paper presented at Renewing Environmental Law: A Conference for Public Interest Environmental Law Practitioners, University of Victoria Environmental Law Centre, West Coast Environmental Law and Ecojustice, 3–4 February, Vancouver.

Preston, B. 2011b. 'The Use of Restorative Justice for Environmental Crime', *Criminal Law Journal* 35, 136–145.

Prez de, P. 2000a. 'Excuses, Excuses: The Ritual Trivialisation of Environmental Prosecutions', *Journal of Environmental Law* 12(1), 65–78.

Prez, de P. 2000b. 'Beyond judicial sanctions: The negative impact of conviction for environmental offences', *Environmental Law Review* 2, 11–22.

Pring, G. and Pring, C. 2009. *Greening Justice: Creating and Improving Environmental Courts and Tribunals*. The Access Initiative.

Robyn, L. 2002. 'Indigenous Knowledge and Technology', *American Indian Quarterly* 26(2), 198–220.

Schlosberg, D. 2007. *Defining Environmental Justice: Theories, Movements, and Nature*. Oxford: Oxford University Press.

Shuttleworth, K. 2012 'Agreement Entitles Whanguanui River to Legal Identity', *The New Zealand Herald*, August 30, 2012.

South, N. and Brisman, A. (eds.) 2013. *The Routledge International Handbook of Green Criminology*. New York: Routledge.

Stone, C. 1972. 'Should Trees Have Standing?: Toward Legal Rights for Natural Objects', *Southern California Law Review* 45, 450–487.

Taylor, M. and Stokes, R. 2005. 'When is a River not a River? Consideration of the Legal Definition of a River for Geomorphologists Practising in New South Wales, Australia', *Australian Geographer* 36(2), 183–200.

Tsing, A. 2005. *Friction: An Ethnography of Global Connection*. Princeton: Princeton University Press.

Walters, R. and Westerhuis, D.S. 2013. 'Green Crime and the Role of Environmental Courts', *Crime Law and Social Change* 59, 279–290.

Westerhuis, D. 2013. 'A Harm Analysis of Environmental Crime', in *Emerging Issues in Green Criminology*, edited by R. Walters, D.S. Westerhuis and T. Wyatt. Basingstoke: Palgrave Macmillan, 197–217.

White, R. 2011. *Transnational Environmental Crime: Toward an Eco-Global Criminology*. London: Routledge.

White, R. 2013a. 'Environmental Crime and Problem-Solving Courts', *Crime, Law and Social Change* 59(3), 267–278.

White, R. 2013b. *Environmental Harm: An Eco-Justice Perspective*. Bristol: Policy Press.

White, R. and Heckenberg, D. 2014. *Green Criminology: An Introduction to the Study of Environmental Harm*. London: Routledge.

Williams, C. 1996. 'An Environmental Victimology', *Social Justice* 23(4), 16–40.

Part III

Alternative Methods to Combat (Transnational) Environmental Crime

9 New Environmental Governance

Environmental Harms, Enforcement and Collaboration

Cameron Holley[1]

Introduction

Environmental harms are arguably the most confounding challenge of our time. Biodiversity loss, pollution from toxic and hazardous materials, climate change and natural resource degradation all continue to defy solutions, largely due to the fact that they cross human borders between and within sovereign states. Traditionally, governments and their agents responded to these harms through enforcement of strict rules and standards set out in legislation and treaties (Gunningham 2009). These laws established a plethora of enforcement functions, powers and procedures on issues such as illegal wildlife trade, hazardous waste and pollution (UNODC 2012, p. 87). An increasingly complex cohort of police, customs, specialist environmental agencies and courts arose to administer these laws (UNODC 2012, p. 87). Yet, despite some success (Cole and Grossman 1999; Najam et al. 2006), this traditional regulatory approach has often proved ineffective and inefficient at arresting environmental harms (Spapens et al. 2014). These weaknesses have been caused by an array of factors, not least the mismatch between the traditional regulatory architecture (which is based on ecologically arbitrary human defined borders) and the transboundary nature of environmental harms (White 2012; United Nations Interregional Crime and Justice Research Institute 2015).

As a range of policy-makers and scholars have pointed out, successfully addressing the transboundary nature of environmental harms requires new approaches that rely on cooperation between states, communities, auspices of government and international bodies (White 2011; Tomkins 2009). This cooperation is essential at the international level, where growth in cross-border environmental harms poses a formidable challenge to discrete nation states and fragmented enforcement communities (UNEP 2007). The need for cooperation is equally compelling at the domestic level, where environmental harms continue to confound regulation by

1 Some elements of this chapter were developed from and first presented at the Environmental Crime and the World Conference, 11–12 November 2013, Tilburg University, the Netherlands and earlier work appearing in Holley (2015b). The author is grateful for the research assistance of Thomas Ellicott and Antonia Ross, and the comments of participants in the Environmental Crime and the World Conference.

disjointed agency 'silos' and territorial tiers of government (Lipman 2013; Gunningham et al. 2007; White 2012).

A recent response to this 'cooperation imperative' has been the so-called New Environmental Governance (NEG), which emphasizes collaboration, integration, participation, deliberative styles of decision-making, adaptation and learning. Complex environmental and social systems cannot readily be governed by a single actor, namely, a government acting alone. Consequently, this new form of governance is distinctively polycentric, with the state no longer necessarily playing the central role in decision-making (McGinnis 1999; Gunningham 2008; Ostrom 2010, p. 643). Under such arrangements, power is diffuse and sanctions, in the absence of state or other regulatory mechanisms, involve public 'shaming' and other forms of informal social control (Gunningham 2008). Although still an evolving literature, a growing number of scholars and policy-makers believe that NEG can substantially improve the effectiveness, efficiency and legitimacy of responses to environmental harms.

This chapter explores the contours of the NEG approach, mapping the shifts in environmental regulation and governance that led to its development, before highlighting the strengths and weaknesses of NEG for addressing transboundary environmental harms.

Before embarking on this discussion it is important to note that much of the scholarship on NEG, including the work discussed in this chapter, has been developed in the fields of law and governance, rather than within the field of criminology, or more specifically green criminology (cf. Bisschop and Verhage 2012). Despite this, NEG scholarship arguably has many points of overlap with work in green criminology, not least because both examine institutions that apply rules (both hard and soft) to create order (Shearing 2013). As this chapter will detail below, much of the NEG work also resonates with the growing focus of green criminologists on broadening definitions of environmental harm, and moving from past-focused processes to forward-looking ones that try to anticipate and prevent the realization of harms (White 2009; Shearing 2013). Like policy-oriented approaches to green criminology, NEG scholarship also shares an interest in examining and identifying the kind of policies that may be effective in controlling environmental harms (Lynch and Stretesky 2011). Moreover, NEG's collaborative and participatory approach echoes the growing trend in criminology and policing scholarship to look beyond the state and Westphalian visions of governance (Krasna 2001) to other auspices and providers of governance (e.g. private and community actors) (Loader 2000). Given these links, the chapter's exploration of NEG (as part of a regulatory frame) hopes to assist green criminology to expand what it can study and how it can be studied, in ways that enable it to recognize, and play a role with respect to, new ways of solving environmental harms (Shearing 2013).

The analysis proceeds in three parts. The first part commences by mapping the path that led to NEG, highlighting shifts in the thinking and arrangements of governing, from traditional environmental regulation to markets, early forms of partnerships and finally NEG. The second part goes on to examine the NEG approach, identifying its distinguishing features, examples in practice and the key benefits that NEG could contribute to effectively governing transboundary environmental harms. Attention is paid to international harms and domestic contexts (including those of weak states), since transboundary environmental problems infiltrate administrative regions at all levels, in addition to crossing sovereign state boundaries (Yu 2011, pp. 188–9). This chapter will highlight recent debates, with a focus on whether NEG can deliver on its promised benefits to offer a more effective, efficient and legitimate resolution to environmental harms. As we will see below, despite NEG's 'new' approach, its success in practice often appears to depend on its coexistence (rather than opposition to) traditional regulatory enforcement (De Burca et al. 2013; Driessen et al. 2012, p. 157). The third part will offer some concluding thoughts and sum up the chapter.

Governing Environmental Harms: Regulation, Markets, Partnerships and NEG

To understand why NEG is considered a promising means of addressing transboundary environmental harms, it is necessary to briefly examine the history of environmental regulation and governance. This historical perspective is important because NEG thinking and arrangements arose out of the perceived limits and failures of 'old governance' (e.g. international treaties and intergovernmental organizations, and domestic regulation) (Abbott and Snidal 2009).

The traditional architecture of national and international environmental regulation arose in the 1970s, against the backdrop of states exercising sovereign ownership over natural resources within their territory (Gess 1964). It is therefore logical that early responses to environmental harm relied on the nation state, or at the international level, groups of states, acting primarily through treaty-based intergovernmental organizations (De Burca et al. 2013; Abbott and Snidal 2009, p. 505). A raft of specific international rules addressing problems such as trade in endangered species and pollution from ships were developed and overseen by international organizations, including the United Nations Environment Programme (Kelemen and Vogel 2010). Under this approach, states believed they understood environmental harms clearly; they could be defined in advance; and managed through mandatory rules (De Burca et al. 2013, p. 730).

A similar example is the 'command and control' approach to environmental regulation adopted by domestic Western governments. This involved centralized legislatures setting blanket environmental targets, such as emission standards, exposure levels or technology standards (the command). Delegated agents, such as environmental protection agencies, were then empowered to monitor environmental targets, oversee compliance and impose penalties where standards were breached (the control) (De Burca et al. 2013; Gunningham et al. 1998).

In some cases, this state-centric approach to law and regulation was relatively effective, achieving a number of gains in halting and reducing environmental harms (Cole and Grossman 1999; Najam et al. 2006). However, this approach also suffered from a number of weaknesses that limited its effectiveness. For example, at the international level, 'treaty congestion' and fragmentation led to claims that international environmental law was too unwieldy, incoherent and ineffective for confronting increasingly serious global environmental challenges (Najam et al. 2006; Scott 2011). International cooperation on crime was also scarce, with states and international organizations struggling with awareness and knowledge of environmental harms, not least because there was little sustained effort to share data among different states, organizations and agencies (White 2009, p. 238; Elliott 2012, p. 95).

Similar claims were levelled at domestic systems, where the centralized and uniform nature of command and control regulation was increasingly criticized as costly, cumbersome and inefficient (Karkkainen 2006). The effectiveness of these approaches was limited due to under-resourced regulators, evidence barriers and limited data gathering and monitoring (particularly when harms crossed domestic boundaries) (White 2012). These challenges were only augmented in the developing world, were the allocation of human and financial resources to environmental harms was extremely scarce (Huisman and Van Erp 2013).

Traditional command and control approaches also suffered from adversarial enforcement by 'stick' waving agencies, particularly in the United States, producing counterproductive resistance from regulated individuals and firms (Lazarus 2004). Such resistance was said to heighten problems such as evasion, concealment and displacement of crime to countries with more lenient inspection regimes (Bisschop 2012).

Another limitation of regulatory approaches was their failure to provide sensitivity to local contexts (Stewart 2001; Karkkainen 2006; Holley et al. 2011). Traditional laws and treaties tended to be single media/issue based and were administered through siloed organizations and agencies. This made it increasingly difficult for traditional regulation to address more complex environmental problems, which often involved multiple polluters and required a more holistic and integrated approach to solving harms (Freeman and Farber 2005; Durant et al. 2004; Holley et al. 2011, p. 2). These challenges were only augmented in federal systems of governance, such as in the United States, Canada and Australia, where conflicting lines of authority made coordination particularly complicated (White 2011).

One final weakness of traditional regulatory approaches was that they were typically only suited to addressing past events, such as cleared forests or dumped pollution in a water body. The regulatory approach was not designed to pre-empt the realization of harms (other than through the deterrence effect of punishment) or encourage norms and behaviour that foster proactive protection and management of the environment. As a result, regulation was ill-suited to accounting for and adapting to the dynamic nature of ecological systems (Holling 1978; Gunderson and Holling 2001) and changing the behaviour of many offenders who had a laggard culture or were well resourced, able to fight, delay and in some cases buy their way out crimes (Ayling 2013; Spapens et al. 2014). For similar reasons, traditional regulation provided a poor response to harms (e.g. wildlife poaching) that arose from actions deeply embedded in local communities with little alternative sources of income (Huisman and Van Erp 2013; e.g. Houfu and Xiaopu 2013; Nellemann et al. 2014).

Together, these numerous challenges conspired to reduce the effectiveness of traditional top-down enforcement. State-centred hierarchy was no longer seen as the *exclusive* response to *all* environmental problems (Durant et al. 2004). Instead, by the 1980s and 1990s, new market-based instruments, partnership and light-handed approaches began to be explored, particularly relating to more complex environmental harms, such as the causes of climate change and diffuse water pollution.

For some scholars and policy-makers, environmental harms were seen to occur as a result of a failure of markets to properly value environmental resources (Cutting and Cahoon 2005, p. 55; Roma 2006, p. 534). This line of thinking gave rise to the creation of market signals and instruments (e.g. climate markets spurred by the UNFCCC and Kyoto; McKibbin and Wilcoxen 2002) that placed a value on and charged appositely for the use of scarce assets (Holley et al. 2011, p. 2). In theory, by creating such markets (e.g. regulated trade in wildlife), those who are likely to harm the environment (e.g. through poaching) will be less inclined to do so because they will see wildlife or other aspects of the environment as a resource worth protecting (Huisman and Van Erp 2013).

Despite some successes, many market-inspired approaches have proven to be less environmentally successful than traditional regulation (Howes et al. 1997). In part, this is because of a variety of practical and contextual difficulties faced by governments who seek to develop and rely on market mechanisms. Although, in theory, *free markets* mobilize knowledge (Hayek 1945), most *market-based* instruments share with command and control a requirement for centralized planning and knowledge, such as setting the right tax, charge or cap levels. This can often be difficult for policy-makers in the absence of an existing market reference (Sabel et al. 1999; Freeman and Farber 2005). Also, tradable rights/pollution need a similar level of compliance and enforcement machinery as traditional performance based regulation. Regulated actors, particularly corporations, also historically opposed the introduction of economic initiatives such as taxes and charges, preferring the certainty of regulation to the uncertainty of novel approaches (Gunningham and Holley 2010).

An alternative to direct regulation, more popular with business and increasingly cash-strapped domestic government regulators, was a variety of voluntary and light-handed initiatives that emerged during the late 1980s and 1990s. These included business-led voluntary and self-regulatory approaches, such as Responsible Care (Lenox and Nash 2003). While they achieved limited success, they typically failed to deliver acceptable levels of industry-wide compliance, particularly where the gap between the private interests of business (not least, making a profit) and the public interest in environmental protection was substantial (Gunningham and Sinclair 2002, pp. 145–8 and 155; Freeman and Farber 2005).

Stronger, but reconfigured, roles for domestic state regulation were accordingly pursued. These approaches typically maintained a state underpinning, but looked to engage with business and NGOs in ways that were considered more effective and efficient, while also maintaining cooperation and trust of regulated actors. This was primarily achieved by: accounting for and facilitating the use of non-state knowledge and capacities; and by harnessing related motivational drivers, such as profit, social licence (e.g. negative business publicity by NGOs); and other informal sanctions (Gunningham and Sinclair 2002).

These reconfigured approaches varied in form, and have been considered and analysed by a variety of theories. These approaches include: environmental partnerships and negotiated agreements in Europe (Orts and Deketelaere 2001); tripartite arrangements between regulators, communities and industry (Ayres and Braithwaite 1992), such as environmental improvement plans in Australia (Holley and Gunningham 2006); informational-based regulation, embodied most prominently in the Toxic Release Inventory in the United States (Karkkainen 2001); eco-modernization that facilitated cooperation and the uptake of new technologies in Europe (Mol and Sonnenfeld 2000); and reflexive law approaches, where firms developed their own process and management system standards designed to achieve regulatory goals (Orts 1995).

While each of these approaches provided greater flexibility to businesses, including facilitating beyond compliance activities, in the absence of more coercive intervention by domestic state regulators, their impact has (for the most part) been very modest and tended to operate more or less at the margins of environmental governance (Gunningham and Holley 2010). Even so, what was unique about these flexible and cooperative programmes was that they signified some of the first steps towards what has become NEG thinking and practice (discussed below), where non-state actors take on a greater role in the 'steering' and 'rowing' of addressing environmental harms (Osborne and Gaebler 1993).

This trend towards non-state steering and rowing was mirrored by unique international changes. For instance, new trans-governmental environmental networks of state officials and private actors emerged to combat the above-mentioned international inertia and fragmentation (Slaughter 2004; De Burca et al. 2013). International organizations also sought to use their mandates and expertise to extend governance beyond the point of state agreement and deepen the application of rules. They did this through partnerships, involving other organizations and actors, and establishing and diffusing new niches of governance (De Burca et al. 2013, p. 734; Glasbergen et al. 2007; Andonova 2010; Shepston Overly 2010). Emblematic of these approaches were new international enforcement collaborations (Pink and Lehane 2011; White 2011) as well as the growing pluralization of policing (e.g. Loader 2000) and NGO engagement in crime monitoring (e.g. Greenpeace and Humane Society whaling monitoring) (White 2012).

These international and domestic developments opened up new forms of non-state auspices and influence, in ways that arguably pioneered NEG. However, as we will see, what makes the NEG phase distinct from these earlier developments is that it demands levels of collaboration, participation, deliberation, flexibility and adaptability that would have been unimaginable years before (De Burca et al. 2013; Holley et al. 2011).

New Environmental Governance

An Overview of NEG Theory and Practice

The NEG enterprise involves collaboration between a diversity of private, public and non-government stakeholders who, acting together towards commonly agreed (or mutually negotiated) goals, hope to achieve more collectively than they could individually (Holley et al. 2011, p. 4). This approach relies heavily upon participatory dialogue and deliberation, flexibility (rather than uniformity), inclusiveness, knowledge generation and processes of learning, transparency and institutionalized consensus-building practices (see generally: De Burca and Scott 2006; Trubek and Trubek 2007). Rather than using law to secure uniform compliance with fixed rules, NEG seeks to use open-ended standards that can accommodate diversity, and tries to solve problems before coercion is necessary (although this does not mean that traditional regulation is entirely abandoned) (Cottrell and Trubek 2012). Through the use of collaboratively developed strategies and partnerships between agencies, community groups and traditional environmental offenders (such as industry), NEG seeks to look beyond government auspices to harness non-government institutions to contribute to preventing harms and enhancing environmental performance (Bricknel 2010; Grabosky and Gant 2000; Ayling 2013; UNODC 2012; Abott and Snidal 2009).

Just as there is no singular green criminology theory (Lynch and Stretesky 2014, p. 77), there is no firm agreement on a definitive 'model' of NEG (Van der Heijden 2013). Rather, a variety of terms and theories have been developed to describe and prescribe how NEG operates. These include 'experimentalism' (De Burca et al. 2013), 'post sovereign environmental governance' (Karkkainen 2004b), 'collaborative governance' (Freeman 1997), 'adaptive governance' (Chaffin et al. 2014) and 'global environmental governance' (Okereke et al. 2009).

These perspectives vary in their emphasis, encompassing different schools of thought and applying distinct institutional and political approaches to a range of environmental harms. However, what binds these theories is a number of common, broad characteristics. These include a focus on the virtues of flexibility, participation, deliberation, collaboration, learning and adaptation. These common characteristics have led a burgeoning group of scholars to collectively refer to these approaches as NEG (Karkkainen 2004a; De Burca and Scott 2006; Holley et al. 2011).

Consistent with evolving understandings of NEG, not all of the above characteristics need be present for a particular practice or programme to fall within this category – indeed there are very few single institutional forms that fully capture the idea of NEG in its entirety. However, the more characteristics that are present, the stronger the claim that they fall within the category of NEG (De Burca and Scott 2006; Holley et al. 2011).

Domestic programmes that fall within this category typically involve a variety of non-state actors assuming administrative, regulatory, managerial and mediating functions previously undertaken by the state (Gunningham 2009; Ostrom 2010, p. 643). Often domestic NEG programmes engage both past 'offenders' (e.g. those who have breached the law and harmed the environment), potential 'offenders' (those who may harm the environment, whether legally or illegally), as well as interested third parties (e.g. NGOs), to develop environmental protection goals, targets and a suit of actions to redress past harm, but also proactively manage and prevent future harm.

These past or future harms often relate to complex environmental challenges such as diffuse water pollution and management of natural resources like land and forests. Many of these problems are already regulated by existing legal instruments, however as discussed above, these instruments have often been ill-suited to resolving the behaviours that have caused environmental harms. For example, in the case of diffuse transboundary water pollution, the problem is often caused not by a single large ship or factory, but rather by the collective discharges of a variety of ships, commercial enterprises, farms and/or households. In such cases, many of the causes are not illegal at the individual level, and only give rise to harm at the cumulative level (White 2009, p. 231). In this context, regulators have little recourse under traditional regulatory enforcement. Even if they have cause for traditional regulation, regulators are often vastly outnumbered by the multitude of causes, or the problems 'fall through the cracks' between different tiers of government or different government agencies which allocate jurisdictional responsibility along ecologically arbitrary, human-defined boundaries (Gunningham et al. 2007, p. 127).

Prominent NEG approaches that have tried to overcome these issues and manage complex environmental harms include regional natural resource management bodies in Australia (Holley et al. 2011); collaborative approaches to water management in New Zealand (Holley and Gunningham 2011); and endeavours of multiple agencies and stakeholders addressing competing demands on water resources in the Bay Delta in the United States (Holley 2015).

NEG has also been identified internationally (and in the interaction between international and domestic levels). These NEG programmes often involve more flexible open-ended standards, multi-level networks, as well as significant decision and implementation roles being given to non-state actors (Cottrell and Trubek 2012, p. 362). Examples included the European Union's Water Framework Directive (Trubek and Trubek 2007) and Forest Law Enforcement Governance and Trade initiative (Overdevest and Zeitlin 2014); the Partnership for the Development of Environmental Law in Africa (PADELIA) (Kimani 2010); the inter-American tropical tuna commission (De Burca et al. 2013) and management of the Great Lakes in the United States/Canada (Karkkainen 2004b).

NEG's Potential Benefits for Addressing Environmental Harms

It is an open question whether NEG theory sufficiently accounts for the practical differences within the evolving NEG examples discussed above (Karkkainen 2004a). Certainly, the shift to NEG has to some extent been shaped by specific contexts and influences (De Burca 2010), but generally speaking it has come about because of the perceived capacity of these more collaborative and adaptive approaches to deliver benefits in circumstances where traditional approaches cannot (Holley et al. 2011, p. 4). For example, prescriptive regulatory standards – and even caps/taxes in some market-based instruments – depend upon a degree of centralized knowledge (e.g. in order to set suitable standards, prices or caps) that is often not available. In contrast, the sort of collaborative, participatory and deliberative approaches contemplated by NEG are said to lead to problem-solving that is inclusive of local circumstances and able to capitalize on the unique knowledge and capacities of multiple public and private actors in managing environmental harms (Holley et al. 2011, p. 4). Kimani's (2010, pp. 50–51) study of PADELIA, for instance, suggests that the kind of collaborative and participatory engagement envisioned by NEG can help state and non-state actors to 'identify their interests, frame issues and enhance implementation' of laws to better address environmental harms. Further, by fostering collaborative decision-making among previously fragmented agencies and non-government actors, NEG may better integrate and respond to increasing connections between different forms of crime. Signs of such an NEG approach are evident in the International Consortium on Combating Wildlife Crime, a coordinated global response to wildlife crime and its connections to money laundering, fraud, counterfeiting and violence (Interpol 2015).

The direct involvement of government and non-government actors in NEG's collaborative styles of implementation, management and monitoring can also help augment and extend the resources of traditional regulators (Ayling 2013; White 2011). For example, government actors engaged in multi-stakeholder collaborative environmental forums may have more formal opportunities to link-up with NGOs to access and better coordinate the use of international resources to fund programmes that address environmental harms (Duffy 2013, p. 232; Kimani 2010). Further, the engagement of local non-government actors in NEG approaches has been shown to bring additional forms of social control to addressing environmental harms (such as peer pressure), as well as expanding the scope of surveillance by bringing together agencies and stakeholders who are close to the problem (Holley and Gunningham 2011; Morrison et al. 2004; Karkkainen 2002, p. 228; Lubell et al. 2005; Freeman and Farber 2005, p. 877). This type of collaboration is likely to have particular benefits for 'weak' states, where government resources and expertise may be otherwise limited, and environmental harms often go unseen (Börzel 2011, p. 13; Braithwaite 2004). Chhetri et al. (2012) provide a nice example of such benefits in their study of community forestry in Nepal. They found that local enforcement in community settings detects far more forest crimes (e.g. illegal extraction of firewood) than enforcement by formal forest authorities.

The involvement of non-government actors in deliberative styles of governance (albeit varying from local citizens to international NGOs) can also foster stakeholder ownership and 'buy-in' (Ayling 2013; Grabosky and Gant 2000; Karkkainen 2001) and can give greater voice to marginalized interests (as contrasted to an exclusive reliance on bureaucratic expertise in hierarchy or on price and competition in markets) (Sabel et al. 1999; Holley et al. 2011, p. 4). Such buy-in and ownership can mean that the perceived costs of compliance are likely to remain low (Cottrell and Trubek 2012, p. 390), as Holley and Gunningham (2011) show in their analysis of a collaborative NEG programme in New Zealand. They argue that the traditional New Zealand regulatory framework had proved unsuccessful at addressing pollution of many streams and other water bodies. By fostering collaboration amongst regulators and those who manage land beside the waterway, including people who had previously breached the law, farmers came to 'buy-in' to the management of the stream environment, and this contributed to demonstrable environmental improvements.

In a similar vein, NEG's deliberative and participatory approaches are argued to be more adept at changing behaviour by focusing on internalized drivers and norms, developed from social context and shared values (Holley and Lawson 2015). NEG may activate these norms by engaging those who may potentially harm the environment directly in decision-making and implementation of environmental programmes, in partnership with government, scientists, NGOs and others. Through collaborative decision-making and dialogue, a shared understanding of environmentally important norms can emerge (Holley and Lawson 2015; Bandura 1997, p. 483; Cottrell and Trubek 2012, p. 390). Such approaches would appear to have particular potential in changing drivers of environmental harm, such as through engaging local communities in developing and implementing conservation processes and ecotourism (Huisman and Van Erp 2013).

NEG's learning and adaptation focus is thought to ensure that it copes better with the dynamism, uncertainty and complexity of environmental harm than either traditional regulation (which can easily ossify, freeze standards at a particular point in time or adopt a one-size-fits-all approach) or many market-based approaches (where significant post-hoc programme corrections to pollution levels and permits risk undermining the security of ownership rights on which the market itself depends or prevent new entrants) (Holley et al. 2011, p. 5). Instead, NEG ideals are said to enable governance processes that 'learn' more easily from changing circumstances 'on the ground' (making the governance framework more responsive to the complexity of crime situations it faces) (Bisschop and Verhage 2012; Abbott and Snidal 2009, pp. 546 and 552; Sabel et al. 1999, p. 3; Durant et al. 2004, p. 4; Lobel 2004, p. 502; Orts 1995).

The most fully formed learning and adaption architecture has been developed by experimentalist strands of NEG theory (De Burca et al. 2013). Experimentalist theories suggest that widespread information sharing can enhance the overall performance and accountability of governance systems, particularly by sharing information and experience between localized groups (horizontally), and/or between localized groups and agencies (vertically), to periodically reformulate and progressively refine minimum performance standards, desirable targets, and preferred means of achieving them (see Karkkainen et al. 2000, p. 690; Scheuerman 2004, p. 115).

Such explicit commitment to knowledge generation is arguably better suited to addressing specific environmental harms of moving species, resources and pollutants across borders, as it demands cross-jurisdictional information sharing between government and non-government collaborators (be they Westphalian state boundaries or domestic ones) (Elliott 2012). Kimani's (2010, p. 51) findings in the case of PADELIA suggests these NEG ideals hold promise, where cross-fertilization of ideas occurred horizontally between developing nations, rather than simply downwards from developed to developing nations. This contributed to 'the creation of local capacity to develop, implement and enforce environmental laws, which would outlive the duration of the project' (Kimani 2010, pp. 50–51).Cottrell and Trubek (2012) offer a more expansive example in their study of the Tuna-Dolphin case, and the subsequent La Jolla Agreement and International Dolphin Conservation Program. These NEG developments gave rise to an ambitious on-board observer programme. Using the information generated, stakeholders were able to meet their objectives by developing recommendations and exchanging best practices protocols (e.g. improving performance with respect to releasing dolphin by-catch alive). According to the authors, 'Flagship states ultimately complied with the La Jolla Agreement and their fleets' performance exceeded expectations, achieving a dolphin kill rate that was "one-tenth the kill rate of the highly regulated U.S. fleet in 1988, using virtually the same technology (but with greater skill and care)" ' (Cottrell and Trubek 2012, p. 389).

NEG Critiques and Debates

Despite the potential benefits of these NEG features, it is important not to overlook the potential weaknesses and challenges of NEG. Perhaps the biggest challenge for NEG is the uncertainty of whether its benefits can actually be achieved in practice (Driessen et al. 2012). Certainly the above studies suggest there are successful examples. But NEG has also faced a litany of criticisms, including claims that it leads to lowest common denominator solutions, rent seeking, dominance by self-interested economic actors, disenfranchised environmental interests and problems sustaining participation after initial bursts of enthusiasm (see generally: Holley et al. 2011). Considerable empirical research is still required to resolve disagreement surrounding the impacts of NEG, as it is the principles and practical conditions that will enable successful NEG experiments to be replicated (Karkkainen 2006; Holley et al. 2011, p. 9).

One particularly fruitful area of research has focused on whether and how NEG interacts with earlier phases of environmental regulation, principally command and control, which remains a bedrock of addressing environmental harms and crimes (e.g. illegally taking water or clearing vegetation) in most countries (Karkkainen 2004a; Lobel 2004; Gunningham 2009, p. 159; Holley and Sinclair 2011; Bartel 2005). Scholars have tentatively identified a range of possible relationships between traditional command and control and NEG, each of which has differing implications for 'success'. Some of the more underexplored hypotheses include: 'gaps' (where law and collaboration conflict and potentially inhibit mutual success); 'penalty default hybridity' (a constructive relationship broadly akin to Ayres and Braithwaite's (1992) regulatory pyramid, where regulation should be set precisely for the purposes of inducing otherwise reluctant people to embrace

NEG); and 'transformative integration' (where the two approaches are merged into an integrated system) (Trubek and Trubek 2007). While debates over these hypotheses continue, a range of NEG theories increasingly recognize that NEG very often needs to operate in hybrid within conventional regulation, so as to prevent abuse and to incentivize actors' participation (Holley and Gunningham 2011; De Burca et al. 2013).

More generally, the few studies that have attempted to grapple with NEG's performance in practice, increasingly suggest that it is no panacea to the globe's continuing environmental harms (De Burca et al. 2013; Holley et al. 2011). Indeed, results have been mixed at best. Arguably this is because NEG is a continuing social experiment that is transiting from a period of testing by trial and error to one of consolidation and refinement. But the success of this new, more mature stage will depend principally upon heeding the lessons of earlier successes and failures and drawing broader lessons from them to make NEG work in practice. A number of scholars have begun this task (De Burca et al. 2013), and a range of identified principles and conditions under which NEG appears likely to work include: the need for significant resourcing; carefully designed incentives; the identification, creation, nurturing and maintenance of governance capacities (particularly for non-government actors); and incorporating effective horizontal, as well as vertical, information-exchange mechanisms into NEG structures (Holley et al. 2011).

Concluding Remarks

Criminologists have expressed concern that their discipline continues to neglect green issues (Lynch and Stretesky 2014). This is not to say progress in green criminology has not been made (South and Brisman 2013; Bisschop and Verhage 2012; Gibbs et al. 2010; White 2012; Spapens et al. 2014). However, more work is needed to 're-create' criminology (Lynch and Stretesky 2014; Spapens et al. 2014; White 2009).

This chapter has sought to contribute to this re-creation. It has done so by examining NEG, a recent development in environmental law and governance scholarship. The chapter tracked the development of NEG, highlighting a shift away from traditional forms of controlling environmental harms, namely regulation, as well as markets and early forms of partnerships. It has outlined the collaborative, participatory, deliberative and flexible learning characteristics of NEG and offered some examples of its operation in practice. The benefits of NEG, for addressing transboundary environmental harms, were identified. These benefits specifically included: resource savings, enhancing on-the-ground monitoring of crimes, accessing new resources and expertise to improve governance responses, enhancing chances of compliance (e.g. by encouraging buy-in, internalizing environmental norms) and diffusing information and innovation to improve performance.

Despite these potential benefits, it is important to caution against seeing NEG as a panacea. There is still a long way to go to understand when and whether NEG may work in practice. Even so, the potentially fruitful benefits of NEG's collaborative, participatory, deliberative and learning architecture appears to warrant further exploration of this new approach to governing environmental harms in the world.

References

Abbott, K. and Snidal, D. 2009. 'Strengthening International Regulation through Transmittal New Governance: Overcoming the Orchestration Deficit', *Vanderbilt Journal of Transnational Law* 42, 501–78.

Andonova, L. 2010. 'Public-Private Partnerships for the Earth: Politics and Patterns of Hybrid Authority in the Multilateral System Global', *Environmental Politics* 102, 25–53.

Ayling, J. 2013. 'Harnessing Third Parties for Transnational Environmental Crime Prevention', *Transnational Environmental Law* 2(2), 339–62.

Ayres, I. and Braithwaite, J. 1992. *Responsive Regulation: Transcending the Deregulation Debate*. New York: Oxford University Press.

Bandura, A. 1997. *Self-Efficacy: The Exercise of Control*. New York: WH Freeman and Company.

Bartel, R. 2005. 'When the Heavenly Gaze Criminalises: Satellite Surveillance, Land Clearance Regulation and the Human-Nature Relationship', *Current Issues in Criminal Justice* 16(3), 322–39.

Bisschop, L. 2012. 'Is it all Going to Waste? Illegal Transports of E-Waste in a European Trade Hub', *Crime, Law and Social Change* 58(3), 221–49.

Bisschop, L. and Verhage, A. 2012. 'The Complex(ity) of Policing Dirty Crime', *Politiestudies: Tides & Currents of Policing* 25, 273–90.

Börzel, T. 2011. 'Move Closer! New Modes of Governance and Accession to the European Union', *Law and Economics Review* 2, 1–22.

Braithwaite, J. 2004. 'Methods of Power for Development: Weapons of the Weak, Weapons of the Strong', *Michigan Journal of International Law* 26, 297–330.

Bricknel, S. 2010. *Environmental Crime in Australia.* Research and Public Policy Series no. 109. Canberra: Australian Institute of Criminology.

Chaffin, B.C., Gosnell, H. and Cosens, B. 2014. 'A Decade of Adaptive Governance Scholarship: Synthesis and Future Directions', *Ecology and Society* 19(3), 56.

Chhetri, B., Overgaard Larsen, H. and Smith-Hal, C. 2012. 'Law Enforcement in Community Forestry: Consequences for the Poor', *Small Scale Forestry* 11, 435–52.

Cole, D. and Grossman, P. 1999. 'When is Command-and-Control Efficient?', *Wisconsin Law Review* 5, 887–938.

Cottrell, M. and Trubek, D. 2012. 'Law as Problem Solving: Standards, Networks, Experimentation and Deliberation in Global Space', *Transnational Law and Contemporary Problems* 21, 359–93.

Cutting, R. and Cahoon, L. 2005. 'Thinking Outside the Box: Property Rights as a Key to Environmental Protection', *Pace Environmental Law Review* 22, 55–90.

De Burca, G. 2010. 'New Governance and Experimentalism: An Introduction', *Wisconsin Law Review* 2, 227–38.

De Burca, G. and Scott, J. 2006. 'Introduction: New Governance, Law and Constitutionalism', in *Law and New Governance in the EU and the US*, edited by G. De Burca and J. Scott. Oxford: Hart Publishing, 1–14.

De Burca, G., Keohane, R. and Sabel, C. 2013. 'New Modes of Pluralist Global Governance', *New York University Journal of International Law & Politics* 45, 723–86.

Driessen, P., Dieperink, C., Van Laerhoven, F., Runhaar, H. and Vermeulen, W. 2012. 'Towards a Conceptual Framework for the Study of Shifts in Modes of Environmental Governance – Experiences from the Netherlands', *Environmental Policy and Governance* 22, 143–60.

Duffy, R. 2013. 'Global Environmental Governance and North–South Dynamics: The Case of the CITES', *Environment and Planning C: Government and Policy* 31, 222–39.

Durant, R., O'Leary, R. and Fiorino, D. 2004. 'Introduction', in *Environmental Governance Reconsidered*, edited by R. Durant, R. O'Leary and D. Fiorino. Cambridge, MA: MIT Press, 1–28.

Elliott, L. 2012. 'Fighting Transnational Environmental Crime', *Journal of International Affairs* 66(1), 87–104.

Freeman, J. 1997. 'Collaborative Governance in the Administrative State', *UCLA Law Review* 45, 1–98.

Freeman, J. and Farber, D. 2005. 'Modular Environmental Regulation', *Duke Law Journal* 54, 795–912.

Gess, K. 1964. 'Permanent Sovereignty over Natural Resources', *International and Comparative Law Quarterly* 13(2), 398–449.

Gibbs, C., Gore, M., McGarrell, E. and Rivers, L. 2010. 'Introducing Conservation Criminology: Towards Interdisciplinary Scholarship on Environmental Crimes and Risks', *British Journal of Criminology* 50(1), 124–44.

Glasbergen, P., Biermann, F. and Mol, A. 2007. *Partnerships, Governance and Sustainable Development*. Cheltenham: Edward Elgar.

Grabosky, P. and Gant, F. 2000. *Improving Environmental Performance, Preventing Environmental Crime*. Research and Public Policy Series no. 27. Canberra: Australian Institute of Criminology

Gunderson, L. and Holling, C.S. (eds). 2001. *Panarchy: Understanding Transformations in Human and Natural Systems*. Washington, DC: Island Press.

Gunningham, N. 2008. *Innovative Governance and Regulatory Design: Managing Water Resources*. Landcare Research No LC0708/137. New Zealand: Landcare Research.

——— 2009. 'Environment Law, Regulation and Governance: Shifting Architectures', *Journal of Environmental Law* 21(2), 179–212.

Gunningham, N. and Holley, C., 2010. *Bringing the 'R' Word Back: Regulation, Environment Protection and NRM*. Canberra: ASSA.

Gunningham, N. and Sinclair, D. 2002. *Leaders & Laggards*. Sheffield: Greenleaf.

Gunningham, N., Grabosky, P. and Sinclair, D. 1998. *Smart Regulation: Designing Environmental Policy*. Oxford: Clarendon Press.

Gunningham, N., Holley, C. and Shearing, C. 2007. 'Neighbourhood Environment Improvement Plans: Community Empowerment, Voluntary Collaboration and Legislative Design', *Environmental and Planning Law Journal* 24(2), 125–51.

Hayek, F.A. 1945. 'The Use of Knowledge in Society', *American Economic Review* XXXV(4), 519–30.

Holley, C. 2015a. 'Crafting Collaborative Governance', *Environmental Law Reporter* 45(4), 10324–37.

Holley, C. 2015b. 'Environmental Regulation and Governance', in *Regulation, Institutions and Networks*, edited by P. Drahos. Canbera: ANU E Press (in press).

Holley, C. and Gunningham, N. 2006. 'Environment Improvement Plans: Facilitative Regulation in Practice', *Environmental Planning and Law Journal* 23, 448–64.

——— 2011. 'Natural Resources, New Governance and Legal Regulation: When Does Collaboration Work?', *New Zealand Universities Law Review* 24, 309–36.

Holley, C. and Lawson, A. 2015. 'Implementing Environmental Law and Collaborative Governance: Water and Natural Resource Management', in *Implementing Environmental Law*, edited by P. Martin and A. Kennedy. Cheltenham: Edward Elgar, 238–59.

Holley, C. and Sinclair, D. 2011. 'Compliance and Enforcement of Water Licences in NSW: Limitations in Law, Policy and Institutions', *Australasian Journal of Natural Resources Law and Policy* 15(2), 149–89.

Holley, C., Gunningham, N. and Shearing, C. 2011. *The New Environmental Governance*. Abingdon: Earthscan.

Holling, C.S. (ed.). 1978. *Adaptive Environmental Assessment and Management*. Chichester: Wiley.

Houfu, Y. and Xiaopu, S. 2013. 'Transfer or not Transfer? It is a Question: The Challenges to and Solutions for the Transfer Procedure of Suspected Environmental Pollution Criminal Cases', *Environmental Practice* 15(3), 271–9.

Howes, R., Skea, J. and Whelan, B. 1997. *Clean and Competitive? Motivating Environmental Performance in Industry*. London: Earthscan Publications.

Huisman, W. and Van Erp, J. 2013. 'Opportunities for Environmental Crime: A Test of Situational Crime Prevention Theory', *British Journal of Criminology* 53(6), 1178–200.

Interpol. 2015. *Task Forces: National Environmental Security Task Forces 2015*. Available at: www.interpol.int/Crime-areas/Environmental-crime/Task-forces (accessed 27 February 2015).

Karkkainen, B. 2001. 'Information as Environmental Regulation: TRI and Performance Benchmarking, Precursor to a New Paradigm?', *Georgetown Law Journal* 89, 257–370.

——— 2002. 'Collaborative Ecosystem Governance: Scale, Complexity, and Dynamism', *Virginia Environmental Law Journal* 21, 189–243.

——— 2004a. 'Reply, New Governance in Legal Thought and in the World: Some Splitting as Antidote to Overzealous Lumping', *Minnesota Law Review* 89, 471–97.

——— 2004b. 'Post-Sovereign Environmental Governance', *Global Environmental Politics* 4(1), 72–96.

——— 2006. 'Information Forcing Regulation and Environmental Governance', in *Law and New Governance in the EU and the US*, edited by G. De Burca and J. Scott. Oxford: Hart Publishing, 293–321.

Karkkainen, B., Fung, A. and Sabel, C. 2000. 'After Backyard Environmentalism: Toward a Performance-Based Regime of Environmental Regulation', *American Behavioral Scientist* 44(4), 690–709.

Kelemen, R. and Vogel, D. 2010. 'Trading Places: The Role of the United States and the European Union in International Environmental Politics', *Comparative Political Studies* 43(4), 427–56.

Kimani, N. 2010. 'A Collaborative Approach to Environmental Governance in East Africa', *Journal of Environmental Law* 22(1), 27–57.

Krasna, S. 2001. *Problematic Sovereignty: Contested Rules and Political Possibilities*. New York: Columbia University Press.

Lazarus, R. 2004. *The Making of Environmental Law*. Chicago: University of Chicago Press.

Lenox, M.J. and Nash, J. 2003. 'Industry Self-Regulation and Adverse Selection: A Comparison Across Four Trade Association Programs', *Business Strategy and the Environment* 2, 343–56.

Lipman, Z. 2013. 'Environmental Crime and Enforcement in Australia', *Australian Environment Review* 28(5), 580–85.

Loader, I. 2000. 'Plural Policing and Democratic Governance', *Social & Legal Studies* 9(3), 323–45.

Lobel, O. 2004. 'Setting the Agenda for New Governance Research', *Minnesota Law Review* 89, 498–509.

Lubell, M., Sabatier, P., Vedlitz, A., Focht, W., Trachtenberg, Z. and Matlock, M. 2005. 'Conclusions and Recommendations', in *Swimming Upstream: Collaborative Approaches To Watershed Management*, edited by P. Sabatier, W. Focht, M. Lubell, Z. Trachtenberg, A. Vedlitz and M. Matlock. Cambridge, MA: MIT, 261–96.

Lynch, M.J. and Stretesky, P.B. 2011. 'Similarities between Green Criminology and Green Science: Toward a Typology of Green Criminology', *International Journal of Comparative and Applied Criminal Justice* 35(4), 293–306.

——— 2014. *Exploring Green Criminology*. Farnham: Ashgate.

McGinnis, M. (ed.). 1999. *Polycentric Governance and Development*. Ann Arbor: University of Michigan Press.

McKibbin, W. and Wilcoxen, P. 2002. 'The Role of Economics in Climate Change Policy', *The Journal of Economic Perspectives* 16(2), 107–29.

Mol, A. and Sonnenfeld, D. 2000. *Ecological Modernisation around the World*. London: Frank Cass.

Morrison, T., McDonald, G. and Lane, M. 2004. 'Integrating Natural Resource Management for Better Environmental Outcomes', *Australian Geographer* 35(3), 243–59.

Najam, A., Papa, M. and Taiyab, N. 2006. *Global Environmental Governance: A Reform Agenda*. Winnipeg: IISD.

Nellemann, C., Henriksen, R., Raxter, P., Ash, N. and Mrema, E. (eds). 2014. *The Environmental Crime Crisis, Threats to Sustainable Development from Illegal Exploitation and Trade in Wildlife and Forest Resources*. Nairobi and Arendal: United Nations Environment Programme and GRID-Arendal. Available at: www.unep.org/unea/docs/rracrime crisis.pdf (accessed 27 February 2015).

Okereke, C., Bulkeley, H. and Schroeder, H. 2009. 'Conceptualizing Climate Governance beyond the International Regime', *Global Environmental Politics* 9(1), 58–78.

Orts, E. 1995. 'Reflexive Environmental Law', *Northwestern University Law Review* 89, 1227–340.

Orts, E. and Deketelaere, K. (eds). 2001. *Environmental Contracts: Comparative Approaches to Regulatory Innovation in United States and Europe*. London: Kluwer.

Osborne, D. and Gaebler, T. 1993. *Reinventing Government: How the Entrepreneurial Spirit is Transforming the Public Sector*. New York: Plume.

Ostrom, E. 2010. 'Beyond Markets and States: Polycentric Governance of Complex Economic Systems', *American Economic Review* 100, 641–72.

Overdevest, C. and Zeitlin, J. 2014. 'Assembling an Experimentalist Regime: Transnational Governance Interactions in the Forest Sector', *Regulation and Governance* 8(1), 22–48.

Pink, G. and Lehane, J. 2011. *Environmental Enforcement Networks: Development of a Network Evaluation Matrix*. Paper presented at the 9th International Conference on Environmental Compliance and Enforcement, 20–24 June.

Roma, A. 2006. 'Energy, Money, and Pollution', *Ecological Economics* 56, 534–45.

Sabel, C., Fung, A. and Karkkainen, B. 1999. 'Beyond Backyard Environmentalism', *Boston Review* October/November, 1–17.

Scheuerman, W. 2004. 'Democractic Experimentalism or Capitalist Synchronization – Critical Reflections on Directly-Deliberative Polyarchy', *Canadian Journal of Law and Jurisprudence* 17, 101–28.

Scott, K. 2011. 'International Environmental Governance: Managing Fragmentation through Institutional Connection', *Melbourne Journal of International Law* 12(1), 177–216.

Shearing, C. 2013. *Whither Criminology*. Speech held at Ottawa University, 30 October (personal communication, 14 November 2013).

Shepston Overly, M. 2010. 'When Private Stakeholders Fail: Adapting Expropriation Challenges in Transnational Tribunals to New Governance Theories', *Ohio State Law Journal* 71, 341–80.

Slaughter, A. 2004. *A New World Order*. Princeton: Princeton University Press.

South, N. and Brisman, A. (eds). 2013. *The Routledge International Handbook of Green Criminology*. London: Routledge.

Spapens, T., White, R.D. and Kluin, M. (eds). 2014. *Environmental Crime and its Victims: Perspectives within Green Criminology*. Farnham: Ashgate.

Stewart, R. 2001. 'A New Generation of Environmental Regulation?', *Capital University Law Review* 29, 21–182.

Tomkins, K. 2009. 'Police, Law Enforcement and the Environment', in *Environmental Crime: A Reader*, edited by R. White. Cullompton: Willan Publishing, 515–27.

Trubek, D. and Trubek, L. 2007. 'New Governance & Legal Regulation', *Columbia Journal of European Law* 13, 540–64.

United Nations Environment Programme (UNEP). 2007. *Networking Counts: Combating Illegal Trade in Ozone Depleting Substances*. Paris: United Nations Environment Programme.

United Nations Interregional Crime and Justice Research Institute. 2015. *Environmental Crimes*. Available at: www.unicri.it/topics/environmental/ (accessed 27 February 2015).

United Nations Office of Drugs and Crime (UNODC). 2012. *Wildlife and Forest Crime Analytical Toolkit*, revised edition. New York: United Nations. Available at: www.unodc.org/documents/Wildlife/Toolkit_e.pdf (accessed 27 February 2015).

Van der Heijden, J. 2013. 'Is New Governance the Silver Bullet? Insights from the Australian Buildings Sector', *Urban Policy and Research* 31(4), 453–71.

White, R. 2009. 'Researching Transnational Environmental Harm: Toward an Eco-Global Criminology', *International Journal of Comparative and Applied Criminal Justice* 33(2), 229–48.

——— 2011. 'Environmental Law Enforcement: The Importance of Global Networks and Collaborative Practices', *Australasian Policing: A Journal of Professional Practice and Research* 3(1), 12–16.

——— 2012. 'NGO Engagement in Environmental Law Enforcement: Critical Reflections', *Australasian Policing: A Journal of Professional Practice and Research* 4(1), 4–7.

Yu, X. 2011. 'Transboundary Water Pollution Management: Lessons Learned from River Basin Management in China, Europe and the Netherlands', *Utrecht Law Review* 7(1), 188–9.

10 Deliberative Democracy and Environmental Law Enforcement

Giuseppe Rotolo

Out of the 'Cave' and Beyond the 'Blindness'

> – And now, I said, let me show in a figure how far our nature is enlightened or unenlightened: Behold! human beings living in a underground den, which has a mouth open towards the light and reaching all along the den; here they have been from their childhood, and have their legs and necks chained so that they cannot move, and can only see before them, being prevented by the chains from turning round their heads. Above and behind them a fire is blazing at a distance, and between the fire and the prisoners there is a raised way; and you will see, if you look, a low wall built along the way, like the screen which marionette players have in front of them, over which they show the puppets.
>
> (. . .)
>
> – And now look again, and see what will naturally follow if the prisoners are released and disabused of their error. At first, when any of them is liberated and compelled suddenly to stand up and turn his neck round and walk and look towards the light, he will suffer sharp pains; the glare will distress him, and he will be unable to see the realities of which in his former state he had seen the shadows; and then conceive someone saying to him, that what he saw before was an illusion, but that now, when he is approaching nearer to being and his eye is turned towards more real existence, he has a clearer vision, – what will be his reply? And you may further imagine that his instructor is pointing to the objects as they pass and requiring him to name them, – will he not be perplexed? Will he not fancy that the shadows which he formerly saw are truer than the objects which are now shown to him?
>
> – Far truer.
>
> (. . .)
>
> – Then, I said, the business of us who are the founders of the State will be to compel the best minds to attain that knowledge which we have already shown to be the greatest of all-they must continue to ascend until they arrive at the good; but when they have ascended and seen enough we must not allow them to do as they do now.
>
> – What do you mean?

> – I mean that they remain in the upper world: but this must not be allowed; they must be made to descend again among the prisoners in the den, and partake of their labours and honours, whether they are worth having or not.
>
> (Excerpts from Plato, *The Republic*, Book VII)

Plato's allegory of the cave has been a very inspiring source of reflection for many disciplines: not only the philosophical or philological, but also the social and political. The origin of the image has been in the spotlight of scholars (Wright 1906), as well as the hidden meaning of the metaphor (Hyland 2004). Considering the political relevance of the allegory, James S. Fishkin has recalled the image of the cave in his proposal of deliberative democracy: he uses the myth as a metaphor for the level of awareness that in our societies a large part of the people have about political instances (Fishkin 1995). The condition of those persons who have been constrained since their childhood to watch the shadows cast on the wall in front of them represents that of the citizens who do not take part in the political debate and who are not involved in the decision-making process. As Fishkin observes:

> In the modern age, our citizens live in a high-tech version of Plato's cave . . . Instead of puppetlike reflections from fire on a cave wall, we watch television images in our living rooms. Instead of echoed voices from the puppet manipulators, we listen to the voices of radio and television talk shows and advertisements. Like the inhabitants of Plato's cave, we tend to take these reflected images and voices as the real world. At least in terms of our roles as citizens, things that do not happen on television have little, if any, force, vividness, or immediacy. It is the reflected images that seem real and important. They constitute the political world rather than what we can see outside 'the cave' with our own eyes.
>
> (Fishkin 1995, pp. 13–14)

The core idea at the basis of the notion of deliberative democracy is that citizens should take active part in the political life of the community they belong to; furthermore, such participation requires a higher level of awareness as a necessary precondition to carry the weight of taking public decisions and, thus, of assuming responsibilities for collective issues. Just like those individuals who were able to get out of the cave and contemplate the world as well as the *light* that cast the shadows on the wall, people need to acquire those skills necessary to bring personal contribution to the public sphere.

Martin Heiddeger studied in depth the allegory of the cave, along with his studies on Truth. In his 1942 essay devoted to the interpretation of Plato's myth, he argued that the passage determines the modification of the concept of *aletheia* (ἀλήθεια), previously intended as *unhiddeness* and then related to the *correctness of vision* (Heiddeger 1997). As the prominent philosopher underlined, this mutation has meant a different conception of the Truth, which has played a relevant role in the future development of our Western societies. Basically, the new theoretical construct has emphasized a subjective attitude towards Truth, as a personal improvement following the path from the cave to get the *light* above. In this perspective, the allegory stands for the educational pathway that a philosopher has to follow in order to gain a higher level of knowledge and, along this way, contemplate the Truth.

Of course, this interpretation of the myth could likewise be consistent with the elitist political ideal expressed by Plato and symbolized with the figure of the *philosopher king*. Nevertheless, eliciting the allegory meaning highlights other aspects coherent with the idea of citizens' involvement in public activities. Not only, as Fishkin points out, since in other works by Plato, especially in the *Laws*, the philosopher proposes the participation of samples of ordinary people on deliberative councils, in charge of making public decisions (Fishkin 1995). In fact, the allegory itself seems to promote the idea of people's participation in the *res publica*: those who made severe efforts to get out and contemplate the world above and the light, as the symbol of the supreme Good, the Being, have a moral duty to go back to the cave. The ethical and political meaning of the myth lies on the necessity for those who got free from the chains of the ignorance to relieve the 'prisoners' (Reale 1998, p. 298). Indeed, their efforts entail the sharing of the deeper knowledge they gained with those who are still blind, although this could be extremely challenging, recalling the metaphor, just like it is very difficult to gaze upon the shadows and the *dark* of the cave for the eyes of those who have experienced the *light* of the reality.

Essentially, the ancient Greek culture stands as a source of inspiration for deliberative democracy: in particular, the role of the citizen in that model of democracy may be understood as the root of deliberative decision-making strategies on public issues (Elster 1998, pp. 2–3; Fishkin 1991, p. 1).[1] If, generally speaking, equality is the distinguishing feature of the role of the ancient Greek citizen, it is also possible to connote that attitude more specifically. Actually, the equality of citizens can be intended as equal dignity of all participants to the republic (*isotimia*; ἰσοτιμία) and also as the parity of rights and duties recognized to the

1 At this stage it is necessary to point out a premise, which is not only terminological, but that can also contribute to clarify the argument. Although the term remains the same, the concept of 'democracy' deeply varies since its foundation in ancient Greece up until today. If after the French Revolution its meaning has been enriched with a political value that we still hold, originally 'democracy' (δημοκρατία) stood merely for the form of government, which recognizes the power (κράτος) to the people (δῆμος). Of course many specific features among several systems of law historically have arisen, as long as this peculiar form of government has been arranged in different ways. When it comes to the case of Athens, the form of democracy was direct (and not representative), this means that the legislative function was assigned to an assembly composed by all the citizens and the institutional offices were fulfilled by some of them randomly selected. Thus, the political power was equally distributed among 'citizens', however the Athenian citizenship was essentially restricted to adult men and excluded some other categories (e.g. foreigners), besides women and slaves. For the evolution of the concept of democracy and the enrichment of its meaning, see Dunn (2005).

people towards the laws (*isonomia*; ἰσονομία), but it is the concept of *isegoria* (ἰσηγορία) which profoundly inspired the deliberative approach to democracy, since the citizens' participation to public decisions is a very distinguishing aspect of that theory. Namely, *isegoria* can be intended as 'an equal right to be heard in the sovereign assembly of the state before public decisions were taken' (Dunn 2000, p. 17).

This chapter aims to evaluate whether deliberative democracy could inspire strategies appropriate to improve the enforcement of environmental law, making it more effective: especially when competing interests are simultaneously relevant (e.g. health and environment to one side; employment to the other side) and the regulation needs a deep evaluation to balance the protection of natural resources and other values. Furthermore, a deliberative approach can foster community participation in the risk management, in order to involve the citizens in prevention strategies and to consider criminal sanctions actually as the *extrema ratio*.

Consistent with this vision, it is first necessary to focus on the main features of deliberative democracy, which – as well – can provide more effectiveness to the regulation concerning environmental issues. Then, several aspects about the implementation of deliberative strategies and instruments will be critically discussed, also presenting pertinent case studies and emphasizing the more controversial points.

Deliberative Democracy: Basic Features

Although no widely shared or formally adopted definition of deliberative democracy can be provided (Elster 1998, p. 8), several characteristics frequently return in the discussion about this approach to public decision-making strategies. Consistent with the purpose of this chapter and trying to underscore the particular attitude of such a theory, here can be shared the conceptualization of deliberative democracy as 'an un-coerced, other-regarding, reasoned, inclusive and equal debate' (Chappell 2012, p. 7).

Considering several comments on the definition proposed, the most representative feature of deliberative democracy – as already outlined – is citizens' participation. As the scope is to solve problems which have a social impact, deliberation requires the commitment of the whole community to address a particular situation and to offer a feasible solution. Moreover, as Zsuzsanna Chappell formulates, 'deliberation is democratic if it includes all substantively affected citizens and all relevant arguments to a sufficient degree and if it does so by guaranteeing at least minimal equality between them' (Chappell 2012, p. 7).

Focusing on this approach, at least two different aspects can be distinguished: about the contents, the way to balance different visions on the same issue and to foster a common point of view on the strategy to promote; and, about the method, a procedure to be followed in order to guarantee full representativeness to citizens' opinions.

Beginning with the former concept, a basic feature of this model of democracy recalls John Rawls' point about a deliberative approach to democratic decision-making: the necessity of pursuing the *common good* (Rawls 1971, pp. 261ff.). For that, political decisions cannot be shaped as a bargaining procedure of many self-interests, supported by different groups of population. As Joshua Cohen recaps:

> When properly conducted, then, democratic politics involves *public deliberation focused on the common good*, requires some form of *manifest equality* among citizens, and *shapes the identity and interests* of citizens in ways that contribute to the formation of a public conception of common good.
>
> (Cohen 1989, p. 19)

From this perspective, public and social institutions should be shaped in a way which is consistent with the aim of seeking to *mirror* the ideal of a fair deliberation (Cohen 1989, p. 20). Assuming the necessity of a deliberative model to take political decisions which could be inspired by the purpose to foster the arrangement of disputes in a deeply shared way, deliberative democracy requires also the definition of a procedure which could be coherent with that goal and, as well, could express prominently public participation and cooperation as main traits. In such a manner, citizens come to gather up their 'commitment to the resolution of problems of collective choice through public reasoning, and regard their basic institutions as legitimate in so far as they establish the framework for free public deliberation' (Cohen 1989, p. 21).

Seeking to evaluate how an ideal procedure of deliberation should be shaped (Cohen 1989, pp. 21ff.), four substantive features arise as fundamental. As a precondition of the deliberative process, freedom of participation is required, not only as an immediate consequence of the attitude towards inclusiveness that characterizes such an approach, but also as a particular aspect strictly related to the legitimacy of the method itself. Indeed, participants to a deliberative process should not be bound to any sort of ideology or prejudice, but to the results of the deliberation. Following the procedure, such a mechanism of deliberation entails a prerequisite of legitimacy that implies that the decision will be binding.

The last point comes with the second basic element with which a deliberative procedure should be consistent. In fact, in order to guarantee the results as legitimate, the procedure has to satisfy several conditions inherent to the fundamental roots of deliberation itself. Any decision should be premised on the strength of the argumentation used to support the proposal, thus the reasoning definitely arises as the basic rule to perform a deliberation. In this sense, Habermas' (1996) idea of discursive democracy comes to relevance: according to this, 'no force, except that of the better argument is exercised' (Habermas 1975, p. 108). Now, the deliberation that is assessed in terms of reasoning is expected to express more meaningful and effective decisions, just because it is rooted in the pertinence and in the relevance of the rationale brought to support them.

At its heart, the reasoning not only constitutes the basic rule of the decision-making procedure according to a deliberative approach, but also confers the epistemic justification to such a process. On the one hand, it is the proceduralism itself that attributes epistemological relevance to the outcome of the deliberation, inasmuch as the decision is perceived as a binding one; on the other hand, according to a pragmatic perspective, the debate oriented to deliberation assures the pursuit of truth through the means of active discussion among all the participants (Chappell 2012, p. 8). Moreover, the pragmatic relevance of such an approach brings to mind the concept of 'street-level epistemology', defined by Russell Hardin as a 'theory of the knowledge of the ordinary people', which heavily diverges from 'standard philosophical epistemology' just as it 'is not about what counts as knowledge in, say, physics, but rather about what counts as your knowledge, my knowledge, the ordinary person's knowledge' (Hardin 2003, p. 165). In Hardin's words, while the former deals with the justifications 'of any claim that some piece of putative knowledge is actually true', on the contrary street-level epistemology is about 'usefulness' and follows John Dewey's 'pragmatic rule' for which '(i)n order to discover the meaning of an idea, ask for its consequences' (Hardin 2003, pp. 165–6).

Thus, when a proposal has been extensively compared and evaluated, and it results in reasonable outcomes supported by adequate arguments, it is assumed to guarantee equality among all the participants to the procedure. But specifically, equality stands for a basic feature of deliberative procedures, as long as it acknowledges equal capabilities to all the persons involved in the process. This aspect implies also a moral meaning, in terms of requiring that citizens have an open attitude towards the needs, the concerns and also the interests of other people involved. In the wake of this point, it has been maintained that the deliberative way of decision-making also contributes to make citizens more other-regarding and less selfish[2] (Chappell 2012, p. 7).

Finally, a basic characteristic of the deliberative approach to public decision-making involves the outcomes expected, which are supposed to be based on the participants' consensus. However, also this general concordance requires, as a precondition, the equality of all the citizens involved, and of their equal capacities to partake in all the steps of the procedure oriented to the deliberation. Otherwise, in situations of unequal opportunities and capacities, it would be more relevant to speak of the risk of group polarization in decision-making activities, that is the phenomenon which occurs when 'members of a deliberating group predictably move toward a more extreme point in the direction indicated by the members' pre-deliberation tendencies' (Sunstein 2003, p. 81). Rather, the deliberation should aim at gaining a commonly shared decision, ideally supported by the agreement of all who are committed to act in accordance with the results of the deliberation, coherently with the necessity to foster the reasoning as a method to make

2 These features are required especially in the case of political decisions on environmental matters, as long as the protection of natural resources has to be intended in a long-term perspective in order to assure their conservation for the 'next generations' (see Jonas 1984). In these terms it is necessary to promote a cultural approach able to go beyond any individualistic or self-interested attitude towards common values.

decisions on issues of collective relevance, even though this purpose could rarely be fully achieved, and in those cases the majority rule would stand in for the consensus-based approach (Cohen 1989, p. 23).

In other words, though the pursuing of a widely shared consensus could only rely on the premises of an ideal model which in practice could not work or, at least, would face hard challenges to be effective, nonetheless a deliberative approach should seek to foster a higher level of agreement among all of the participants to the decision. After all, the degree of consensus reached with the deliberative procedure could express the level of improvement of all the participants in terms of information, knowledge and awareness about the issues on which deliberation is focused. Indeed, it has been argued that the attitudes related to the social capital can facilitate the decision-making process over issues of collective relevance, since the participation in civic groups or associations can assure the chance to improve knowledge and information over relevant collective issues (Fishkin 1995, p. 148; Chappell 2012, p. 5, pp. 123–4). For all intents and purposes, the basic idea on which the social capital theory counts 'is that social networks have value'; in particular ' "social capital" calls attention to the fact that civic virtue is most powerful when embedded in a dense network of reciprocal social relations' (Putnam 2000, p. 19). Furthermore, studying the differences among the Italian regional governments, Robert Putnam highlights the concordance between the political outcomes and the level of social capital in each region (Putnam 1993a), also recognizing relevance to 'strong traditions of civic engagement' like – for instance – 'voter turnout, newspaper readership, membership in choral societies and literary circles' (Putnam 1993b, p. 36).

In such a sense, the point emphasized by the social capital theory and its connection with the deliberative approach recalls the interpretation of Plato's metaphor of the cave discussed above. Just like those who have walked in the direction of the 'light' and the 'truth' experience the moral duty to share their knowledge with those who still face the darkness of the cave, the deliberative approach, while pursuing the most widely shared consensus over the contents of the deliberation itself, lets the community improve its capabilities and guarantees the achievement of a wide deliberated opinion, though not always accompanied by unanimity.

After all, three overlapping ways have been hypothesized in responding to issues surrounding consensus: first, as to specific contents, when there is no way to deliberate a commonly agreed decision, compromise might simply refer to a recognized space in which to compromise and bargain; second, the object of consensus could be intended not to be the particular decision, but the framework in which the decision occurs; and, third, consensus could be referred to as the deliberative procedure in terms of the legitimization criterion for such a decision-making strategy (Chappell 2012, pp. 105ff.).

Bringing Deliberative Democracy into Practice: The Example of Deliberative Polls

Moving to a practical perspective, many social and political experiences, also at a local level, can be seen as attempts to perform the deliberative approach over collective issues: starting from the example of the Town Hall Meetings realized by the communities of the New England states since the seventeenth century to the first experiments of Participatory Budgeting, that is a year-round procedure aimed at involving citizens in funding allocation and in assessment of priorities for the municipality (Chappell 2012, pp. 141ff.).

Among these tools, the deliberative poll can be implemented in many contexts and situations and, as proven by past experiences, even when applied under different circumstances has always consistently exhibited the same standard shape. James S. Fishkin defines it as follows:

> The deliberative poll is unlike any poll or survey ever conducted. Ordinary polls model what the public is thinking, even though the public may not be thinking very much or paying much attention. A deliberative poll attempts to model what the public *would* think, had it a better opportunity to consider the questions at issue.
>
> (Fishkin 1995, p. 162)

Recalling Plato's myth of the cave elicitation mentioned above, the activity of deliberative polling seems able to ensure an appropriate condition of awareness about the issue under discussion: fostering the citizens' participation and stressing the relevance of information and of the learning processes, the 'path' from the darkness of the cave to the light above can be walked through.

> The idea is simple. Take a national random sample of the electorate and transport those people from all over the country to a single place. Immerse the sample in the issues, with carefully balanced briefing materials, with intensive discussions in small groups, and with the chance to question competing experts and politicians. At the end of several days of working through the issues face to face, poll the participants in detail. The resulting survey offers a representation of the considered judgments of the public – the views the entire country would come if it had the same experience of behaving more like ideal citizens immersed in the issues for an extended period.
>
> (Fishkin 1995, p. 162)

Accordingly, collecting in the same room the 'nation', represented by randomly selected samples, guarantees on one hand the inclusiveness of the deliberation through dynamics of immediate discussion among all the participants – 'face to face' as Fishkin points out – in this way making any opinion relevant and avoiding the effects of the *rational ignorance.* Indeed the last concept, coined by Anthony Downs, consists in one's belief that his/her vote is not significant for the definitive decision, so that it is convenient invest his/her own time on more urgent matters (Fishkin 2006).

On the other hand, the criterion of selection adopted ensures equality of access, warding off the negative consequences of what has been defined as a 'SLOP' – Self-selected Listener Opinion Poll – in which, on the basis of a volunteer participation, only citizens directly interested in the issue could be incentivized to partake. Rather, a randomly selected sample is consistent with the necessity of a wide representativeness of the whole community involved and, thus, also of the stakeholders concerned with that particular issue, as a part of the whole (Fishkin 2011, pp. 612–13).

Another relevant point lies on the role of the experts who are in charge of facilitating and promoting the discussion, together with the enhancement of the arguments used to support each opinion and thereby caring about the learning process among the participants by sharing relevant information over the selected issues (Fishkin 2011, pp. 615–16). The effectiveness of the procedure can be evaluated by analysing how many people changed their mind after the discussion. Since the first experiment of a deliberative poll, carried out in Manchester on 15 March 1994, on the issue of criminal policies, it has been clear that impressive changes in the opinions about policy strategies occurred as a result of the people's engagement and of the related improvement of knowledge. Very meaningful is an excerpt of this experiment, which makes clear the significance of the learning processes:

> In particular, there seem to have been four or five major shifts. The first was an increased sense of the limitations of prison as a tool for fighting crime. Twelve of sixteen items under the 'punishment' heading showed statistically significant net change, and all twelve of the significant changes were towards less punitive attitudes. Participants left wanting to send fewer criminals to prison, less inclined to stiffen criminal sentences, and more willing to support alternatives to prison for 'criminals who are not a big threat to society'. They became more hesitant about imposing a life sentence automatically for all murders. Forced to choose between punishing criminals and reforming them, they left more inclined to try reform. Regarding 'juvenile offenders', similarly, the significant changes were that two proposals for dealing leniently with first-timers – that they be just warned or sent to a special institution – received increased support, while one proposal for dealing strictly with them – that they be sent to ordinary prisons – received decreased support.
>
> (Luskin et al. 2002, pp. 467ff.)

Deliberative Democracy and Environmental Law

At this stage we turn now to focus on the role which the deliberative decision-making model could play on the field of environmental law. As a basic point the current regulation of environmental matters is characterized by a lack of effectiveness. Indeed, the institutions and the legal tools available seem too obsolescent to cope with such problems (Laslett 2003). According to this, it has also been argued that the attitude of the courts has to be oriented to a problem-solving approach (White 2013). Furthermore, particularly managing environmental issues of second generation, it would be necessary to adopt a more flexible, adaptive and dynamic system, which could recognize space for participation and inclusiveness for all people concerned (Camacho 2011). That entails not only a rearrangement of management attitudes – which should be shaped on the model of green management (DiMento and Forti 2001) – but also the necessity of providing an alternative legal framework.

In particular, 'uncertainty' represents a recurring feature of environmental issues and concurs to stress the obsolescence of well-known institutions, since it jeopardizes the effectiveness of any legal tool not flexible enough to address the complexity of such problems (Laslett 2003). In addition, other severe limits of our ordinary legal systems can be found in the field of criminal sanctions, namely the severest form of institutional reaction to the infringement of environmental laws, which should better be rooted in a condition of plain certainty. Facing such huge difficulties, the involvement of all the actors concerned – not only the institutional ones – seems a reliable answer, as long as sharing information and managing singular situations allow its effectiveness to improve. Hence, it should not be surprising that the French legislative reform started in 2003, which has consisted in the acknowledgement of the constitutional relevance of the environment, had been preceded by a year-round process of popular consultation, in which both experts and citizens were involved, by responding to national questionnaire on this issue or by partaking in seminars, round tables, workshops. Furthermore, it is now a constitutionally acknowledged right of all the citizens to receive full knowledge of data regarding environmental matters (Forti 2003, pp. 1371–2).

The participation in political choices relevant to the environmental field has always been considered as a way to foster higher levels of consensus and, as such, is an undeniable premise for designing a clearer, fairer and more rational regulation (DiMento 1986, p. 108). Among the new models of environmental governance the deliberative approach has progressively achieved more relevance. As Cameron Holley, Neil Gunningham and Clifford Shearing have specified, the 'new environmental governance' (hereafter NEG):

> involves collaboration between a diversity of private, public and non-government stakeholders who, acting together towards commonly agreed (or mutually negotiated) goals, hope to achieve far more collectively, than individually. It relies heavily upon participatory dialogue and deliberation, devolved and decentralized decision-making, flexibility (rather than uniformity), inclusiveness, knowledge generation and processes of learning, transparency and institutionalized consensus-building practices.
>
> (Holley et al. 2012, p. 4)

Effectively, this approach is rooted in the basic idea that, rather than prescriptive regulation, the adaptive attitude of a system which fosters learning processes, the sharing of relevant information and the participation of the stakeholders in the decision-making, can assure more effective protection, in particular when it comes to facing delicate issues such as uncertainty and complexity.

These writers also illustrate several examples from the Australian experience that show efforts to implement deliberative ideals in the regulation of environmental problems, conceptualized with different features, but all aimed at enhancing the voluntary participation and performed to guarantee a more flexible approach to regulation (Holley et al. 2012, pp. 70ff.; see also Chapter 9, this volume). Obviously, such attempts of innovation are not simple at all and face many difficulties: fair deliberation is obstructed mainly by the risk of power imbalance among the participants and by the absence of instruments that could provide incentives for institutional actors to share information with the other parties.

As previously highlighted, the lack of equality among participants to a deliberative process – also determined by different levels of knowledge on the particular issue or different capacities – could facilitate the polarization of consensus. Besides, in the case of voluntary participation in the procedure, the risk of a SLOP could emerge: the prevalence of self-interests could overpower the pursuing of the common good. Furthermore, it has been argued that, under certain circumstances and in particular when the issue entails conflicting interests, this seriously challenges the enhancement of a deliberative approach, since the evaluation should take into account also the power imbalances of the parties involved together with the exit costs, in order to strengthen the weaker actors in the decision-making process (Shapiro 2003).

Indeed, it can be appropriate to recall that Holley et al. (2012) focus on several points appropriate to properly express a deliberative attitude: the development and strengthening of participation – particularly in the case of widespread interests, to which people could also not feel directly concerned – and the rebalance of the differences among participants. In the case of the latter strategy, education and culture as well as social policies directed to improving the capacities of the whole community are considered as overriding:

> Our findings point to the importance of designing other mechanisms canvassed in the NEG literature to enhance the meaningful input of non-governmental stakeholders. For example, provision of education and training in deliberation and problem-solving may improve both government and non-government actors' adherence to ideals of negotiation. Funding and technical support also plays an important role in reducing the capacity of government officers or of private industry to take advantage of informational asymmetries. As the experience of 'civic environmentalism' in the United States suggests, opportunities for non-governmental actors to input into decision-making seem more likely to arise under conditions where decision-making is centred around an 'independent' person who represents no particular substantive interest.
>
> (Holley et al. 2012, p. 98)

Moreover, arranging a fair deliberation requires the presence of a third party or – when necessary – of tools which could rebalance the *weight* of each proposal:

> Our findings have also provided support for suggestions in the literature that the use of mediators, agency assistance and mechanisms, such as VEPA and community pressure, can effectively overcome or at least mitigate power imbalances. However, we found that although these conditions were effective

> for local issues, this was not the case when knowledge and capacity differences between non-governmental stakeholders and industry were amplified (i.e., more technical issues). In the latter circumstances, industry was able to exploit their technical knowledge and capacity to dominate decision-making and overwhelm government officers. Where knowledge imbalances are large (e.g., between industry and local resident) fair deliberative decision-making may require conditions such as funding for technical assistance, training in deliberation . . . and effective countervailing power.
>
> (Holley et al. 2012, p. 98)

From a more practical perspective, the adoption of deliberative polling thus could bring about advantages. First, the randomized sample can strengthen the equality among participants who would represent all the concerned community parties. Second, a relevant role should be recognized to the facilitators responsible for the development of the learning process and for balancing the weight of the proposals, independently of their authors and consistently with the strength of the argumentations. Therefore, it is the maximization of the knowledge available, also by sharing the relevant information held by the key actors, that is the pivotal factor on which the process should be based so as to pursue a fair deliberation.

How to Regulate Competing Values?

According to Chappell's definition of deliberative democracy mentioned earlier, the political aspect of this approach can arise as long as the decision-making activity is focused on moral issues, as the decision is on how to allocate scarce resources to foster the achievement of different social goals. As well, the collective relevance emerges in connection with public choices regarding issues which involve competing or conflicting interests.

Some suggest that environmental law is supposed to manage topics that are incisively related to moral issues (Bach 2014). Other views suggest a scientific model of environmental protection. In both, to safeguard the environment means to protect public health at the same time; this implies that, in order to provide healthy standards of life to the whole community, it is necessary to prevent harms to the ecosystems. Furthermore, the need for environmental protection arises also in a diachronic perspective: providing high quality standards for natural resources not only contributes to assure public health, but also represents the premise that we need to guarantee the same conditions for future generations (Uhlmann 2014).

Although the framework of environmental law can be assessed from a human-centric approach, such regulation cannot be considered as univocal and uncontested. Rather, it requires a deep evaluation to define the most appropriate and balanced policy in relation to human and wider ecological interests. As David M. Uhlmann details:

> The extent to which we emphasize public health, biodiversity, and ecological concerns has significant practical implications. We regulate toxic substances

> differently when our concern is human exposure rather than protecting other species. We set different water quality standards when our goal is fishable and swimmable streams rather than promoting healthy ecosystems for all aquatic life. We pursue different climate change mitigation efforts when our focus is safeguarding cities and towns from extreme weather rather than preventing the loss of habitat for polar bears in the Arctic Circle or the acidification of the oceans, although eventually the melting of polar ice and the loss of carbon sinks in the oceans will have dramatic public health ramifications.
>
> (Uhlmann 2014, p. 237)

Even in defining environmental law enforcement consistently within the human-centric perspective, many questions surrounding managing competing values arise. For instance, environmental regulation involves activities that produce benefits and positive externalities, and the cost of such activities is ordinarily assessed in relation to relevant thresholds of harm and degrees of scientific uncertainty (Osofsky 2014).

Though trade-offs between economic interests and the safeguarding of basic values such as public health and environment are very common, a more incisive perspective can turn up many additional questions. Namely, regulating risks can frequently allow or even foster further risks to emerge, as ancillary risks – sometimes very difficult to discover – or produce other fundamental harms, like unemployment and poverty (Sunstein 1998, pp. 246–7). The issue of assessing economic development as well as the environmental impact of its related activities holds considerable social relevance as the studies of environmental justice have already shown (Bullard 2000) and requires scrupulous evaluation of potential trade-offs.

How, then, are competing values to be managed so as to achieve an adequate and balanced regulation? Here, an inclusive and deliberative approach is preferred, as it allows for the appraisal of many perspectives and the involvement of all the actors concerned – each one with his/her own view on the issue and his/her own knowledge on the related problems – who then can provide a more informed basis for the decision. Indeed, such a 'hybrid structure' has the function to gather 'the various overlapping formal and informal regulatory vehicles and numerous public and private stakeholders', so 'combining multiple institutions or actors, often across levels of governance and the public/private divide' (Osofsky 2014, p. 270).

Consider the case of a municipality of 30,000 inhabitants that has to decide whether to allow or prohibit the establishment of a controversial industrial facility (see Susskind 2009; Fishkin 2011). On the one hand, the new firm would create new employment; on the other hand, the level of pollution would get higher. Under these circumstances, Susskind suggests an alternative solution based on a consensus-based approach, with the aim to go beyond several limits he bestows to the deliberative democracy model. The framework of decision-making process suggested is that:

> (The) city council hires a professional neutral – a mediator – to meet privately and confidentially with all relevant stakeholders, both in and outside the city,

> to learn their concerns about the proposed project. Along with the developer of the proposed facility and appointees from a range of city and regional departments, carefully selected stakeholder representatives are invited to engage in joint fact-finding to see if they can resolve their differences. After a year of highly transparent and mediator facilitated problem-solving, the forty (or so) stakeholder representatives sign an agreement. It spells out the circumstances under which they can all support a revised version of the project. It also commits them to making a series of voluntary payments and other contingent commitments from the developer and the city – maybe even the state and federal government, too – that go well beyond what the city has a statutory right to require. They all present the agreement to the city council, which ratifies it. Its details are added as conditions to the various formal permits granted to the developer. The agreement creates a joint monitoring committee whose staff is paid by the project developer. The project goes forward with little or no political opposition.
>
> (Susskind 2009, p. 395)

It can first be observed that this proposal is not so different from the deliberative approach, since the methods and the aims of both seem to be in common (Fishkin 2011, p. 611). The most significant differences can be seen in the relevance of the consensus and the categories of citizens to involve.

Beginning with the latter point, if deliberative democracy requires the citizenry to be randomly represented, the consensus-based approach of Susskind requires the selection and the consultation only of the stakeholders, that is, of those directly involved. Of course, the stakeholders generally have more technical and detailed information over a particular issue. However, limiting the deliberation only to this category could run the risk of a self-selected participation. Besides, the more delicate the issue is to evaluate, the more it is necessary to share the available knowledge and to enhance the learning process, thus it would be appropriate to involve as many parties as possible. Perhaps the best scenario would be arranging a wide representation of both categories: randomly selected citizens together with the stakeholders directly involved.

When it comes to the former point, Susskind suggests pursuing the widest possible form of consensus, while according to deliberative democracy a less extensive group agreement – although appreciable – may be sufficient. As long as unanimity cannot be reached, perhaps the public decisions on social issue should be rooted in the 'collective, shared understanding of the society' rather than in the individuals' consent (Fishkin 1992, p. 63). After all, a full and wide consensus can be a long-term goal to achieve, also going through deliberative democracy experiences. In this case, both approaches seem able to ensure a proper level of collective sharing on the decision under discussion and to foster the widest consensus reachable under those circumstances, which are fundamental features for environmental law enforcement in order to prevent not only harms to the ecosystems, but also any other social conflict coming up from unbalanced evaluations of competing interests.

The Claim for Health versus the Claim for Employment: A Case from Southern Italy

Some questions still remain unresolved: what could happen in the aftermath of an episode of pollution or when the latent consequences of it emerge, in instances where no form of community participation had previously been fostered? Which are the perceivable benefits of an approach more dynamic and flexible like in the case of forms of inclusiveness and deliberation?

A relevant case taken from the Italian experience can help to answer these questions. The events at the big steel plant located in Taranto recall the ideal situation discussed by Susskind and Fishkin, except for the city size, since it is much more populated than the town in the theoretical example, with more than 200,000 inhabitants. In particular, this *story* lets emerge the costs on the social field of a very rigid regulation, one which does not acknowledge any role to non-institutional actors' voices. The Italian system of environmental law enforcement can be considered a centralized one, rooted mainly in criminal provisions and sanctions in case of administrative regulation infringement; in more explicit terms, no space is left for the community to participate in the rule-making. Very recently a new range of environmental crimes has been introduced in the Italian penal code through L. 22 May 2015, No. 68, which should guarantee criminal enforcement in case of more severe harms to ecosystems and natural resources. As well, no form of public participation has been so far fostered.

In the 1960s the industrial area had risen quickly, becoming one of the biggest in Europe: in the early 1980s the main corporation operating in that branch employed about 43,000 people, either directly or through other satellite activities. Recent epidemiological studies – embedded in the 'SENTIERI project' – have analysed the incidence of several diseases related to long-term exposure to pollutants in the area of Taranto, which was previously included in the range of Italian polluted sites (IPS): for both genders, instances of cardiovascular and respiratory diseases, as well as cancer, are often higher than the national and the regional average; infant mortality also exceeds national averages. The environmental exposure to pollutants is determined by the presence, not only of the steel plant, but also of a refinery, a harbour area and waste landfills. In addition, in the same area illegal dumping sites have also been identified (Comba et al. 2012).

In the summer of 2012, because of a criminal charge involving ILVA – the company owner of the steel plant – and its CEOs for the long-term pollution of the surrounding neighbourhoods, the facility ran the risk of closure. The proceedings are actually ongoing, thus it seems appropriate and fair to abstain from expressing any opinion; however, it could be very useful sketching some considerations about the consequences of this situation on the affected society and public opinion; as well it would be interesting to verify how political institutions have intervened in such a delicate scenario.

It is easy to imagine how the after-effect of this situation has been marked by social conflict among several groups within the local population: those who wanted the facility to continue with its activity, because of basic economically related self-interests (i.e. to preserve their jobs); on the opposite side, those who wanted the production to close, in order to preserve human health and restore the standards of a safe and healthy environment. This social conflict featured prominently in the mass media exposure, so much so that, in accordance with the fair trial principle, the defendants made a petition to move the proceeding to another territorial court (although this was rejected).

The eruption of social conflict shows how inadequate ordinary strategies have been so far and how ineffective the law enforcement could be: when coping with competing basic values a balancing act is necessary to define the best management of the trade-off. Conversely, in the case of Taranto no commonly shared decision was taken on the degree of the bearable pollution or on the impact of both reduction and improvement of the industrial activity. What is more, not even the legal provisions have been able to placate the conflict. The political institutions were eventually forced to intervene when thorny consequences already arose: first, a national law was approved with the scope to preserve the production, despite the previous measures undertaken (D.l. No. 207, 3 December 2012, then converted in L. No. 231, 23 December 2012); subsequently, the Constitutional Court consulted by the tribunal of Taranto held that is the Parliament that is in charge, with the trade-off between industrial policies and the basic values at stake, and ruled that those values (health and the right to employment) have to be reciprocally balanced, since none of them should be allowed to prevail over the other (Corte Cost. judgment No. 85, 9 April – 9 May, 2013).

Reading the Taranto case, some evidence in favour of deliberative democracy initiatives can be inferred. The basic idea is that such a model would be able to monitor the situation in depth and to prevent damages, but at the same time it would help in avoiding or reducing the social conflict in the background, providing an instance in which at a local level all parties could feel represented. Hypothetically, this kind of approach would lead to a much fairer deliberation through a process of knowledge sharing and learning improvement with a bottom-up strategy. Such an idea does not imply that this *modus operandi* is easier or invulnerable; simply that it is more democratic and dialogical, aspects that are extremely valuable when the interests to balance are those related to health, the environment, and basic personal interests (as with employment, in this case).

Conclusions

This chapter aimed to highlight several basic features of deliberative democracy that could support decision-making strategies on environmental issues and around environmental law enforcement.

Inevitably, implementing deliberative democracy will cost relevant amounts of money. For instance, in accordance with the model of deliberative polls proposed by Fishkin, in order to incentivize popular participation the format suggests a payment for all the randomly selected people plus the reimbursement of all the associated expenses. Indubitably, this aspect could threaten the experiment feasibility but it is our belief that the costs of a well performed framework, including forms of participation and assuring good effectiveness in terms of prevention, would contribute to substantial savings from a long-term perspective. Consider only how expensive the measures taken to reclaim polluted areas are and that in many cases the population is compelled to live in a unhealthy environment for a long period because of the scarce resources available. Surely, these kinds of assessments would require more and more complex analysis of political, economic and social data, whose results are essential to figure out a more rational environmental policy for the decades to come. Indeed, such an inclusive and participative approach like the one we have tried to draw here would invest more resources in personal capabilities, improving the level of both the human and the social capital of the community, hopefully opening up new perspectives and frontiers.

References

Bach, T. 2014. 'Protecting Human Health and Stewarding the Environment: An Essay Exploring Values in U.S. Environmental Protection', *Michigan Journal of Environmental & Administrative Law* 3, 260–70.

Bullard, R.D. 2000. *Dumping in the Dixie: Race, Class and Environmental Quality*. Boulder and Cumnor Hill: Westview Press.

Camacho, A.E. 2011. 'Transforming the Means and Ends of Natural Resources Management', *North Carolina Law Review* 89, 1405–50.

Chappell, Z. 2012. *Deliberative Democracy: A Critical Introduction*. Basingstoke and New York: Palgrave Macmillan.

Cohen, J. 1989. 'Deliberation and Democratic Legitimacy', in *The Good Polity: Normative Analysis of the State*, edited by A. Hamlin and P. Pettit. Oxford and New York: Basil Blackwell, 17–34.

Comba, P., Pirastu, R., Conti, S., De Santis, M., Iavarone, I., Marsili, G., Mincuzzi, A., Minelli, G., Manno, V., Minerba, S., Musmeci, L., Rashid, I., Soggiu, E. and Zona, A. 2012. 'Environment and Health in Taranto, Southern Italy: Epidemiological Studies and Public Health Recommendations', *Epidemiologia & Prevenzione* 36, 305–20.

Corte Costituzionale. 2013. 'Judgement No. 85 of 9 April – 9 May 2013', *Giurisprudenza costituzionale*, 1424–93.

DiMento, J. 1986. *Environmental Laws and American Business: Dilemmas of Compliance*. New York: Springer.

DiMento, J. and Forti, G. 2001. 'Green Managers Don't Cry: Criminal Environmental Law and Corporate Strategy', in *Contemporary Issues in Crime and Criminal Justice. Essays in Honor of Gilbert Geis*, edited by H.N. Pontell and D. Shichor. Upper Saddle River: Prentice Hall, 253–64.

Dunn, J. 2000. *Western Political Theory in the Face of the Future*. Cambridge: Cambridge University Press.

——— 2005. *Setting the People Free: The Story of Democracy*. London: Atlantic Books.

Elster, I. 1998. 'Introduction', in *Deliberative Democracy*, edited by I. Elster. Cambridge: Cambridge University Press, 1–18.

Fishkin, J.S. 1991. *Democracy and Deliberation: New Directions for Democratic Reform*. New Haven and London: Yale University Press.

——— 1992. *The Dialogue of Justice: Toward a Self-Reflective Society*. New Haven and London: Yale University Press.

——— 1995. *The Voice of the People: Public Opinion and Democracy*. New Haven: Yale University Press.

——— 2006. 'The Nation in a Room: Turning Public Opinion into Policy', *Boston Review*, March 1.

——— 2011. 'Making Deliberative Democracy Practical: Public Consultation and Dispute Resolution', *Ohio State Journal on Dispute Resolution* 26, 611–26.

Forti, G. 2003. 'Tutela ambientale e legalità: prospettive giuridiche e socio-culturali', *Rivista italiana di diritto e procedura penale* 46, 1353–77.

Habermas, J. 1975. *Legitimation Crisis*. Boston: Beacon Press.

——— 1996. *Between Facts and Norms: Contributions to a Discourse Theory of Law and Democracy*. Cambridge, MA: MIT Press.

Hardin, R. 2003. 'Street-Level Epistemology and Democratic Participation', in *Debating Deliberative Democracy*, edited by J.S. Fishkin and P. Laslett. Malden and Oxford: Blackwell Publishing, 163–81.

Heidegger, M. 1997. *Platons Lehre von der Wahrheit*. Frankfurt am Main: Klostermann Vittorio Gmbh (first edition 1942).

Holley, C., Gunningham, N. and Shearing, C. 2012. *The New Environmental Governance*. Abingdon and New York: Earthscan.

Hyland, D.A. 2004. *Questioning Platonism: Continental Interpretations of Plato*. Albany: State University of New York Press.

Jonas, H. 1984, *The Imperative of Responsibility: In Search of an Ethics for the Technological Era*. London and Chicago: University of Chicago Press.

Laslett, P. 2003. 'Environmental Ethics and the Obsolescence of Existing Political Institutions', in *Debating Deliberative Democracy*, edited by J.S. Fishkin and P. Laslett. Malden and Oxford: Blackwell Publishing, 212–24.

Luskin, R.C., Fishkin, J.S. and Jowell, R. 2002. 'Considered Opinions: Deliberative Polling in Britain', *British Journal of Political Science* 32, 455–87.

Osofsky, H.M. 2014. 'Complex Value Choices at the Environment-Energy Interface', *Michigan Journal of Environmental & Administrative Law* 3, 261–72.

Putnam, R.D. 1993a. *Making Democracy Work: Civic Traditions in Modern Italy*. Princeton and Chichester: Princeton University Press.

——— 1993b. 'The Prosperous Community: Social Capital and Public Life', *American Prospect* 13, 35–42.

——— 2000. *Bowling Alone: The Collapse and Revival of American Community*. New York: Simon & Schuster.

Rawls, J. 1971. *A Theory of Justice*. Cambridge, MA: Harvard University Press.

Reale, G. 1998. *Platone. Alla ricerca della sapienza segreta*. Milano: Rizzoli.

Shapiro, I. 2003. 'Optimal Deliberation?', in *Debating Deliberative Democracy*, edited by J.S. Fishkin and P. Laslett. Malden and Oxford: Blackwell Publishing, 121–37.

Sunstein, C.R. 1998. 'Health-Health Trade-Offs', in *Deliberative Democracy*, edited by I. Elster. Cambridge: Cambridge University Press, 232–59.

——— 2003. 'The Law of Group Polarization', in *Debating Deliberative Democracy*, edited by J.S. Fishkin and P. Laslett. Malden and Oxford: Blackwell Publishing, 80–101.

Susskind, L. 2009. 'Deliberative Democracy and Dispute Resolution', *Ohio State Journal on Dispute Resolution* 24, 395–406.

Uhlmann, D.M. 2014. 'Environmental Law, Public Health, and the Values Conundrum', *Michigan Journal of Environmental & Administrative Law* 3, 231–42.

White, R. 2013. 'Environmental Crime and Problem-Solving Courts', *Crime, Law and Social Change* 59(3), 267–78.

——— 2014. 'Eco-Justice and Problem-Solving Approaches to Environmental Crime and Victimisation', in *Environmental Crime and its Victims: Perspective within Green Criminology*, edited by. T. Spapens, R. White and M. Kluin. Farnham and Burlington: Ashgate, 87–101.

Wright, J.H. 1906. 'The Origin of Plato's Cave', *Harvard Studies in Classical Philology* 17, 131–42.

11 Deterring Corporate Environmental Crime

Lessons from the Waste Industry in the Netherlands

Karin van Wingerde[1]

Introduction

When corporations and their managers violate environmental laws and regulations, effects on the health and safety of human life and on our natural environment can be disastrous. As just one of many examples, the dumping of toxic waste by the ship the *Probo Koala* in Abidjan, Ivory Coast in the summer of 2006 has led to a crisis with social, economic and sanitary consequences (White 2008; Amnesty International and Greenpeace Netherlands 2012; Van Wingerde 2015). People who were exposed to the waste complained of nosebleeds, diarrhoea, nausea, irritated eyes and respiratory problems. Moreover, there was a major displacement of people living near the dump sites. Last but not least, there were demonstrations all over Abidjan and the government of Ivory Coast resigned a couple of weeks after the incident (Amnesty International and Greenpeace Netherlands 2012, pp. 51–67; Van Wingerde 2015, p. 264).

Since the birth of environmental law and policies in the 1970s, governments have sought to deal with environmental crimes by so-called command-and-control policies; by regulation and enforcement (Braithwaite and Drahos 2000; Gunningham 2009). Especially in the wake of a disaster or crisis, politicians, the media and the public call for increased supervision and harsher, more deterrent, sanctions.

Alternatively, there also has been an effort to shift more and more regulation away from the state, such as efforts to stimulate voluntary compliance and self-regulation and civil society organizations that are increasingly pressurizing firms to reduce the adverse impacts of their activities (Braithwaite and Drahos 2000; Braithwaite 2008; Braithwaite et al. 2007; Cashore et al. 2011; Parker and Lehmann Nielsen 2011).

Yet, despite the fact that criminalization and enforcement are no longer the sole instruments in the regulatory toolbox, imposing sanctions is still one of the most dominant approaches in regulatory enforcement (Braithwaite and Drahos 2000; Wenzel 2004; Tyler 2011; Van Wingerde 2012; Parker 2012, 2013). One of the main goals is deterrence: the belief that the more severe the penalty, the more effectively it will deter firms from criminal behaviour in the future.

1 Parts of this chapter have been previously published in Van Wingerde (2012, pp. 373–83).

As legal enforcement is expensive and requires a lot of personnel and means, it is crucial to understand how important deterrent threats are in motivating firms to comply with environmental regulation, compared to social pressures, on the one hand, and efforts from within firms to comply with the law, on the other. This chapter presents the results of a qualitative empirical study of 40 firms in the Dutch waste industry designed to explore this question.

This chapter is organized as follows. First I will summarize the existing literature on corporate deterrence. The research design and methodology will then be described. The following three sections present the results of this study and connect the findings with the particularities of the case study, the waste industry in the Netherlands. The final section summarizes and discusses the findings and sets out the implications, particularly for regulatory policy.

How Does Deterrence Work?

Deterrence finds its roots in the classical school of criminology influenced by Cesare Beccaria (1982 [1764]) and Jeremy Bentham (2007 [1823]). Deterrence is based on the notion that business firms are rational, amoral calculators that base the decision to comply or violate on the weighing of the perceived costs and benefits of their actions. Only if the costs of criminal behaviour exceed the benefits, will they then comply with the law. In other words, firms will only comply with the law if it is economically sensible to do so (Kagan and Scholz 1984).

Deterrence therefore assumes that only the fear of tough legal penalties that exceed the benefits of rule violation will motivate firms to comply with regulatory demands. Important factors influencing the decision to comply or violate are the risk of detection, the certainty of punishment, and the severity of the punishment. Each sanction, it is assumed, sends a threat message that communicates the potential costs if firms violate the law (Zimring and Hawkins 1973; Geerken and Gove 1975). As the perceived risks and costs increase, there will be a greater likelihood of compliance with the law.

Usually two types of deterrence are distinguished. Specific deterrence covers the notion that the actual experience of inspection or punishment deters future criminal behaviour. In this perspective the offending firm *itself* will be deterred from reoffending. General deterrence, on the other hand, assumes that the target group of potential offenders learns about the sanction (including hearing about particular instances where it has been applied against a specific firm), fears the possible consequences of rule violation, and as a result complies with the law to prevent the possibility of penal consequences. This chapter is specifically concerned with general deterrence, meaning the extent to which the mere *threat* of punishment deters businesses from environmental violations.

Is Deterrence Effective?

Soon after its adoption by Beccaria and Bentham, deterrence theory was abandoned by more positivist approaches to crime and crime control. However, interest in the deterrence approach was renewed in the late 1960s when economist Gary Becker wrote his seminal article 'Crime and Punishment: An Economic Approach' (1968). Ever since, deterrence theory has been one of the most dominant approaches in regulatory enforcement, and empirical research into the deterrent effects of sanctions has continued to grow. For example, in their recent review of the corporate deterrence literature, Simpson et al. (2014) reckoned over 2,700 published documents that reported results on corporate deterrence. And these were just the publications before 2004. Moreover, in another recent review, Gray and Shimshack (2011) described over 60 relatively recent studies on the effectiveness of environmental enforcement.

The popularity of the deterrence approach might be the result of the fact that deterrence theory not only offers an explanation for crime ('people choose to commit crime if they believe that the benefits outweigh the costs'), but it also provides an easy solution: making this choice less attractive by increasing the costs of misconduct (Pratt et al. 2006, p. 367). What can we learn from this previous research on corporate deterrence?

Notwithstanding the large amount of literature reporting empirical results on deterrence, the review of this literature shows that empirical support for deterrence is far from conclusive (Simpson 2002; Thornton et al. 2005; Pratt et al. 2006; Paternoster 2010; Kagan et al. 2011; Simpson et al. 2013, 2014). Most studies show that the deterrent effect of sanctions is not as strong as expected. Due to the relative small likelihood of detection and the lack of penalties that outweigh the profits of most business firms, the impact of formal legal sanctions can often be better understood as 'weak signal, weak threat' (Thornton et al. 2005; Van Wingerde 2012; Simpson et al. 2013, 2014). Nonetheless, the prior literature identified several key dynamics explaining the relationship between deterrence and compliance that are important for this study.

First, in the 1970s and early 1980s many researchers began to study deterrence as a perceptual process, meaning that 'deterrence is most likely to depend on what the certainty and severity of punishment were thought to be rather than on their actual levels' (Paternoster 1987, p. 174). Consequently, studying deterrence means that the perceptions of the risks and costs of non-compliance should be taken into account. In the case of business firms, most perceptual deterrence researchers study the perceptions of relevant managers within the firm that are then extrapolated to the firm itself (Parker and Lehmann Nielsen 2011). Moreover, most perceptual studies show that in so far as sanctions lead to compliance behaviour this is the result of the perceived risk of getting caught and not the result of the perceived severity of the sanction (Braithwaite and Makkai 1991; Cohen 2000; Simpson 2002; Gray and Shimshack 2011). In one of the first studies on corporate deterrence, Braithwaite and Makkai (1991) for example showed that amongst the most effective pressures on business compliance was the risk of detection. Similarly, in their review of the corporate deterrence literature, Simpson et al. (2014) found almost no support for the relationship between the severity of the penalty and business compliance. In so far as sanctions produced compliance related behaviour this effect was the result of the risk of discovery by regulatory authorities.

Second, perceptions of and responses to deterrence generally are far more complex than the 'fear of detection and sanction severity model' would lead one to believe. For instance, several studies on deterrence indicate that even when frequent inspections and severe legal penalties appear to be absent, many business firms still invest in costly environmental improvements in order to comply with regulatory demands and some firms even go 'beyond compliance' (Braithwaite 1989, p. 349; Vandenbergh 2003; Kagan et al. 2011, p. 41). Using data on 116 paper mills, Gray and Shadbegian (2005) for example found that although these paper mills were inspected rather infrequently, only 16 per cent violated water pollution regulations. Furthermore, comparative research has found no differences between the level of compliance of regulated firms in the United States and Europe and Asia, although enforcement regimes in the United States are often characterized as tougher than their counterparts in Europe and Asia (Gunningham et al. 2003).

Socio-legal research suggests some explanations for these findings. For example, most business managers are relatively unaffected by formal legal sanction threats (Kagan et al. 2011, p. 41). Negative publicity that affects the firm's reputation and pressure from environmental interest groups, the local community and the public are far more threatening than the risks of legal penalties. Furthermore, research shows that some firms feel the moral obligation to comply with the law. These firms have internalized the social norms that underlie regulatory norms and are morally bound to do 'the right thing'. For those firms, one might assume that deterrence is irrelevant, contributing hardly anything to a culture of compliance (Thornton et al. 2005, p. 264).

These findings suggest that research on deterrence should be sensitive to a variety of costs, benefits and motives for compliance, including legal enforcement, social pressures and moral commitments within firms (Kagan and Scholz 1984; Ayres and Braithwaite 1992; Paternoster and Simpson 1996; Huisman 2001; Simpson 2002; Vandenbergh 2003; May 2005; Kagan et al. 2011; Lehmann Nielsen and Parker 2012).

As described above, legal enforcement is expensive and requires a lot of enforcement capacity. Moreover, previous research shows that a persistent focus on deterrence as a tool for social control may lead to a 'rat race' increasingly proposing harsher and more deterrent enforcement actions (see Parker 2013). At the same time, regulators will not be able to implement such actions as they often lack juridical, economic or political support (Coffee 1981; Braithwaite 2002; Parker 2006). Given the weight of these public interests, it is important to understand if, how and why deterrence 'works'. The next section describes the research approach designed to explore this question.

Data and Methodology

This chapter aims at providing a detailed understanding of the role and importance of general deterrence compared to social pressures and the ways in which firms themselves give shape and meaning to compliance. In doing so, it reports the results of a qualitative empirical study among 40 companies in the waste industry in the Netherlands (Van Wingerde 2012).

The companies involved in this study were selected from the membership lists of two trade organizations. Together these organizations represent almost the entire Dutch waste industry. The sample includes smaller independent firms as well as medium-sized and large internationally operating firms.

The data in this study were collected using several research methods. On-site, in-depth interviews were held with environmental managers of waste companies. Environmental managers were chosen as key respondents because they are the most knowledgeable in environmental compliance matters. The interviews were designed to gain insight into the firm's activities, its environmental management and compliance system, its relationship and history with regulators, their knowledge and reactions to enforcement actions against other firms, the characteristics of and relationship with the social environment and the ways in which the interviewed companies gave shape and meaning to environmental compliance measures.

In most cases, I also interviewed company directors, industry association officials, public regulators, and representatives of environmental interest groups or the local community. In total the data includes transcripts of 70 in-depth interviews. The data obtained during the interviews was complemented and confronted with company documents, including permits, annual reports, environmental plans, the results of (internal) environmental audits; on-site observations; and the analysis of media content.

Studying Deterrence

As mentioned above, this chapter focuses on *general deterrence* as the chief driver for compliance behaviour. In their study on general deterrence and corporate environmental behaviour, Thornton et al. (2005) identified three key elements of general deterrence. First, in order to deter potential offenders, companies have to be aware of sanctions against other companies, because if they do not learn about sanctions against other firms it is not likely that they will be deterred by it.

Second, in response to hearing about enforcement actions against other companies, companies have to fear the possible consequences in terms of the risk of getting caught and being punished, because if they do not fear the consequences, it is not likely that they will translate the information about the sanction into new behaviour.

Lastly, in order for deterrence to work, the potentially offending firm also has to be willing and able to take costly compliance measures to improve its behaviour. Thornton et al. (2005) chose eight significant enforcement actions ('signal cases') by the Environmental Protection Agency. They then conducted a telephone survey identifying whether corporate officials in 233 business firms knew about the enforcement actions, how they responded to the type and the size of the penalties imposed as well as to the risk of being found in violation, and the extent to which they had improved their compliance behaviour in response to hearing about these sanctions. Thornton et al. (2005) found that the firms in their study were relatively unaware of enforcement actions against other firms. However, a majority of their respondents reported that hearing about enforcement actions against other firms had urged them to further improve environmental performance. Thornton et al. (2005, p. 280) suggest that this is the result of a more implicit general deterrence effect: to firms that are already in compliance, sanctions might serve as a 'reminder' to check whether they still operate in accordance with their previous commitment to comply with the law; or as a 'reassurance' by sending the message that 'bad apples' are caught and punished, reaffirming their commitment to invest in costly compliance measures.

This study follows an approach similar to that of Thornton et al. (2005). To examine how important deterrent threats are in motivating companies to comply with environmental regulations, two cases were selected: a criminal and a regulatory case. These cases were selected on the basis of the timeframe in which the sanctions were imposed, the attention they attracted from the media, and the type of violations. Both sanctions were imposed in 2007, so that respondents could remember the cases. Moreover, they received at least some attention in the media, and included rule violations that were recognizable to other firms in this industry. A description of the two cases is presented below.

Case 1: ATF [Waste Terminal Friesland]

The storage hall of ATF, a company specialized in the collection, separation, and treatment of hazardous waste, was completely destroyed by fire. Approximately 480 tons of hazardous waste was stored at the company at the time of the fire. The authorities took thorough measures to control the effects of the fire; within 30 kilometres of the fire the cattle had to be taken of the lands and milk of the cows was not allowed to be sold. The Prosecution Office suspected that the company collected waste materials in violation of what their licence allowed and held the company liable for the improper working of the fire prevention system. The company and three individual executives were criminally prosecuted.

Case 2: Edelchemie

Edelchemie specializes in processing chemical and hazardous waste. Ever since its foundation, the local community started complaining about odours from the facility. In addition, regulators detected several environmental violations, for example processing waste materials without having a licence for these materials. The company appeared not to be able to process the waste properly and stored it at their premises. The company was notified several times to stop the violations. The regulator decided to start administrative enforcement measures.

During the interviews, the environmental managers were provided with these case descriptions and then were asked questions about their knowledge and awareness of the enforcement actions, their reactions towards the imposed sanctions, and the extent to which they had taken compliance measures in response to hearing about these sanctions.

General Deterrence: Knowledge and Fear of Enforcement Actions

As described above, deterrence assumes that each sanction sends a threat message communicating the potential risks and costs of misconduct. Being rational, amoral calculators, firms monitor their environment for information about inspections and enforcement actions. When they perceive enforcement actions as impacting their potential rewards, they translate this information to their own situation and respond by taking measures to ensure that they are in compliance with regulations. Otherwise, corporate actors ignore enforcement actions.

The interviews showed that this communication process malfunctions in practice. It became clear that sanctions did not have much effect in terms of the awareness that they created. Although most of the respondents remembered at least one enforcement action against some other firm, hardly anyone recalled the actual penalties imposed (Table 11.1).

Looking at the signal cases, 63 per cent of respondents (N=31) remembered the first example in which the company and its executives were criminally prosecuted much better than the regulatory case (35 per cent; N=17). However, even in the criminal case, only two (4 per cent) respondents could recall the punishment. As such this is not very surprising because criminal cases tend to receive more attention in the media as compared to regulatory sanctions. However, although the respondents were asked to describe the *sanctions* that they remembered, they spoke about the cases more in general. In fact, in most cases the respondents only remembered what had happened and the violations that

Table 11.1 Knowledge and awareness signal cases (N = 49)[2]

	Recognizes the case		*Recognizes the sanction*	
	Yes	*No*	*Yes*	*No*
Case 1 (criminal)	31	18	2	47
Case 2 (regulatory)	17	32	0	49

Source: van Wingerde (2012, p. 165).

2 In some firms I interviewed more than one official.

had led to the penalty. For example, in the criminal case there was a huge fire that caused a lot of damage to the local surroundings. Most of the environmental managers recalled the fire and its consequences in terms of pollution, while only two of them knew that both the company and its three executives were criminally prosecuted.

One explanation for these findings is that sanctions only provide a very weak signal and therefore impose only a weak threat on business firms. Most of the interviewees believed that penalties for environmental violations are relatively insignificant compared to the profits of waste companies. For example, in the *Probo Koala* case that was mentioned in the introduction to this chapter, Trafigura, the owner of the waste, was sentenced to pay a fine of €1 million in the Netherlands in 2011. At the same time, however, the firm achieved a net profit close to US$1 billion (Van Wingerde 2015, p. 268).

Moreover, many of the environmental managers interviewed stated that sanctions are often imposed for violations that in their opinion were either administrative or quite technical in nature, such as failure to fill out a form in a timely manner. This is problematic because these types of rule violations do not have the same moral message as, for example, dumping toxic chemicals in the water, and being punished for committing such relatively minor offences (i.e. administrative rather than substantive) does not involve the same loss of face. On the contrary, these types of violations are characterized as trivial and insignificant which undermines the potential deterrent effect that the sanction may have.

At the same time, however, during the interviews the environmental managers provided many illustrations of the importance of social licence pressures.

Social Licence Pressures

Next to governments, public interest groups, local communities and the media have also pressured firms to reduce the adverse consequences of their activities. In the literature on organizational responses to regulation, this has been conceptualized as the regulated firms' 'social licence', which refers to the demands and expectations from the local community and environmental interest groups (Joyce and Thomson 2000; Gunningham et al. 2003, 2004; Lynch-Wood and Williamson 2007).

Many environmental managers in this study spoke about their relationship with their neighbours and about 'keeping their social licence'. Firms that have a good reputation and relationship with the local community also receive trust and legitimacy from their social environment. This in turn could make it easier to recruit well-trained employees, to renew the firm's environmental licence, and to receive governmental approval on new developments or new activities. In other words: investing in the firm's social licence might be good for business in the future (Gunningham et al. 2004).

The same is true for the opposite. Firms that lack the trust of their social environment may be confronted with negative publicity, reputational damages and even protests. According to the interviews, to most firms in the waste industry in the Netherlands negative publicity that affects their reputation as well as pressure from environmental interest groups is far more threatening than the risk of legal sanctions. The following responses are typical:

> 'When you are working with waste, you are owned by the public'.
>
> (Case 13)

> 'Reputation is what it is all about!'
>
> (Case 8)

> 'It works against you when you don't establish a good relationship with the public. Being a good neighbour is crucial, or you will create a potential problem'.
>
> (Case 12)

So it is not the public regulator who inspects only once or twice a year who is the central driver for compliance, but the firm's neighbours whom they see every day and vice versa, who smell and see the company every day.

Some research even suggests that the conditions of the social licence might be tougher than those of the regulatory licence, resulting in 'beyond compliance' behaviour (Prakash 2000; Huisman 2001; Simpson 2002; Gunningham et al. 2003, 2004; Hutter and O'Mahony 2004; Van Rooij 2006). For instance, in one case a company hired two 'odour experts'. They drove through the local area twice a day trying to locate any smells coming from the incinerator of the company. This has not been compelled by regulations, but it did help to improve their reputation with the local community (Case 10).

In another case, the company obtained a legal licence for a mobile installation for the demolition of construction waste. Because those installations tend to produce a lot of dust and noise, the local community had often expressed their concerns and they were fairly hostile towards the installation. Even though the firm legally obtained the licence, it decided not to use it because of its relationship with the public (Case 26).

There are, however, limitations to the effectiveness of the social licence. In order to be able to pressure firms, the social environment first needs to be able to recognize potential harms. It is clear that while odours, noise and dust are quite easily detected, other more serious environmental problems remain undetected by the local community (see Gunningham et al. 2004).

Second, the social environment should also be able and willing to enforce the demands of the social licence. It is clear that not all social environments have the means, knowledge or the political power to address complex environmental and legal issues. Finally, the interviews showed that social licence pressures not always lead to meaningful compliance. Business firms respond in different ways to the pressures of the local community. Some firms have been able to effectively neutralize the pressure from their local community by manipulating the information about their environmental performances, by making an offer to buy the houses of local citizens who were considered to be 'annoying' plaintiffs, or by relocating their activities to jurisdictions where the local community was expected to be less powerful.

In examining general deterrence we also need to analyse how and why regulated actors shape compliance within their own organizations.

Regulating from the Inside

Of course, the degree to which sanctions actually penetrate the regulated actors' business depends largely on the responsibility taken within the firm to comply with regulations. A key concept in this regard is the *social responsiveness* of the regulated actor (Van de Bunt 1992). This refers to the firm's ability to take into account the adverse consequences of its actions and respond to the demands and expectations from the regulatory and the social environment.

According to Van de Bunt (1992), the concept of social responsiveness comprises two aspects. First, responsive business firms need to have an adequate perception of the consequences of their activities for their social environment.

Second, socially responsive actors must act based on these perceptions in order to prevent the adverse consequences of their actions to occur. Van de Bunt (1992) shows that unresponsive actors are more likely to violate the law because they are unable or unwilling to take into account the consequences of their actions. These firms may not even be aware of the applicable legal norms and the sanctions that may be imposed when violating these norms.

Alternatively, the more responsive the firm is, the sooner it will view a sanction as a signal to check whether it still operates in compliance with the law and, if not, take measures to improve its behaviour. At the same time, however, my research shows that more responsive firms are also often large and complex organizations that do not always perceive a sanction as a meaningful suggestion to business compliance. This is the result of the fact that a sanction usually only communicates *that* a violation has occurred. However, it does not provide information about the causes of the violation and the blameworthiness of the offence, two aspects that are crucial to actually make any behavioural changes. During the interviews, the environmental managers provided several examples that indicated that sanctions did not provide them with the information necessary to adjust their behaviour. For example, one of the respondents mentioned that it is important to create a culture of compliance in which the firm actually improves its environmental performance and she was not sure that a sanction would help them do that (Case 7).

In another case example, the company collected batteries to have them recycled in the near future. Regulations prescribe that batteries need to be stored in a special box to avoid leakages. On one of the busiest days of the week, right before a public holiday, a couple of batteries fell out of the box, at which point in time the company was inspected and fined €1,500. The environmental manager commented: 'Technically it is a violation, but to us compliance isn't about whether or not batteries are stored in a box, but about governing that emissions are within the safety margins and about making sure that the risks of a chemical fire of spill are minimized. This inspection is just a snapshot of compliance, you need to be in control all the time' (Case 13).

Thornton et al. (2005) suggest that to these more responsive firms, sanctions might serve as a 'reminder' to check whether they still operate in accordance with their previous commitment to comply with the law; or as a 'reassurance' by sending the message that 'bad apples' are caught and punished, reaffirming their commitment to invest in costly compliance measures. However, in order to serve as a reminder or a reassurance, sanctions have to condemn the penalized behaviour and create consensus about the blameworthiness of the sanctioned offence. Most of the sanctions studied in this research project, however, lack those qualities.

Discussion

The above findings can be put into perspective by examining the history and character of the waste industry in the Netherlands. At present, the Dutch waste industry is an important economic branch of industry with large, internationally operating firms. The 25 largest firms all have an annual turnover of €25 million and the five largest firms together achieve an annual turnover of €2.1 billion and all pursue high level innovations to improve environmental performance (Noordhoek 2014). However, this has not always been common practice.

The waste industry in the Netherlands is a relatively young branch of industry. It developed rapidly during the 1970s and 1980s when due to environmental regulations the treatment and processing of waste suddenly became profitable. This attracted a lot of entrepreneurs who tried to make it in this industry. At the same time, however, this also attracted businesses that were less inclined to properly handle the waste. During the 1980s and early 1990s, when environmental policy was still developing, the Netherlands was alarmed by several huge environmental scandals in the waste industry. The best-known Dutch scandal is a case involving a company named Tank Cleaning Rotterdam. In this case the executives were sentenced to six years' imprisonment and the affair even led to a parliamentary inquiry in 1996 into the role of the government subsidizing this company (Huisman 2001).

In reaction to these scandals a regulatory climate has emerged that obliges waste companies to meet intensified regulatory pressures and which is characterized by a climate of great distrust between regulators and waste companies. Only since the beginning of this century, things have begun to change (Huisman 2001). Waste companies have become more and more aware that in order to secure their future they needed to change their behaviour and gain the trust of regulators as well as of the general public. So they have put a lot of effort into professionalization; waste companies have invested a lot in environmental performance; they have hired highly educated professionals responsible for environmental compliance; and they have invested in their reputation towards the public. At present, most firms in the Dutch waste industry do not portray themselves as waste companies, but as environmental specialists.

To these large multinational firms the sanction itself and the public regulator imposing it, is only one of the incentives for compliance with regulatory standards. 'And of these, the law is not likely to occupy the foreground of the businessman's attention' (Stone 1975, p. 40).

Conclusion: Sanctions as Moral Messages

The aim of this chapter was to provide insight into the role and importance of general deterrence in motivating firms in the Dutch waste industry to comply with environmental regulations and to provide insight into the interaction between deterrence, social licence pressures, and management-based regulation.

This study showed that deterrent threats hardly have a direct effect on business compliance in the waste industry in the Netherlands. Instead, this study provides support for a more indirect general deterrent effect of sanctions (Thornton et al. 2005). First, as far as sanctions influence the compliance behaviour of waste companies, this effect runs through the social environment. Negative publicity, reputational damages and pressures from the local community are far more threatening than formal legal sanctions. Second, this indirect effect depends on the degree of social responsiveness of the regulated actor. The more responsive the business firm, the sooner it views signals from outside the firm as meaningful to corporate compliance. The paradox of deterrence therefore is that it works best for those firms that least need it.

In conclusion, this study shows that deterrence works much better if there are other pre-existing normative systems that influence the behaviour of companies. These are either the social environment that pressures firms to comply, or moral commitments within the firm. Regulators that effectively want to influence the behaviour of these firms should make use of and interact with these private mechanisms of social control.

Sanctions can contribute to that, but then the sanction has to communicate a moral message instead of a threatening one, emphasizing that the penalized behaviour is condemned and creating consensus about the blameworthiness of the penalized offence. As such the sanction may create discussion amongst the regulated community about the offence, it may change perceptions about right and wrong, and it may result in meaningful compliance.

References

Amnesty International and Greenpeace Netherlands. 2012. *The Toxic Truth: About a Company Called Trafigura, a Ship Called the Probo Koala, and the Dumping of Toxic Waste in Côte d'Ivoire*. London and Amsterdam: Amnesty International and Greenpeace Netherlands.

Ayres, I. and Braithwaite, J. 1992. *Responsive Regulation: Transcending the Deregulation Debate*. New York: Oxford University Press.

Beccaria, C. 1982 [1764]. *Over misdaden en straffen* [*On Crimes and Punishment*] (Dutch translation by J.M. Michiels). Antwerpen and Zwolle: Kluwer and Tjeenk Willink.

Becker, G.S. 1968. 'Crime and Punishment: An Economic Approach', *Journal of Political Economy* 76(2), 169–217.

Bentham, J. 2007 [1823]. *An Introduction to the Principles of Morals and Legislation.* Mineola: Dover Publications Inc.

Braithwaite, J. 1989. *Crime, Shame, and Reintegration.* Cambridge: Cambridge University Press.

——— 2002. *Restorative Justice and Responsive Regulation.* New York: Oxford University Press.

——— 2008. *Regulatory Capitalism: How it Works, Ideas for Making it Work Better.* Cheltenham: Edward Elgar.

Braithwaite J. and Drahos, P. 2000. *Global Business Regulation.* Cambridge: Cambridge University Press.

Braithwaite, J. and Makkai, T. 1991. 'Testing an Expected Utility Model of Corporate Deterrence', *Law & Society Review* 25, 7–39.

Braithwaite, J., Coglianese, C. and Levi-Faur, D. 2007. 'Can Regulation and Governance Make a Difference?', *Regulation and Governance* 1(1), 1–7.

Bunt, van de H.G. 1992. *Organisatiecriminaliteit* [*Corporate Crime*]. Arnhem: Gouda Quint.

Cashore, B., Auld, G. and Renckens, S. 2011. 'The Impact of Private, Industry and Transnational Civil Society Regulation and their Interaction with Official Regulation', in *Explaining Regulatory Compliance: Business Responses to Regulation,* edited by C. Parker and V. Lehmann Nielsen. Cheltenham: Edward Elgar, 170–95.

Coffee, J.C. 1981. '"No Soul to Damn: No Body to Kick": An Unscandalized Inquiry into the Problem of Corporate Punishment', *Michigan Law Review* 79(3), 386–459.

Cohen, M.A. 2000. 'Empirical Research on the Deterrent Effect of Environmental Monitoring and Enforcement', *The Environmental Law Reporter* 30(4), 10245–52.

Geerken, M.R. and Gove, W.R. 1975. 'Deterrence: Some Theoretical Considerations', *Law & Society Review* 9(3), 497–513.

Gray, W.B. and Shadbegian, R.J. 2005. 'When and Why do Plants Comply? Paper Mills in the 1980's', *Law & Policy* 27(2), 238–61.

Gray, W.B. and Shimshack, J.P. 2011. 'The Effectiveness of Environmental Monitoring and Enforcement: A Review of the Empirical Evidence', *Review of Environmental Economics and Policy* 5(1), 3–24.

Gunningham, N. 2009. 'Environmental Law, Regulation and Governance: Shifting Architectures', *Journal of Environmental Law* 21(2), 179–212.

Gunningham, N., Kagan, R. and Thornton, D. 2003. *Shades of Green: Business, Regulation, and Environment.* Stanford: Stanford University Press.

——— 2004. 'Social License and Environmental Protection: Why Businesses Go Beyond Compliance?', *Law & Social Inquiry* 29, 307–41.

Huisman, W. 2001. *Tussen winst en moraal. Achtergronden van regelnaleving en regelovertreding door ondernemingen* [*Between Profit and Morality: Compliance and Violations by Businesses*]. Den Haag: Boom Juridische uitgevers.

Hutter, B.M. and O'Mahony, J. 2004. *The Role of Civil Society Organizations in Regulating Business.* Center for Analysis of Risk and Regulation, discussion paper no. 26. London: London School of Economics and Political Science.

Joyce, S.A. and Thomson, I. 2000. 'Earning a Social License to Operate: Social Acceptability and Resource Development in Latin America', *The Canadian Mining and Metallurgical Bulletin* 93(1037), 49–52.

Kagan, R.A. and Scholz, J.T. 1984. 'The "Criminology of the Corporation" and Regulatory Enforcement Strategies', in *Enforcing Regulation*, edited by K. Hawkins and J.M. Thomas. Boston: Kluwer, 67–95.

Kagan, R.A., Gunningham, N. and Thornton, D. 2011. 'Fear, Duty and Regulatory Compliance: Lessons from Three Research Projects', in *Explaining Regulatory Compliance: Business Responses to Regulation*, edited by C. Parker and V. Lehmann Nielsen. Cheltenham: Edward Elgar, 37–58.

Lehmann Nielsen, V. and Parker, C. 2012. 'Mixed Motives: Economic, Social, and Normative Motivations in Business Compliance', *Law & Policy* 34, 428–62.

Lynch-Wood, G. and Williamson, D. 2007. 'The Social License as a Form of Regulation for Small and Medium Enterprises', *Journal of Law & Society* 34(3), 321–41.

May, P.J. 2005. 'Compliance Motivations: Perspectives of Farmers, Homebuilders and Marine Facilities', *Law & Policy* 27, 317–47.

Noordhoek, F.K. 2014. *Afval! Jaarboek 2013* [Waste! Yearbook 2013]. Utrecht: Noordhoek Publishers.

Parker, C. 2006. 'The "Compliance" Trap: The Moral Message in Responsive Regulatory Enforcement', *Law & Society Review* 40, 591–622.

——— 2012. 'Economic Rationalities of Governance and Ambiguity in the Criminalization of Cartels', *British Journal of Criminology* 52, 974–96.

——— 2013. 'The War on Cartels and the Social Meaning of Deterrence', *Regulation & Governance* 7, 174–94.

Parker, C. and Lehmann Nielsen, V. (eds). 2011. *Explaining Regulatory Compliance: Business Responses to Regulation*. Cheltenham: Edward Elgar.

Paternoster, R. 1987. 'The Deterrent Effect of the Perceived Certainty and Severity of Punishment: A Review of the Evidence and Issues', *Justice Quarterly* 4(2), 173–217.

——— 2010. 'How Much Do We Really Know About Criminal Deterrence?', *The Journal of Criminal Law & Criminology* 100, 765–824.

Paternoster, R. and Simpson, S. 1996. 'Sanction Threats and Appeals to Morality: Testing a Rational Choice Model of Corporate Crime', *Law and Society Review* 30, 549–83.

Prakash, A. 2000. *Greening the Firm: The Politics of Corporate Environmentalism*. Cambridge: Cambridge University Press.

Pratt, T.C., Cullen, F.T., Blevins, K.R., Daigle, L.E. and Madensen, T.D. 2006. 'The Empirical Status of Deterrence Theory: A Meta-Analysis', in *Taking Stock: The Status of Criminological Theory*, edited by F.T. Cullen, J.P. Wright and K.R. Blevins. New Brunswick: Transaction Publishers, 367–96.

Rooij, van B. 2006. *Regulating Land and Pollution in China: Lawmaking, Compliance, and Enforcement; Theory and Cases*. Leiden: Leiden University Press.

Simpson, S.S. 2002. *Corporate Crime, Law, and Social Control*. New York: Cambridge University Press.

Simpson, S.S., Gibbs, C., Rorie, M., Slocum, L.A., Cohen, M.A. and Vandenbergh, M. 2013. 'An Empirical Assessment of Corporate Environmental Crime Control Strategies', *The Journal of Criminal Law & Criminology* 103, 231–78.

Simpson, S.S., Rorie, M., Alper, M. and Schell-Busey, N. 2014. 'Corporate Crime Deterrence: A Systematic Review', *Campbell Systematic Reviews* 2014:4. Available at: www.campbellcollaboration.org/lib/project/199/ (accessed 26 May 2014).

Stone, C.D. 1975. *Where the Law Ends: The Social Control of Corporate Behavior*. New York: Harper & Row.

Thornton, D., Gunningham, N.A. and Kagan, R.A. 2005. 'General Deterrence and Corporate Environmental Behaviour', *Law & Policy* 27(2), 262–87.

Tyler, T. 2011. 'The Psychology of Self-Regulation: Normative Motivations for Compliance', in *Explaining Regulatory Compliance: Business Responses to Regulation*, edited by C. Parker and V. Lehmann Nielsen. Cheltenham: Edward Elgar, 78–99.

Vandenbergh, M.P. 2003. 'Beyond Elegance: A Testable Typology of Social Norms in Corporate Environmental Compliance', *Stanford Environmental Law Journal* 22(1), 55–144.

Wenzel, M. 2004. 'The Social Side of Sanctions: Personal and Social Norms as Moderators of Deterrence', *Law and Human Behavior* 28, 547–67.

White, R. 2008. 'Toxic Cities: Globalizing the Problem of Waste', *Social Justice* 35(3), 107–19.

Wingerde, van C.G. 2012. *De afschrikking voorbij: Een empirische studie naar afschrikking, generale preventie en regelnaleving in de Nederlandse afvalbranche* [Beyond Deterrence: Deterrence, Prevention, and Compliance in the Dutch Waste Industry]. Nijmegen: Wolf Legal Publishers.

——— 2015. 'The Limits of Environmental Regulation in a Globalized Economy: Lessons from the Probo Koala Case', in *The Routledge Handbook of White-Collar and Corporate Crime in Europe*, edited by J.G. van Erp, W. Huisman and G. Vande Walle. Oxford: Routledge, 260–75.

Zimring, F.E. and Hawkins, G.J. 1973. *Deterrence: The Legal Threat in Crime Control*. Chicago: University of Chicago Press.

12 Enforcing the European Emissions Trading System within the EU Member States

A Procrustean Bed?

Floor Fleurke and Jonathan Verschuuren[1]

Introduction

Since the late 1990s, the EU has explicitly decided to take the lead in action addressing climate change, and has made common action against global warming an important part of its foreign environmental policy (European Commission 2008). The EU has laid down this goal in its *Climate and Energy* package of 2010, in which it committed to a reduction of 20 per cent in greenhouse gas emissions by 2020 relative to a 1990 baseline (European Commission 2010). In October 2014, the Council of the EU adopted a reduction target of 40 per cent as part of the 2030 Framework for Climate and Energy Policies (European Council 2014, p. 1). The flagship of this policy is the EU emissions trading system (EU ETS), as laid down in Directive 2003/87 (hereafter 'the Directive') (Official Journal 2003a). This will remain so in the period until 2030,[2] despite major challenges to the EU ETS that emerged during the economic crisis. These were mainly caused by a growing surplus of emission allowances, which undermined the trade in the carbon market. Although the EU ETS is now in its third trading phase, so far the outcomes in terms of emissions abatement have been minor (Department of Energy and Climate Change 2013). The price for CO_2 has simply remained too low to encourage the industry to invest in low carbon technology. This, in turn, was caused by a cap that was set too high; the financial crisis, which caused a reduction in production; 'offsetting' of emission reduction abroad; and a reduced need for electricity caused by warm weather.[3]

Moreover, the carbon market – as the world's fastest growing commodities market – is at risk of being targeted and undermined by criminals. In fact, the system has been plagued by incidences of fraud that have been covered extensively

1 This chapter summarizes the main findings of a research project that received funding from the European Union's Seventh Framework Programme for research, technological development and demonstration under grant agreement no. 308481. For the full report see Verschuuren and Fleurke (2014).

2 See European Council (2014, p. 2). In December 2014, the European Commission started work on the revision of the EU ETS Directive for post-2020. See European Commission (2014).

3 A structural reform of the EU ETS is underway to deal with these challenges, see the European Commission's website for details: http://ec.europa.eu/clima/policies/ets/reform/index_en.htm.

in the media (see HETQ 2014; Mason 2011; *The Economist* 2010). It requires proper monitoring and enforcement to ensure both the environmental and financial integrity of the EU ETS system. Its effectiveness and reliability depends for a substantial part on the level of compliance in each of the 31 participating states.[4] A lack of compliance in even one or just a few participating countries may harm the functioning of the ETS in the entire EU. It is here that we are confronted with a Procrustean dilemma: is there a fit between the centralized and standardized EU ETS and the decentralized, individual enforcement practices and enforcement cultures of the different member states? In Greek mythology, Procrustes was a rogue smith who stretched people or cut off their legs, so as to make them fit the size of his bed.

Against this background we examine the enforcement side of the EU ETS. The chapter is organized as follows. First, we will explain the compliance cycle of the EU ETS. We will also briefly pay attention to the various amendments that were adopted over the years, and especially in the run up to the third trading phase: how has the EU legislature tried to improve the compliance mechanism? In the third section, we explain the core legal obligations for market players to which all compliance efforts are directed, and in the fourth section we will deal with the sanctions that apply in case of non-compliance.

The fifth and sixth sections then provide the findings of an empirical study of the compliance mechanism of the EU ETS in six different member states: Germany, the Netherlands, Poland, Greece, the United Kingdom and Hungary. These member states were chosen because they represent both smaller and larger countries as well as old and new member states. Here, we turn to the question of how the compliance mechanisms have played out in the context of the EU ETS at the domestic level, drawing on experiences in different member states, with a focus on organization and compliance instruments respectively. We have studied and compared national legislation and analysed the organizational and administrative structures, including monitoring instruments. Data were gathered by means of desk research and interviews with representatives from various institutions involved in the compliance mechanism.[5] In the final section, we will draw some conclusions on whether in the third phase the compliance mechanism of the EU ETS has sufficiently improved in terms of effectiveness, and what prospects – from a compliance perspective – exist for stepping up the EU's emission reduction efforts while relying on the EU ETS as the main instrument, to achieve the 2030 targets.

Complying with the EU ETS

The EU ETS is the largest trading programme in the world, designed with the aim to combat global climate change. The key concept of emissions trading is the establishment of a market mechanism to mitigate greenhouse gasses. After a cap

4 Participating states are the 28 member states of the EU and Norway, Iceland and Liechtenstein.

5 For a full overview of the findings, see Verschuuren and Fleurke (2014). Transcripts of all interviews are available with the authors. We would like to thank all persons that have participated in the interviews for their time and valuable insights.

is set and potential polluting firms have obtained allowances to emit (either distributed freely, or through auctioning), they can either (1) reduce their emissions and sell their allowances by for example investing in technological innovation; (2) use their allowances in order to cover their emissions; or, (3) increase their emissions by buying additional allowances on the market.

The crucial importance of a well-developed and operationalized compliance chain has been neglected in the original design. In fact, a striking paradox of the EU ETS is that while it is based on the idea of a free market the system only functions if it operates in a well-regulated context. Market participants must have the confidence that the system is transparent and consistent, and that it guarantees a level playing field for all actors in the participating states. In this regard, information on emission allowances, on the amount of allowances that are surrendered, and information on actual emissions is essential. Monitoring, reporting and verification of this process are therefore of vital importance for the functioning of the system and compliance.

In order to be compliant covered installations must operate in accordance with the requirements of the EU ETS. Inspections and enforcement actions are necessary to monitor and ensure this (IMPEL 2007, p. 3). The Commission already emphasized the importance of oversight and enforcement in its Green Paper on emission trading in the year 2000, by stating that:

> The purpose of strict compliance provisions and enforcement is to enhance confidence in the trading system, make it work in an efficient way in accordance with the rules of the internal market and at the same time increase the likelihood of achieving the desired environmental result.
>
> (European Commission 2000, p. 24)

In reality, however, not much attention was dedicated to this important aspect of environmental compliance.[6] The initial EU ETS legislation left a considerable amount of discretion to member states. This particularly concerned operational elements of emission trading, such as registration, monitoring, verification, reporting and enforcement issues. It was only when European law enforcement agencies reported signals that in some European countries carbon trading fraudsters accounted for up to 90 per cent of all market activity, with proceeds of crime running into billions, that compliance issues started to receive increased attention (Interpol 2013a).

As mentioned above, the effectiveness and reliability of the EU ETS to a significant extent depends on compliance in each of the member states and differences in compliance strategies in the member states may distort the entire market for greenhouse gas allowances. Earlier reports have indicated that this decentralized approach pursued in the Directive has adversely affected the effectiveness of the system and gradually, however, a series of amendments of the scheme's

6 M. Peeters was an early signaller of this important issue (Peeters 2006).

operational aspects have been adopted to reduce the level of decentralization.[7] The latest changes made to the EU ETS, the ones that apply to the current trading phase (2013–20), have greatly centralized the EU ETS. Provisions on compliance and enforcement have now for the most part been harmonized. Particularly regarding enforcement issues various elements of the ETS however remain within the domain of the member states (Ellerman 2009).[8] Nevertheless, member states remain the most important actors responsible for ensuring compliance with of the EU ETS. The active role of member states in setting up compliance strategies is also important for ensuring that competition of the industry covered is not seriously distorted, and that there remains a 'level playing field' (Peeters 2006, p. 179).

Compliance issues in emission trading differ from those flowing from standard command and control regulations typical for environmental law. As Peeters pointed out, the classical command and control enforcement method is imposing static obligations on firms, such as binding limit values for their emissions, and requirements to apply specific techniques (Peeters 2006, p. 178). To the firms to which such obligations apply these do not change unless the permit is amended. In emissions trading, however, the requirements set in the emission permit are dynamic: the amount of allowances that need to be surrendered fluctuates with the exact amount of CO_2 emitted (Peeters 2006). Monitoring this is a challenging and highly complex task for the operators of installations covered by the system and also requires continuous control and oversight by member state authorities. Weishaar (2014, p. 150) in this regard even suggests that the EU ETS 'necessitates a system that may perhaps be even more stringent than in the case under comparable command and control instruments'.

When thinking of compliance and inspection as an ongoing effort of both operators and competent authorities, one has to bear in mind the entire *compliance cycle*. This includes the following activities:

- information and communication facilities;
- site visits and consideration of the results;
- monitoring achievements;
- verification of self-monitoring and self-reporting;
- controlling equipment;
- controlling systems and procedures;
- controlling the relevant records and measurement systems;
- controlling the emission permit to ensure that the activities described in the monitoring plan reflect the reality of the site in relation to the consistency and completeness of the monitoring of the emissions;
- controlling the verified emissions reports (IMPEL 2007).

7 See, for a detailed discussion of all the regulatory changes, Verschuuren and Fleurke (2014).

8 Negotiations are currently underway with Switzerland. Plans to link the EU ETS to the Australian ETS were abandoned after the Australian parliament repealed the emissions trading scheme in July 2014.

Ideally, a compliance assessment by the competent authority will be produced based upon a risk assessment taking into account the complexity of the installation, the level of emissions, the compliance history of the installation and its operator, the time required for visits and for drawing up the verifier report. Here, 'instrument sequencing', whereby enforcement agencies dispose of a range of instruments, ranging from soft to hard, is also of relevance. Within the dynamic context of the EU ETS it is particularly important for regulators and firms to foster good relationships to ensure sustained and long-term compliance. Therefore, upon becoming aware of an infringement, enforcement agencies will first seek to educate and persuade rather than resort immediately to the more extreme coercive instruments that they also have at their disposal. The fact that enforcement agencies may revert to coercive instruments higher up the escalation ladder accounts for the effectiveness of less draconic enforcement policies. Socio-legal scholars explain this dynamic by referring to it as 'negotiating under the shadow of the law' (Gunningham and Grabosky 1998).

As has become clear from the country reports in this study, the extent to which the member states apply the different instruments depends upon the regulatory approach the competent authorities choose. Their choices depend on factors such as regulatory tradition, the principles underlying their enforcement strategy and how it is implemented, but also on available resources.

The EU ETS Compliance Forum has been established to promote better harmonization (European Commission 2012). Participation is voluntary and open to all member states. The Forum is used to exchange information and best practices and to discuss challenges concerning the operation of the EU ETS. Task forces are organized to address specific priorities. A second instrument to foster harmonization and compliance is standardized IT systems as is for example used to register the EU ETS.

Key Legal Obligations of Participating Operators in the EU ETS

Before discussing concrete compliance issues relating to the EU ETS, we briefly explain the core legal obligations applying to the market's actors. The essential requirement for the actors is a permit necessary for entering the emissions market obliging them to monitor, report and verify emissions. Registration obligations are included as well, as the integrity of the Register is crucial to the functioning of the EU ETS. In our chapter we do not address auctioning since it does not directly relate to questions of enforcement and compliance in the context of the EU ETS.[9]

9 Compliance with the auctioning system is part of the report on which this chapter is based (Verschuuren and Fleurke 2014).

The Greenhouse Gas Emissions Permit

As explained above, the core of the EU ETS is that the emissions of every installation falling within the scope of the system must equal its annual emission rights. Since operators without a GHG emissions license may no longer emit CO_2 this permit is the key legal instrument of Directive 2003/87 (hereafter: 'The Directive'). The competent authority can only issue such a permit after having established that the operator is capable of monitoring and reporting emissions.[10] In the permit, the specific activities of the installation(s) are described, as well as the main conditions for operating within the EU ETS: the operator must surrender allowances equal to the total emissions of the installation in each calendar year, within four months following the end of that year.[11] In addition, the operator is required to inform the competent authority of any changes that affect the functioning of the installation, for example an extension that might require an update of the emission permit.[12]

Monitoring, Reporting and Verification (MRV)

The Directive requires that the GHG emissions permit contains a monitoring plan, specifying detailed, complete and transparent documentation, including a risk assessment.[13] The monitoring plan is of paramount importance, because without it the permit cannot be granted.[14] Emissions must be monitored in accordance with the rules of the Commission Regulation 601/2012/EU on the monitoring and reporting of greenhouse gas emissions, and the competent authorities must ensure that each operator of an installation reports the emissions from that installation during each calendar year after the end of that year (Official Journal 2012). An update of the monitoring plan is not necessarily labelled as 'a change' that also requires a revision of the GHG emissions permit.[15]

Monitoring provisions require the use of certain monitoring methodologies and detailed specific sector rules. Operators must take into account different aspects, such as the location and calibration of measurement equipment, and quality assurance and control, missing data and uncertainties (Official Journal 2012).[16] The principle of constant improvement of performance in monitoring and reporting emissions hence should encourage in continuously finding new, improved approaches, hereby supported by the verifier.

10 Art. 4 of the Directive.
11 Art. 6(2) (e).
12 Art. 7.
13 Art. 6(2) (c), Art. 12.
14 Art. 6(2) (c) and (d), Arts. 14 and 15.
15 Art. 6(2) (c) of the Directive.
16 Section 3 and Art. 57. There are specific provisions for the aviation sector.

In addition to the monitoring requirements, according to Article 6(2)(d) of the Directive the operator must draft and submit an emission report.[17] Ultimately, the member states must confirm that all operators of an installation report the emissions from that installation during each calendar year to the competent authority after the end of that year. Independent and certified verifiers commissioned by the operator must approve the emission reports.[18] The verification report must conclude with 'reasonable assurance' that the operator's report is free from 'material misstatements'.[19] The verifier must carry out his activities with 'an attitude of professional scepticism recognizing that circumstances may exist that cause the information in the operator's report to contain material misstatements'.[20] These provisions should guarantee the quality and reliability of the system of self-monitoring and self-report.

Importantly, since 2012 the verifier is obliged to include irregularities in the monitoring plan even if the competent authority accepts the verification report. Detailed rules prescribe the verification process. For example, data should be tested in detail and be traced back to the primary source and cross-checked with information from external sources. Site visits must be conducted during the verification process to assess the operation of measuring devices and monitoring systems and to conduct interviews.[21] Although it is very important that the verification tasks are carried out 'in the public interest', member state authorities remain ultimately responsible in checking whether compliance exists.

Register

Operators must submit all transactions within the EU ETS electronically to a Register to ensure the availability of accurate data on transfers and submission of emissions. The quality of the transaction logs is crucial to the functioning of the EU ETS. A breach of the integrity of the Register can lead to substantial fraud and cybercrime, for instance to double counting of surrendered allowances and identity theft.[22] In 2009, it was observed that there was a significant increase in the occurrence of VAT-fraud, money laundering and other criminal activities (Interpol 2013a). To secure the integrity of the registration, the national registries were replaced by a single Union Registry and a European Union Transaction Log (EUTL) in the third phase (2013–20) of the EU ETS (Official Journal 2008).

This was deemed necessary to improve the coherence of the registry, and also to better guarantee the robustness of the system and to reduce its vulnerability

17 See also Official Journal (2009), Arts. 14 and 15 and Official Journal (2012) on the verification of greenhouse gas emission reports and tonne-kilometre reports and the accreditation of verifiers pursuant to the Directive.

18 Art. 15 of the Directive and Regulation 600/2012/EU.

19 Art. 7 of Regulation 600/2012/EU.

20 Art. 7 of Regulation 600/2012/EU.

21 Art. 21 of the Directive.

22 See for example on the fraud hitting the EU ETS: Interpol (2013b).

to fraud.[23] One measure was to tighten regulations on the persons involved in the transaction administration. National administrators, for instance, can now refuse to open an account in case the person who requests the opening of the account is a suspect under investigation in cases of fraud involving allowances or Kyoto units, money laundering, terrorist financing and other serious crimes to which the account may be instrumental, or any other reason set out in national law.[24] Any violations of these requirements may result in the European Commission instructing the EU Central Administrator to suspend the acceptance of some or all processes (i.e. automated technical means to carry out an action relating to an account or a unit in a registry).[25] Automated checking of all processes is required.[26] If discrepancies are discovered, the process concerned has to be terminated and the relevant account holder has to be informed on this.[27]

Interestingly, there exists no market inspection yet as a CO_2 allowance is not considered to be a financial product. However, the Market Abuse Directive (Article 43) does apply to the EU ETS (Directive 2003/6/EC, Official Journal 2003b). According to that Directive authorities have the right to: (a) access any document in any form whatsoever, and to receive a copy of it; (b) demand information from any person; (c) carry out on-site inspections; (d) request existing telephone and existing data traffic records; (e) request the cessation of any practice that is contrary to the provisions adopted in the implementation of the above provisions; (f) suspend trading; (g) request the freezing and/or sequestration of assets; and (h) request temporary prohibition of professional activity.[28] Member states have the obligation to impose effective, proportionate and dissuasive administrative sanctions against the persons responsible for non-compliance. Criminal proceedings may also be instituted if a member state so decides.[29]

Since the national competent authorities responsible for the enforcement of the EU ETS do not possess specific expertise on criminal behaviour it is important that they cooperate closely with other enforcement agencies and government agencies, such as the tax authorities or the authorities on competition (NEa 2010).

23 In addition, accounts have to have at least two authorized representatives next to the person opening the account, and the obligations of these persons (account holder and authorized representatives) have been laid down in Annex VI of Regulation 920/2010/EU, such as the duty to ensure that the posted data are accurate. Regulation 920/2010/EU also contains many provisions with technical requirements of the registries system aimed at preventing security breaches. If there is a security breach, the Central Administrator may suspend access to the EUTL.

24 Art. 13(4) of Regulation 920/2010/EU.

25 Art. 65(2) of Regulation 920/2010/EU.

26 Art. 66 of Regulation 920/2010/EU.

27 Art. 67 of Regulation 920/2010/EU.

28 Art. 12 of Directive 2003/6/EC.

29 Art. 14 of Directive 2003/6/EC.

Sanctions

The EU ETS Directive requires member states to put in place a system of penalties which is effective, proportionate and dissuasive, though the nature of the penalties is almost completely left to member state discretion.[30] There exists an important exception to this rule: the aforementioned obligation for operators of an installation to surrender each year by 30 April at the latest a number of allowances equal to the total emissions from that installation during the preceding calendar year.[31] Failure to comply with this requirement will result in an excess emissions penalty of €100 for each tonne of CO_2 equivalent emitted without sufficient allowances.[32] This may result in huge penalties keeping in mind that large installations may emit millions of tonnes of CO_2 annually.[33] The financial penalty may further increase in accordance with the European index of consumer prices.[34] In addition, the Directive also requires the names of the offending operators to be published.[35] The latter penalty, of 'naming and shaming', is a novelty in European secondary environmental legislation. The idea is that covered installations are usually conscious about their reputation and therefore this penalty would increase compliance (Gunningham and Grabosky 1998). Finally, the operator is still obliged to surrender an amount of allowances equal to the excess emissions.[36]

In EU environmental law such detailed requirements for the kind of sanctions the member states must include in their national legislation are rare. Consequently, this raised questions about how much room this leaves to the national courts to apply domestic sanctioning case law. In the *Billerud* case, a Swedish court, for example, asked the Court of Justice of the EU (CJEU) whether the principle of proportionality had to be applied in a case where the operator did have a sufficient number of allowances on 30 April, but did not surrender these as a result of an oversight, an administrative error or a technical problem, and whether the penalty could be waived or reduced under certain circumstances.[37] The CJEU gave a more or less negative answer to these questions and stressed the relevance of a centralized sanctioning system for the functioning of the EU ETS, at least as far as the surrendering of allowances is concerned.[38]

30 Art. 16(1) of the Directive.

31 Art. 12(3) of the Directive.

32 Art. 16(3) of the Directive.

33 Europe's biggest emitter is a Polish coal-fired power plant emitting 37 million tonnes of CO_2 annually (Gutmann et al. 2014, p. 10).

34 Art. 16(4) of the Directive.

35 Art. 16(2) of the Directive; the Directive does not specify where or how the names of operators who are in breach of requirements to surrender sufficient allowances under Article 12(3) should be published.

36 Art. 16(3) of the Directive.

37 Case C-203/12, *Billerud Karlsborg AB, Billerud Skärblacka AB* v. *Naturvårdsverket* of 17 October 2013.

38 The Court noted that imposing sanctions for any other conduct contrary to the Directive, is left to the discretion of the member states.

According to the CJEU in the *Billerud* case, the Directive does not aim to penalize 'polluters' generally, but rather those operators whose number of emissions for the preceding year exceeds the number of allowances listed in the centralized registry in the section of the surrendered allowance table for their installations for that year. This – and not the emissions which are per se excessive – is how the concept of 'excess emissions' is to be construed.[39] The Court of Justice therefore concluded that the obligation imposed by Directive 2003/87 is not a mere obligation to have in their possession the allowances covering the emissions for the preceding year on 30 April of the current year, but is an obligation to surrender those allowances by 30 April in order to have them cancelled in the registry, which is intended to ensure the accuracy of the accounting record of the allowances.[40] Although the ultimate purpose of the EU ETS is environmental protection, the infrastructure needed to attain that purpose is the strict accounting of the issue, holding, transfer and cancellation of allowances.[41] Implementation of a uniform sanctioning regime throughout the EU is necessary in the pursuit of the legitimate objective of establishing an efficient carbon dioxide equivalent allowance trading scheme, in order to prevent certain operators or market intermediaries from being tempted to circumvent or manipulate the scheme by speculating abusively on prices, quantities, time limits or complex financial products.[42]

The message for operators is a simple one: if you do not keep a proper administrative record you risk paying a substantial fine. The fact that this fine may reflect earlier expectations of market prices which, with the benefit of hindsight, have now proved to be unrealistically high is not in itself a reason to question the wisdom of the Court to deny a role for national courts to take the sharp edges off Article 16(3) by allowing them to sweeten the pill through a general recourse to the principle of proportionality. If, for whatever reason, the penalty system thus imposed proves to be disproportionate, it is for the EU legislator to intervene by amending the Directive's relevant provisions. To allow national courts to perform this role by opening the door for national and inconsistent applications of the principle of subsidiarity would give rise to the kind of distortions which the Directive intends to prevent.

As mentioned above, for all other breaches of the obligations concerning the functioning of the EU ETS, such as on the rules on MRV, member states have to put in place a system of penalties that is effective, proportionate and dissuasive.[43] This for example concerns penalties for not complying with monitoring

39 Case C-203/12, *Billerud Karlsborg AB, Billerud Skärblacka AB* v. *Naturvårdsverket* of 17 October 2013, para. 28.

40 Case C-203/12, *Billerud Karlsborg AB, Billerud Skärblacka AB* v. *Naturvårdsverket* of 17 October 2013, para. 30.

41 Case C-203/12, *Billerud Karlsborg AB, Billerud Skärblacka AB* v. *Naturvårdsverket* of 17 October 2013, para. 27.

42 Case C-203/12, *Billerud Karlsborg AB, Billerud Skärblacka AB* v. *Naturvårdsverket* of 17 October 2013, para. 39.

43 Art. 16(1) of the Directive.

and reporting obligations causing essential data to be missing or to be inaccurate, which in turn may lead to problems in establishing how many allowances the operator must surrender. Obviously this can seriously impair the effectiveness of the EU ETS, and member states thus have an obligation to establish an enforcement strategy that includes sanctions for these infringements. Considering the diversity in enforcement strategies among the member states, Article 21 of the Directive is of specific interest. According to this provision member states are required to report every year on the application of the Directive. The European Commission has developed a format for this questionnaire that also addresses the compliance issues we have discussed above.[44] The format has been expanded as of 2013; reports now have to include much more detailed information on all issues relating to the functioning of the EU ETS. Based on these national reports the Commission must publish a report on the application of the Directive within three months of receiving the reports of the Member States.[45] In the past, the Commission has used the 'Article 21 Reports' for making improvements in future trading periods.

Organization of Enforcement

Considering how important the organization of the administrative arrangements within the 31 participating states is for the functioning of the EU ETS, it is remarkable that the Directive gives minimal directions on how implementation is to be organized. Article 18 only requires the 'designation of the appropriate competent authority or authorities, for the implementation of the rules of this Directive'. This flexibility is reflected in differences in the organization of the implementation and enforcement of the Directive in the Member States.

Generally speaking, we can distinguish three approaches: (1) a single competent authority responsible for all tasks regarding the functioning of the EU ETS (e.g. the Netherlands, UK, Hungary); (2) a clear separation between the authorities responsible for the issuing of the GHG permit and the enforcement of the EU ETS respectively, with a coordinating role for the Designated National Authority (e.g. Germany, Greece); and (3) a decentralized network of several local or regional authorities for the assessment and issuance of permits and accepting of monitoring plans, as well as separate Inspectorates for Environmental Protection responsible for the enforcement of the EU ETS (e.g. Poland).

In environmental law, it is usually considered wise to task separate authorities with the issuing of permits on the one hand and inspection and enforcement on the other. This seems to be different for the EU ETS. Given the complexity of the system and the emphasis on compliance assistance, the emissions authority seems to be best placed to oversee the entire process, from the issuing of the GHG permit

44 Official Journal (2006). The Art. 21 reports are available at: http://cdr.eionet.europa.eu/ (accessed 11 April 2015).

45 Art. 21(3) of the Directive. See for example EEA (2008).

to the sanctioning of non-compliance. In the Netherlands, for example, this set-up has enhanced communication and quality throughout the compliance chain.[46] In this case all employees operate according to a functional division between departments in order to account for checks and balances.

In addition, to enforce the EU ETS cooperation with regular environmental inspection, authority is necessary (e.g. joint site inspections), since environmental law inspectors will usually have a long-standing relationship with operators. Knowing the operator's past (compliance) performance in other environmental areas can be useful when checking compliance with the EU ETS.

Among the member states, there exist notable variations in terms of the quality and number of staff employed with the competent authorities. This is also visible in the level of assistance that is provided to operators falling under the scope of the Directive. In some of the member states the competent authorities are very active in providing assistance through their helpdesks in particular to small emitters. They view this as part of their 'Compliance Assistance' strategy.[47] In these cases, websites provide online guidance and assistance in the permit application process. The competent authority actively notifies stakeholders of new procedures and introduces these through emails, newsletters, stakeholder workshops and updates of respective websites where appropriate. By comparison, other member states do not have a helpdesk (Hungary) or provide very limited assistance (Greece).

At the EU level, some member states (the United Kingdom, Germany, the Netherlands and, to a lesser extent, Italy and Poland) are active contributors to the Compliance Forum. The Forum is regarded as a valuable platform to test thoughts, exchange best practices and answer frequently asked questions. However, most of the member states are not participating at all.[48] The variety in enforcement styles could affect the level playing field that is needed throughout the EU to ensure an efficient and effective EU ETS.[49]

Compliance Instruments

Monitoring and Reporting in the Member States

This section provides insights into the compliance and enforcement practices of the six member states included in our study. In Germany and the Netherlands the authorities required operators of existing installations to submit their monitoring plans for the third trading period at least five and four months, respectively, before its start.[50] They deemed these periods necessary for the completion of the

46 Interview Netherlands emissions authority NEa, 14 April 2014.
47 In particular the UK, the Netherlands and Germany.
48 Interview German emissions authority DEHSt, 7 April 2014.
49 Interview Netherlands emissions authority NEa, 14 April 2014.
50 Treibhausgas-Emissionshandelsgesetz Appendix 2, Part 1, §1(a) TEHG.

collaborative process involving the competent authority and the operator to achieve the desired quality of the monitoring plan. In the UK, too, we found that the ex-ante process is an elaborate one during which the monitoring plan is scrutinized and qualified as a 'dialogue between the operator and the regulator'.[51]

After the operator has submitted the application for a permit and the monitoring plan, the national emissions authority decides on granting the permit within four months. The validation process involves active correspondence with the applicant, and usually requires the remedying of omissions at least once. Interestingly, the UK has developed and installed an online Emissions Trading System Workflow Automation Program (ETSWAP) in which all monitoring plans and reports must be submitted in a standardized electronic format. This online system is capable of checking anomalies relative to previous entries.[52] The online system may even refuse certain information if it differs substantially from the values of previous years.

Once the competent authority approves the monitoring plan the operator is obliged to continuously update it if significant changes occur. This also means that there has to be constant oversight. In Germany, for example, the operators must comply with a system of ongoing ex-post control, which includes continuous measurement of source streams, and providing information on new emission sources and scales for example. This system constantly generates items the operator must update in the monitoring plan. As of 2014, site visits also generate input for this process (see below). Finally, the yearly emissions registry cycle is also important for the ex-post control mechanism because here the verifiers check the annual emissions reports against the monitoring plan.[53]

In Greece, Hungary and Poland, we found much less collaborative processes between operators and the authorities. The operators here seem to be much more on their own in figuring out how to comply with the requirements on monitoring and reporting. We also found that ex-post control is much less a continuous process. Instead, the authorities in these countries primarily rely on the verified report. In Greece, the authorities complained that most of the operators send the verified report to them on the final day.[54] This is problematic because then they have to check everything within a very short time period.[55]

Verification and Inspection

As mentioned above, in accordance with Regulation 600/2012 an independent verifier must verify the annual emission report.[56] The EU has completely

51 Interview UK Environment Agency, 7 April 2014. The research on UK practices did not include Scotland and Northern Ireland.

52 Interview UK Environment Agency, 7 April 2014.

53 Interview German emissions authority DEHSt, 7 April 2014.

54 Interview Greek Emissions authority GEDE, 28 March 2014.

55 Ultimately, though, operators, after being pressured by GEDE, hand in what is needed also because of the influence of the verifiers. Interview GEDE, 28 March 2014.

56 Art. 15 of the Directive and Regulation 600/2012/EU.

harmonized the provisions for the accreditation of verifiers, more specifically the conditions for granting and withdrawing an accreditation and the requirements for mutual recognition and peer evaluation of accreditation bodies.

The number of accredited verifiers varies per country. In 2014, in Poland the number of accredited verifiers was insufficient and this resulted in a late submission of the emission reports.[57] Not all member states exercise continuous oversight after the verifier has been accredited, but we did find some best practices. For example, the United Kingdom Accreditation Service (UKAS) regularly inspects verifiers to ensure they continue to meet with their accreditation obligations. In Greece, verifiers are obliged to notify the Hellenic Accreditation Board (ESYD) and the Competent Authority on their schedule of site visits. ESYD can choose to join them in these site visits as part of the verification process.[58]

The competent authorities must subsequently check the verified emission report. How thoroughly this is conducted varies greatly between the member states we researched. In the UK, the regulator carries out independent checks on all verified reports and sends its comments back to the operator. Certain reports are selected for detailed analysis; this is done on the basis of classification of an installation in one of the categories laid down in Regulation 601/2012.[59] The verified reports have to include information on insignificant non-conformities and misstatements.[60] Operators subsequently address such non-material non-conformities and misstatements in improvement reports they are required to submit to the competent authority by 30 June each year.[61] The German DEHSt does not review the work of the verifiers but instead performs additional checks. It, for instance, compares different years and different source streams.[62] So far, in Germany, two methods are used to detect non-compliance. First and most importantly automated systems of the competent authority detect suspicious data automatically, such as big differences compared to previous years. It will then investigate these signals in-depth. Second, inspectors who compare data from various sources and do cross-checks may detect irregularities. The authorities expect that the newly planned site visits will further improve detection of non-compliance.[63] Upon detection of non-compliance, the DEHSt corrects the report if necessary and the operator must pay a financial penalty that follows from the corrected data.

In the Netherlands, the Dutch NEa does not review every emission report but only a random sample. If the NEa detects inaccuracies it will substitute the report by conducting its own measurements. There have been incidences where the NEa found omissions in the verified reports, and subsequently sent a complaint to the

57 Questionnaire Polish National Centre for Emissions Balancing and Management KOBIZE, received 7 May 2014.

58 Interview Greek Emissions authority GEDE, 28 March 2014.

59 Art. 19(1).

60 See for the exact number of non-material misstatements and non-conformities UK Art. 21 Reports.

61 Greenhouse Gas Emissions Trading Scheme Regulations 2005 Regulations, 89(4)(d).

62 Interview German emissions authority DEHSt, 7 April 2014.

63 Interview German emissions authority DEHSt, 7 April 2014.

verifier and the Council for Accreditation. In Greece the competent authority also randomly checks a sample of the reports.[64]

The Hungarian reports pursuant to Article 21 of the Directive for the period of 2008–12 stated that all verified reports were checked for completeness and that most were reviewed in full detail, with the conclusion that no non-satisfactory reports were received.[65] However, although Hungary has implemented inspection and enforcement obligations in its national legislation, practice is quite different. Companies falling under the scope of the Directive are not checked ex-ante and do not receive assistance. There exists ex-post control of the monitoring protocol, but only in an electronic way. The competent authority does not perform individual checks and site visits. During the first phase, a priority system for regular checks was developed but it was never put into operational use.[66]

Site Visits

In the UK, the competent authority regularly conducts site visits as part of its enforcement strategy; 5 per cent of the operators are audited each year. Operators receive notice of these audits since their purpose is more to check than to inspect, although formally the regulator could use its power of entry to perform an unannounced inspection.[67] Regulators in England and Wales have developed a common format for reporting the results of site visits, which are entered into an electronic database. The details include a summary of the visit, any instances of non-compliance detected and the follow-up actions that have been agreed with the operator. The findings of the site visit may also be shared with other government bodies. Non-compliance is explicitly recorded to create a database of historical performance for future reference. Follow-up varies from a phone call or a visit to slightly more invasive forms such as a warning.

By comparison, until 2013, inspections in Germany were mainly an administrative process as described above. Until recently the federal emissions authorities performed physical inspections of installations, but not the DEHSt. However, the emissions authorities did not focus on GHG emissions. In retrospect, this was the biggest loophole in the German EU ETS compliance mechanism.[68]

In the Netherlands, the NEa has developed an Inspection Strategy that is published on its website. It states that all new entrants operating in the EU ETS shall be audited within three years to test their monitoring plan. The frequency of audits of other operations depends on a risk-based assessment, taking into account the location and complexity of the operation, the size of emissions, past compliance behaviour and external signals. In addition, the NEa conducts random audits. The

64 Interview GEDE, 30 April 2014.

65 Reports available on the Internet at: http://cdr.eionet.europa.eu/.

66 Interview of 17 July 2014.

67 Interview UK Environment Agency, 7 April 2014.

68 Interview DEHSt, 7 April 2014.

audits are generally announced and the NEa provides a 'what to expect' list to help operators prepare for the audit. This exemplifies the strategy of persuasion of the NEa: throughout the entire compliance cycle the NEa deliberately communicates and assists operators in their efforts to comply with the EU ETS.

The Greek legislation provides the GEDE with the power to perform site visits to installations but at the time of writing these have not yet taken place in practice.[69] The low number of staff (four) employed in the GEDE, and a lack of funding combined with 160 facilities that require inspection explains this outcome.[70] In Hungary, site visits are also rare. In 2013, for example, the Inspectorate reported only two on-site inspections of installations.[71]

In Poland, inspection is decentralized: when the emissions authority detects cases of non-compliance it lists and forwards these to the relevant Regional Inspectorate for Environmental Protection for further factual inspection.[72] Inspection is considered 'a useful tool that could be used in more problematic cases, such as the lack of an emission report in case of cessation, bankruptcy or closure. However, due to the high costs and capacity limitations each Regional Inspectorate decides for itself on when and how to organize an inspection'.[73]

Mandatory Sanctions

As mentioned above, the Directive requires that all member states impose fixed penalties in case the operator fails to surrender the required allowances by 30 April. All member states have implemented these mandatory sanctions in their national legislation. The UK, however, changed its regulations in 2013. If an operator that initially failed to surrender the allowances timely and correctly did notify the regulator of their mistake and surrender the correct allowances before the regulator noted their non-compliance, a penalty of only €20 per ton CO_2 applies instead of €100 per ton.[74] Imposing the penalty in cases of self-rectification was seen as disproportionate and this amendment allows operators to self-rectify under-reporting of emissions in previous years. The UK government argues that this amendment is compliant with the aim of the Directive 2003/87/EC to ensure the monitoring, report and accountability of all relevant emissions of greenhouse gases. The lower penalty only applies to *under-reporting* and not to *under-surrendering*. However, critics have suggested that operators can thus deliberately leave reportable emissions out of their reporting obligation and benefit from a lower penalty (Department of Energy and Climate Change 2013). Given the *Billerud* case discussed above, it is unlikely that the mandatory penalty of Article 16(3) is a discretionary penalty. The UK government was well aware of the legal

69 Interview GEDE, 30 April 2014.
70 Interview GEDE, 30 April 2014.
71 Interview, 17 July 2014.
72 Art. 66 (1) ETS Act. See also Art. 63 (1), (2) and (3) ETS Act.
73 Questionnaire KOBIZE, received 7 May 2014.
74 Greenhouse Gas Emissions Trading Scheme Regulations 2005, 54.

risk it took by including this new provision and stated that 'the legal position may in the longer term have to be clarified by the UK courts' (Department of Energy and Climate Change 2012, p. 23).

Overall, the excess emissions penalty has not been imposed very often in the different member states. In the Netherlands, for example, this happened only three times between 2006 and 2014; with two penalties imposed in 2013. In the UK, 21 excess emission penalties were imposed in the years 2008–11.

The naming and shaming sanction does not seem very effective either. Most member states make the information publicly available in the national official journal. Not all member states publish the data on their own website. According to the German authority, DEHSt, NGOs do not follow up on this information (so far). NGOs do identify the dirtiest power companies from the reports, but are more concerned with the level of emissions than with compliance issues.[75] As a consequence, it can be doubted whether the public will have learned of such publicly available information.

Other Sanctions

Most member states have in place a system of both administrative and criminal sanctions for non-compliant behaviour. An exception is the UK where for the third trading phase (that commenced in 2013), its policy on penalties has substantially changed by moving to a strategy based entirely on administrative penalties.

The discretion given to the member states is such that they can: (a) refrain from imposing a penalty; (b) choose the nature or maximum of a penalty; (c) extend the time for payment of a financial penalty; (d) withdraw a penalty; or (e) substitute a lower penalty. When comparing the different enforcement and sanction policies the member states apply, a range of approaches appear. For example, to the Dutch competent authority (NEa) compliance assistance rather than imposing sanctions is key to the enforcement strategy. If the NEa detects non-compliance it will first issue a warning and try to persuade the operator into compliant behaviour. A directive drawn up by the NEa issuing guidelines on which penalty should be applied in which case distinguishes between 'essential obligations', 'important obligations' and 'other obligations'. To each type of obligation, a different penalty applies (Staatscourant 2011). In practice the NEa will only impose penalties when a non-complying operator is very persistent in its behaviour. Similarly, in Greece the competent authority, GEDE, invites the non-complying operator for an interview before handing the dossier to its superiors in the Ministry of Environment, Energy and Climate Change (YPEKA) for possible enforcement measures. According to the Polish emissions authority, financial fines work mainly as a deterrent. The Polish authority sends reminders before each important deadline.[76]

75 Interview DEHSt, 7 April 2014.
76 Questionnaire KOBIZE, received 7 May 2014.

While some member states have detailed what penalties can be imposed under what conditions, others have no such guidelines (Greece, Hungary). The UK competent authority DECC, for example, determines the value of the EU ETS carbon price used by the regulator to calculate administrative penalties. In February 2013, the Secretary of State issued a Ministerial Direction to instruct regulators on how the penalty for operating without a permit should be calculated.[77] The Direction provides a transparent methodology for estimating the economic benefits derived from operating without a permit. Regulators are also required to set the penalty 5 per cent above this estimate to ensure it exceeds the benefits and produces the desired deterrent effect.

Throughout the EU, member states achieve a compliance rate of 97 per cent, with some even achieving a near-perfect record (Dechezleprêtre 2013). These figures seem to illustrate the effectiveness of the enforcement strategy. In 2005, the first year of emissions trading, the DEHSt imposed administrative sanctions on operators in 180 cases. That numbers fell to 58 in 2006 and to 32 in 2007. In 2008, the DEHSt only had to take action in 21 cases. According to the DEHSt, the rapid fall in the number of sanctions imposed shows that emissions trading procedures have become part of normal business routine. It is clear that there is a continuous decline of non-compliance. Nowadays in Germany, 1,900 installations annually produce an estimated 30 cases of non-compliance.[78]

The first obvious reason for the high compliance rate is the falling price of emissions; there is simply not an incentive for deviant behaviour. In fact, we can attribute most cases of non-compliance to unfamiliarity with the legislation and the fact that the EU ETS is not part of the core business of the operator. The majority of offences concerns the operation of a CO_2 installation without holding the required permit, exceeding the deadline for submitting the emission report or not monitoring in accordance with the monitoring plan.[79] It is also believed that the verification process pays off: many mistakes are discovered during that process and subsequently rectified.[80] An important question is undoubtedly whether this high compliance rate holds when the price for carbon allowances increases substantially above the current price of €3–4.

Criminal investigation usually follows upon suspicions of fraud. For example, when the VAT fraud hit Germany hard (in 2011, German prosecutors announced that the German state lost €850 million in this scheme), a German court in 2011 sentenced six people to prison terms of between three years and seven years and 10 months in a trial in a case of tax evasion related to carbon permits.[81]

77 See www.gov.uk/government/uploads/system/uploads/attachment_data/file/80705/penalties_n.pdf.

78 Interview DEHSt, 7 April 2014.

79 Interview NEa, 14 April 2014.

80 Interview DEHSt, 7 April 2014.

81 Many VAT fraud related court cases are still ongoing.

Conclusions

Data suggest that compliance with the EU ETS has been extremely high. This positive result cannot automatically lead to the conclusion that the enforcement of the EU ETS is effective. Since the prices of ETS allowances are very low, the majority of allowances are surrendered and not traded. Hence, the EU ETS has not been tested to the full yet, and it remains to be seen whether compliance will be as high in a market under stress (with high prices of carbon credits due to limited availability of allowances). Our study shows that, contrary to general belief, monitoring and enforcement efforts of an emissions trading market mechanism must be much more intensive compared to regular command and control type instruments due to the inherently complex character of an EU ETS and its constant fluctuations of emissions and allowances.

We have researched whether in the third phase the compliance mechanism of the EU ETS has sufficiently improved in terms of effectiveness, and what prospects – from a compliance perspective – exist for stepping up the EU's emission reduction efforts while relying on the EU ETS as the main instrument, to achieve the 2030 targets. In this section, we present our main findings.

Our first conclusion is that the dozens of additional rules and regulations of various legal form that were adopted after the first phase to secure a reliable compliance mechanism for the EU ETS have greatly improved the quality of the regulatory framework for compliance through providing for tightened rules at EU level and, generally, centralization of the EU ETS. Such measures as adopting harmonized rules for verifiers, and adopting rules to combat VAT fraud, money-laundering and other criminal activities have improved the resilience of the EU ETS. Similar improvements stem from linking the EU ETS to the EU's financial regulatory instruments (Market Abuse Directive and Anti-Money Laundering Directive), tightened rules on transactions, the range of available sanctions, centralizing auctioning and registration processes, etc.

However, it is important to stress that centralization and harmonization does not encompass the entire compliance cycle: the national competent authorities remain responsible for inspection and sanctioning, and are in charge of reviewing compliance of operators with the MRV process. Therefore, achieving full compliance with the EU ETS still largely depends on the efforts of national competent authorities of the participating countries.

Here, our conclusions are less positive. We have found that compliance strategies and their implementation still differ substantially between the member states. In some member states, all competences regarding the functioning of the ETS (issuing of permits, inspection and sanctioning) are bundled in one agency. In others, different authorities hold different competences. In addition, there are notable variations in capacity and staff employed at the competent authorities. Although verifiers detect most of the anomalies and take the necessary follow-up actions, we found that some member states largely depend on the verification process without developing their own inspection policy. More in general, we found tremendous differences between the member states in the style of inspection and enforcement. A remarkable finding, for example, is that site visits are not yet part of the standard enforcement strategy in most of the member states we studied. Only the UK and the Netherlands have a well-developed blueprint for conducting regular site visits based on risk assessments. There is a considerable risk that non-compliant behaviour will remain undetected when inspectors rely on data provided by the automated system ('paper reality') (for a similar conclusion with respect to the United States, see Stretesky 2006).

Many differences were discovered with regard to compliance assistance. Since most detected infringements were caused by 'genuine mistakes' and lack of knowledge usually related to the complexity of the rules, we think it is important that competent authorities offer assistance throughout the whole compliance cycle. Currently, the member states differ profoundly in this respect: some have an active helpdesk, regular mailings and meetings. Other countries hardly provide operators with any assistance at all. The use of ICT as a compliance assistance tool is very useful here, but again, variation between the member states is substantial. The UK online ETSWAP system for example could serve as a basis for a more harmonized compliance in this respect.

Although there exists a harmonized automatic sanction of €100 per ton CO_2 equivalent emitted by an installation for which the operator did not surrender allowances, there are major differences in other administrative and criminal sanctions that can be imposed in case of evasion of rules, fraud, etc. These additional penalties in some member states include huge fines (in the range of millions of euros) and substantial prison terms (up to 10 years), whereas in others rather low fines apply (as low as €1,500) without the possibility to press criminal charges. Further empirical analysis of the applications of such sanctions is warranted. The sanction of 'naming and shaming' is not actively applied in all member states researched. The names of the installations that did not surrender sufficient allowances are available in reports on the websites of the emissions authorities, but are far from easy to find. Consequently, the intended effect of reputation loss is yet hardly achieved. More in general, we found that the information provided by the member states in the reports pursuant to Article 21 of the Directive do not provide a complete picture of actual compliance with and enforcement of the EU ETS. The new format for reporting introduced in 2013 has solved this problem to some extent, but the distributed data are still insufficient to allow the European Commission to fulfil its role as the 'watchdog' of the EU ETS.

These findings lead to the conclusion that the final, essential element of the compliance cycle, i.e. administrative and criminal enforcement by the domestic authorities in the member states, is not overall effective. It is of the utmost importance that the EU's central instrument to achieve future climate change targets is resilient and reliable. Hence, we feel that much more attention should be focused on the role of domestic enforcement, even though most member states are reluctant to have the EU encroach upon domestic enforcement. Some not too far-reaching suggestions for improvement are a further harmonization of the additional penalties and/or bringing the EU ETS Directive under Directive 2008/99/EC on the protection of the environment through criminal law. Overall, more efforts should be undertaken to harmonize the *practice* of the national competent authorities responsible for the enforcement of the EU ETS, for instance by transforming the now voluntary EU ETS Compliance Forum into a compulsory platform in which best practices are exchanged. Other light forms of harmonization could be applied as well, for instance through issuing guidelines for inspection and enforcement.

Although Procrustes perhaps was not the nicest person, an EU-wide ETS only functions in a fully harmonized market, which definitely also includes the enforcement phase. Some stretching and cutting off legs cannot be avoided in the process . . .

References

Dechezleprêtre, A. 2013. *Report on the Empirical Assessment of Monitoring and Enforcement of EU ETS Regulation*. London: LSE. Available at: http://entracte-project.eu/research/report-monitoring-and-enforcement-eu-ets-regulation/ (accessed 11 April 2015).

Department of Energy and Climate Change. 2012. *Consultation Summary of Responses: Transposition of EU Directive 2009/29/EC revising EU Directive 2003/87/EC (2012)*. URN 12D/351. London: Crown.

——— 2013. *Amendments to UK Greenhouse Gas Emissions Trading Scheme and National Emissions Inventory Regulations: A Public Consultation*. URN 13D/198. London: Crown.

The Economist. 2010. 'The Wrong Sort of Recycling', 25 March.

Ellerman, D. 2009. *The EU's Emissions Trading Scheme: A Prototype Global System?* Cambridge, MA: Joint Program on the Science and Policy of Global Change, Report No. 70.

European Commission 2000. *Green Paper on Greenhouse Gas Emissions Trading*. Brussels, 8 March, COM/2000/87.

——— 2008. *EU Action Against Climate Change: Leading Global Action to 2020 and Beyond*. Brussels.

——— 2010. *Analysis of Options to Move Beyond 20% of Greenhouse Gas Emission Reductions and Assessing the Risk of Carbon Leakage*. Brussels, 26 May, COM(2010)265 final.

——— 2012. 'EU ETS Compliance Forum 7–8 February 2012', conference webpage. Available at: http://ec.europa.eu/clima/events/articles/0050_en.htm (accessed 11 April 2015).

——— 2014. 'European Commission Starts Written Consultation on Revision of the EU Emission Trading System (EU ETS) Directive for Post-2020', press release, 21 December. Available at: http://ec.europa.eu/clima/news/articles/news_2014121901_en.htm (accessed 11 April 2015).

European Council. 2014. *European Council (23 and 24 October 2014) – Conclusions*. Brussels, 24 October, EUCO 169/14, CO EUR 13/CONCL 5.

European Environment Agency (EEA). 2008. *Application of the Emissions Trading Directive by EU Member States – Reporting Year 2008*. Copenhagen, EEA.

Gunningham, N. and Grabosky, P. 1998. *Smart Regulation: Designing Environmental Policy*. Oxford: Oxford University Press.

Gutmann, K., Huscher, J., Urbaniak, D. White, A., Schaible, C. and Bricke, M. 2014. *Europe's Dirty 30: How the EU's Coal-Fired Power Plants are Undermining its Climate*

Efforts. Brussels: CAN Europe, WWF European Policy Office, HEAL, the EEB and Climate Alliance Germany.

HETQ. 2014. 'United Kingdom: Four Men Jailed for Carbon Credit Cyber-Heist', 25 September. Available at: http://hetq.am/eng/news/56580/united-kingdom-four-men-jailed-for-carbon-credit-cyber-heist.html (accessed 11 April 2015).

IMPEL. 2007. *Options and Proposals for Consistency in the Implementation of the EU Emissions Trading Scheme. Report 4: Good Practice in Compliance and Enforcement*. Available at: http://impel.eu/wp-content/uploads/2012/09/IMPEL-Report-4-Compliance-and-Enforcement-Report-FINAL.pdf (accessed 11 April 2015).

Interpol. 2013a. 'Guidance to Carbon Trading Crime', media release. Available at: www.interpol.int/en/News-and-media/News/2013/PR090/ (accessed 11 April 2015).

——— 2013b. *Guide to Carbon Trading Crime*. Lyon: Interpol.

Mason, R. 2011. 'The Great Carbon Trading Scandal', *Telegraph*, 30 January.

Nederlandse Emissieautoriteit (NEa). 2010. *Onderzoeksrapport: Frauderisico's bij handel in emissierechten*. The Hague.

Official Journal of the European Union (Official Journal). 2003a. *Directive 2003/87/EC of the European Parliament and of the Council of 13 October 2003 establishing a scheme for greenhouse gas emission allowance trading within the Community and amending Council Directive 96/61/EC*. Brussels, October 2003, OJ L 275/32.

——— 2003b. *Directive 2003/6/EC of 28 January 2003 of the European Parliament and of the Council on insider dealing and market manipulation (market abuse)*. Brussels, April 2003, OJ L 96/16.

——— 2006. *Commission Decision of 23 November 2006 amending Decision 2005/381/EC establishing a questionnaire for reporting on the application of Directive 2003/87/EC of the European Parliament and of the Council establishing a scheme for greenhouse gas emission allowance trading within the Community and amending Council Directive 96/61/EC*. Brussels, November 2006, OJ L 329/38.

——— 2008. *Commission Regulation (EC) No 994/2008 of 8 October 2008 for a standardised and secured system of registries pursuant to Directive 2003/87/EC of the European Parliament and of the Council and Decision No 280/2004/EC of the European Parliament and of the Council*. Brussels, October 2008, OJ L 271/3.

——— 2009. *Directive 2009/29/EC of the European Parliament and of the Council of 23 April 2009 amending Directive 2003/87/EC so as to improve and extend the greenhouse gas emission allowance trading scheme of the Community*. Brussels, June 2009, OJ L 140/63.

——— 2012. *Commission Regulation 601/2012/EU of 21 June 2012 on the monitoring and reporting of greenhouse gas emissions pursuant to Directive 2003/87/EC of the European Parliament and of the Council*. Brussels, July 2012, OJ L 181/30.

Peeters, M. 2006. 'Inspection and Market-Based Regulation through Emission Trading: The Striking Reliance on Self-Monitoring, Self-Reporting and Verification', *Utrecht Law Review* 2(1), 177–95.

Staatscourant. 2011. 'Besluit van 8 september 2011, nr. IenM/BSK-2011/114418, houdende wijziging van de Beleidsregels voor het bestuur van de Nederlandse emissieautoriteit inzake het bepalen van de hoogte van een last onder dwangsom of een bestuurlijke boete bij de handhaving van de regels voor de handel in emissierechten', 14 September. Available at: https://zoek.officielebekendmakingen.nl/stcrt-2011-16636.html (accessed 11 April 2015).

Stretesky, P.B. 2006. 'Corporate Self-Policing and the Environment', *Criminology* 44(3), 671–708.

Verschuuren, J. and Fleurke, F. 2014. *Report on the Legal Implementation of the EU ETS at Member State Level*. Tilburg: Tilburg Sustainability Center. Available at: http://entracte-project.eu/research/report-legal-studies/ (accessed 11 April 2015).

Weishaar, S.E. 2014. *Emissions Trading Design: A Critical Overview*. Cheltenham: Edward Elgar.

Part IV

(Transnational) Environmental Crime and Criminological Research

13 Criminal Networks and Black Markets in Transnational Environmental Crime

Lorraine Elliott

Introduction

Environmental crime has become 'serious, transnational and organized' (Banks et al. 2008, p. 2). Crimes associated with illegal extraction, harvest and waste are serious because of their environmental consequences, because of the ways that they undermine the rule of law and good governance at local, national and global levels, and because of their links with violence, corruption and a range of cross-over crimes such as money laundering. They have become increasingly transnational as those involved take advantage of a globalizing economy characterized by freer trade, increases in the frequency and volume of commodity shipments, fewer border controls, and the opportunity to launder profits into legitimate enterprise through financial and banking systems that have a global reach. And this area of criminal activity is sufficiently systematic and organized that it now merits consideration alongside other forms of transnational organized crime. These particular forms of organized illegal trade fit the definition of what makes crime transnational set out in the UN Convention Against Transnational Organized Crime. That is, they are either committed in more than one state or are committed in one state but with a substantial part of the preparation, planning, direction or control taking place in another state (United Nations 2000, Article 3). In effect, the products, the perpetrators and often the profits move across borders with the knowing intention of obtaining illegal gain.

Indeed, transnational environmental crime, defined here to include wildlife smuggling, timber trafficking and the black market in ozone depleting substances (ODS), is reputed to be one of the fastest growing areas of criminal activity, globally worth billions of dollars in profit to criminal groups around the world. In the early 2000s, the monetary value of transnational environmental crime was estimated to be between US$31 billion a year and US$40 billion a year or more (see Lauterback 2005; Lovell 2002). By 2014, the United Nations Environment Programme and Interpol were reporting estimates for what they called 'transnational organized environmental crime' of US$70 billion to US$213 billion a year (Nellemann et al. 2014, p. 7). Estimates are also available for individual sectors. The annual value of the illegal timber trade, for example, has been estimated at a 'minimum of $US11 billion' (Nellemann and Interpol Environmental

Crime Programme 2012, p. 13). Illegal wildlife trade is calculated to be worth US$50 billion to US$150 billion a year (UNEP 2014, p. 25).

The seriousness of key transnational environmental crime sectors has been acknowledged at the global level. In March 2012, Interpol convened the first ever meeting of International Chiefs of Environmental Compliance and Enforcement. Delegates expressed their worries about 'the scale of environmental crime and the connection with organized transnational crime, including . . . issues of smuggling, corruption, fraud, tax evasion, money laundering, and murder' (Interpol 2012, p. 2). Two years later, governments attending the 2014 London Conference on the Illegal Wildlife Trade drew attention to the 'significant scale and detrimental economic, social and environmental consequences of the illegal trade in wildlife', highlighting the 'organised and widespread criminal activity, involving transnational networks' that facilitate these kinds of illegal markets (London Conference on the Illegal Wildlife Trade 2014, paras 1–2). The purpose of this chapter, then, is to gain a better understanding of ways in which those markets in illegally produced, harvested or extracted environmental commodities operate illicitly and covertly across borders. This chapter analyses criminal networks involved in the trafficking of protected wildlife, illegally logged wood and the black market in ODS. In order to understand this business of organized crime, this chapter draws on criminological social network analysis, and approaches to networks developed in the fields of public policy and management and transaction cost economics. In doing so, it builds a cross-disciplinary model of criminal networks that is relational (social), organizational (governance) and transactional (production). From this model follow four aspects at the core of this analytical framework: nodes; specialization and differentiation; relationships of supply and exchange; and the efficiency of mechanisms of social control.

The Market for Protected Wildlife, Timber and ODS: Demand and Supply

The illegal trade that constitutes much of transnational environmental crime relies on a political economy of 'lootable commodities' – those that are 'high in value but have low economic barriers to extraction' (Farah 2010, p. 2) – and on 'uncritical markets [that] ensure that there are buyers for goods at the right price, regardless of how they are obtained, processed or transported' (Nellemann et al. 2010, p. 34). These markets are driven by both price and cost differentials: when expected returns (price) are higher than for analogue legal trade, when 'demand exceeds the supply of legal products' (in the case of timber, for example) (OECD 2011, p. 7), and when compliance with regulations (cost) can be avoided through illegal practices as is the case in the black markets in ODS and hazardous waste.

Each of these illegal market sectors reflects patterns of demand and supply. In the illegal wildlife trade supply follows demand. Private collectors and zoos in developed and developing countries want rare and unusual species. Consumer preferences create niche markets for components of protected plants and animals that are used in traditional Asian and African medicines, for exotic foods such as bushmeat and reef fish, and for fashion items that use ivory, tortoise shell or shatoosh (the wool of the endangered Tibetan antelope, the chiru, which has to be killed for the wool to be collected). The Asia-Pacific region is thought to account for up to three-quarters of the illegal wildlife trade either as source or destination. But South America has also become a wildlife crime 'hot spot' with up to 15 per cent of the illegal trade now estimated to be sourced in Brazil alone (Giovanini 2006, p. 27). Developed countries are not immune. Countries such as Australia and New Zealand, for example, are prime targets for poachers and smugglers seeking wild birds, reptiles and native insects for sale to collectors in the international marketplace (see UNODC 2013, ch. 7). Wild birds of prey are smuggled from the United Kingdom to the falconry market in the Middle East (Smith 2010). Poachers have targeted North American bears for the Asian medicine trade (Interpol 2014). The trade in illegally logged timber, which one observer describes as being of 'industrial scale' (Lawson 2004a, p. 1), is driven by a global demand for cheap timber and by specific market demand for high-value species such as rosewood and mahogany. It is also a consequence of private sector efforts to generate quick profits through evading government fees and taxes and avoiding the costs of compliance with environmental regulations.

The black market in ODS is, somewhat ironically, a direct but unintended demand-driven consequence of international efforts to protect the ozone layer through restricting and then prohibiting the production and consumption of such chemicals. Demands for cheap ODS (rather than substitutes that required expensive retrofitting) went 'underground', first in developed countries and then in developing countries as the provisions of the 1987 Montreal Protocol and its amendments made production and consumption effectively illegal. The illegal trade in hazardous waste, on the other hand, is explicitly supply-driven as those who produce waste seek to avoid high disposal costs and those who export it for illegal disposal seek quick profit. While much of it ends up in developing countries, Interpol's Pollution Crimes Working Group has identified a profitable trade between developed countries. Organized 'waste laundering' between the United States and Canada, for example, is estimated by Interpol to generate criminal profits of CAN$2.48 million a year (2006, p. 2).[1]

Understanding TEC Networks from a Criminological, Commodity Chain and Governance Perspective

In simple terms, networks are 'actors . . . linked to each other through stable formal or informal relationships of communication and exchange' (Sangiovanni 2005, p. 7). They are usually distinguished from markets on the one hand and hierarchies (states or firms) on the other, a distinction that draws its impetus from Coase's work on theories of the firm. In pure markets, 'prices capture all the

1 Interpol describes this as a 'an organised process to export and "launder" hazardous wastes through companies in the USA and return the waste to Canada' (2006, p. 2).

relevant information necessary for exchange' (Powell 1990, p. 297). In contrast, ideal-type hierarchies involve tight coupling between nodes, and centralized governance structures that, in turn, demand varying degrees of formal decision-making. Nevertheless, hierarchies themselves do not come with a one-size-fits-all format and this applies equally to transnational crime. In a report for the UN Office of Drugs and Crime (UNODC 2002), for example, the Centre for International Crime Prevention described a typology of hierarchies ranging across standard, regional and clustered forms. In contrast to hierarchies, networks are loosely organized, decentralized and more fluid (in theory at least) in the way that information is managed and decisions made. In contrast to pure markets, they are iterative in a way that establishes more enduring patterns of interaction, and rely on signals other than those offered just by price to determine patterns of exchange. Williams suggests that networks (and we might assume that this applies equally to illegal networks) function as a complement to pure markets, 'making them more efficient, reducing transaction costs and providing increased opportunities for both buyers and sellers' (2001, p. 65). In this context, he also distinguishes between directed networks where a 'core of organizers . . . want to use [a network] for a specific purpose' and transaction networks which emerge 'spontaneously . . . to add efficiency to the functioning of a market' (Williams 2001, p. 69).

Much of the toolkit available for analysing networks, including criminal ones in this case, and the way they function draws on three bodies of literature – the criminology literature and in particular its focus on social network analysis; the literature on transaction cost economics which offers insights into production and value chains; and the public management literature that explores governance mechanisms within markets and networks. Of these three only the first – criminology – is explicitly concerned with the illicit economy and those engaged in it. Despite their different methodologies and intent, they have in common the claim that networks are at the very least organizationally different, and perhaps even ontologically distinct from the orthodox units of analysis that have characterized each particular field of inquiry: hierarchical crime groups, markets and states, and forms of production centralized in the firm. Networks are 'typically treated as varying along three related dimensions: the number of nodes; the . . . frequency of interaction between nodes; and the structure of the network, defined as the pattern of connection between nodes' (Lake and Wong 2009, p. 129). Drawing on these three bodies of literature, this basic analytical framework is adjusted to provide a more multi-faceted and, potentially, more operationally useful approach to investigating the nature of transnational environmental crime networks and the management of illegal trade.

Social Network Analysis of Crime

Contemporary criminology challenges long-held views that domestic and transnational crime is managed by hierarchically structured and tightly-controlled mafia or cartel arrangements in which family or ethnic ties are dominant. Research on sectors including the drug trade, human trafficking and the arms trade confirms that organized crime 'increasingly operat[es] through fluid network structures' (Williams 2001, p. 64). This shift in research focus – from hierarchy to networks – has been accompanied by new methodologies and analytical frameworks that have sought to understand crime networks as *social* artefacts rather than just a new form of institutional arrangement. Social network analysis (SNA) proceeds from the assumption that 'criminals are embedded in a network of relationships' (Ballester et al. 2004, p. 1). It seeks to document relationships between offenders in order to identify and understand the density and social complexity of those links and to determine the characteristics of the roles that individuals play within criminal networks.

SNA also has a distinctly applied purpose. More effective, realistic and evidence-based modes of understanding criminal activity is argued, indeed assumed, to provide a crucial basis for better law enforcement outcomes. This form of SNA therefore relies on sufficient information about the relationships between particular known individuals (Bright et al. 2012, p. 157) to map the nominal and relational aspects of crime networks. Those datasets are usually gathered through in-depth research that can include analysis of open sources such as court proceedings, judicial statements and interviews with (former) offenders. When deployed by enforcement agencies, it will also include intelligence from covert sources. That level of detail is network- and case-specific. It can tell us something about known, individual TEC networks, but is less useful for capturing patterns of transnational illicit behaviour across space and time.[2] At the more abstract level, however, SNA does offer some useful conceptual scaffolding for research into the institutional forms and likely internal dynamics of networks associated with transnational environmental crime and its associated markets. In particular, it provides a language for describing individuals or actors (nodes) in illicit networks in functional and positional terms and for analysing the dynamics of connection and coordination within those networks. That language includes concepts of brokerage, centrality and density, redundancy and structural holes which are examined more closely later in this chapter.

Commodity Chain/Value Chain Analysis

In contrast to the focus on social networks associated with contemporary criminology, commodity chain or value chain analysis, which draws in turn on transaction cost economics (TCE), brings a production-based approach to our understanding of illicit networks.[3] Commodity chain analysis is primarily concerned with

2 See, for example, a specific illegal network for the trade in big cats described by the EIA (2014, pp. 9–12).

3 Sturgeon explains that the term 'value' was introduced to what had previously been described as commodity chains to overcome colloquial images of commodities as singular goods such as oil or bulk agricultural products, and also to encapsulate the idea that value is or can be added at each stage of the commodity production chain (2008, p. 8).

the 'spatial organisation of [licit] production . . . in a globalised world economy' (Potts 2006, p. 2) and the 'geographical regions within which specific processes and chain relationships occur' (Potts 2006, p. 3). As an analytical tool, it focuses on the processes by which material and labour inputs are sourced and managed, the role of technology in the way those inputs are assembled, and the nodes and networks (or chains) through which a finished commodity is produced and distributed. The core assumption that underpins global commodity chain analysis is that in production for the global market, processes in which most or all aspects of production were in the past contained and controlled *within* multinational firms have given way to vertically disintegrated structures that take network form (see Gereffi et al. 2005).

The emphasis on transaction costs ensures that the material factors of supply, production and information, as well as those of bargaining and enforcement, will play a central role in decisions about how commodity or value chains are managed spatially and functionally as well as by whom. As with chains of custody associated with illicit trade, those networks will be characterized by efforts to balance high profits against low costs. In general, we might expect that transactions costs will be higher in covert or illicit networks than in networks of production or exchange that function in the legitimate economy. Those costs are associated with the demands for complicated forms of coordination that derive from the need for concealment and minimizing the risk of exposure to law enforcement action.

Commodity chain analysis can help to shed some light on 'the nodes . . . that are operational along a supply chain' (Potts 2006, p. 3), decisions about 'outsourcing' in illicit networks, about the value or otherwise of decentralized structures, and the nature of *supply* relationships between nodes rather than focusing on them primarily in associational terms. The goods that are traded across TEC chains of custody are likely to adopt some but not all of the characteristics of the commodities usually under scrutiny in value or commodity chain analysis. While some TEC commodities are placed on the market in the same raw form in which they were extracted or harvested, others are transformed through various degrees of 'production' as they move through the illegal chain of custody. For example ivory is almost always carved in some fashion before reaching its final market destination. Illegal wildlife products can also be tanned (as skins), or stuffed, or turned into wearable products (shoes or belts from reptile skins) or treated in some form for consumptive and medicinal purposes. For some commodities, that production process attracts a high degree of asset-specificity – that is, a skill set or knowledge specific to that particular transaction or transformation or where tasks are complex or difficult. The geography of supply, on the other hand, particularly for wildlife smuggling and timber trafficking, will be constrained by factors other than cost. It is, in effect, non-negotiable except in cases where there is little asset specificity involved (for example if the species of timber is irrelevant) or where individuals of species can be sourced from multiple and easily accessible range states.

Organizational Models: Public Policy and Management

Public policy and management approaches to networks share some similarities with commodity chain analysis, in particular the interest in governance structures. But whereas the former understands intra-network governance as a function of pricing signals and supply/purchaser relationships and as a synonym for coordination, specifically of the linkages between the nodes in a chain, the latter identifies governance structures and processes in the formal and informal rule-making that arises from the policy-relevant 'actions of networks of actors' (Klijn 2005, p. 329). This shares some similarities with Kahler's (2009) conceptualization of networks as structure, by which he means to focus less on specific organizational forms (networks as actors in his typology) and more on the way that those forms influence the behaviour of the members of that network and, 'through them, produce consequential network effects' (2009, p. 4). In both licit and illicit spaces, therefore, networks function to sustain collective action and cooperation through 'sequential transactions within the context of a general pattern of interaction' (Powell 1990, p. 301).

As suggested above, criminal market networks are 'organised into a structure of relations between thieves, smugglers, facilitators, sellers and buyers of illicit commodities' (Mackenzie 2011, p. 69). The form of that organization will almost certainly differ across TEC sectors and even within them. In the licit economy, differences in network structures are 'contingent on the information processing requirements imposed by the characteristics of a product and its market' (Baker and Faulkner 1993, p. 838). In contrast, in the illicit economy those differences 'appear to be related to legal and financial risks associated with the crimes in question' and, in turn, to the 'required levels of trust between collaborating criminals' (Bruinsma and Bernasco 2004, p. 79). In TEC as in other areas of transnational criminality, the organizational form that criminal chains of custody take will also be influenced in part by the complexity of logistic trails. This includes the geographic distance across which goods are transported to link source with market, the volume or bulk of shipments, and the ease or otherwise with which goods or profits can be laundered into the legitimate economy.[4]

Raab and Milward argue that illegal networks will generally demonstrate a tendency towards decentralized structures 'unless the task necessitates a centralised one' (2003, p. 434). However the literature is divided on the relationship between task demands and decentralization. With respect to legitimate production networks or commodity chains, Baker and Faulkner have suggested that 'difficult, complex [and] ambiguous tasks are performed more effectively in decentralised structures' (1993, p. 844). In contrast, Powell points to the importance of more centralized arrangements in situations of high-asset specificity, that is, where the complexity of the task requires 'knowledge specific to the transaction' (1990, p. 297).

4 Laundering is understood here as 'all consequential handling . . . devoted to conceal the results of a predicate crime for profit' (Van Duyne 2002, p. 4).

The most common organizational forms are chain networks and hub-and-spoke networks (sometimes also called star or wheel networks).[5] Chain networks most closely approximate the ideal-type network: the structure is organizationally flat and loosely coupled rather than centralized or hierarchical (although there might well be hierarchical arrangements at any particular nodal point). As Kenney describes it, independent nodes or cells perform specific tasks and conduct arm's length transactions directly with other nodes 'without mediation and oversight with core groups' (2007, p. 244). Hub-and-spoke networks, on the other hand, involve core groups that coordinate activities among 'functionally specific nodes' such as suppliers, transporters and distributors (Kenney 2002, p. 3). While these networks display higher levels of density or interconnectedness between nodes than chain networks, they are still constructed on a need-to-know basis in which communication between nodes is managed to limit the risks of discovery. Links between core groups are likely to be more dense than those between peripheral nodes such as those involving poachers or chain saw operators who are likely to have little contact with the 'main architects behind the trade' (Aning 2007, p. 200). Capabilities are unlikely to be evenly distributed and core groups or individuals can function as 'multi-task enterprises' (Kenney 2007, p. 242). Hub-and-spoke networks also provide more scope for, or are the consequence of, a kingpin strategy. In this organizational form, kingpins direct all aspects of an illicit chain of custody even if they also sometimes rely on trusted intermediaries as a way of buffering themselves against claims of criminal activity.

Networks for Black Markets

The varying forms of network arrangements that characterize black markets in ODS, smuggled wildlife and trafficked timber link together poachers, harvesters, producers, traders, brokers, purchasers and retailers to manage illicit chains of custody. Some of this illegal commercial exchange is managed through simple, amateur efforts involving a small number of people, uncomplicated routes and unsophisticated forms of concealment (disorganized crime). The criminal networks that sustain larger-scale TEC, on the other hand, are professional and well organized with complex transnational relationships of communication and exchange that span the illicit and licit economies and that link local harvest, extraction and waste production to a global marketplace. They involve multiple participants in the logistic trail, complex trade and transportation routes, and sophisticated methods of concealment.

The three approaches to networks in the previous section of this chapter provide both a language and the analytical tools to contribute a more nuanced understanding of illicit TEC networks in social, organizational and transactional terms.

5 Arquilla and Ronfeldt (2001) add to this the all-channel network where everyone is connected to everyone else. There is little evidence that this form – which in many respects is hardly a network at all – applies in any TEC sector.

Not only does it help to track the nature of nodes in logistic trails but it also shines light on specialization and role differentiation, and on supply and exchange relationships. As noted above, the concept of 'nodes' (and those who occupy them) has been central to social network analysis in particular although transaction cost economics also uses the term, particularly in discussions of global production and commodity chains as touched on above and described in more detail below. As discussed earlier in this chapter, that production and commodity chain literature explores material factors of supply and production in both licit and illicit networks. In doing so, and in focusing attention on factors such as asset specificity and the kinds of supply relationships that exist between production nodes, it points to the importance of also asking questions about the extent and nature of role and production specialization or differentiation. Finally, the overview of public policy and management approaches outlined in the previous section offers insights into the internal organizational structures of illicit networks and the way that those networks are governed or managed. In particular, the focus in that literature on the degree of centralized or decentralized organizational arrangement generates propositions about the importance of mechanisms of social control.

Nodes

The idea of a 'node' offers a conceptual and empirical starting point for understanding illicit networks. A node is the location at which some form of supply, exchange, production or transformation in a commodity (or the profits of such) takes place. It can be occupied by an individual or a group of individuals, including those that take on a more formal structure such as a company, a public or private agency or similar. Nodal roles can be described in functional terms. Within a TEC logistic trail or chain of custody individuals or groups might be poachers, harvesters, chain-saw operators, purchasers or collectors, exporters, transporters, cutters and carvers, or retailers. They might also be delinquent professionals – accountants, lawyers, financiers or shipping agents, for example – who act in various ways to launder profits, facilitate links to the upperworld, and minimize or even cause to disappear the threat of prosecution. Depending on the nature of the supply and exchange relationships, nodes (whether individuals or small groups or cells) can function with varying degrees of autonomy, possibly even offering their services to more than one network or market arrangement.

Nodes in TEC networks are designed to contribute to or manage illicit trade flows. The links between those nodes, therefore, consist not just of social relations but also relationships of illegal commercial exchange. The sophistication of these networks – constituted by the links between nodes – makes it possible for bulk consignments of illegal wildlife, timber, waste and ODS to be moved across borders by ship, barge, truck and plane. To make detection more difficult, illicit environmental goods are often moved along complex routes through multiple nodes or transhipment points where surveillance and enforcement is lax. Timber from the Congo basin is being moved through companies in Burundi, Rwanda and Uganda before being exported to the European Union, the Middle East, China and other

Asian countries, with support from financiers in the United States (Nellemann et al. 2010, p. 6). Intelligence on merbau smuggling syndicates in Southeast Asia shows that they involve timber brokers in Jakarta, companies and individuals in Malaysia who oversee the actual logging, agents in Singapore who charter cargo vessels and who arrange false documentation, and brokers in Singapore and Hong Kong who connect sellers in places such as Papua with buyers in India and China (Newman and Lawson 2005, p. 9). The illegal trade in elephant tusks from Africa into Asia is reported to involve interlocking webs of shell companies, Southeast Asian and African nationals, and smuggling routes that trade from Africa across multiple borders and through several Asian ports before reaching its final destination (Banks et al. 2007). Ivory that ends up in China or Japan may have come from the Democratic Republic of Congo, Cameroon and Nigeria, through ports including Hong Kong, Macau and Taiwan. Jernelov (2005) reports complicated distribution lines in chlorofluorocarbons (CFCs) from Spain via Singapore or Dubai, through India to Nepal or Bangladesh and then back again to the market in India, often relabelled or with fraudulent documentation.

The number of nodes that can be identified in an illicit network – either directly or indirectly – reveals the size of a network. The size of a network and the geographic location of the nodes within it can tell us something about the likely complexity involved in logistic trails. But it says little about the division of labour within a network or the rationale for such a division. This requires examining nodes and the relationships between them in the transactional or production terms favoured by commodity chain analysis. This is somewhat akin to the distinction that Curtis and Wendel make between social organization and technical organization, the former referring to issues of cooperation, differential responsibilities, and power and authority relationships, the latter to include 'physical location . . . procedures, [and] technology' (2000, p. 128). As indicated earlier in this chapter, we need to understand both – the social and the technical (including transaction arrangements) – to understand the nature of illicit trade networks.

Specialization and Role Differentiation

Commodity chain analysis, and its accompanying emphasis on modes of production, can offer further insights into the form and function of illicit networks for transnational environmental crime by directing attention to the nature and degree of specialization and role differentiation within TEC networks (see Bright et al. 2012). This pays less attention to individual nodes or actors and 'focuses instead on the business of organized crime' (Mcillwain 1999, p. 303). Questions about specialization focus on whether particular skills are required in either the production or transaction process, broadly understood, or whether individuals can easily switch roles: this relates to the asset-specificity dimension introduced above. The related question about differentiation examines whether different people perform different roles or whether individuals can or do occupy multiple nodes, that is whether they perform more than one role in the chain of custody.

Specialist skills can also take the form of particular production expertise within a network as well as the ability to channel information in situations of knowledge asymmetries, or to undertake tasks such as laundering profits seamlessly into the legitimate economy. Different kinds of illicit environmental commodities, and the markets associated with them, will require different levels of specialization. Roles such as operating chain saws for illegal logging can usually be done by unskilled or semi-skilled workers, as can timber milling. Tiger poaching, on the other hand, requires expertise: skins that are damaged in the killing process are of little value on the illicit market. While smuggling ODS across borders might require few commodity-specific skills, the illegal production of ODS is asset-specific, usually drawing on expertise within the legitimate industry. The modes by which illicit environmental commodities are transported along a logistic chain (for example in bulk or in small consignments, by air, sea or road) will also create demands for different capabilities and skills.

The answers to questions about specialization and differentiation in illicit environmental networks will also reveal something about redundancy and criticality within those networks. Within TEC networks, in-built redundancy – that is, more than one person or node able to fulfil any particular task – can arise at a number of points in the chain of custody. As Kenney points out, multiple nodes also 'provide enterprise leaders with a range of options in planning their illicit activities' (2002, p. 13). Critical nodes, on the other hand, are those without which the network would cease to function easily, or the loss of which would make the network more susceptible to further disruption and decapitation. Critical nodes are more likely in markets and illicit trade networks which have a high degree of specialization and a low level of differentiation. As with licit markets, critical nodes in illicit TEC networks are likely to exist in functional terms at the point of production, harvest or capture; at the point of export or import, and the point of retail or final use. Critical nodes can also be defined in entrepreneurial or positional terms, sometimes captured in concepts such as 'middleman' [*sic*] or in terms of brokers and brokerage.

Robust redundancy, or minimal criticality, is more likely for those commodities for which few specific harvesting or production or transportation skills are required. The illegal trade in pangolin, prized for their meat and their scales for use in traditional Asian medicine, requires little specialization in terms of harvest and therefore comes with a high degree of in-built redundancy at that part of the chain of custody at least. In their range states in Southeast Asia, pangolin are mainly sourced from farmers who know that if they come across a pangolin it is worth money if they can get it to a local buyer. But the buyers do not rely on *specific* farmers as extraction nodes. As noted above, poaching tigers from the wild, whether alive for specialist collectors or zoos or dead for their skins, requires greater skill. The networks that manage wild-tiger chains of custody are therefore more likely to be vulnerable to harvest/extraction criticality though even this will depend in part on the pool of available 'labour'. The same is the case for, say, ivory carving. This is a specialist skill but evidence suggests that there is still a reasonable labour pool, particularly in parts of China and Southeast Asia. Therefore the extent of redundancy or criticality embedded in any *particular* ivory smuggling network will depend on access to carvers.

Relationships of Supply and Exchange

In their discussion of commodity chains and the technology that is used to produce specific components of a commodity, Gereffi et al. (2005) distinguish between different kinds of supply arrangements. These can be mapped, albeit with a bit of conceptual flexibility, onto those that supply chains that function within illicit networks. While Gereffi and colleagues categorize overall chains as either supplier-driven or producer-driven, the term 'supply' is used in this part of the chapter to capture the provision of goods and services within illicit TEC networks. That is, while those networks are primarily driven by demand for illicit environmental goods (with the exception of hazardous waste) the internal technical organization nevertheless involves nodes who supply products, skills or expertise to the chain of custody.

Gereffi et al. (2005) identify three main forms of supply relationship that can exist between nodes: commodity suppliers, captive suppliers and turn-key suppliers. Commodity suppliers are those who provide standard, undifferentiated products at arm's length from any specific market demand. This concept can capture processes such as timber milling where the technology and skill set is standard and can be called on equally for illicit as for licit production. It may apply to transport supply such as the use of tobacco boats (so-called because they have been used to smuggle tobacco) also being used to smuggle cylinders of illegal ODS from the Caribbean to the United States. It may also capture supply sectors such as those associated with some parts of the illegal pet trade or the illegal fur trade for which there is a parallel or analogue legal trade.[6]

Captive suppliers, in contrast, make products using processes that are 'dedicated to customers' needs' under conditions where the suppliers are 'transactionally dependent' on those for whom they produce or to whom they sell (Gereffi et al. 2005, pp. 83–4). These might be specialist manufacturers who are more likely to work in forms similar to artisan craftspeople in the legitimate economy. In the TEC context, this captive supply can take the form of skills or products for a specific illicit market, for example expert preparation of the components used in traditional Asian medicines, or illegally produced (and transported) ODS, or ivory that has to be cut to reach its highest value on the black market.

The final category – that of turn-key suppliers – produce to a customer's specifications but (recalling the focus of commodity or value chain analysis on technological inputs to production) do so with machinery or processing techniques or expertise that has the flexibility to adapt to meet the needs of different buyers.

6 For example, Bouchard and Wilkins (2009, p. 4), referring to Wyatt's work, note that the 'illegal fur trade is populated by individuals who are already involved in the legal fur trade, creating smuggling channels along already existing legitimate structures'.

In the TEC context, turn-key suppliers might include so-called 'swing plants' (Liu 2007, p. 7) that have been able to adjust from producing CFCs to producing HCFCs (hydrochlorofluorocarbons). Such suppliers might include 'processing plants' such as those reported by IFAW that have been set up to butcher and package pangolin meat. It can also include tanning and taxidermy skills that can be applied to different contexts (such as reptile skins being imported illegally into the United States or tiger skins being exported from South Asia). Such production suppliers are not always co-located with the source of the illegal commodity. EIA, for example, reports buyers of tiger skins in Inner Mongolia who divert skins to professional tanners in Hebei Province.

Efficiency and Mechanisms of Social Control

Understanding the relationship between production nodes and the way they function in commodity chains, in an enterprise structure, is a necessary but not necessarily sufficient condition for analysing TEC networks and associated trade. In criminal networks, the efficiency dividend that might come from 'outsourcing' and open lines of communication associated with commodity chains in the licit economy conflicts with the need for security. As well as the kind of efficient communication, supply and transfer that sustains transnational market exchange in the licit economy, TEC networks are likely to place a high value on physical and descriptive concealment of various kinds – of the commodities that are being traded, of the shipments, and of the profits and the criminal actors. This demands that personal contact across a network is limited or controlled, especially if participants in illicit markets are likely to cooperate in 'complex and unpredictable ways' (Williams and Godson 2002, p. 323). The networks that sustain illicit transnational environmental markets also require effective mechanisms of social control. Doing business in the illicit economy therefore influences the ways in which intermediaries in the network establish and maintain contacts, the ways in which bonds of trust are sustained in the absence of formal hierarchy and, as Edwards and Gill point out, the ways in which 'criminal expertise is transferred' (2003, p. 62). The more effective these webs of affiliation and mechanisms of social control are, the less likely is the risk of exposure and the more resilient a network will be in protecting logistic trails and sustaining illicit markets. In that sense, trust functions in criminal networks in much the same way as in transnational inter-firm networks – to 'dampen opportunistic behaviour' and to make possible 'more complex . . . divisions of labour' (Gereffi et al. 2005, p. 81).

Local communities who provide labour for illegal logging, timber processing or wildlife poaching are often integrated into criminal networks through patron–client relationships. These are likely to involve semi-feudal connections to local timber barons or local officials who control aspects of criminal activity, or through social coercion that takes advantage of economic vulnerability in situations where alternative livelihoods are not available. Local communities are sometimes also 'bought off' to minimize protests in areas where resource extraction is known to be illegal (see, for example, the case studies of Cameroon in Van Oijen and

Angerand 2007). Those engaged in illicit TEC market activity have also moved to take advantage of the 'upperworld' of corrupt officials and politicians, enabling them to evade control mechanisms and protect illegal chains of custody. Indeed, some commentators suggest that corruption should best be understood not as a pathology of the state, but rather as an instrument of risk management – a strategy for doing business – for criminal groups (Williams 2002, pp. 174–5). Local officials, customs officers, police and the judiciary are bribed to overlook illegal shipments, to assist with false paper trails and forged documentation, to help evidence disappear during prosecutions, to delay or drop prosecutions, and even to return no convictions when cases are brought to trial. Syndicates running timber smuggling enterprises in Indonesia, for example, are reported to have 'bought off local Indonesian customs officials and harbour masters' and used their influence to 'have any attempted shipments by competitors stopped' (Lawson 2004b, p. 13). Companies in Ukraine have 'negotiated' with customs officers to facilitate the importation of 'uncontrolled' ODS (Demkine 2001, p. 10) and companies involved in timber theft in Papua are reported to be 'aided every step of the way by officials from the military, police and forestry departments, as long as the requisite bribe is paid' (Newman and Lawson 2005, p. 7).

Conclusion

The focus of this chapter was on exploring ways in which illicit trade in environmental commodities can be analysed and understood. In effect, the focus here has been on (illegal) trade as the business of criminal activities that are organized across borders. Using examples from the illegal wildlife trade, timber trafficking and the black market in ODS, this chapter has drawn on the toolkits provided by social network analysis, commodity chain analysis (as a feature of transaction cost economics) and public policy approaches to intra-network governance. The interest has been in networks less as a function of social or associational relationships and more as a structure of supply chains and transactional or exchange relationships. It has argued that we need to take account of spatial organization of the kinds of production that are involved as illicit commodities 'travel' from source to market destination, and to explore the nature of nodal specialization, differentiation and asset-specificity. The framework sketched in this chapter can also help to correct for the focus in much literature on end-points rather than pipelines, on poachers, smugglers, timber-barons, 'kingpins' and the 'eco-mafia' rather than those who collect and warehouse illicit goods in border towns, or carve ivory, or tan tiger skins, or construct false walls in trucks, or carry contraband commodities in ones and twos across borders. The latter may be equally crucial to logistic trails and the black trade – getting a saleable commodity to market – as the former.

References

Aning, K. 2007. 'Are There Emerging West African Criminal Networks? The Case of Ghana', *Global Crime* 8(3), 193–212.

Arquilla, J. and Ronfeldt, D. 2001. 'The Advent of Netwar (Revisited)', in *Networks and Netwars: The Future of Terror, Crime and Militancy*, edited by J. Arquilla and D. Ronfeldt. Santa Monica: RAND, 1–25.

Baker, W.E. and Faulkner, R.R. 1993. 'The Social Organization of Conspiracy: Illegal Networks in the Heavy Electrical Equipment Industry', *American Sociological Review* 58(6), 837–60.

Ballester, C., Calvó-Armengol, A. and Zenou, Y. 2004. *Who's Who in Crime Network: Wanted the Key Player*. Working Paper no. 617. Stockholm: The Research Institute of Industrial Economics.

Banks, D., Gosling, J., Newman, J., Noble, R. and Rice, M. 2007. *Upholding the Law: The Challenge of Effective Enforcement*. London: Environmental Investigation Agency.

Banks, D., Davies, C., Gosling, J., Newman, J. Rice, M., Wadley, J. and Walravens, F. 2008. *Environmental Crime: A Threat to Our Future*. London: Environmental Investigation Agency.

Bouchard, M. and Wilkins, C. 2009. 'Introduction', *Global Crime* 10(1), 1–5.

Bright, D.A., Hughes, C.E. and Chalmers, J. 2012. 'Illuminating Dark Networks: A Social Network Analysis of an African Drug Trafficking Syndicate', *Crime, Law and Social Change* 57(2), 151–75.

Bruinsma, G. and Bernasco, W. 2004. 'Criminal Groups and Transnational Illegal Markets', *Crime, Law and Social Change* 41(1), 79–94.

Curtis, R. and Wendel, T. 2000. 'Toward the Development of a Typology of Illegal Drug Markets', *Crime Prevention Studies* 11, 121–52.

Demkine, V. 2001. 'Facing the Challenge in Countries with Economies in Transition', *OzonAction Newsletter* Special Supplement no. 6, 9–12.

Edwards, A. and Gill, P. 2003. 'Measurements and Interpretations', in *Transnational Organised Crime: Perspectives on Global Security*, edited by A. Edwards and P. Gill. London: Routledge, 59–64.

Environmental Investigation Agency (EIA). 2014. *In Cold Blood: Combating Organized Wildlife Crime*. London: EIA.

Farah, D. 2010. *Transnational Crime, Social Networks and Forests: Using Natural Resources to Finance Conflicts and Post-Conflict Violence*. Washington, DC: Program on Forests [PROFOR].

Gereffi, G., Humphrey, J. and Sturgeon, T. 2005. 'The Governance of Global Value Chains', *Review of International Political Economy* 12(1), 78–104.

Giovanini, D. 2006. 'Taking Animal Trafficking Out of the Shadows: RENCTAS Uses the Internet to Combat a Multi-Billion Dollar Trade', *Innovations* 1(2), 25–35.

Interpol. 2012. *International Chiefs of Environmental Compliance and Enforcement: Summit Report*. Lyon: Interpol Secretariat.

——— 2014. *Assessment on Illegal Bear Trade*. Lyon: Interpol Environmental Security Sub-Directorate.

Interpol Pollution Crimes Working Group. 2006. *Assessing the Links Between Organized Crime and Pollution Crimes*. Lyon: Interpol Secretariat.

Jernelov, A. 2005. *The Ozone Mafia*. Project Syndicate Print Commentary.

Kahler, M. 2009. 'Networked Politics: Agency, Power and Governance', in *Networked Politics: Agency, Power and Governance*, edited by M. Kahler. Ithaca: Cornell University Press, 1–20.

Kenney, M. 2002. *The Challenge of Eradicating Transnational Criminal Networks: Lessons from the War on Drugs*. Paper prepared for the 2002 Annual Meeting of the American Political Science Association, 29 August to 1 September.

——— 2007. 'The Architecture of Drug Trafficking: Network Forms of Organisation in the Columbian Cocaine Trade', *Global Crime* 8(3), 233–59.

Klijn, E.-H. 2005. 'Designing and Managing Networks: Possibilities and Limitations for Network Management', *European Political Science* 4, 328–39.

Lake, D.A. and Wong, W.H. 2009. 'The Politics of Networks: Interests, Power and Human Rights Norms', in *Networked Politics: Agency, Power and Governance*, edited by M. Kahler. Ithaca: Cornell University Press, 127–50.

Lauterback, A. 2005. *Statement by the Chair*. Interpol Environmental Crimes Committee to the 5th International Conference on Environmental Crime, Lyon, 2 and 3 June.

Lawson, S. 2004a. *The Ramin Racket: The Role of CITES in Curbing Illegal Timber Trade*. London: Environmental Investigation Agency.

——— 2004b. *Profiting from Plunder: How Malaysia Smuggles Endangered Wood*. London and Bogor: Environmental Investigation Agency/Telapak.

Liu, N. 2007. *Illegal Trade in Ozone Depleting Substances*. Bangkok: United Nations Environment Programme.

London Conference on the Illegal Wildlife Trade. 12–13 February 2014. *Declaration*, paras 1–2. Available at: www.gov.uk/government/uploads/system/uploads/attachment_data/file/281289/london-wildlife-conference-declaration-140213.pdf (accessed 25 March 2015).

Lovell, J. 2002. 'Eco-Crooks Outwitting Law Agencies', Reuters News Service, 28 May. Available at: www.planetark.org/dailynewsstory.cfm/newsid/16164/newsDate/28-May-2002/story.htm (accessed 19 September 2012).

Mcillwain, J.S. 1999. 'Organized Crime: A Social Network Approach', *Crime, Law and Social Change* 32(4), 301–23.

Mackenzie, S. 2011. 'The Market as Criminal and Criminals in the Market: Reducing Opportunities for Organised Crime in the International Antiquities Market', in *Crime in the Art and Antiquities World: Illegal Trafficking in Cultural Property*, edited by S. Manacorda and D. Chappell. New York: Springer, 69–86.

Nellemann, C. and Interpol Environmental Crime Programme. 2012. *Green Carbon, Black Trade: Illegal Logging, Tax Fraud and Laundering in the Worlds Tropical Forests. A Rapid Response Assessment*. Nairobi: United Nations Environment Programme/GRIDArendal.

Nellemann, C., Redmond, I. and Refisch, J. 2010. *The Last Stand of the Gorilla: Environmental Crime and Conflict in the Congo Basin*. Norway: UNEP GRID Arendal.

Nellemann, C., Henriksen, R., Raxter, P., Ash, N. and Mrema, E. 2014. *The Environmental Crime Crisis – Threats to Sustainable Development from Illegal Exploitation and Trade in Wildlife and Forest Resources: A UNEP Rapid Response Assessment*. Nairobi/Arendal: United Nations Environment Programme and GRID-Arendal.

Newman, J. and Lawson, S. 2005. *The Last Frontier: Illegal Logging in Papua and China's Massive Timber Theft*. London and Bogor: Telapak/Environmental Investigation Agency.

Organisation for Economic Co-operation and Development (OECD). 2011. *Illegal Trade in Environmentally Sensitive Goods: Draft Synthesis Report*, COM/TAD/ENV/JWPTE(2011)45. Paris: OECD Trade and Agriculture Directorate/Environment Directorate.

Potts, J. 2006. *Global Commodity Chain Sustainability Analysis: Explanations and Examples*. Prepared for the Planning Meeting of the Task Force on China's sustainable development and global markets. Winnipeg: IISD.

Powell, W.W. 1990. 'Neither Markets nor Hierarchy: Network Forms of Organization', *Research in Organizational Behaviour* 12, 295–336.

Raab, J. and Milward, H.B. 2003. 'Dark Networks as Problems', *Journal of Public Administration Research and Theory* 13(4), 413–39.

Sangiovanni, M.E. 2005. 'Transnational Networks and Security Threats', *Cambridge Review of International Affairs* 18(1), 7–13.

Smith, S. 2010. 'Halting Illegal Bird Trade to Gulf'. BBC News [online]. Available at: www.bbc.co.uk/news/science-environment-11086707 (accessed 13 March 2015).

Sturgeon, T.J. 2008. *From Commodity Chains to Value Chains: Interdisciplinary Theory Building in an Age of Globalization*. Working Paper Series WP-2008–02. Pittsburgh: University of Pittsburgh Industry Studies Association.

UN Office of Drugs and Crime (UNODC). 2002. *Results of a Pilot Survey of Forty Selected Organized Criminal Groups in Sixteen Countries*. Vienna: UNODC Global Program against Transnational Organized Crime.

——— 2013. *Transnational Organized Crime in East Asia and the Pacific: A Threat Assessment*. Bangkok: UNODC.

United Nations 2000. *UN Convention Against Transnational Organized Crime*. General Assembly Resolution 55/25, 15 November.

United Nations Environment Programme (UNEP). 2014. *UNEP Yearbook: Emerging Issues in Our Global Environment*. Nairobi: UNEP Division of Early Warning and Assessment.

Van Duyne, P.C. 2002. 'Introduction: Upper- and Underworld Cross-Border Crime Economy', in *Upperworld and Underworld in Cross-Border Crime*, edited by P.C. van Duyne, K. von Lampe and N. Passas. Nijmegen: Wolf Legal Publishers, 1–10.

Van Oijen, D. and Angerand, S. 2007. *Illegally Logged Wood from Cameroon on the Dutch Market*. Amsterdam and Paris: Milieudefensie/Les Amis de la Terre.

Williams, P. 2001. 'Transnational Criminal Networks', in *Networks and Netwars: The Future of Terror, Crime and Militancy*, edited by J. Arquilla and D. Ronfeldt. Santa Monica: RAND, 61–97.

——— 2002. 'Transnational Organized Crime and the State', in *The Emergence of Private Authority in Global Governance*, edited by R.B. Hall and T.J. Biersteker. Cambridge: Cambridge University Press, 161–82.

Williams, P. and Godson, R. 2002. 'Anticipating Organized and Transnational Crime', *Crime, Law and Social Change* 37(4), 311–55.

14 Eliciting Narratives on the Experiences of Environmental Victimization

A Qualitative Visual Method

Lorenzo Natali[1]

Introduction

'Ultimately, Photography is subversive not when it frightens, repels, or even stigmatizes, but when it is *pensive*, when it thinks' (Barthes 2000 [1980]). These sentiments and thoughts capture the essence of the methodology I describe in this chapter. As Diane Heckenberg and Rob White (2013; see also White and Heckenberg 2014) maintain, the study of environmental crime requires new modes of observation of the world, and new methods capable of synchronizing the spatial dimensions (global/local) and the temporal dimensions of the ongoing changes occurring in and to our environment (see also Brisman and South 2014, p. 121). Drawing on a case study described in previous work (Natali 2010), this chapter asks: What new horizons are made available for the green criminologist by the development and application of methodological instruments using visual dimensions? What unheard 'appropriation' of the world and of its representations can one achieve, renovating and reviving some of the modes through which one sees, looks at, glances at and observes the world (Robins 1996, pp. 8–9)?

This chapter describes a visual approach useful for carrying out qualitative research in green criminology, and suggests some analytical perspectives that can be stimulated by the use of the photographic image (see Ferrell and Van de Voorde 2010, pp. 37–8; Holm 2008, p. 338; Van de Voorde 2012, p. 215). The proposed observational method has the advantage of bringing together the multiple and complex nature of the experiences of those who live in polluted areas, describing in detail and from their point of view what they know, think of, and feel about the reality in which they find themselves living. This method casts doubts on simplistic conceptions about the way victims relate to the 'uncomfortable truth' of pollution and of environmental harm. In particular, this chapter attempts to demonstrate the value of visual methods generally, and photo-elicitation specifically, as part of green cultural criminology (Brisman and South 2013b, 2014; Brisman et al. 2014). A detailed examination of the methodological aspects of this new

1 I would like to thank Avi Brisman, Jeff Ferrell, Eamonn Carrabine, Valentina Anzoise and Elisa Bignante who made precious suggestions and comments on the original version of this chapter. Mirella Giulidori helped me with the translation of the text.

source for generating qualitative data in the green criminology field is followed by some excerpts that illustrate how images can provide a means of eliciting narratives from interviewees. The chapter concludes with a call to use a qualitative visual approach for carrying out research in green criminology designed to open the way for new explorations of environmental harms and crimes.

Towards a Visual Green Criminology Approach

Green criminology is a criminological area that allows the meeting of a wide range of theoretical orientations aimed at connecting a series of issues of crucial importance for today's world: environmental crimes, harms and various forms of (in)justice related to the environment, the animal species and the planet.[2] More specifically, green criminology represents a unique 'conceptual umbrella' under which to re-think and examine from various perspectives the bio-physical and socio-economic consequences of the diverse sources of environmental harm, such as pollution, the deterioration of natural resources, the loss of biodiversity and climate change (see Ruggiero and South 2013; South et al. 2013, pp. 28–9). While emerging within the framework of critical criminology, green criminology is marked by a constitutive openness that allows it to go beyond the boundaries of a specific criminological tradition to become a theoretical laboratory for thinking about 'environmental issues' in the richest and broadest sense of the word (see Sollund 2012, p. 4; South et al. 2013). In this sense, green criminology seems to promote new 'ways of looking' at the human–environment relationship – a peculiar 'green gaze' that can expand the criminological understanding and imagination of environmental crimes beyond the existing criminological frames (White 2003).

Since its inception, cultural criminology has called for the development of a form of criminological *Verstehen* capable of exploring the universes of sense and the emotional processes related to crime and to its control (Ferrell 1998, 2001; Ferrell et al. 2008). Recently, describing the connections between green and cultural criminology, Jeff Ferrell (2013) suggested that cultural criminology is a theoretical perspective capable of offering new observational and analytical frames, and of exploring the visual dimension not only as an essential criminological object in a mediatic society (see also Hayward and Presdee 2010), but also as a *tool* for criminological study.

These aspects may be profitably put in dialogue with what Avi Brisman and Nigel South (2013b, pp. 15–16, 2014) conceptualize as a 'green cultural criminology' – a criminological perspective that tries to imagine new modes of analysing critically the intersection of culture, crime, justice and environment. On this theoretical basis, a qualitative visual method may represent one of the possible avenues of and for a

2 Without becoming a single unity, these approaches come together within an emerging broad *perspective* (see, e.g., Ruggiero and South 2013; South et al. 2013, p. 28; White 2008, p. 14; see also Halsey 2004, p. 834; Lynch and Stretesky 2003; Walters 2010; White 2011).

green cultural criminology (Brisman and South 2013b, 2014). Thus, my proposal for a visual green criminology approach finds its natural habitat in the area where green criminology and cultural criminology meet (Brisman and South 2013b, 2014; Brisman et al. 2014; Ferrell 2013, p. 349), while at the same time, trying to forge new ground.

Before turning to my discussion of photo-elicitation interviews with environmental victims, one final point is in order. As Nicole Rafter (2014, p. 129) elucidates, if criminology is the study of crime, visual criminology may be defined as 'the study of ways in which all things visual interact with crime and criminal justice, inventing and shaping one another'. More importantly, its aim is to develop 'its own theoretical and methodological approaches', suggesting new visual ways of exploring and critically analysing social and power relations, harm, suffering and justice in the criminological field (see also Brown 2014, p. 181; Schept 2014, p. 203). Cultural criminology has played an important role in the revaluation of visual criminology (Hayward 2009; Hayward and Presdee 2010; Rafter 2014, p. 131). In this regard, some criminologists (e.g. Brisman 2012; Ferrell 2006; Ferrell 2013; Van de Voorde 2012) have attempted not just to devote attention to already existing visual representations of criminal phenomena, but to generate *their own* visual images of crime and crime control (see also Carrabine 2011, p. 463; Ferrell et al. 2008, pp. 174, 184–5; Greek 2009). Moreover, in the specific field of green criminology, other scholars have contemplated visual representations of environmental harms (Brisman and South 2013b; Kohm and Greenhill 2013). However, the use of visual mediums for gathering data on environmental harms, rather than just as a subject of analysis, remains unexplored (see also Natali 2013a).

Photo-Elicitation Interviews and Environmental Victims

In a previous research, I examined a town in southern Spain, Huelva, heavily polluted by a neighbouring industrial chemical plant established during the 1960s (Natali 2010, 2014). In this investigation, my choice of a visual method was intended as a means to capture and explore the harmful reality of environmental crime starting from the knowledge of those social actors who were the most direct victims of its consequences. In particular, I tried to capture some sensitizing dimensions, including the uniqueness of the biographical experiences and social perceptions about contamination; narratives of the personal experiences of environmental injustice; and consciousness of the environmental harm and the concomitant processes of denial and of habituation that make such a confusing situation acceptable for the residents or motivate them to oppose it.

To this end, the methodological technique used as a new source of qualitative data for green criminology was the photo-elicitation interview (Anzoise and Mutti 2012; Bignante 2010, p. 2; Lapenta 2011; Rose 2012, pp. 304–17). As visual sociologist Douglas Harper (2001, p. 16) explains, 'photo-elicitation interview' is 'a process of organizing interviews around photographs'. The assumption is that the meaning of the image rests in the mind of the viewer (see also Becker 1974;

Holm 2008, p. 328; Pauwels 2011, p. 12). As Cécile Van de Voorde (2012, p. 206) explains, photography as a methodological tool for criminological research may be used by collaborating with social actors, 'resorting to photo-elicitation to probe the participants' visual meanings and gain new knowledge from their personal narratives'.[3] This generates a sort of 'visual Verstehen' (see also Schept 2014, p. 207) where the photographs create a deeper unity between the subjects' and researcher's understanding.

Photographs as a visual tool allowed a detailed exploration of the object of study, starting directly from the perspectives of those who live the experience of pollution 'in the first person' (the 'subject' of the narrative) rather than from other narratives offered by *outsiders* with respect to that context.[4] In particular, photo-elicitation interviews proved to be useful in enhancing the active role of social actors and in placing their perceptions in the context of the social and cultural worlds in which they are embedded.

As with other qualitative research in green criminology, a visual approach should always consider adequately the nature of the object under study. This delicate phase requires a sensitivity to the symbolic perspectives of the social actors observed (see also Heckenberg and White 2013), in their narratives and 'ways of seeing' (Berger 2008 [1972]; Rose 2012, p. 13), getting closer to the 'truths' expressed in the narratives of the participants involved in the research process and interpreted by the researcher. To avoid imposing predetermined schemes on the reality under observation (Blumer 1969) does not mean accepting everything at face value, however (see also Bignante 2010, p. 11; Schept 2014, p. 209). It is necessary to establish the right distance, already deeply political, to allow a critical view capable of highlighting, for example, all those phenomena of denial that construct and distort the interpretative processes of certain environmental harms (see Heckenberg and White 2013). As I will describe below, the use of a 'critical visual methodology' (Rose 2012) helps in taking into account these various aspects.

How to Operate in the Field: A First Visual Exploration

Far from 'decorating' social research, photography represents a core methodological tool and heuristic device (see Rose 2012, pp. 297–301; Suchar 1997; Van de Voorde 2012, p. 203). As Harper (1993, p. 26) explains, the researcher may start by photographing a subject or a social environment. Concretely, the exploratory

3 In visual sociology, photo-elicitation has become a familiar, if underused, qualitative method. John Collier (1967) first describes the use of this method in research on rural assimilation into urban centres in Canada.

4 In this perspective, a green, cultural and visual victimology would be able to explore 'the symbolic environments created by victims . . . as they come to terms with their experiences' (Ferrell et al. 2008, p. 190) and, for this very reason, would become a significant method 'to account for meaning, situation, and representation, and to confront the harms of injustice and inequality' (Ferrell et al. 2008, p. 187).

phase of my study was directed at finding and capturing the visual dimensions that would indicate the presence of the pollution in the town of Huelva and its environs, focusing on the social and environmental harm produced. I endeavoured to do so from a great number of possible visual angles – what might be called a 'cubist approach' (Auyero and Swistun 2009, pp. 16, 166). In this phase, the 'visual lens' through which I approached the field included foreground shots that represented in detail the specific subjects portrayed, as well as wider shots that situated the subject within a larger context (e.g. the geographical, architectural and communitarian spaces of the reference setting). It was, therefore, a methodological perspective that considered the details but at the same time was capable of including a 'panoramic' view.[5]

Attempting to find the symbolic perspectives of the inhabitants of Huelva in their daily life, I tried to focus upon those 'social objects' (Mead 1963 [1934]; Athens 2007; Natali 2010) on which the perception of present environmental degradation and pollution are based.[6] Of course, capturing these 'shots' required prior familiarization and immersion in the social and environmental worlds to be studied (see also Ferrell and Van de Voorde 2010, p. 46).[7] Thus, this initial phase allowed entry into that socio-environmental world, experiencing it 'first hand' and collecting visual material for the next phase. During this process, it is important to bear in mind that, although these images produce what can be considered to be 'empirical data', they don't represent 'objective truth': '[t]he very act of observing is interpretative, for to observe is to choose a point of view' (Harper 2000, p. 721; see also Chalfen 2011, pp. 26–7). Thus, the decisions of the image-maker have profound consequences for the kinds of sociological (and criminological) statements that will result from the images (see also Ferrell and Van de Voorde 2010, p. 41).

In this context, the photographs were real 'shots' which helped weave the circular process between the reality investigated and the progressive construction of an emergent theoretical perspective (see also Pauwels 2010, pp. 559–62). The gathering and analysing of the photographic images shot at the site of the environmental harm that I was investigating promoted continuous revisiting of the initial hypothesis until a satisfactory refining of the concepts was reached (see also Suchar 1997).

5 Furthermore, when taking photographs for the purpose of photo-elicitation interviews, one need not ignore 'background noises' or 'interferences' (see also Auyero and Swistun 2009). Instead, such 'noises' or 'interferences' enhance the interview by providing further heuristic tools approaching that reality.

6 The expression 'social object' refers to the radical interactionist perspective that informs my approach (see Athens 2002).

7 'As with W. Eugene Smith's years in Pittsburgh or Minamata, as with Robert Capa's years in the Spanish Civil War or Indochina, the decisive moment emerges from the countless moments of cultural immersion and human commitment that have preceded it' (Ferrell and Van de Voorde 2010, p. 47).

How to Navigate the Space of the Image?

The exploratory phase of my study was oriented by the goal of finding and capturing the visual dimensions that would indicate the presence of the chemical plant and the pollution it was generating in the town of Huelva and its surrounding environment. As a green criminologist, my attention was focused on the environmental harm in Huelva and its visual traces and, after this exploratory phase, I had many photographs – and many questions. Indeed, the visual data one collects offers considerable information, while still posing many questions, and reveals much about the 'objects' observed and 'caught' in precise contexts.

Barthes (2000 [1980], p. 100) contends, however, that '[s]uch is the Photograph: it cannot *say* what it lets us see'. Thus, the images I captured during the visual exploration stage were still too 'silent' – they did not retain (or reveal) the *meaning* of an event or place. The technique of photo-elicitation helped make such images more eloquent. In fact, to gain access to the possible meanings of the images, it was necessary to reposition the immediacy of the photographic image within the temporal flux of the narrative that the observer could develop using the photograph as a starting point. The words and the narratives of the interviewees constituted, in other words, the text that focused and defined the context for the reading and the interpretation of the images presented to them (see also Ferrell and Van de Voorde 2010, p. 45). As Anders Vassenden and Mette Andersson (2010, p. 152) warn:

> for an image to work as an entry into meaning, feelings and sense-making . . . it has to resonate somehow with the informant, be it related to biography, perception or imagination . . . [D]ifferent images strike different chords with different viewers. Put another way, the degree of openness and 'closedness' of an 'image space' varies among observers.

In this process, a photograph that evoked elements of the respondents' worlds gave rise to associations, definitions or ideas that would have otherwise gone unnoticed: my interviewees suggested to me how to read the photographs from a different perspective (see also Harper 2002, p. 13; Anzoise and Mutti 2012).

Thanks to this methodological tool that enhanced the polysemy of the image (see Parmeggiani 2006, p. 35; Harper 2002, p. 15; Barthes 1978; Bignante 2010, p. 2), an interpretative process of co-construction and re-negotiation between the interviewer (me) and interviewee began.[8] Every single photograph acquired a meaning that was the result of the active and reflexive interpretation of the interviewee through acts of 'self-indication' regarding the 'social objects' (see Athens

8 Van de Voorde (2012, p. 207) writes: 'Barthes (1981) and Sontag (1977) further suggest a visual semiotics attuned to the layering of meanings, with *denotation* focusing on what or who is depicted, and *connotation* emphasizing the various ideas and values that are expressed through the content and structure of representation'.

2007; Blumer 1969; Mead 1963 [1934]; Natali 2010) shown in the photographs. It was in this fertile ground that the symbolical interpretations of the interviewees clarified what that 'social object' meant for them as inhabitants of that place and as people who interact with and within that socio-environmental context, rooted in that specific history and with their own personal and unique experiences. In other words, I, as the researcher, *read meanings in their worlds* but they, the interviewees, suggested *where* to read (Harcourt 2006, p. 121; see also Pauwels 2010, p. 565).

This cooperation allowed the emergence of narratives that defined the context of the photograph. Such a 'co-construction' must not be thought of in a linear manner; the significant interaction between images and words operated *radially*, 'that is to say with an enormous number of associations all leading to the same event' (Berger 1991 [1980], p. 64). As Berger (1991 [1980], p. 67) explains:

> Words, comparisons, signs need to create a context for a printed photograph in a comparable way; that is to say, they must mark and leave open diverse approaches. A radial system has to be constructed around the photograph so that it may be seen in terms which are simultaneously personal, political, economic, dramatic, everyday and historic.

Criminological imagination in the green field may find here an appropriate context and a fertile ground. The strategy of data collection described ensured, for me, access to the wide variety of ways of seeing the human–environment relationship, reconstructing an articulated range of personal landscapes. Each of us, in fact, when looking at a landscape, always does so through one's 'mindscape' – an image constructed and organized prospectively, stratified through biographical and social time. Among those 'landscapes' are also the time-scapes through which we observe reality (Natali 2010, 2013b, pp. 78–80). In this way, by studying the answers of the interviewees when faced with the image of the polluted landscape, it was possible for me to investigate the 'invisible' present in the 'visible' (see also Schept 2014, p. 218).

The Photographic Picture Shown to the Interviewees

The theoretical ideas described so far – together with the results of the first visual exploration – spilled over and coalesced into the photographic collage proposed to the single interviewees, shown in Figure 14.1.

If it is true that the limits of a horizon are also the conditions of the existence of many points of view, then the line that separates the single images is the condition of the possibility of the co-existence of many different points of view in the same picture. Specifically, this photographic picture suggests the co-existence of many spatial points of view and many temporal dimensions. In this way, perceptions of space and time mutually re-form each other (see also Degen and Rose 2012, p. 3; Rose et al. 2010, p. 341).

Como hemos venido a la capital, he querido que Platero vea El Vergel... Llegamos despacito, verja abajo, en la grata sombra de las acacias y de los plátanos, que están cargados todavía. El paso de Platero resuena en las grandes losas que abrillanta el riego...

Figure 14.1 The photographic collage used in the interviews (Huelva, Spain 2008). Photographs by Lorenzo Natali[9]

In my study, the photographs (re)presented *just one possible* version of the many, often conflicting, dimensions that emerged from an explorative observation of the environmental context of Huelva:[10]

- The old photograph, placed in the centre of the picture, suggests the historical stratifications of the contaminated landscape and of the vision of the local inhabitants, orienting their seeing according to a vanishing point through the time scale. This temporal dimension allowed the narratives to develop around a 'now and then' – a before and after – with reference to the 'perceptual

9 'Since we have come to the capital, I have wanted Platero to see the orchard. We walk very slowly along the iron grille in the grateful shade of the acacias and banana trees, which are still loaded with fruit. Platero's footsteps resound on the pavement, which is moistly bright from its watering' (translated by Eloise Roach).

10 In this sense, it is possible to imagine that by arranging and re-arranging the images new theoretical perspectives could evolve (see also Suchar 1997).

memory' (see Degen and Rose 2012, p. 13) of the creeping disaster in the town of Huelva.[11]

- Satellite photo: seeing the town from the perspective of the satellite used for Google Earth, my interviewees were able to visualize and interpret the extent of the contamination. Because the most serious effects are sometimes those that are least visible, it is important to introduce images from above and afar.
- The remaining images, chosen from among those shot during the explorative phase (e.g. the workmen, the demonstration to defend the jobs, the fishing activities), suggested many levels of interpretation. For example, the factories' chimney stacks, aside from representing their specific reality, also stood as visual metaphors (Todd and Harrison 2008, pp. 482, 491) of the tragic reality of pollution and of socio-environmental harms.
- The sentence at the lower edge of the picture (Figure 14.1), like a caption, is the sentence seen on the façade of the Combined Cycle Gas Turbine Endesa to highlight the 'green image' of the plant (Natali 2010). When this plant was built, particular attention was devoted to its aesthetic appearance: a light blue background, which recalls Huelva's colours, bears a quotation from an important work by the Spanish Nobel Prize winner Juan Ramón Jiménez, *Platero y yo*, which celebrates the beauty of Huelva's environs. If cities 'can be thought of as a palimpsest which is constantly being written, repainted and re-populated' (Pauwels 2009b, p. 263), whose objects and artefacts are continuously filled with new meanings, these visual strategies of 'green washing' represent a relevant aspect to be investigated.[12]

The photographic pictures, then, worked as a palimpsest blending different modes of perception and vision and promoting 'contaminations' among the various images (see also Robins 1996, p. 165). During the interviews, rather than present individual images in a sequence,[13] I showed the interviewees this single but multiple visual picture (Figure 14.1), containing different and oxymoronic perspectives of the macrocosm under observation.

This methodological strategy has the advantage of allowing a great degree of interpretative and narrative freedom in the symbolic interaction between the

11 In the field of visual sociology, this comparison between 'before' and 'here and now' can be caught by the technique called 're-photography' or 'chrono-photography', which enables one to disclose environmental continuity or change (see Parmeggiani 2006, p. 16; see also Anzoise et al. 2005).

12 These tactics of persuasion meant to construct and highlight the 'green' image of productive activities inevitably dangerous and harmful for the environment have been known, since the end of the 1990s, as 'green washing' (cf. Brisman 2009; Katz 2010, p. 304; Walters 2010, p. 315; White 2008). In this context, the image plays a decisive role because of the pervading and communicative power it has in late modern society (Szasz 1994).

13 Harper writes (2000, p. 724): 'To expand the idea of empirical data in single images to a sequence of photos is to introduce the concept of visual narrative . . . The most respected photojournalists have used this narrative form to great advantage. Eugene Smith and Aileen Smith's (1975) visual narrative of a social movement surrounding the lethal poisoning of a fishing village by a corporation describes the scenarios of several social groups'.

iconic and verbal level. Indeed, if one does not create a pre-established visual narrative, that is, a sequential order for the reading of the images, one allows the interviewees to organize the images according to their own point(s) of view. By choosing the image from which to start the interview and those that follow, the interviewees can create their own sequence and edit the pictures as stages in their own story – a story that, even within the horizon delimited by the framing choice of the researcher, is personal and unique. While 'editing' the pictures, the interviewees develop *micro* and *macro* visual narrative plots about the contaminated environment, moving, progressively or suddenly, from the detail (micro dimension) to a panoramic view (macro dimension), increasing the complexity of the interpretative process and enhancing the multifocal view presented.

Thus, the photographic images are seen as 'windows' – with surfaces sometimes transparent, sometimes opaque and ambiguous (see also Pauwels 2010, p. 550) – opening on to the social perception of pollution and the socio-environmental conflict considered. Cities, in fact, 'constitute at once a battle field for conflicting interests, a playground of ideas and a theatre for our senses, orchestrated by different agents with different temporal referents and audiences in mind' (Pauwels 2009b, p. 264). The interest in the continuous re-generation of meaning in the symbolic interaction in urban places (and the conflicts over it) is a relevant aspect of green criminology and of green cultural criminology (Brisman and South 2014, pp. 18, 21). As Brisman and South (2014, p. 21) remark: '[g]reen criminologists have drawn attention to the environmental victimization of poor, minority communities suffering from the effects of chemical plants . . . and other polluting industries . . . Are these not issues regarding the politics of urban space?' Visual qualitative approaches may help in investigating these relevant urban aspects of green harm, looking at them from different angles (see also Degen and Rose 2012, p. 2; Pauwels 2009a, p. 54; Rose 2012, p. 298).

At the same time, the images work as 'entries' or 'keys' for other dimensions and depths of the reality investigated and not necessarily found among the images selected and presented by the researcher. In essence, the photo-elicitation interview provides a 'verbal expansion of the scene' going beyond what is shown by the framing (see Parmeggiani 2006, p. 32). This approach is consonant with that of Anders Vassenden and Mette Andersson (2010, pp. 151–2), albeit in a different context:

> we suggest that an image might be conceptualized as more of an open space, compared with an oral question . . . This open space of a photograph can be both an advantage and a problem. It is an advantage in the sense that it might allow informants to articulate the unspoken . . . as it can show the range and complexity of the interpretative repertoires employed in meaning-making. When the observer explores this 'open space', images might display inner complexity. At the same time, the 'open space' is sometimes the problem of an image . . . It requires that you are actually willing to explore it. It requires that you are willing to employ your creative capacity to navigate the multiple interpretative repertoires that this particular photograph might point to.

Eliciting Narratives on the Experience of Environmental Contamination and Harm: An Example

The interviews were carried out in the streets, in bars or shops, asking people who were in the various areas of the town if they were willing to participate. I decided not to have a statistical sample of the inhabitants of Huelva: in a symbolic interactionist perspective 'a small number of well-informed informants are . . . a better sample than much larger samples of minimally involved subjects' (Harper 2001, p. 27). In fact, my purpose was not to generalize from my empirical results,[14] but to focus on and propose some 'sensitizing' perspectives (Blumer 1969) suitable for the observation of 'sensitive' environments.[15]

Moreover, as Auyero and Swistun (2009, pp. 15–16) remark, when studying the experiences of pollution by those who live in degraded environments, one needs to pay attention not only to what certain businesses and those who manage them 'are' and do 'in reality', but to explore how people *perceive* those activities and the consequences they produce, to what extent they *know* about them, how they *feel* and *think* about their environment, and how they make sense of it. From this perspective, it was not important to know what the photographs *really* represented: the main focus was on the meanings that the interviewees connected to those images. The objective was not to value or 'verify' the truth of the narratives or the significant vocabularies that emerged during the interviews, but rather to understand the meanings – the possible symbolic and emotive 'lenses' – that directed those visual perspectives (see also Bignante 2010; Silverman 2000, p. 823).

Another important aspect of these interviews was that they took place in different locations in the town, within a certain landscape that sometimes became part of the narratives of the interviewees as a further reality upon which to comment – a reality presenting itself with a power even stronger and more compelling than the two-dimensional photographic images. The interviewee, therefore, was immersed in the real consequences of the visual encounter proposed, an encounter that put him/her in contact with the 'social objects' that represented environmental harm and conflict. Essentially, what was brought into play during the visual exploration was not only the 'sight' but also, and above all, the 'being in the world'. As Robins (1996, p. 33) suggests, '[t]o see is to be in the world, to be "caught in the fabric of the world", and to be open to the world'. The observer is never detached from the world, indeed, he/she is immersed in it – 'in the disorder of the real world' (Robins 1996, p. 34). Thus, his/her observations are always placed in a specific experiential context, a real 'web of life' (see also Degen and Rose 2012; Kearns

14 As for the possibility of generalizing, or not, from the results drawn from a case study, Diane Heckenberg and Rob White (2013, p. 96) recall the concept of 'naturalistic generalization' described by Sherri Melrose (2010).

15 The interviewees in this study ranged in age from 18 to 90 and were both male and female. As the speakers' background characteristics influence how they interpreted the images (Harper 2001, p. 18), I chose at least one representative of each category, asking them if they were workers, students or residents.

2010) – far from the ideal of a 'detached' or impersonal observation, often at the core of traditional scientific methods (see Blumer 1969).

To make these theoretical and methodological reflexions more concrete, I present an example of what can happen during a photo-elicitation interview. The interview excerpts show how images elicit information that ranges from individual to broader cultural and historical interpretation (see Harper 2000, pp. 726–7). Below is a conversation generated during a photo-elicitation interview that took place in a shop using the photographic picture described in the previous paragraph.

Case 46

Interviewer: Let me show you this visual picture . . . start from whichever photo you prefer . . .

A: I live in district X. From my house you can see the factories and also smell the stink quite well . . . I am from the Sierra . . . I was not born in Huelva. I have worked in this shop for 20 years . . .

[commenting on the photo with 'Polo no, ría si']: 'Polo no, ría si': I agree with that . . .

. . . *UGT*, the workers' union, is against the *Mesa de la Ría* . . . The old photo . . . I have not seen it personally, but it would be wonderful to be able to enjoy this beach again . . .

The plant doing the most damage is Fertiberia . . . I wouldn't eat the fish caught in that area . . . even if there are many people who fish there . . . I do not know if they are aware of the contamination . . . if they eat it or throw it away after catching it . . . [looking at the phrase from *Platero y yo* by Jiménez]: There is a great passage of time with respect to what this phrase can communicate now . . . it's a paradox . . . that is a highly polluted area . . .

The most representative photo is the one with the writing 'Polo no, ría si'.

At this point a client (**B**) came into the shop of the interviewee (**A**), and became a new participant in the conversation. The client (**B**) tried to impose her 'truth' on the description proposed so far by the interviewee. This was a particularly significant and unexpected moment of my photo-elicitation interview. Indeed, as the research process is a continuing building process, 'unexpected texts' may become extremely relevant: '[a]s a reflexive researcher, you must remain open to such unexpected possibilities' (Waitt 2010, p. 223).

B: [looking at the antique photograph]: This [the beach of *Punta del Sebo*], my husband says, has never been possible . . .

A: But it was!

B: No! . . . because from the time of the Romans the mines of the río Tinto have been worked and 'shit' has come from the top to the bottom (of the river) . . . the residues of the washing of the minerals . . . I know people older than me who say they did bathe here, but my husband says they bathed in 'shit' . . .

there was already pollution even before the factories were built . . . it was at the confluence of the río Tinto and the río Odiel . . .

This [the beach of *Punta del Sebo*] is utopian . . . they bathed here because it was the nearest beach and not because it was not contaminated . . . for a few years now the water has vastly improved because the plants use filters that are less polluting . . .

A: but your husband works . . .

B: Yes, my husband unloads raw material for the factories . . .

But to take away the factories is utopian . . . Huelva was a village before they came, there was no pollution but there was no wealth either, there was nothing . . . we must be practical: many people here make a living from this . . . I cannot see any alternatives . . . I think the *Mesa de la Ría* people are utopians . . . it would be great but it's utopian . . . let's keep our feet on the ground, instead of dreaming, OK?

In this specific example it is possible to note the importance of the use of photographs to 'indicate' (Blumer 1969) and share common, though conflicting, realities – becoming a bridge not only between the subjects and the researchers (see Harper 2000, pp. 725, 731, note 4) but also among other social actors. In the case of Huelva, these images are old photographs, dating back to the 1950s. As such, they depict Huelva prior to the installation of the factories, showing a beach, the so-called *Punta del Sebo*, where the residents of Huelva used to bathe. Those photographs are there to prove that such a time 'has really been' (Barthes 2000 [1980]; Natali 2010, pp. 198–9). More generally, because these worlds are 'sensitive' worlds, where conflicts are expressed and suffering felt, a qualitative method working with both words *and* images will have a decisive role in the process of approaching and empathizing with the different visions of others, revitalizing both our disciplinary and non-disciplinary imagination (see also Brisman and South 2014, pp. 119–20).

Conclusion: Open Perspectives Being Defined

As I have tried to suggest, using photo-elicitation interviews in the field of green criminology can allow access to the hybrid multiplicity of perspectives directed at the human–environment relationship, including the perspective of the environmental victims (Williams 1996; Hall 2013; Natali 2015). Keeping itself open to interdisciplinary attitudes and to methodological 'contamination' (see also Brisman and South 2014, pp. 119–20; Rafter 2014, p. 130), this approach sees the visual experience of the social world in action as its most central and qualifying moment (see also Van de Voorde 2012, p. 215). More analytically, visual ethnographic research in the field of green criminology – and specifically, photo-elicitation interviews – may help in exploring the silent knowledge of social actors and in bridging cultural and natural worlds, thereby crossing the dichotomous divide between what is natural and what is social (Natali 2013b; Natali 2015; see also Rose et al. 2010, pp. 334–5). Moreover, because the nature of photography 'entails an *objective representation* (a mechanical record of something factual) and a *subjective interpretation* (a representation of the paradigm in which it was constructed) with meanings ascribed to the image by the photographer and the viewer' (Van de Voorde 2012, p. 212; see also Ferrell and Van de Voorde 2010, pp. 41–2), it seems that photography can capture the paradox, or rather the oxymoron, typical of environmental phenomena: they are *socially defined and described* but *at the same time* they are *real* (Brisman and South 2013a).

Drawing on Pauwels (2009b, p. 264), we might say that criminology and photography 'represent distinct "ways of looking" at society. But they are both about "making the familiar strange", about questioning the seemingly obvious and "reframing" it (as social facts or processes or visual statements)'. In this way, the photographic image becomes a tool for investigating and knowing social reality – a means for activating an interpretative process of the visual and symbolic contents of the reality under observation by both the researcher and the interviewees. It is here that the visual image deploys one of its most significant abilities, inviting the researcher to imagine himself inside other people's worlds and to empathize with their 'inhabiting it' (see Pink 2001, 2008). The technique of the photo-elicitation interview, then, makes it possible to weaken the conditionings and the judgments that the formulation of a 'verbal' question can hardly avoid. These two ways of 'asking' are, indeed, different as they work on levels that are not immediately super-imposable (see Berger 1991 [1980]). In addition, in all examples of photo-elicitation research, the photograph loses its claim to 'objectivity' and shows its ability 'to unlock the subjectivity of those who see the image differently from the researcher' (Harper 2000, p. 729).

Finally, these methods of 'attentive observation and compassionate analysis' can also help 'ourselves and others to understand and confront the everyday reality of injustice' (Ferrell et al. 2008, p. 192). As Ferrell et al. (2008, p. 192) further contend, in '[e]xposing injustice, unpacking ideologies of crime and victimization, giving voice to those unheard and unnamed, such methods can make for some decidedly dangerous knowledge'. To this end, it seems necessary to develop not only flexible methods, but also flexible conceptual tools – instruments sensitive enough to critically capture the 'vagueness' and elusiveness of environmental issues without severely diminishing their multiple and synchronous dimensions. The complex and 'open' nature of the photographic image helps in that direction (see also Carrabine 2014, p. 149; Brown 2014, p. 182). Considering that the relationship between criminological knowledge and the notion of crime is reflected in a specific concept of society (see White and Haines 2002, pp. 216–17), we can ask ourselves: which are the social and natural worlds that green criminology observes and imagines? Which tools of observation are used? Which socio-natural universes are privileged and which remain unexplored? Which other worlds can be discovered if new methodological tools are used? How can the visual dimensions of an environmental crime and of its harmful consequences help in revealing individual and collective categories, interpretations and perceptions that concern its empirical and normative dimension? Taking into account the visual dimensions and using photographs as tools of qualitative research represent unparalleled and unlimited means for addressing these complex questions.

References

Anzoise, V. and Mutti, C. 2012. 'Integrating Photo Elicitation and Mental Maps in the Study of Urban Landscape', in *Sociology of the Visual Sphere*, edited by R. Nathansohn and D. Zuev. New York and London: Routledge, 129–59.

Anzoise, V., Liberatore, L., Mutti, C. and Torricelli, A. 2005. 'Re-Photographies: A Comparative Visual Synthesis of Territorial Change', in *La Bicocca e il suo territorio*, edited by E. dell'Agnese. Milan: Skira, 100–29.

Athens, L. 2002. '"Domination": The Blind Spot in Mead's Analysis of the Social Act', *Journal of Classical Sociology* 2(1), 25–42.

——— 2007. 'Radical Interactionism: Going Beyond Mead', *Journal for the Theory of Social Behaviour* 37(2), 137–65.

Auyero, J. and Swistun, D. 2009. *Flammable: Environmental Suffering in an Argentine Shantytown*. Oxford and New York: Oxford University Press.

Barthes, R. 1978. *Image-Music-Text*. New York: Hill and Wang.

——— 2000 [1980]. *Camera Lucida: Reflections on Photography*. London: Vintage.

Becker, H.S. 1974. 'Photography and Sociology', *Studies in the Anthropology of Visual Communication* 1, 3–26.

Berger, J. 1991 [1980]. *About Looking*. New York: Vintage International.

——— 2008 [1972]. *Ways of Seeing*. London: Penguin.

Bignante, E. 2010. 'The Use of Photo-Elicitation in Field Research: Exploring Maasai Representations and Use of Natural Resources', *EchoGéo* 11, 1–18.

Blumer, H. 1969. *Symbolic Interactionism: Perspective and Method*. Berkeley and Los Angeles: University of California Press.

Brisman, A. 2009. 'It Takes Green to Be Green: Environmental Elitism, "Ritual Displays", and Conspicuous Non-Consumption', *North Dakota Law Review* 85(2), 329–70.

——— 2012. 'Coda: An Elevated Challenge to "Broken Windows": The High Line (New York)', *Crime Media Culture* 8(3), 381.

Brisman, A. and South N. 2013a. 'Introduction: Horizons, Issues and Relationships in Green Criminology', in *Routledge International Handbook of Green Criminology*, edited by N. South and A. Brisman. London and New York: Routledge, 1–21.

——— 2013b. 'A Green-Cultural Criminology: An Exploratory Outline', *Crime Media Culture* 9(2), 115–35.

——— 2014. *Green Cultural Criminology: Constructions of Environmental Harm, Consumerism and Resistance to Ecocide*. London and New York: Routledge.

Brisman, A., McClanahan, B. and South, N. 2014. 'Toward a Green-Cultural Criminology of "the Rural"', *Critical Criminology* 22(2), 479–94.

Brown, M. 2014. 'Visual Criminology and Carceral Studies: Counter-Images in the Carceral Age', *Theoretical Criminology* 18, 134–58.

Carrabine, E. 2011. 'The Iconography of Punishment: Execution Prints and the Death Penalty', *The Howard Journal* 50(5), 452–64.

——— 2014. 'Seeing Things: Violence, Voyeurism and the Camera', *Theoretical Criminology* 18, 134–58.

Chalfen, R. 2011. 'Looking Two Ways: Mapping the Social Scientific Study of Visual Culture', in *The SAGE Handbook of Visual Research Methods*, edited by E. Margolis and L. Pauwels. London and Thousand Oaks: Sage, 24–47.

Collier, J. 1967. *Visual Anthropology: Photography as a Research Method*. New York: Holt Rinehart and Winston.

Degen, M. and Rose, G. 2012. 'The Sensory Experiencing of Urban Design: The Role of Walking and Perceptual Memory', *Urban Studies* 49(15), 3271–87.

Ferrell, J. 1998. 'Criminological *Verstehen*: Inside the Immediacy of Crime', in *Ethnography at the Edge: Crime, Deviance and Field Research*, edited by J. Ferrell and M. Hamm. Boston: Northeastern University Press, 20–42.

——— 2001. 'Cultural Criminology', in *The Sage Dictionary of Criminology*, edited by E. McLaughlin and J. Muncie. London: Sage, 75–7.

——— 2006. *Empire of Scrounge: Inside the Urban Underground of Dumpster Diving, Trash Picking, and Street Scavenging*. New York: New York University Press.

——— 2013. 'Tangled Up in Green: Cultural Criminology and Green Criminology', in *Routledge International Handbook of Green Criminology*, edited by N. South and A. Brisman. London and New York: Routledge, 349–64.

Ferrell, J. and Van de Voorde, C. 2010. 'The Decisive Moment: Documentary Photography and Cultural Criminology', in *Framing Crime: Cultural Criminology and the Image*, edited by K. Hayward and M. Presdee. Abington and New York: Routledge, 36–52.

Ferrell, J., Hayward, K. and Young, J. 2008. *Cultural Criminology: An Invitation*. London: Sage.

Greek, C. 2009. 'Documenting and Framing Police Public Interaction with Citizens: A Study in Visual Criminology', *Criminal Justice Matters* 78(1), 18–20.

Hall, M. 2013. 'Victims of Environmental Harms and Their Role in National and International Justice', in *Emerging Issues in Green Criminology: Exploring Power, Justice and Harm*, edited by R. Walters, D. Westerhuis and T. Wyatt. Basingstoke: Palgrave Macmillan, 218–41.

Halsey, M. 2004. 'Against "Green" Criminology', *British Journal of Criminology* 44(6), 833–53.

Harcourt, B. 2006. *Language of the Gun: Youth, Crime and Public Policy*. Chicago and London: University of Chicago Press.

Harper, D. 1993. 'Orizzonti sociologici. Saggio di sociologia visuale', *Sociologia della comunicazione* 10(19), 15–31.

——— 2000. 'Reimagining Visual Methods: Galileo to Neuromancer', in *Handbook of Qualitative Research*, second edition, edited by N.K. Denzin and Y.S. Lincoln. Thousand Oaks: Sage, 717–32.

——— 2001. *Changing Works: Visions of a Lost Agriculture*. Chicago and London: University of Chicago Press.

——— 2002. 'Talking about Pictures: A Case for Photo Elicitation', *Visual Studies* 17(1), 13–26.

Hayward, K.J. 2009. 'Visual Criminology: Cultural Criminology-Style', *Criminal Justice Matters* 78(1), 12–14.

Hayward, K.J. and Presdee, M. (eds). 2010. *Framing Crime: Cultural Criminology and the Image*. Abingdon and New York: Routledge.

Heckenberg, D. and White, R. 2013. 'Innovative Approaches to Researching Environmental Crime', in *Routledge International Handbook of Green Criminology*, edited by N. South and A. Brisman. London and New York: Routledge, 85–103.

Holm, G. 2008. 'Visual Research Methods: Where Are We and Where Are We Going?', in *Handbook of Emergent Methods*, edited by S.N. Hesse-Biber and P. Leavy. New York and London: The Guilford Press, 325–41.

Katz, R.S. 2010. 'The Corporate Crimes of Dow Chemical and the Failure to Regulate Environmental Pollution', *Critical Criminology* 18, 295–306.

Kearns, R.A. 2010. 'Seeing with Clarity: Undertaking Observational Research', in *Qualitative Research Methods in Human Geography*, edited by I. Hay. Oxford and New York: Oxford University Press, 241–58.

Kohm, S. and Greenhill, P. 2013. '"This is the North, Where We Do What We Want": Popular Green Criminology and "Little Red Riding Hood" Films', in *Routledge International Handbook of Green Criminology*, edited by N. South and A. Brisman. London and New York: Routledge, 365–87.

Lapenta, F. 2011. 'Some Theoretical and Methodological Views on Photo-Elicitation', in *The SAGE Handbook of Visual Research Methods*, edited by E. Margolis and L. Pauwels. London and Thousand Oaks: Sage, 201–13.

Lynch, M.J. and Stretesky, P.B. 2003. 'The Meaning of Green', *Theoretical Criminology* 7(2), 217–38.

Mead, G.H. 1963 [1934]. *Mind, Self and Society: From the Standpoint of a Social Behaviorist*. Chicago: University of Chicago Press.

Melrose, S. 2010. 'Naturalistic Generalization', in *Encyclopedia of Case Study Research*, edited by J. Mills, G. Durepos and E. Wiebe. Thousand Oaks: Sage, 600–2.

Natali, L. 2010. 'The Big Grey Elephants in the Backyard of Huelva', in *Global Environmental Harm: Criminological Perspectives*, edited by R. White. Cullompton: Willan Publishing, 193–209.

——— 2013a. 'Exploring Environmental Activism: A Visual Qualitative Approach from an Eco-Global and Green-Cultural Criminological Perspective', *CRIMSOC: The Journal of Social Criminology. Special Issue: 'Green Criminology'*, Autumn, 64–100.

——— 2013b. 'The Contemporary Horizon of Green Criminology', in *Routledge International Handbook of Green Criminology*, edited by N. South and A. Brisman. London and New York: Routledge, 73–84.

——— 2014. 'Green Criminology, victimización medioambiental y social harm. El caso de Huelva (España)', *Revista Crítica Penal y Poder* 7, 5–34.

——— 2015. 'A Critical Gaze on Environmental Victimization', in *Green Harms and Crimes*, edited by R. Sollund. Cheltenham: Palgrave Macmillan, 63–78.

Parmeggiani, P. 2006. *Fotografare il territorio. Nuovi contributi della sociologia visuale*. Udine: Quaderni del Dipartimento EST.

Pauwels, L. 2009a. 'Photo Essay: The Urban Canvas', *Contexts* 17, 54–61.

——— 2009b. 'Street Discourse: A Visual Essay on Urban Signification', *Culture Unbound* 17, 263–72.

——— 2010. 'Visual Sociology Reframed: An Analytical Synthesis and Discussion of Visual Methods in Social and Cultural Research', *Sociological Methods and Research* 38(4), 545–81.

——— 2011. 'An Integrated Conceptual Framework for Visual Social Research', in *The SAGE Handbook of Visual Research Methods*, edited by E. Margolis and L. Pauwels. London and Thousand Oaks: Sage, 3–23.

Pink, S. 2001. *Doing Visual Ethnography: Images, Media and Representation in Research*. London: Sage.

——— 2008. 'An Urban Tour: The Sensory Sociality of Ethnographic Place-Making', *Ethnography* 9, 175–96.

Rafter, N. 2014. 'Introduction to Special Issue on Visual Culture and the Iconography of Crime and Punishment', *Theoretical Criminology* 18, 127–33.

Robins, K. 1996. *Into the Image: Culture and Politics in the Field of Vision*. London and New York: Routledge.

Rose, G. 2012. *Visual Methodologies: An Introduction to Researching with Visual Materials*. London: Sage.

Rose, G., Degen, M. and Basdas, B. 2010. 'More on "Big Things": Building Events and Feelings', *Transactions of the Institute of British Geographers* 35(3), 334–49.

Ruggiero, V. and South, N. 2013. 'Green Criminology and Crimes of the Economy: Theory, Resarch and Praxis', *Critical Criminology* 18, 245–50.

Schept, J. 2014. '(Un)seeing like a Prison: Counter-Visual Ethnography of the Carceral State', *Theoretical Criminology* 18, 198–223.

Silverman, D. 2000. 'Analyzing Talk and Text', in *Handbook of Qualitative Research*, edited by N.K. Denzin and Y.S. Lincoln. Thousand Oaks: Sage Pubblications, 821–34.

Sollund, R.A. 2012. 'Introduction', in *Eco-Global Crimes: Contemporary Problems and Future Challenges*, edited by R. Ellefsen, R. Sollund and G. Larsen. Farnham: Ashgate, 3–14.

South, N., Brisman, A. and Beirne, P. 2013. 'A Guide to a Green Criminology', in *Routledge International Handbook of Green Criminology*, edited by N. South and A. Brisman. London and New York: Routledge, 27–42.

Suchar, C.S. 1997. 'Grounding Visual Sociology Research in Shooting Scripts', *Qualitative Sociology* 20(1), 33–55.

Szasz, A. 1994. *Ecopopulism: Toxic Waste and the Movement for Environmental Justice*. Minneapolis: University of Minnesota Press.

Todd, Z. and Harrison, S.J. 2008. 'Metaphor Analysis', in *Handbook of Emergent Methods*, edited by S.N. Hesse-Biber and P. Leavy. New York and London: The Guilford Press, 479–93.

Van de Voorde, C. 2012. 'Ethnographic Photography in Criminological Research', in *The Sage Handbook of Criminological Research Methods*, edited by D. Gadd, S. Karstedt and S.F. Messner. London and Thousand Oaks: Sage, 203–17.

Vassenden, A. and Andersson, M. 2010. 'When an Image Becomes Sacred: Photo-Elicitation with Images of Holy Books', *Visual Studies* 25(2), 149–61.

Waitt, G. 2010. 'Doing Foucauldian Discourse Analysis – Revealing Social Realities', in *Qualitative Research Methods in Human Geography*, edited by I. Hay. Oxford and New York: Oxford University Press, 217–40.

Walters, R. 2010. 'Toxic Atmospheres Air Pollution, Trade and the Politics of Regulation', *Critical Criminology* 18, 307–23.

White, R. 2003. 'Environmental Issues and the Criminological Imagination', *Theoretical Criminology* 7, 483–506.

——— 2008. *Crimes against Nature: Environmental Criminology and Ecological Justice*. Cullompton: Willan Publishing.

——— 2011. *Transnational Environmental Crime: Toward an Eco-Global Criminology*. London and New York: Routledge.

White, R. and Haines, F. 2002. *Crime and Criminology: An Introduction*. Oxford: Oxford University Press.

White, R. and Heckenberg, D. 2014. *Green Criminology: An Introduction to the Study of Environmental Harm*. London and New York: Routledge.

Williams, C. 1996. 'An Environmental Victimology', *Social Justice* 23, 16–40.

15 Organized Crime and Illegal Waste Disposal in Campania

Pasquale Peluso

Introduction

According to ISPRA in Italy 7.2 million tons of special, industrial and toxic waste were produced in 2012 (ISPRA 2012). Yet, every year about 30 million tons of waste disappears. Such a quantity of waste has been compared to a cylinder 2,000 metres high with a base three hectares wide (Osservatorio Ambiente e Legalità di Legambiente 2010). In Italy, a crime against the environment is committed every 17 minutes.

The illicit cycle of waste represents an interesting study case in the region of Campania in southern Italy. The illegal waste disposal is the cause of two emergencies: the first one, the so-called 'waste emergency', is well known. This emergency lasted 17 years from 1994 when rubbish invaded the city streets in Campania because the waste dumps were full of industrial waste from northern Italy. The second emergency is connected to the *illegal* waste disposal that started in Campania in 1989 and still goes on. It is 25 years since the emergency started and it is far from being solved (Capacchione 2008, p. 157).

The Waste Disposal in Campania

To understand the real problem of waste disposal in Campania it is necessary to distinguish urban solid garbage from special waste. About 42 per cent of the special waste consists of inert waste derived from building and demolition activities. The remaining part is made up of special waste from handicraft, farming and business activities (Osservatorio Ambiente e Legalità di Legambiente 2008a). Campania became the special place for illegal waste disposal since the end of the 1980s when the international traffic of waste, directed to the underdeveloped countries, and especially to Africa and the Balkans, was discovered and the criminals were forced to look for new, simple and cheap routes to follow, without any control or having to get through customs (Osservatorio Nazionale Ambiente e Legalità 2005). The increase of controls at the customs points induced criminal groups to choose internal routes for the waste disposal in order to bypass harbours (Massari and Monzini 2004).

Unscrupulous entrepreneurs, politicians and leaders of organized crime saw a chance of making a profit from waste disposal. As a consequence, in 1989 they met in Villaricca in order to divide the territory and business and regulate the waste traffic in Campania (Iacuelli 2008). Such an agreement was fostered by the relationships among Camorra organizations, freemasonry, politicians and entrepreneurs. There is a close connection between some clans from Naples (capital of Campania) and the Casalesi clan, the historical family operating around Caserta (a town a dozen miles north of Naples). The Casalesi clan had been implicated as being particularly busy with the shipment and disposal of toxic waste. Some connections to freemasonries and secret services have also emerged in order to explain why tons of toxic waste, produced by northern Italy industries, have arrived in Campania (Capacchione 2008, p. 156).

According to Iacuelli (2007a), the Casalesi were the first to start the illegal waste disposal, taking advantage of their presence in the territory's towns and countryside, their clan power structure that controls the inhabitants of the same area, the violence of their actions, their relationship with politicians, and their alliance with other criminal organizations such as the Mafia. Some of the clan's most important spokespersons of Pianura and Flegrea area and Casalesi took part at the meeting at the 'La Lanterna' Hotel. Ferdinando Cannavale, as a freemason and a friend of local politicians, was given permission by Raffaele Perrone Capano, the council member in the Ecology Department in the province of Naples, to receive extra regional waste. Several owners of rubbish dumps in Naples and Caserta area also took part at the mentioned meeting: Gaetano Vassallo, owner of the Novambiente Srl and council member of the town of Cesa, Gaetano Cerci, Francesco Bidognetti's nephew, and Francesco Schiavone's man Friday, holder of the 'Eighty-nine Ecology Company', transporting and disposing wastes and mediator between the Casalesi and Licio Gelli. Licio Gelli, as freemason and leader of the 'P2 Lodge' supplied the contacts of entrepreneurs in northern Italy who were interested in the illegal disposal of waste produced in their companies in order to save money (Iacuelli 2007a).

According to the judicial inquiries, in the province of Caserta the lawyer and entrepreneur Cipriano Chianese played an important role as mediator between local entrepreneurs and the clans (Capacchione 2008). Chianese was arrested in January 2006. The Villaricca agreement laid down that the Camorra took a kickback of 25 lire for each kilo of garbage. Ten lire were destined to the council member Perrone Capano and his political party and 15 lire to the Casalesi clan. In an examination of the Spartacus trial, the treasurer of the Casalesi clan, Dario De Simone, explained to the judges how the waste traffic was executed. It was managed by the Casalesi organization through the so-called 'Eighty-nine Ecology Company' whose engineer Gaetano Cerci, a relative of boss Francesco Bidognetti, was the leader. The company's aim was to manage the shipment of waste from northern Italian industries. Mario Caterino and Francesco Di Puorto were the men procuring the means for transport in northern Italy and they worked in Tuscany. The majority of northern industries knew the people belonging to the organization to whom they could turn to in order to have the waste disposed. The lawyer Chianese was another man of the Casalesi clan as regard the judicial facts. The entrepreneurs were in contact with the 'Eighty-nine Ecology Company' or Chianese himself, both of whom had always been receiving requests to dispose of the waste. Between them, they used to discuss the modalities of waste disposal and the prices that ought to apply. The material was subsequently dumped in particular fields and, as well, holes were dug for all sorts of waste (Capacchione 2008).

The illegal dumping was possible because there was no plan for waste disposal in Campania before 1996. This absence made the illegal waste disposal blend with the legal waste disposal. Today the difference between lawful management of waste and illegal manipulation with regard to their compliance with health regulations is very narrow, and the health risks are rising. (Senior and Mazza 2004).

In 1994, the negative management of waste and the lack of a regional plan for disposal blocked the collection and left thousands of tons of waste along the streets (Iovene 2008). In this way the first waste emergency was born in Campania. In order to solve this problem an Extraordinary Emergency Commissioner was appointed. The Commissioner adopted measures such as the requisition of a large number of dumps in the territory, that were managed by private citizens, in order to increase the opportunity to get rid of waste and remove garbage quickly from the streets.

Another consequence was the summoning of several Camorra clans to transport and dispose of solid urban waste. This was an opportunity for the clan to dispose of municipal waste and also special waste (Pasotti 2010). The disposal of special waste in the dumps built for the urban waste meant that space for the latter underwent a contraction. To solve the problem of the saturation of the open dumps, the criminal organizations requested new spaces from companies, clans and farmers. One of the peculiar traits of the Camorra is its ability to quickly reorganize (D'Alisa et al. 2010). The Alfieri clan, which is allied to the Casalesi clan, was involved in the territory expansion of the Camorra as regards the waste disposal in Nola. The Alfieri clan had the same professional competences as the Casalesi clan. In fact the main clan activities pertain to illegal construction and the production and use of concrete. Several companies mining sand from illegal quarries and working in the ecological sector were connected to the clan (Iacuelli 2008).

In 1994, a state of emergency was declared in Campania and the urban waste started to be disposed in several dumps of different sizes (De Crescenzo 2007). There are no documents about these dumps and only a part of the waste could be legally disposed in them. In fact these dumps often were simple non-waterproofed holes, without any plant for the collection of percolate. In Campania two dumps for the urban waste disposal belonged to private companies, the Resit in Giugliano and the Di.Fra.Bi in Pianura. Chianese and Vassallo were the owners of a dump, named Setri, in Giugliano (Campania).

The inquiries revealed that the Resit, whose manager was the lawyer Chianese, owned two quarries in Scafarea, near Giuliano; they were called X and Z. Thanks to the friendship with some important men of the Casalesi clan, Chianese could buy some fields at rock-bottom prices, where he started the disposal of waste. During the waste emergency in 2003, the Commissioner took over these dumps, which were to be closed and then reclaimed in order to dump urban waste. The Resit invoiced €35 million to the Commissioner. Once the legal sites such as the Novambiente were filled, the waste disposal activities continued in illegal sites. In addition to urban rubbish, a huge quantity of dangerous special waste, mostly produced by northern Italian companies, was dumped by the Camorra into these sites. From an enquiry of the Naples Public Prosecutor's Office it emerged that during the waste emergency (2008–10) the Director-General of the Department of the Environment, Gianfranco Mascazzini, authorized the illegal disposal of percolate produced by landfill sites in the province of Naples (Baccaro and Musella 2013).

From the 2008 report 'Rifiuti S.p.a' of Legambiente it emerged that 316 of Campania's 459 dumps were unauthorized, according to monitoring that started in 1990 (Osservatorio Ambiente e Legalità di Legambiente 2008b). Nowadays, the number of authorized landfill sites is lower because many were impounded due to irregularities or because they filled up. These urban and special waste disposal activities contributed to the opening of new illegal dumps. Vassallo's sites were going to have a long life. During the long waste emergency they were expropriated by the Commissioner who paid about €2.5 million to dump the garbage of Naples into full and illegal hollows. Sooner or later these dumps were going to overflow, but the Casalesi dumps kept on disposing illegally, taking advantage of the permission, but using new sites, built without any system of percolate control or collection tanks. The measures adopted by the Extraordinary Commissioner for the waste emergency, gave the Mafia the opportunity to dump special waste mixed with urban garbage in private landfills. Evidence of this can be found in the declarations of the informer Domenico Bidognetti. During questioning he declared that, at first, the waste was northern Italy was disposed of in the dumps. Then the clan decided to stop disposing of the garbage in authorized places in order to avoid filling them up, but rather began to use unauthorized sites (Massari 2004).

According to Iacuelli (2007a), until its closing in 1996, 40 million cubic metres of wastes had been disposed of in the Pianura dump. From 1987 to 1994 more than 800,000 tons of industrial mud, asbestos dust, contaminated soil and chemical industry waste, produced in northern Italy, were dumped there. In Giugliano municipality there were other dumps beside Resit's, including the Noavambiente dump owned by Vassallo, the instigator of the toxic waste traffic from northern Italy to Campania, as well as the Masseria del Pozzo dump, Schiavi's dump and Giuliani's quarry. These dumps owned by companies and people connected to the Casalesi clan were built without respecting the safety rules. The perimeter of these dumps was not known and this has allowed them to keep on being used for illegal dumping. With reference to these dumps, Vassallo himself declared that 'as the dumps were filling, the garbage was buried everywhere. In such cases the entrepreneurs were ignored, but sometimes the use of the clan stamps was requested in order to cover and justify the waste disposal of Northern Italy producers' (Capacchione 2008).

In Castel Volturno, in the province of Caserta, some illegal quarries belonging to the Camorra were used to extract sand for the production of concrete. Once exhausted, they were exploited to dump any kind of waste. As the quarries were filling up, they were dug deeper and deeper. Eventually the layer of soil able to hold back a nearby body of water broke and the ditch was flooded, creating a little lake (Osservatorio Ambiente e Legalità di Legambiente 2008a).

The appointment of the Commissioner was justified by the need to manage the emergency through quick procedures, deliberately avoiding the laws in force. The Extraordinary Commissioner took the place of local authorities, depriving them of any decision-making power. The Commissioner eliminated the democratic control of municipalities and other territorial districts and reduced the jurisdictional supervision exercised by the TAR (Regional Administrative Court) and Supreme Administrative Court. In reality, the Commissioner produced a unique deed, a 'Regional Plan for Urban Solid Waste Disposal', that was presented by the Extraordinary Commissioner Rastrelli. The plan provided for the building of two incinerators and seven systems for the production of refuse derived fuel (RDF). These systems were to create bales of selected garbage to be burned in the incinerators (Rabitti 2008).

According to Iacuelli (2007b) the plan was only partially carried out. In 2001 the RDF systems were built, but no plan to separate rubbish collection was put into effect. No incinerator system was completed, although the agreement with FIBE, the contractor for the Acerra incinerator, envisaged building the plant in just 300 days. Therefore, the RDF systems started producing unselected garbage bales that were against the regulations expected for bales to burn in the incinerators. These bales have been stockpiling in the territory.

In 2001, a new emergency occurred when the dumps originally confiscated in 1994 became saturated and over eight million bales were stocked in several sites in Campania, waiting to be burned. Since there was still not a real plan to differentiate and reduce waste collection, in 2007 a new and further emergency occurred, thus requiring the opening of new garbage dumps that, in turn, caused strong protests and resistance by citizens. This induced the federal government to declare sites in which garbage dumps, RDF systems and incinerators were to be located as sites of national strategic interest, with the same status as military bases. Since March 2009, the incinerator of Acerra has been working by burning the RDF bales produced, but not respecting any rules and without a disposal plan for the residuals of combustion. The incinerator has been working in fits and starts due to several technical issues and the overrun of the annual emission limit permitted by law (Iacuelli 2007b).

Waste in the streets, full garbage dumps, the risk of possible epidemic, and a new emergency quickly induced the Commissioner to identify new agencies that were available to conduct the garbage collection in peculiar circumstances. In the event, the Commissioner suggested municipality companies that were connected to the Camorra. He identified the subjects to which the contracts were to be awarded and indicated the suppliers to local authorities, all without waiting for the time of a competitive bid process. In this way the transport companies winning the contracts for the waste collection in the small municipalities could enter into the tips and dump special waste mixed with urban garbage (Rabitti 2008).

The Techniques of Illegal Waste Disposal

As time goes by, the techniques of illegal and special wastes disposal have changed (Massari 2004). Initially, they were rather simple. Taking advantage of disused illegal quarries for the extraction of sand, the organized crime groups filled them with toxic waste dumped by trucks during the night and then immediately covered this with materials coming from the excavations for the foundations of buildings that were used to make the ground compact. Upon those sites they used to build villas, roads and so on. Nowadays this technique is no longer used. The clans or organised crime groups do not use big trucks for the transport of the toxic barrels any more, and instead prefer to use intermediaries who offer temporary stocking docks. Their couriers pick up a few barrels and abandon them in the illegal dumps, repeating the same operation several times.

With the closing of the dumps, the modus operandi changed and today the so-called *giro bolla* is widely used, that is the turning shipping note technique. The waste is directly collected from the producer and transferred into the temporary stocking docks. There, both the waybill (packing list) and the accompanying form for any kind of waste (from which it would be possible to deduce that it is toxic waste) are forged, so the producer appears to be the same stocking centre and the garbage loses its codification as special waste. The false forms are often delivered directly by the drivers of the organization to entrepreneurs when the drivers go to the company to pick up the toxic barrels.

The technique of *giro bolla* – turning shipping note – has been joined by a new technique, the so-called *theory of prevailing code*. It is based on a triangulation too, like the other one. Even if only virtually, wastes are sent to recycling or composting plants to downgrade the type of treated waste, changing the weight or composition through a mix with other waste. Each waste has its own ERC (European waste catalogue) code. The mixture of two or more kinds of waste is classifiable according to the waste code of the prevalent kind. Then the mix of toxic waste such as arsenic in small doses with urban solid waste allows the overall waste to obtain a mixture classification as non-hazardous waste, identifiable as solid urban waste.

There are less pragmatic and refined techniques to get rid of toxic waste when they arrive at the dumps. In the less monitored industrial areas the *smoking drain* technique prevails. Tanker trucks, travelling with the drain hose already connected, arrive in these areas and spill toxic substances derived from the processing of inks or metal plates. When these substances come in contact with the sewage, they generate white smoke. The disposal in unsuitable plants takes place thanks to the use of public dumps where toxic wastes are disposed by mixing the urban solid garbage without forming any mixture. Sometimes, toxic wastes are disposed in legal dumps mixed with inert wastes deriving from building or demolition activities (Osservatorio Ambiente e Legalità di Legambiente 2008b).

Another very profitable technique consists of the *white spills*. The toxic wastes, especially the muddy and liquid ones, are transferred to composting plants and are mixed in with compost. In the mixture obtained there are no traces of toxic waste and it is sold as a fertilizer for agriculture. In the last few years, thanks to the statements of informers, it has been discovered that the Camorra disposed of toxic waste through the so-called *tombamento*, that is, the entombment in reinforced concrete used to build public buildings, roads and foundations of buildings (Giordano and Chiariello 2015). In other cases, the Camorra forced farmers *to bury barrels of toxic waste* and put them on their land. Sometimes, farmers themselves were conniving with the Camorra, allowing the burial of waste on their land in exchange for payment (Osservatorio Ambiente e Legalità di Legambiente 2007).

Finally, the easiest and best known modality, thanks to their exposure in the media in recent times, is the *wild spill along roadsides*. In this case the waste is burned on the road, giving rise to continuous blazes. The techniques used are simple and easy. Old tyres filled with toxic waste are placed on the ground before the garbage deposit. The tyres are covered with fuel-soaked rags which are then set on fire. The fire destroys the wastes and scatters toxic substances in the atmosphere. The origin of the expression *Terra dei fuochi* (land of the fires) derives from this practice. This expression refers to a large area of Naples and Caserta provinces where waste is burnt every day (Saviano 2006).

Analysing the illegal waste disposal's production chain, it is very interesting to explain how this system can be exported and how firmly rooted it is in the local area. In addition to the final disposer – managing dumps, fields, compost plants and no longer used quarries – there are the drivers moving the wastes to the disposal places; stocking centres play an important role with reference to *giro bolla* and *prevailing code*; and there is white-collar criminality made up of technicians who put their expertise at the service of organized criminality in falsifying delivery notes, and corrupted public employees who authorize the importation or spills of special waste as inert waste. Finally, there are waste producers, entrepreneurs or managers of important companies who are ready to dispose of the waste products illegally from their plants, in order to save money. The intermediary plays a very important role. He keeps in touch with companies and entrepreneurs and tries to understand which services they need. Then he offers them the best solution and relative price table (Iacuelli 2007b).

From the Local to the Global Level

These modalities are particularly alarming because they can be exported in many cases. In 2008, for example, the Camorra tried to export toxic waste illegally to Germany. Hamburg expressed the intention to help Naples to solve the garbage crisis that had worsened again by taking waste to burn in its incinerators. The agreement was temporary and would have contributed to solving the Naples emergency. A daily train of 56 freight cars containing 700 tons of urban garbage was planned. A few weeks later the disposal plan was interrupted because a small quantity of medical and radioactive waste mixed with urban garbage was found in a wagon (Smoltczyk et al. 2010). Since April 2007, freight cars full of waste have left Campania for the German town of Großpösna every day. However, since 2005, German laws have established that the solid urban garbage cannot be disposed in dumps but it has to be burnt down or subjected to particular treatments.

An enquiry carried out by Carabinieri inspecting some foul-smelling freight cars pointed out that the garbage consisted of urban solid waste that had never been treated. It was calculated that 7,500 containers arrived in Germany. It was a lucrative business for the disposal company which received €86 per disposed ton, even though they were violating the German laws. The Minister of the Environmental Department found out that 300,000 tons of waste were disposed of illegally in the dump of Freyburg-Zeuchfel city, in the Saxon Anhalt region. The Neapolitan urban solid waste sent to Saxony-Anhalt was classified as mineral garbage to be disposed of illegally (Rosenthal 2008).

Illegal garbage disposal has found further ways in Italy too, especially when it could not be shipped abroad. The Camorra and criminal entrepreneurs did not limit their polluting behaviour to large areas in Campania, as the informer Schiavone has recently revealed. According to him the areas in which toxic waste were hidden in the ground include the Domitio seaboard, Caserta hinterland, the northern area of Campania, the area around Acerra, Marigliano and Nola, and so on (Vito 2008). In order to diversify the final destinations of the illegal traffic, the dangerous special waste turned up in regions such as Molise and Umbria. Toxic wastes were discovered in some areas in Puglia. In Supersano, in the province of Lecce, scraps of a local company producing chromium plating for shoes and buckles were discovered. According to the informer of the United Sacred Crown, Silvano Galati, the company involved would have been the Corrado Group. In Puglia the local criminal groups did not manage the cycle of waste directly, as in Campania, but kept in touch with companies that had to eliminate dangerous waste, making themselves available to dispose of the possible load (Foschini 2013).

Molise represented a land of conquest for the Camorra where it used some areas such as Venafro, Isernia and a coast area in order to dispose of toxic waste illegally. Trucks from Naples used to arrive in the industrial area of Pozzilli, go into the warehouse and some hours later return to Naples. According to the Report of the National Anti-Mafia Directorate, the Casalesi clan used the Caturano trucking company to load and unload toxic waste. The yellow and red trucks of Caturano drove the same route every day from Caianello through Venafro, Isernia, Bojano and Campobasso area, where they disappeared mysteriously and appeared again along state road eighty-seven in the opposite direction (De Chiara 2010).

Recently some enquiries have pointed out that hexavalent chrome waste slags (which are particularly carcinogenic) have been discovered under the third lane of toll road A4 in the province of Brescia. The concentration of hexavalent chrome is about 1,400 times higher than the Italian laws allow. This is not the only case of this kind of illegal waste disposal in northern Italy. The technique to conceal the dangerous waste under the *blacktop carpets* had been used in the case of the toll road A31 (Valdastico) too. In order to build 18 kilometres of toll road from

Longare to Agugliaro in the province of Vicenza, 155,000 cubic metres of materials containing waste slags of not reclaimed steelworks were used. According to the results of the enquiry by the public prosecutor's office, someone spread high polluting materials instead of harmless gravel (Petenzi 2013).

Several small companies in Veneto, Brescia and Emilia Romagna have been involved in the enquiry with the prosecution of illegal waste disposal. In northern Italy, when the burial of waste was not possible, the quarries were also used to dispose of the dangerous industrial waste illegally. The technique is always the same; it consists of dumping toxic waste in the quarries. These wastes were transported with falsified documents that allowed their disposal, by covering them with correctly disposed garbage in order to conceal them. For this reason several quarries have been confiscated between Martinengo and Mornico al Serio in the province of Bergamo (Tosca 2013).

It is evident that the organized crime preferred using Campania areas in order to dispose of the waste illegally. Southern Italy and Campania have been transformed into a huge trashcan, 'a lunar waste land where toxic wastes have been buried' (Capone et al. 2006). The effects of these criminal actions are known, as the informer Schiavone had revealed in advance during a deposition at the Anti-Mafia Commission in 1997. The illegal waste combustion, garbage entombment and the dispersion in the fields have resulted in the emission of carcinogenic substances that have caused an increase in mortality rates, innate deformity, leukemia and child cancer, especially in the first year of life (Nadeau 2004).

The Reclaims Issue

It is calculated that in Campania there are 5,220 potentially polluted sites. According to the Report by the Regional Agency for Environmental Protection in Campania, 461 sites are characterized by a high level of pollution. As regards the reclaims, it is necessary to clarify the issue (Vito 2008).

In Italy, the most important recoveries were planned between 2007 and 2010 when Mascazzini was the general director of the Department of the Environment. Reclaiming an area by removing toxic waste is very expensive, as indicated in the case of the coastal Domitio between Naples and Caserta or the large area in Giugliano in Campania which were polluted by several activities of illegal garbage disposal. For the recovery of the dumps Resit 1 and Resit 2, belonging to Cipriano Chianese and then confiscated by the Commissioner, in which had been dumped a great amount of toxic waste for a long time thanks to the Casalesi clan, €50 million had been allocated (Donadio 2011). On the top of the tuff layer there are the dumps. Poisons are going to pollute dozens and dozens of square kilometres. The delineated picture drawn by the recovery commissioner Mario De Biase is more dramatic. According to him it is useless to talk about the recoveries of the Resit areas and the five dumps next to them. Building a sarcophagus 30 metres underground would be the only possible solution (Russo 2013). Because of this serious situation the position of 'Commissioner for the Land Reclamation Emergency and Water Protection' was established in Campania in 2001. The conspicuous sums of money allocated captured the attention of criminal companies that recognized an opportunity to make more profit from the environment through *ghost recoveries* (Puglia 2013).

The case of the Jacorossi company is emblematic. This is a Roman company specializing in environmental requalification contracted to reclaim 80 municipalities on the Domitio-Flegreo coast from 350,000 tons of toxic and dangerous wastes. The Commissioner chose the Jacorossi company without any competitive bid process but it had to employ 380 community service workers who would be paid by the state. The company subcontracted the work to many companies related to the Camorra. The Jacorossi workers have never worked whereas the subcontract companies' workers have been doing the work (Sodano and Trocchia 2010).

Another important feature of the so-called 'Mascazzini method' was to clean the sites without removing the polluted area. According to Mascazzini the recoveries would be more advantageous if they took place in the site itself. In the Jacorossi case, the areas have never been reclaimed and the wastes have been moved from one area to another. Forty thousand tons of toxic wastes were disposed of in unsuitable structures (Baccaro and Musella 2013).

As regards the dump Di.Fra.Bi in Pianura, it contained 30 million cubic metres of polluting waste and the Commissioner allocated 2.5 billion lire in order to reclaim and make safe the area, but the recovery has never been carried out (Vito 2008).

The Lack of Laws

The large number of legislation gaps is one cause of such a situation. Nowadays national specific legislation (similar to EU legislation regarding the transportation and circulation of waste)[1] has run out. The Department of the Environment introduced the SISTRI monitoring system (the system of control for waste tracing) but it has been revealed to be ineffective. The SISTRI system was introduced in 2009 on behalf of the Department of the Environment and Protection of the Territory and the Sea in order to digitize the production chain of special wastes at the national level and the urban garbage in Campania. The Carabinieri supervised the software management to ensure that suitable environmental safeguards were put in place (Boldrin 2013).

To make the system work the involved subjects (companies producing waste, truck drivers, and final addressees interested in the treatment of waste slags) will receive an electronic device to access the system, transmit the data and sign them electronically and be able to monitor the route of trucks from companies to dumps. Video surveillance devices are going to be installed in dumps and incinerators and

1 It is impossible to trace the waste route as well as the addressees and intermediaries involved because the truck drivers are not obliged to present the Modello unico di dichiarazione ambientale (MUD, the Unique Environmental Statement Form).

connected to the web. To monitor the movements of special waste along the production chain, the SISTRI supports the intermodal transport, where the final phase of waste disposal is controlled by an analysis electronic system and the flux of trucks is carefully observed. The SISTRI is supposed to be a good system to check the movement of special waste (De Simone 2013). Unfortunately the SISTRI is subject to possible manipulations by users and its adoption is not mandatory for foreign trucks. Logically, the illegal shipments are being committed to foreign trucks. This system has been at the centre of enquiries not only for the several delays in its deployment but also for the illegal earnings of the leading spokespersons of the public sector and companies taking part in the project (Trocchia 2013).

The interest of criminal organizations in the market of illegal waste disposal originated from the lack of a national normative that could make crime repression more effective. However, in fact the principle that the 'One who pollutes, must pay for it'. is scarcely attainable. For the most part, trials accusing company managers, public directors, politicians and *mafiosi*, and convicting them for crimes against the environment have been relatively few. It is important to point out that in the Italian penal code there is not a sanction available for punishing environmental crime or disaster. In most cases the criminally relevant behaviours against the environment have been prosecuted under article 434 of the penal code. This article is a generic rule punishing the building collapse or other malicious disaster (disaster with the deliberate intention of committing a crime or harming something). This rule punishes the behaviours that have been considered dangerous for public safety or the malicious disaster. The crime of environmental disaster counts in such a penal circumstance. But the rule demands the psychological element of malice in order to configure a crime, and this is hard to demonstrate. As a consequence it is extremely difficult to punish the crime of environmental disaster if there is not the deliberate intention of committing crime. In Italy, the majority of illegal actions against the environment can only be prosecuted as violations of civic or administrative rules. Sometimes, the illegal actions against the environment are materialized in contraventions that are minor crimes, which are barred after five years.

The legal provision punishing the crime of illicit waste trafficking is important. Article 260 of the Environmental Code allows the law enforcement agency, the security force and the magistrates to apply special investigative methods such as listening in on telephone conversations in cases of environmental crime. This provision still bars the crime of illicit waste traffic after six years, which is a short term if one considers the nature of the crime and its gravity. However, thanks to the law 136 adopted in 2010, this crime has been included in the anti-Mafia jurisdiction and this has increased the bar term from six to twelve years. This term only applies to crimes committed after 2010. As regard crimes other than illicit waste traffic, as there is no specific law they count in the environmental disaster law and the term of bar passes when the illicit conduct stops, or in case of continuation of behaviour from the date of judgment of the first degree.

Under active consideration of the extremely unhealthy and poor environmental quality of some Campania areas, the legislator introduced some changes on sanction discipline regarding wastes law contained in the Environmental Code (Law 152/2006) (Corbo 2013). By the time the Decree Law 136/2013 transformed into the 6/2014 Law, a new criminal offence of illegal waste combustion has been introduced to the Environmental Code. The third article of 136/2013 Law Decree provides three different types of offence. This provision makes it a criminal offence to set fire to waste left or abandoned uncontrolledly in an unauthorized area by a reclusion of two to five years.

Another circumstance of crime is provided in the second part of the new article 256bis where the same behaviours are punished by the reclusion from three to six years if they involve dangerous wastes.

The third circumstance of crime consists in the illegal abandonment of wastes with the illegal combustion aim. For this type of offence a reclusion of two or five years is provided. The legislator provides an aggravating circumstance in subsection number three of the new article. It states that the sanction increases by one-third if the crimes are committed by a firm's business or otherwise organized activity.

Subsection four states that the sanction increases if the crimes are committed in a territory in which the waste emergency has been declared. If vegetation waste deriving from green areas (i.e. gardens, parks and cemetery areas) are burnt illegally, administrative and financial sanctions are provided by article 225 of the Environmental Code on the abandonment of wastes. The fines vary between 300 and €3,000.

Subsection five of the new article 256bis provides for the requisition of the area where the crime has been committed and the requisition of the means of transport used for crimes, except if the means belong to someone who had nothing to do with it and it has been demonstrated that its use occurred without him/her knowing it and in absence of a neglecting behaviour. The law has been written quickly and has a large number of gaps in juridical technical terms (Vergine 2014). However, it is an important starting point in the fight against the environmental crimes even if repression is not always an effective instrument (Vergine 2013). It would be better to implement the control and monitoring system, operating during the prevention of crimes and not in the pathological phases when the crime has been committed.

The Decree-Law 136/13 provided that the perimeter actions of agricultural fields should start within 150 days of its approval in order to map soils and water strata and assess which fields have to be reclaimed or can be cultivated. The Decree establishes a sum of €600 million on top of the €300 million already allocated by Campania Region for the recovery of fields polluted by the dumping of toxic waste.

The trials against the Environmental Mafia are very complex and sometimes end with acquittal because the bar terms are exceeded even at the first judgment (Musella 2013). From the commission of an environmental crime to the discovery of an entombment of barrels several years may pass. The statistics show that the environmental enquires last from two to four years with reference to environmental crimes; six or seven years pass before the court of first instance issues a sentence. The trial duration may be over 10 years. In this way, dishonest entrepreneurs, corrupted politicians and subjects belonging to organized crime groups have found a way to escape in the first judgment. Managers, politicians and *mafiosi* invest in judicial activity in order to take advantage of the trial's long terms and obtain the impunity for the committed crimes.

In the Cassiopea trial, conducted by prosecutor Donato Ceglie against several companies from Veneto, Lombardy, Piemonte and Tuscany that dumped toxic wastes in the province of Caserta, the enquiries started in 1999 when after an inspection a company was charged for producing hot mix in the province of Naples and burying special wastes of northern Italian companies in the fields. In 2002 the enquires were closed down with the request of 98 pre-trial detention orders at the expense of entrepreneurs, drivers, owners of quarries and fields with the charge of criminal conspiracy, environmental disaster, water poisoning, management of abusive quarries, dangerous disposal and abuse of authority (Rai News Ambiente 2003). In 2003 there was the first request for indictment for the persons under investigation. The trial ended in 2011, not with the imposition of penal sanctions on the persons under investigation but with their acquittal (Saviano 2011).

The Bassolino-Impregilo trial with 27 persons under investigation had the same result. Among them was Antonio Bassolino, the governor of Campania Region, and Extraordinary Commissioner for Wastes Emergency from 2000 to 2004, and the managers of the Romiti family running the Impregilo company that had been managing the waste cycle through FIBE[2] in Campania for many years. They were accused of fraud, falsehoods, waste trafficking, and authority abuse for the management of the waste cycle in Campania that created six million bales that were never disposed of and are nowadays stocked in temporary sites, polluting the sites with percolate spillage. In this case Bassolino, Romiti and the others were absolved because the bar terms had been exceeded (Del Gaudio 2013).

The Pellini trial ended for the same reason. Here the suspects were the brothers and Acerra entrepreneurs Giovanni and Cuono Pellini. They were accused of burying industrial wastes, such as Porto Marghera muds, in the fields. The prosecutor had demanded a prison sentence of 18 years. After a trial lasting for seven years and 102 judicial hearings, the brothers Giovanni and Cuono Pellini, owners of the eponymous company of transport and waste disposal, were sentenced to six years for illicit waste trafficking. In addition, the other brother, Salvatore, who was a policeman and an active supporter of the family activity, was given a four-year prison term. The environmental disaster crime originating from toxic waste traffic was established, but it was declared barred for the Pellini case and the accused were not charged with membership of a Mafia-type association (*La Repubblica* 2014). In January 2015 the Court of Appeal of Naples (President Jacobins) imposed a prison sentence of seven years on Giovanni Cuono and

2 In 2000, the FIBE (acronym obtained from the names of the companies Fisia, Impregilo, Babcock and Evo) was awarded the contract for the entire cycle of collection and disposal of industrial waste in the Campania region.

Salvatore Pellini for the crime of causing aggravated environmental disaster. The court of first instance had already convicted them for waste trafficking (Marconi and Geremicca 2015).

One further step was undertaken in 2011 that involved changing the Decree-Law 231/01 at 22 article subsection 4 of Decree-Law 121/11 to implement the 2008/99 CE directive on the penal protection of the environment. This directive includes the suspension of bar terms for companies after commitment for trial. So, if there is a commitment for trial regarding societies and companies under investigation for environmental crimes, bar terms are suspended during the trial.

Several popular committees against the waste fires, established in many towns in the provinces of Naples and Caserta, have recently been playing an important role in drawing attention to the environmental problems and health risks deriving from the illegal waste disposal. A Fires Committees Coordination Group has been coordinating the activities of the different committees since July 2012 and with more than 60 associations and local committees it is now a force to be reckoned with. Its goal is to promote concrete proposals to contrast the measures taken by the government without citizens' consultation. Several protests have been organized with demonstrations attended by thousands of citizens to denounce the immobility of the institutions against such crimes. An action, signed by over 32,000 people, has been started to stop the illegal disposal of toxic waste through the uncontrolled spillage of urban and industrial waste, which have been burned giving off toxic substances (Del Giudice 2012).

Due to this legal deed, the judges have recently indicted 20 mayors of the province of Naples. From July 2014 the Prefecture of Naples has set up an online portal, *Prometheus*, on which it is possible to report the burning of toxic waste anonymously. At the same time the Minister of the Interior, the Region Campania, the ANCI (National Association of the Italian Municipalities), the provincial government and the municipalities of Naples and Caserta signed the *Pact for the Land of Fires*. This agreement allocated €5 million from the Region Campania to monitor the burning of toxic waste, and all involved agencies (including 80 municipalities) are committed to prevent other toxic waste from being spilled illegally and burnt (*Avvenire* 2013).

Conclusion

In Italian legislation and the political and administrative action of the state and of the local authorities, there has been no rule or substantive action regarding the environment for a long time. The lack of legislation allowed the politicians not to debate the centrality of the country's development, so neglecting the problems regarding industrial settlements, citizen health, dangerous industries and the pollution of territory and environment. The recent changes in rules are insufficient to start the process of change needed for environmental requalification in a way that would allow better protection of the environment. Public pressure is mounting, however, for stronger action to be taken on these matters. Such deficiency has been strongly denounced by those members of society who are more sensitive to the future generations. There is still much to do. There is the habit to talk about the Environmental Mafia as being in the past, but the consequences of environmental disaster are present and will continue into the future. It is necessary and essential to establish specific legislation that allows the judges to effectively repress crimes against environment. In this way Italy could become the well-known *Bel Paese*.

References

Avvenire. 2013. 'Napoli, firmato il patto per la "Terra dei fuochi" ', *Avvenire.it*, 11 July. Available at: www.avvenire.it/Cronaca/Pagine/cardinale_sepe_terra_fuochi.aspx (accessed 8 April 2015).

Baccaro, A. and Musella, A. (eds). 2013. *Il Paese dei veleni: Biocidio. Viaggio nell'Italia contaminate*. Roma: Round Robin Editrice.

Boldrin, C. 2013. *Sistri, così i rifiuti sono diventati sistema di mazzette*. Venezia: Osservatorio ambiente e legalità.

Capacchione, R. 2008. *L'oro della camorra*. Milan: BUR.

Capone, N., Cuccurullo, A. and Micillo, F. (eds). 2006. *Allarme rifiuti tossici. Cronaca di un disastro annunciato*. Naples: Assise della Città di Napoli e del Mezzogiorno d'Italia.

Corbo, A. 2013. *Novità legislative: D.L. 10 dicembre 2013, n. 136 'Disposizioni urgenti direte a fronteggiare emergenze ambientali e industriali ed a favorire lo sviluppo delle aree interessate'*. Rome. Available at: www.cortedicassazione.it/cassazione-resources/resources/cms/documents/Relazione_III_04_2013.pdf (accessed 8 April 2015).

D'Alisa, G., Burgalassi, D., Healy, H. and Walter, M. 2010. 'Conflict in Campania: Waste Emergency or Crisis of Democracy', *Ecological Economics* 70, 239–49.

De Chiara, P. 2010. 'Rifiuti, i camion della camorra in Molise', *La Voce del Molise*, 25 October.

De Crescenzo, D. 2007. 'La truffa dell'emergenza rifiuti. La compagnia delle ecoballe', *Narcomafie* Luglio-Agosto.

De Simone, A. 2013. 'I viaggi dei veleni', in *Il Paese dei veleni. Biocidio viaggio nell'Italia contaminate*, edited by A. Baccaro and A. Musella. Rome: Round Robin, 67–74.

Del Gaudio, L. 2013. 'Ciclo rifiuti, processo Bassolino-Impregilo: tutti assolti, il fatto non sussiste', *Il Mattino*, 4 November.

Del Giudice, A. 2012. 'Trentamila firme per arrestare la Terra dei Fuochi', *Napoli Città Sociale*, 21 October. Available at: www.napolicittasociale.it/portal/primo-piano/2214-trentatremila-firme-per-arrestare-la-terra-dei-fuochi.html (accessed 8 April 2015).

Donadio, G. 2011. 'Partono le bonifiche nell'area ex Resit', *L'inchiesta*, 28 July. Available at: www.inchiestanapoli.it/articolo/partono-le-bonifiche-nell%E2%80%99area-ex-resit-1 (accessed 8 April 2015).

Foschini, G. 2013. 'I verbali del pentito Schiavone: in Puglia le discariche della camorra', *La Repubblica*, 2 November. Available at: http://bari.repubblica.it/cronaca/2013/11/02/news/i_verbali_del_pentito_schiavone_in_puglia_le_discariche_della_camorra-70072396/ (accessed 8 April 2015).

Giordano, A. and Chiariello, P. 2015. *Monnezza di Stato. Le terre dei fuochi nell'Italia dei veleni*. Argelato: Minerva Edizioni.

Iacuelli, A. 2007a. *Schede*. Naples: Monitor.

——— 2007b. *Campania senza sbocchi*, 8 March. Available at: http://articoli.alessandroiacuelli.net/?p=87 (accessed 8 April 2015).

——— 2008. *Le vie infinite dei rifiuti. Il sistema campano*. Rome: Rinascita edizioni.

Iovene, B. 2008. *Campania Infelix*. Milan: BUR.

Istituto Superiore per la Protezione e la Ricerca Ambientale (ISPRA). 2012. *Special Waste Report*. Available at: www.isprambiente.gov.it/it/pubblicazioni/rapporti/rapporto-rifiuti-speciali-edizione-2012 (accessed 8 April 2015).

Marconi, L. and Geremicca, M. 2015. 'Pellini, L'Appello aumenta condanne sul filo della prescrizione: "Disastro"', *Corriere del Mezzogiorno*, 2 January. Available at: http://corrieredelmezzogiorno.corriere.it/napoli/cronaca/15_gennaio_29/pellini-l-appello-aumenta-condanne-filo-prescrizione-disastro-97967c88-a7da-11e4-a919–1a402233c54b.shtml (accessed 8 April 2015).

Massari, M. 2004. *Ecomafias and Waste Entrepreneurs in the Italian Market*. Paper presented at the 6th Cross-Border Crime Colloquium, Berlin, September.

Massari, M. and Monzini, P. 2004. 'Dirty Business in Italy: A Case Study of Trafficking in Hazardous Waste', *Global Crime* 6, 285–304.

Musella, A. 2013. 'Ecomafie. Inquinare non è reato', *Left*, 13 July.

Nadeau, B. 2004. 'Under the Volcano II', *Newsweek*, 8 November. Available at: www.newsweek.com/under-volcano-ii-124453 (accessed 8 April 2015).

Osservatorio Ambiente e Legalità di Legambiente. 2007. *Rapporto Ecomafia 2007. I numeri e le storie della criminalità ambientale*. Milan: Edizioni Ambiente.

——— 2008a. *Rapporto Ecomafia 2008. I numeri e le storie della criminalità ambientale*. Milan: Edizioni Ambiente.

——— 2008b. *Dossier 'Rifiuti Spa', Dentro l'emergenza in Campania: i numeri e le storie di un'economia criminale*. Milan: Edizioni Ambiente.

——— 2010. *Ecomafia 2010. Le storie e i numeri della criminalità ambientale*. Milan: Edizioni Ambiente.

Osservatorio Nazionale Ambiente e Legalità. 2005. *Dossier 'Rifiuti Spa', Radiografia dei traffici illegali*.

Pasotti, E. 2010. 'Sorting Through the Trash: The Waste Management Crisis in Southern Italy', *South European Society and Politics* 15(2), 289–307.

Petenzi, W. 2013. 'Rifiuti tossici sotto la A31: indagati 5 bresciani', *Corriere di Brescia*, 1 October. Available at: http://brescia.corriere.it/brescia/notizie/cronaca/13_ottobre_1/rifiuti-speciali-sotto-autostrada-valdastico-indagati-cinque-bresciani-lonati-portamb-2223398312650.shtml (accessed 8 April 2015).

Puglia, I. 2013. 'La bonifica fantasma e la Jacorossi. Basta, abbiamo già dato. Il duro richiamo della Corte dei conti: danni per 43 milioni e 10 anni sprecati', *Parallelo 41*, 20 October. Available at: www.paralleloquarantuno.it/articoli/la-bonifica-fantasma-e-la-jacorossi-basta-abbiamo-gia-dato.html (accessed 8 April 2015).

Rabitti, P. 2008. *Ecoballe. Tutta la verità su discariche, inceneritori, smaltimento abusivo dei rifiuti*. Rome: Aliberti.

Rai News Ambiente. 2003. 'Operazione Cassiopea, sgominata ecomafia che gestiva traffico di rifiuti tossici denunciata', *Rainews24*, 6 November.

La Repubblica. 2014. 'Processo ecomafie rischia prescrizione', *laRepubblica.it*, 17 January. Available at: http://ricerca.repubblica.it/repubblica/archivio/repubblica/2014/01/17/processo-ecomafie-rischia-prescrizione.html (accessed 8 April 2015).

Rosenthal, E. 2008. 'A Whiff of Naples Arrives in Hamburg', *New York Times*, 9 June. Available at: www.nytimes.com/2008/06/09/world/europe/09trash.html?pagewanted=all&_r=0 (accessed 8 April 2015).

Russo, R. 2013. 'Altro che bonifica, per Giugliano ci vuole un sarcofago come Chernobyl', *Corriere del Mezzogiorno*, 6 June. Available at: http://corrieredelmezzogiorno.corriere.it/napoli/notizie/cronaca/2013/6-giugno-2013/altro-che-bonifica-giugliano-ci-vuole-sarcofago-come-chernobyl-2221510622719.shtml (accessed 8 April 2015).

Saviano, R. 2006. *Gomorra. Viaggio nell'impero economico e nel sogno di dominio della camorra*. Milan: Mondadori.

——— 2011. 'Colpo di spugna sui rifiuti tossici 'Cosi uccidono Gomorra', *La Repubblica*, 18 September. Available at: www.repubblica.it/cronaca/2011/09/18/news/cassiopea-21828715/ (accessed 8 April 2015).

Senior, K. and Mazza, A. 2004. 'Italian "Triangle of Death" Linked to Waste Crisis', *The Lancet Oncology* 5(9), 525–7.

Smoltczyk, A., Ulrich, A. and Wassermann, A. 2010. 'The Garbage of Naples: How the Mafia Helped Send Italy's Trash to Germany', *Der Spiegel*, 4 March. Available at: www.spiegel.de/international/europe/the-garbage-of-naples-how-the-mafia-helped-send-italy-s-trash-to-germany-a-681469.html (accessed 8 April 2015).

Sodano, T. and Trocchia, N. 2010. *La peste: La mia battaglia contro i rifiuti della politica italiana*. Milan: BUR.

Tosca, P. 2013. 'Certificati falsi per i rifiuti. Sigilli alla cava Locatelli', *Corriere della Sera*, 23 October. Available at: http://bergamo.corriere.it/bergamo/notizie/cronaca/13_ottobre_23/certificati-falsi-rifiuti-sigilli-cava-locatelli-03547c60-3bb5-11e3-ac98-5d5614d1875c.shtml (accessed 8 April 2015).

Trocchia, N. 2013. 'Sistri, domiciliari a Malinconico. 'Appalti in cambio di consulenze per un milione', *Il Fatto Quotidiano*, 17 April. Available at: www.ilfattoquotidiano.it/2013/04/17/inchiesta-sistri-malinconico-ai-domiciliari-a-lui-milione-in-consulenze-per-indirizzare/565354/ (accessed 8 April 2015).

Vergine, A.L. 2013. 'Il cd. "disastro ambientale". L'involuzione interpretativa dell'art. 434 c.p', *Ambiente & Sviluppo* 6, 534–41.

——— 2014. 'Tanto tuonò . . . che piovve! A proposito dell'art.3 d.l. 136/2013', *Ambiente & Sviluppo* 1, 7–12.

Vito, M. (ed.). 2008. *Siti contaminati in Campania*. Naples: ARPAC.

16 Putting Our Own Animals First!

On the Criminalization of the Migration of Other than Human Animals

Janine Janssen

> PVV: Immigrant Animals Should Be Expelled
> PVV Gelderland [a local branch of the PVV [i.e. the right-wing Freedom Party – Partij voor de Vrijheid – led by Geert Wilders] wants to ban imported animals from local nature. Olof Wullink, a candidate for the provincial Council, believes that Scottish Highlanders had better stay in Scotland and that the Konik horses should go back to where they belong: Poland. Meanwhile, nature lover Wilfred Reinhold has been fighting against newcomers in the land of animals for years, with his 'Platform to Stop Invasive Exotics'. But he pleads for a different approach to that of Olof Wullink: 'the priority should be with animals like the raccoon, the tiger mosquito and the red fire ant, these you need to keep as much as possible away from our borders. They are really harmful and pose a major threat to the Dutch animal world'. At present, Scottish Highlanders and Konik horses function as a kind of guest workers. They are taken to the Netherlands for curtailing groves and the preservation of biodiversity in natural areas. Natuurmonumenten [an environmental organization] calls the PVV-proposal 'absurd'. Staatsbosbeheer [the Forestry Commission] is opposed to the plan to expel the Scots and the Poles. 'They fulfil the role within the Dutch ecosystem that originally was fulfilled by wild ungulates, but all of these creatures have been killed', says a spokeswoman. Furthermore, the PVV organization is left with many questions: 'should rabbits, pheasants but also sheep and goats be expelled? They also do not stem from this country'.
>
> (Spitsnieuws 2011)[1]

Introduction

On this planet humans are not the only creatures that migrate. Other animals[2] do so too. As the paraphrased English language version of the newspaper clipping above illustrates, humans do not only worry about human migrants. Migratory

1 As a reaction some people created a satirical site on which it was claimed that the PVV pleaded for expelling the Egyptian goose after 'molesting our real Dutch goose' for several years. Party leader Geert Wilders was not amused and even considered taking these practical jokers to court. See: www.nrc.nl/nieuws/2011/02/21/pvv-satire-wekt-woede-geert-wilders/ (accessed 25 March 2015).

2 In this chapter, 'animal(s)' refer(s) strictly to other than human animals; where referring to people, I will use the terms 'humans' or 'human animal(s)'.

movements by other species are watched carefully and at times they can cause as much upheaval as human migration. Migration by other species is at times even called 'invasive'. But are these creatures really out to get us? In this chapter a comparison will be made between migratory movements of humans and animals in the Dutch context.[3] In the first section attention will be paid to the vocabulary used describing non-native species – humans and other animals – in Dutch media and policies regarding animal migration. The starting point is the first policy memorandum on invasive species that was published in 2007. How the animal migrants are described in this text, and why their migration to the Netherlands is considered to be dangerous, are discussed. The key issue of differences and similarities in human and animal migration is then considered. The chapter then examines the particular ideas and outlooks on society that have most influenced the worries about migratory processes. Finally some remarks will be made on the fundamental question of how migrants – human or other animal – can become 'native' and therefore a fully appreciated member of society.

Migrating Animals

Human and Other Animal Migration and Dutch Vocabulary

Before exploring the processes of migration by other than human animals, some attention will be paid to the Dutch vocabulary that is frequently used in discussions regarding migration and the heritage of human migrants. The Dutch tend to use the term 'allochtoon' to describe everyone who is not born and bred in the Netherlands compared to families who were already settled there for generations.[4] The Dutch Central Bureau for Statistics (CBS) uses the following, more explicit definition: people with at least one foreign parent (born abroad). The indigenous population is described as 'autochtoon' (Janssen 2012).[5] Recently it has been suggested by the Council for Social Development (Raad voor Maatschappelijke Ontwikkeling), an influential advisory board for the Dutch government and parliament, to abandon the use of these words. According to the Council this categorization does little justice to the roots that an individual has grown in the Netherlands: even if a person was born in the Netherlands, has gone through the Dutch education system and

3 While writing this chapter the author also made use of a Dutch text that she published previously (see Janssen 2009).

4 'Allochtoon' comes from the Greek words 'allos' (meaning 'other') and 'chtoon' (meaning 'country'). In 1961 the word is mentioned for the first time in *Van Dale*, the dictionary of the Dutch language. It is only mentioned as an adjective and described in its original geological sense: 'transported from elsewhere, formed from material that was transported from elsewhere'. In 1971 Hilde Verwey-Jonker, a prominent Dutch sociologist, started applying 'allochtoon' as an alternative for 'guest worker', 'migrant' and 'foreigner'. See: https://onzetaal.nl/taaladvies/advies/allochtonen (accessed 25 March 2015).

5 This is not a typical feature of the Dutch language. In French the same terms are used: 'allochtone' and 'autochtone' for human and other migrants and the indigenous population. See Rémy and Beck (2008).

participates in Dutch society, he or she is still considered to be 'allochtoon' if one of his or her parents was born outside the Netherlands. That means that a great deal of value is attributed to an aspect that lies in fact outside the influence and control of that particular person. Furthermore, the Council states that ethnic categorization once had a function regarding the development of policies for *including* these migrant communities in Dutch society. But nowadays the differences within several ethnic groups are so huge (for example differences in income and level of education) that categorization based on ethnic background does not help policy-makers to gain any relevant insight (RMO 2012).

Although the use of the words 'allochtoon' and 'autochtoon' has met serious criticism, these terms are still frequently used in Dutch media and policies. Their use is not limited to human society, but they are also applied for describing other than human animals, plants and other life-forms.[6] In the quote at the beginning of this chapter in Dutch the reference is to 'allochtone' animals. To underpin the otherness of certain migrant animals next to 'autochtoon' one also encounters use of the adjective 'exotic'.

Animal Migration: Some Developments Over Time

According to figures from the Environment and Nature Compendium (Milieu- en Natuur Compendium) of the CBS, the number of exotic species has increased over the years. Compared to preceding centuries their number has particularly increased considerably since 1900. There are also clues that indicate that the numbers of alien species have increased sharply during the last two decades, particularly among the vertebrates, molluscs and crustaceans. According to the CBS the number of alien species has more than doubled since 1900, to the extent that, nowadays, alien species outnumber native species in the large Dutch rivers (CBS 2015; NRC.Next 2014). Although there are still native species to be found, it is not clear to what extent the newcomers are invasive and capable of replacing native ones (Ministry of Economic Affairs 2014).

Dutch Policies

The Convention on Biological Diversity (CBD) provides the basis for the EU Biodiversity Strategy to 2020. Dutch biodiversity policy is in line with that European strategy and the CBD. In 2011 the European Community adopted a new strategy to fight the loss of biodiversity by 2020. In this strategy the so-called 'Aichi-targets' are elaborated.[7] One of the targets – Aichi target 9 – is to establish tighter control

6 This chapter is limited to a description of migration processes of animals. Plants and other life-forms such as micro-organisms are excluded. For a witty and original description of 'vagabond plants' see Mabey (2010).

7 The parties under Convention of Biodiversity (CBD) meet at regular intervals. At their 10th meeting parties agreed that previous biodiversity protection targets had not been achieved and new targets were formulated. This meeting was held in Aichi, in Japan.

on invasive alien species: 'By 2020, invasive alien species and pathways are identified[8] and prioritized, priority species are controlled or eradicated and measures are in place to manage pathways to prevent their introduction and establishment' (Ministry of Economic Affairs 2014). The Netherlands is committed to the implementation of this strategy and uses it as a framework for its national biodiversity work (Ministry of Economic Affairs 2014). The control of invasive species is based on the implementation of the Dutch Policy Memorandum 'Invasive Alien Species' (IAS) (Ministerie van Landbouw, Natuur en Voedselkwaliteit 2007). The central coordinating authority regarding the implementation of the IAS policy is the Dutch Food and Consumer Product Safety Authority (Nederlandse Voedsel- en Waren Autoriteit, NVWA). The NVWA advises competent ministries on risks regarding the introduction, establishment and spreading of IAS and ways to deal with these risks. Therefore the NVWA plays an important role in the detection and monitoring of IAS and the raising of public awareness.[9]

Policy Memorandum 'Invasive Alien Species'

Let us take a closer look at the Policy Memorandum 'Invasive Alien Species' (Ministerie van Landbouw, Natuur en Voedselkwaliteit 2007) that is considered to be the starting point in Dutch policy on invasive species. How are these dangerous animal migrants described? 'An exotic species is a non-native plant, animal or micro-organism that is not capable of reaching the Netherlands on its own, but has reached Dutch nature due to human activity (transport, infrastructure)'. An 'exotic' can become 'invasive' when it settles in and develops explosive numbers. Then 'invasive alien species may constitute a threat to the native biodiversity, public health and safety. Exotics can be a burden for society and also lead to economic damage'. Nevertheless, in this memorandum it is mentioned that species with a natural habitat in areas surrounding the Netherlands and that are capable of entering this country independently are not covered by this definition. The reason for this is that less damage is to be expected of species that arrive on their own – their numbers are controlled because animals of prey migrate together with their predators – compared to species that were directly introduced due to human activity. In addition, it is almost impossible to stop these species from entering the country.

What kind of damage do policy-makers fear? First and foremost there is the fear of ecological damage. Chances are that an exotic species threatens biodiversity by competing with native species. Furthermore, there is the danger of infection, predation, parasitism and the transfer of infectious diseases towards native

8 In September 2013 the European Commission published a legislative instrument on invasive alien species that is also supported by the Netherlands. The Netherlands will collaborate with other member states in order to establish a European list of invasive alien species (Ministry of Economic Affairs 2014).

9 See, for a more elaborate description of these activities, Bureau Risicobeoordeling en Onderzoeksprogrammering (Team Invasieve Exoten) and de Divisie Landbouw & Natuur (2013).

species. Finally, there is a risk that mixing of native and invasive species will result in the creation of new sub-species and the disappearing of characteristics of native (sub-)species. In the memorandum several examples are presented: the comb jelly, the multi-coloured Asian ladybug and the muntjac. Since 2006 the comb jelly has been located in several Dutch waters. This species is native to the temperate and subtropical estuaries along the Atlantic coast of North and South America. Around the 1980s this animal ended up in the Black and the Caspian Sea via ballast water of ships.[10] It turned out that this creature had the same diet as native species and this had its effect on the whole food chain. The decline in the number of dolphins and seals is partly attributed to the rise of the comb jelly. The multi-coloured Asian ladybug was initially imported as a biocontrol of aphid. Now the animal has spread all over Europe. Because of its gluttony, it is seen as a threat to native species. The muntjac, a small deer of Indian descent, has escaped from deer parks and camps. In a large part of England they are seen as a real nuisance, because their presence results in the displacement of local species. It is estimated that the economic damage caused by invasive species – animals and plants – is about €1.3 billion per year (Van der Weijden et al. 2005).

Furthermore, damage to public health is reported. The Asian tiger mosquito, for example, stepped up as a stowaway in international transport. This insect comes from China and is known as an 'aggressive stabber' that can infect humans with dangerous viruses such as Dengue Fever. Finally, the migration of the muskrat can serve as an example of economic damage and security risks. This North American animal was introduced at the beginning of the twentieth century in Europe because of its precious fur coat. But their numbers went through the roof. Dangerous is their tendency to dig tunnels, for example under train trajectories or – what is even more scarier for the Dutch and their constant battle against the water – under dikes that can lead to sinkage of these structures. Meanwhile, an entire industry emerged, which focuses on the fight against these creatures.

According to the Ministry of Agriculture, Nature and Food Quality (Landbouw, Natuur en Voedelkwaliteit, LNV),[11] there are three options for dealing with invasive exotics: prevention, isolation and management of the population, and elimination. A lot is expected of prevention. The general idea is that after an invasive species has settled itself, it becomes really hard to get rid of it. Awareness should be raised and next to that agreements – on a voluntary basis – should be made

10 Ballast water provides stability and manoeuvrability to a ship. Usually this coastal water is pumped into tanks after a ship has delivered cargo to a port and is departing with less or no cargo. Large ships can carry millions of gallons of ballast water containing all kinds of species. In 2010 the Netherlands signed the International Convention for the Control and Management of Ships' Ballast Water and Sediments (BWM) that was set up by the International Maritime Organization (IMO). According to this agreement ships must have an approved ballast water treatment plant which removes organisms. The convention was still not in force in January 2014 (Ministry of Economic Affairs 2014).

11 This ministry ceased to exist in 2010. Nowadays the tasks of this former ministry are executed by the Ministry of Economic Affairs.

with trade and industry (for example, importers, garden centres and transporters). On the basis of a 'Pest Risk Analysis' (PRA), the risks that come with the import of certain species should be defined. The most drastic measure is elimination. But elimination is thought to be only feasible in the early stages of the process of settlement when the numbers are still relatively low. The responsibility for excluding and eliminating invasive alien species lies with the ministry of LNV.

Migration of Humans and Migration of Other than Human Animals

Similarities

There are similarities between the migration of humans and other than human animals. Regarding human and other than human animals it is, for example, not always clear at what point the subjects are considered to be 'legitimate' and to be 'native', if ever. With human migration criminologists and other experts often make a distinction between legal and illegal ways of migrating. As we have seen in the policy paper discussed above, the migration of other than human animals is also presented as a security problem, just as illegal migration by humans. The jelly comb is of course an excellent example of an illegal migrant: the creature travels as a stowaway on international shipping routes. A special form of illegal migration is that in which other than human animals become the victim – just as unfortunately happens to humans all over the world – as a result of trafficking and smuggling. In the Netherlands the Flora and Fauna Act (Flora en Fauna wet) prohibits, among other things, the possession and trade of certain exotic animals and plants and letting these species run free in the wild. And there are international standards that prohibit these acts such as the Convention on International Trade in Endangered Species of Wild Fauna and Flora (CITES). Among the other than human migrants one can also find guest workers. They have entered the country on a legal basis. Just as human guest workers, they were considered to be useful. But somewhere down the road the receiving community was not that pleased with certain aspects of the guest's behaviour. This is, as a matter of fact, what happened to the muntjac and the multi-coloured Asian ladybug. And finally there is the 'cute factor'. Physical appearance might also be a reason for migration. Not only models and people that are looking for a partner are crossing borders. Some animals were imported by humans because of their looks. The fact that the already mentioned muntjac from India was in introduced in European deer parks must have had something to do with its looks: humans find them attractive to look at.[12]

12 See also Knegtering (2009). He described on what characteristics humans select species for conservation programmes in the Netherlands. There is a tendency to protect larger species more than smaller ones. Legislation, on the other hand, tends in the other direction – the law provides better protection to the smaller species. Knegtering: 'This is possibly because larger species were more interesting to hunt or fish, and that's why they received protection much later. The legislator probably often chose the most socially acceptable line'. The 'cuddle' factor is important, but there's

As stated before, migration by humans as well as migration by other than human animals is often described in terms of safety and security by policy-makers. The adjective 'invasive' says it all and needs no further explaining in this regard. A closer look at the vocabulary makes it clear that the language applied by the department of LNV could easily be used by professionals in law enforcement.[13] Popular buzz words are: 'signalling', 'monitoring', 'prevention', 'control', 'enforcement' and 'liability'. One of the few terms that cannot be spoken out loud in both arenas is that of PRA. That tool is reserved strictly for other than human animals.

Differences

Although in the policy paper mentioned above it is stated that humans play an important role in the migration of alien species and are therefore also responsible for damages as a consequence of this migration process, the outlook on other than human animals differs considerably from the vision on human migrants. Even if humans see themselves as animals, they often see themselves as more complex and therefore 'higher creatures'. In other words, this worldview is human-centred and speciesistic (Cazaux 2002; Beirne 2007). As a consequence humans have created measures for other species – such as elimination of invasive aliens – that – it goes without saying – are not fit for fellow human beings. Bringing 'elimination' into practice in human society would be considered as murder, manslaughter, a war crime or a crime against humanity. But there is no equivalent term in relation to other than human animals, although Beirne (2014) has suggested the use of the term 'therocide' to describe all types of killing of non-human animals by humans. Humans grant themselves additional rights than other animals. Decades ago Margaret Mead (1964) pointed out that as soon as humans label certain animals as 'dangerous' or 'bothersome', than it becomes easier to kill these creatures: most humans will not lose a night of sleep over using a mouse trap to kill mice, but drowning a young and cuddly kitten is a different matter altogether. Contemporary authors have demonstrated that humans still tend to attribute different social status positions to different species (Herzog 2010; Smith 2012).

And there is another difference. In debates on the migration of other than human animals frequently the issue pops up of the risk of diminishing biodiversity as the guests eradicate already present species by taking over their habitat or

---

more to it. Birds clearly receive more attention and protection than mammals, but the latter are generally regarded as cuddlier. All sorts of sentiment play a role here, thinks Knegtering: 'Mammals hide much more and their colours are significantly more boring than birds'. 'You'd be well advised not to be small, ugly and an invertebrate', according to Knegtering (Rijksuniversiteit Groningen 2009).

13 It also goes the other way around: Vasquez et al. (2014) describe how violent criminal acts are sometimes described using animal metaphors. Their findings suggest that an animalistic description of these acts leads to more retaliation against the perpetrator by inducing the perception that he is likely to continue engaging in violence.

change these animals as a result of interbreeding. Although some fear that human migrants will take over guest societies, antagonists of human migration use the argument concerning diversity the other way around. That is, they do not refer to diminishing diversity as the problem. Rather, they fear that human migration will result in too much diversity in their particular society. Living in a poly-ethnic and multicultural world might result in the natives thus losing their identity. While human migrants are not capable of changing their human hosts in a biological way, some do expect that in the future we will see fewer natural blonds, redheads and blue-eyed people as a consequence of interracial relationships in multicultural societies (*National Geographic* 2013, 2014).[14] Such fears and concerns implicitly reinforce the idea that humans are intrinsically different according to certain 'racial' and 'ethnic' characteristics, regardless of the essential biological unity of the human species.

Organicism

Nature or Nurture?

At first glance it might seem that the debate on invasive species has to do with 'nature'. But if nature is defined as those parts of earth that were nether influenced by humans (see also Wolch and Emel 1998), than we can conclude that there is no nature in the Netherlands. All over the world people learn that the Dutch have practically created their own land: without the construction of impressive dikes about one-third of this small country would be flooded by water (Vossestein 2012). That means that the question of which species do belong in this country, does not belong to the realm of 'nature' but to that of 'nurture'. Biological and other scientific knowledge is, nevertheless, indispensable in order to develop understanding of what is happening in the world surrounding us, including the inter-relationship of different species. But the way humans perceive their environment is influenced and coloured by ideas and prejudices formed through personal experience (growing up in geographical spaces with certain pre-established ecological characteristics) and historical trends (such as the establishment of the Netherlands as a distinct country).

The Human Body as a Metaphor

The concept of 'organicism' refers to the use of the body as a metaphor for human culture and society. The Dutch sociologist Schinkel used organicism in order to explain some aspects of the debate surrounding the integration of migrants in Dutch society (2008). Schinkel argues that organicism has been *en vogue* during many instances in history. The body as a metaphor is particularly attractive because the body is a defined unit. All the different organs – like the heart, the

14 See, for a critical comment, *The Hairpin* (2014).

liver, the stomach and so on – have a different function and together they make the body work. They cannot do it on their own and outside the body they are not capable of functioning: an ingenious organ like the heart will simply stop beating.

According to Schinkel a very import characteristic of organicistic thinking is the preoccupation with the wholeness of the social body, that is, a particular human society. The order in the body is seen as a harmonic order. A disruption of that balance immediately leads to feelings of unrest. Schinkel thinks that this is what is happening in the debate on integration: people are scared that the social body, society, is out of balance due to migration and the development of multicultural society. He thinks that the fear is so exaggerated that he has coined a new term to describe that feeling: 'social hypochondria'. This refers to a spasmodic fixation on diseases that threaten the wholeness of the social body in order to avert the attention of its coming death. Or in plain English: organicism can be understood as a dichotomy between parts that belong and, what Germans so beautifully refer to as *Fremdkörper*, those parts that do not belong to the body. But this dichotomy is more than a division of place in space (in or outside the body). That what belongs to the social body is valued more than the parts that are considered to be alien.[15] At the end, for social hypochondriacs it all comes down to the ultimate dichotomy: 'them' versus 'us'.

Organicism and Other than Human Migrating Animals

Organicism frequently pops up in worries of humans regarding the migration of other species. Constantly there is concern about the question of whether some other than human animals have the right to live in this country or if they belong somewhere else. In the media and on the Internet one often finds articles and postings – just like the one at the beginning of this chapter – in which worries regarding the future of native species are expressed. On 7 July 2008, the NRC, a quality newspaper, came up with a headline that could be understood as a reference to the invasion of the Netherlands by the German army at the beginning of the Second World War: 'Raccoons Cross German Border'. In the article it was mentioned that the raccoon was not native to the Netherlands and that it was considered to be an opportunistic wolverine that poses a threat to the ecosystem, meaning that the eggs of water and grassland birds were no longer safe (NRC 2008).[16] The ring-necked parakeet has also been accused of being destructive towards the Dutch ecosystem. Debate over this little bird was even capable of destroying harmony in a Dutch political party, the Christian Democratic Appeal (CDA).[17] Representative Ormel, a party member of minister Verburg of LNV, believes that these bright

15 Compare the classical dichotomy described by Douglas: purity and danger (1966).

16 It is interesting that according to a scientific report by Alterra, an institute that is part of the Wageningen University and Research Centre, the economic, agricultural, veterinary and ecological risks related to the presence of raccoons in the Netherlands are considered to be low (Lammertsma et al. 2008).

17 CDA is a Christian democratic party. It is a centrist and moderate party in Dutch politics.

coloured birds rob the nests of native birds and that they displace native species such as blackbirds, thrushes and sparrows. According to Ormel, ‘the Netherlands are no safari park’. With this he means that action should be undertaken to protect birds that are considered to be typically Dutch, such as the black-tailed godwit or the lapwing. Others within his party argued, however, that any measures taken should be proportionate rather than extreme (*NU.nl* 2008).

An important part of organicistic reasoning is the belief that native species are good because they belong to the social body and that therefore migrants are bad. According to biologist Ken Thompson, this is one of several myths concerning migration of animals and other life forms. Aliens are not always to blame. In his thought-provoking work *Where Do Camels Belong?* (2014) he gives several examples of cases where migrant animals were wrongly accused of causing costly damages: ‘many observers seem happy to believe that an increase in alien X must be the cause of the decline in native Y, if the increase and decline happen around the same time’ (Thompson 2014, p. 205). It is as if observers mix up vague correlations with cause and effect. Troublesome also is that humans not only tend to judge other species by their origins (Davis 2011), but they often do not know very much about the history and geographical movements of these species. For example, Thompson (2014) explains that we instinctively might think that camels originally came from the Middle East, but the camelids actually evolved in North America about 40 million years ago.

Noah's Ark: Who's In and Who's Out?

This chapter should not be understood as a plea for an ecological *laissez-faire* policy. All of us that live in the Netherlands are glad that the Dutch government has taken measures against the dike-weakening activities of the muskrat. But attention for this obviously risk-related behaviour should not blind us to more fundamental issues that this comparison between the discourses on human and other than human animal migration in the Dutch context highlights. Although several differences and similarities have been described in this chapter, the most important issue in both debates is the question of belonging: who's in and who's out? When does a human migrant become a member of society? Which species and habitus should be protected? When are migrants – be it humans or other species – finally considered to be natives? These fundamental questions on societal inclusion and exclusion are not new. They were already addressed in the Bible in the tale of the flood and Noah's ark (Weitzman 1988). But even on the ark not all species received the same hospitality. As a matter of fact, the Lord told Noah: ‘Take seven pairs of every kind of animal that can be used for sacrifice and one pair of all the others’ (Genesis, 7, 2).[18] Another parallel with this biblical story is the idea that humans can manage what is happening in the natural world surrounding them.

18 So kosher animals were favoured in terms of getting access to the ark. See, for a description of which animals are considered to be kosher, Janssen (2014).

Instead of instinctively giving in to the urge of putting our own animals first, we should do some soul-searching and ask ourselves the critical question as to what extent this idea of human control over nature is realistic. Is it not possible that we are indeed suffering of some form of social hypochondria in relation to the other than human migrants?

References

Beirne, P. 2007. 'Animal Rights, Animal Abuse and Green Criminology', in *Issues in Green Criminology: Confronting Harms Against Environments, Humanity and Other Animals*, edited by P. Beirne and N. South. Cullompton: Willan Publishing, 55–83.

——— 2014. 'Therocide: Naming Animal Killing', *International Journal for Crime, Justice and Social Democracy* 4(3), 50–67.

Bureau Risicobeoordeling en Onderzoeksprogrammering (Team Invasieve Exoten) and Divisie Landbouw & Natuur. 2013. *Invasieve Exoten. Werkplan 2013*. Utrecht: NVWA.

Cazaux, G. 2002. *Anthropocentrism and Speciesism Regarding Animals Other Than Human Animals in Contemporary Criminology: Analysing the Concept 'Animal Abuse' in Criminological Science and in Belgian Legislation Regarding the Protection and Welfare of Animals*. Gent: Faculty of Law, University of Gent.

CBS. *Exoten in de Nederlandse fauna, 1900/2012*. Available at: www.compendiumvoordeleefomgeving.nl/indicatoren/nl1375-Exoten-in-de-Nederlandse-fauna.html?i=2–41 (accessed 25 March 2015).

Davis, M.A. 2011. 'Don't Judge Species on Their Origins', *Nature* 474, 153–4.

Douglas, M. 1966. *Purity and Danger: An Analysis of Concept of Pollution and Taboo*. New York: Routledge & Kegan Paul.

The Hairpin. 'Cancel What Americans Would Look Like in 2014', 11 April. Available at: http://thehairpin.com/2014/04/cancel-what-americans-will-look-like-in-2050 (accessed 25 March 2015).

Herzog, H. 2010. *Some We Love, Some We Hate, Some We Eat*. New York: Harper Perennial.

Janssen, J. 2009. 'Eigen dieren eerst! Over de criminalisering van de migratie van dieren', in *Diverse kwesties. Liber amicorum prof. dr. Frank Bovenkerk*, edited by Ch. Brants and S. van der Poel. The Hague/Utrecht: Boom Juridische uitgevers/Willem Pompe Instituut voor Strafrechtswetenschappen, 27–34.

——— 2012. *Weaving Social Networks: Tips for Police Officers and Other Professionals about Building and Maintaining Networks in a Multi-Ethnic Society*. The Hague: Eleven.

——— 2014. 'On the Relationship between Animal Victimization and Stigmatization of Ethnic Groups: The Case of Ritual Slaughter', in *Environmental Crime and its Victims: Perspectives within Green Criminology*, edited by T. Spapens, R. White and M. Kluin. Farnham: Ashgate, 205–17.

Knegtering, E. 2009. *The Featheries and the Furries: Species Characteristics and Tendencies in Public Species Conversation*. Groningen: University of Groningen.

Lammertsma, D., Groot Bruinderink, G. and Broekhuizen, S. 2008. *Wasberen (Procyon lotor L. 1758) in Nederland*. Wageningen: Alterra. Available at: www.wageningenur.nl/en/Publication-details.htm?publicationId=publication-way-333638323633 (accessed 25 March 2015).

Mabey, R. 2010. *Weeds: How Vagabond Plants Gatecrashed Civilisation and Changed the Way We Think About Nature*. London: Profile Books.

Mead, M. 1964. 'Cultural Factors in the Cause and Prevention of Pathological Homicide', *Bulletin in the Menninger Clinic* 28, 11–22.

Ministerie van Landbouw, Natuur en Voedselkwaliteit. 2007. *Beleidsnota Invasieve Exoten*. The Hague: Ministerie van Landbouw, Natuur en Voedselkwaliteit.

Ministry of Economic Affairs. 2014. *Convention on Biological Diversity. Fifth National Report of the Kingdom of the Netherlands*. The Hague: Ministry of Economic Affairs.

National Geographic. 2013. 'The Changing Face of America', October. Available at: http://ngm.nationalgeographic.com/2013/10/changing-faces/funderburg-text (accessed 25 March 2015).

——— 2014. 'National Geographic Imagines What The "Average American" Would Look Like In 2050', 13 April. Available at: http://designtaxi.com/news/365031/National-Geographic-Imagines-What-The-Average-American-Would-Look-Like-In-2050/interstitial.html/?v=1&advertiser=External&return_url=http%3A%2F%2Fdesigntaxi.com%2Fnews%2F365031%2FNational-Geographic-Imagines-What-The-Average-American-Would-Look-Like-In-2050%2F%3Finterstital_shown%3D1 (accessed 25 March 2015).

NRC. 2008. 'Wasberen steken de Duitse grens over', 7 July. Available at: http://vorige.nrc.nl/binnenland/article1934712.ece/Wasberen_steken_de_Duitse_grens_over (accessed 25 March 2015).

NRC.Next. 2014. 'Nederland is kampioen biodiversiteitsverlies. In Europa', 26 June.

Nu.nl. 2008. 'Halsbandparkiet hoort hier niet', 18 June. Available at: www.nu.nl/wetenschap/1618902/halsbandparkiet-hoort-hier-niet.html (accessed 12 October 2015).

Raad voor Maatschappelijke Ontwikkeling (RMO). 2012. *Tussen afkomst en toekomst. Etnische categorisering door de overheid*. The Hague: RMO.

Rémy, E. and Beck, C. 2008. 'Allochtone, autochtone, invasif: catégorisations animales et perception d'autrui', *Politix. Revue des sciences sociales et politique* 21(82), 193–209.

Rijksuniversiteit Groningen. 2009. *Birds and 'Cuddly' Animals More Likely to be Protected*. Press release, 17 November. Available at: www.rug.nl/news/2009/11/178_09?lang=en (accessed 25 March 2015).

Schinkel, W. 2008. *De gedroomde samenleving*. Kampen: Uitgeverij Klement.

Smith, K.K. 2012. *Governing Animals: Animal Welfare and the Liberal State*. Oxford: Oxford University Press.

Spitsnieuws. 2011. 'PVV: allochtone dieren uitzetten', 18 February.

Thompson, K. 2014. *Where Do Camels Belong? The Story and Science of Invasive Species*. London: Profile Books.

Vasquez, E.A., Loughnan, S., Gootjes-Dreesbach, E. and Weger, U. 2014. 'The Animal in You: Animalistic Descriptions of a Violent Crime Increase Punishment of Perpetrator', *Aggressive Behavior* 40, 337–44.

Vossestein, J. 2012. *The Dutch and their Delta: Living below Sea Level*. The Hague: Holland Books.

Weijden, van der, W.J., Leeuwis, R. and Bol, P. 2005. *Biologische globalisering. Omvang, oorzaken, gevolgen, handelingsperspectieven. Achtergronddocument voor de Beleidsnota Invasieve Soorten van het ministerie van Landbouw, Natuur en Voedselkwaliteit*. Culemborg: CLM, Milieu en Natuurplanbureau and TU Delft.

Weitzman, M.L. 1998. 'The Noah's Ark Problem', *Econometrica* 66, 1279–98.

Wolch, J. and Emel, J. (eds). 1998. *Animal Geographies: Place, Politics, and Identity in the Nature-Culture Borderlands*. London: Verso.

Index

For Product Safety Concerns and Information please contact our EU
representative GPSR@taylorandfrancis.com
Taylor & Francis Verlag GmbH, Kaufingerstraße 24, 80331 München, Germany

www.ingramcontent.com/pod-product-compliance
Ingram Content Group UK Ltd.
Pitfield, Milton Keynes, MK11 3LW, UK
UKHW022011180926
475701UK00003B/302
9781138606562